Port of Last Resort

Refugees arriving at the port of Shanghai. Courtesy of the Leo Baeck Institute, N.Y.

Port of Last Resort

THE DIASPORA COMMUNITIES OF SHANGHAI

Marcia Reynders Ristaino

STANFORD UNIVERSITY PRESS

STANFORD, CALIFORNIA

Stanford University Press
Stanford, California
© 2001 by the Board of Trustees of the
Leland Stanford Junior University

Printed in the United States of America
on acid-free, archival-quality paper

Library of Congress Cataloging-in-Publication Data
Ristaino, Marcia R.
Port of last resort : diaspora communities of Shanghai /
Marcia Reynders Ristaino.
     p.   cm.
    Includes bibliographical references and index.
    ISBN 0-8047-3840-8 (alk. paper)
    ISBN 0-8047-5023-8 (pbk. : alk. paper)
    1. Shanghai (China)—Social conditions.
   2. Aliens—China—Shanghai.   I. Title.
HN740.S484 R57   2001
306'.0951'132—dc21   2001020087

Original printing 2001

Last figure below indicates year of this printing:
11   10   09   08   07   06   05   04   03

Designed by Janet Wood
Typeset by BookMatters in 10/14 Janson

For my daughter Elizabeth and in memory of Aunt Evelyn

CONTENTS

ILLUSTRATIONS

TABLES

I was drawn to the research for this book by the opportunity to examine two large and generally overlooked communities, one Jewish and the other Russian Orthodox, whose members found refuge in Shanghai. Together, they at one point numbered more than 50,000 people, most of them refugees from war and revolution, crowded into China's major port city. And as I came to know their experiences, I found much that resonated with what we hear today of societies in conflict, dislocated populations, and the human suffering and painful alienation that accompany those upheavals.

Although they were Western in tradition, the presence of these substantial groups in Shanghai has been largely overlooked. Scholarly attention has focused instead on the Western elites who governed most of Shanghai, and, more recently and intensively, on the Chinese presence in its different forms, levels, stations, and phases, in what was, after all, a Chinese city. The paucity of knowledge of even the most basic kind about the 30,000-member Slavic community comes across in the uncertainty even among scholars over whether there were more Russians than British in the Western settlements in the city. It is well known that at their peak influence, the British numbered about 10,000.

Even the most serious scholarship tends to see the Russians and other Slavs in Shanghai chiefly as bodyguards to rich Chinese or dance hostesses, or, worse, in terms of their involvement in the city's notorious underworld of vice and crime. The Jews are singled out for their relationships to the trades as menders, fixers, or, most often, as owners of colorful small cafés. Neglected are the rich textures of the refugee communities that contributed to the unique diversity of Shanghai society in the 1930s and 1940s. Their involvement in the arts, music, their religious ceremonies and institutions, their internal tensions, and broader community affairs are generally overlooked. In recent years, there has been a welcome addition to our knowledge of the Jewish experience provided by memoirs of years spent in Shanghai. One can at least hope for similar contributions in the near future from the Slavic community, former members of which have thus far apparently resisted any temptation to revisit their generally difficult and sometimes tragic Shanghai experiences.

Formed out of historical circumstances and living in diaspora, these two multi-ethnic groupings, each involving several religious and cultural traditions, are deserving of our close attention. How did such diverse groups, living under very difficult circumstances, nonetheless form a community; articulate and preserve their national identities; experience and resolve group tensions; choose their leaders; find gainful employment; cope with an alien culture and a lack of essential language skills; educate and raise their young; and deal with the other severe political and economic challenges they faced? Taken together, the answers to these questions add a new dimension to what we know of the foreign communities in Shanghai. The communities studied here both experienced the Japanese occupation of the city during World War II directly, albeit differently. Survival dictated the need to accommodate the Japanese military authorities, but the two communities responded in different ways. Still, the resourcefulness of the two communities, laboring under the sway of Western concession holders, followed by a succession of Japanese military control measures, is further evidence that groups struggling to cope in the shadow of privileged ruling elites deserve our serious attention.

I am indebted to a number of people for the wisdom and guidance they offered along the path of creating this work. Frank Joseph Shulman recommended early on that I look in the Shanghai Municipal Police files, which I had been researching, for information about the Jewish and Slavic communities. When my preliminary findings grew into a book-length manuscript, Christian Henriot had the patience to read it and offered welcome criticism and suggestions. Robert Bickers read the manuscript in full at a later stage and offered many additional useful suggestions for its further development. Finally, Parks Coble gave welcome encouragement and provided excellent criticism, which helped me to see some of the forest through the trees. My thanks also go to Chiara Betta, who kindly read Chapter 2, clarifying certain issues and calling additional sources of information to my attention.

I am very grateful as well to those who gave support to this project through their abstracts and translations of key sources. Cecil Uyehara worked with me on Japanese Foreign Ministry files and other Japanese sources. Kurt Maier provided similar help with German-language documents, as Boris Boguslavsky and Leo Orleans did with Russian material. I am also grateful to Peter Dreyer and Dick Ristaino for their patient editorial suggestions. Of course, I assume complete responsibility for any errors of fact or important material overlooked.

Certainly, I owe special gratitude to the numerous people who were willing to be interviewed and share with me what were sometimes painful experiences during their lives in Shanghai. The Bibliography lists these interviews, and I renew my thanks to them here. My work with Muriel Bell of Stanford University Press smoothed the process of creating the book and led to its successful outcome.

I would also like to note the interest and kind support of colleagues at the Library of Congress, among them Yoko Akiba, Barbara Dash, Sharon Horowitz, Zbigniew Kantorosinsky, Kenneth Nyiradi, Peggy Pearlstein, and Gail Shirazi, as well as of Jerry Berkeley, Barbara Brooks, Joshua Fogel, Amy Knight, Jonathan Goldstein, Pan Guang, Tess Johnston, Daniel Kwok, Marilyn Levine, William McCloy, Patricia Polansky, Guido Samarani, John Stephan, Patricia Stranahan, John Taylor, Frederic Wakeman, Jr., Phyliss Waldman, John Witek, S.J., Kache Yip, and Yu Maochun. My thriving friendships with Roderick Engert, Joyce Haney Williamson, and Betty McIntosh contributed to this project too.

This work was supported by a Grant-in-Aid from the American Council of Learned Societies/Social Science Research Council, which made research in Shanghai possible. The Library of Congress gave me time off to undertake that research and related work. Another grant, provided by the American Jewish Archives at Hebrew Union College, made work in those archives possible and allowed for the interactions that were helpful in shaping my perspective. Dr. Abraham Peck, the former director of the archives, provided able assistance.

I have used the pinyin spelling system for most names and place-names mentioned in this work. But to respond to many Western readers and their familiarity with the period under review, the traditional Wade-Giles spelling system is retained for some important names, including Chiang Kai-shek (Jiang Jieshi). Some of the places noted in this study are known by more than one name. The name Manchuria is familiar to English speakers, but when it came under Japanese control in 1932, it became known as Manchukuo (Manzhouguo). Its port city Dalien (Ta-lien) is "Dairen" in Japanese and "Dal'nyi" in Russian. Harbin (Ha'erbin in pinyin) was the Manchurian rail-road center. Beijing (Pei-ching), or "northern capital," became Beiping (Pei-ping), or "northern peace," after Chiang Kai-shek established the capital of the Republic of China at Nanjing (Nan-ching or Nanking), but it reverted to Beijing in 1949 as the capital of the new communist regime. Before 1949, Chongqing (Ch'ung-ch'ing or Chungking) served as the wartime capital of Chiang's government. Unless otherwise indicated, all dollar amounts cited refer to Chinese silver dollars used before November 1935 and Chinese yuan or currency notes issued after November. The two were roughly of equivalent value. A listing of former Shanghai street names with their contemporary equivalents has been included at the end of the book.

AJJDC	American Jewish Joint Distribution Committee
BREM	Bureau of Russian Emigrant Affairs
CENTREJEWCOM	Ashkenazi Committee for Assistance to the Refugees from Central Europe (Shanghai)
CFA	Committee for Assistance of European Refugees (Speelman Committee)
CNRRA	Chinese National Relief and Rehabilitation Administration
DNB	Deutsches Nachrichten Büro
EASTJEWCOM	Committee to assist Jewish refugees from Poland, Lithuania, Latvia, and Estonia (Shanghai)
HIAS	Hebrew Immigrant Aid Society
HICEM	Acronym combining the names HIAS, ICA, and Emigdirect; an organization founded in 1927 by amalgamating three Jewish migration agencies: the New York-based HIAS (Hebrew Immigrant Aid Society); the Paris-based ICA (Jewish Colonization Association); and the Berlin-based Emigdirect.
IRO	International Refugee Organization
JEWCOM	Committee for Assistance to Refugees (Kobe, Japan)
ORT	Obschestvo Remeslenovo i zemledelcheskovo Trouda (Society for Trades and Agricultural Labor)
RFP	Russian Fascist Party
ROVS	Russian General Military Union
SACRA	Shanghai Ashkenazi Collaborating Relief Association
SAJCA	Shanghai Ashkenazi Jewish Communal Association
SJYA	Shanghai Jewish Youth Association

SORO	Council of United Russian Public Organizations at Shanghai
UNRRA	United Nations Relief and Rehabilitation Administration
WJC	World Jewish Congress

The Exile's trade is: hoping.

— *Bertolt Brecht, 1943*

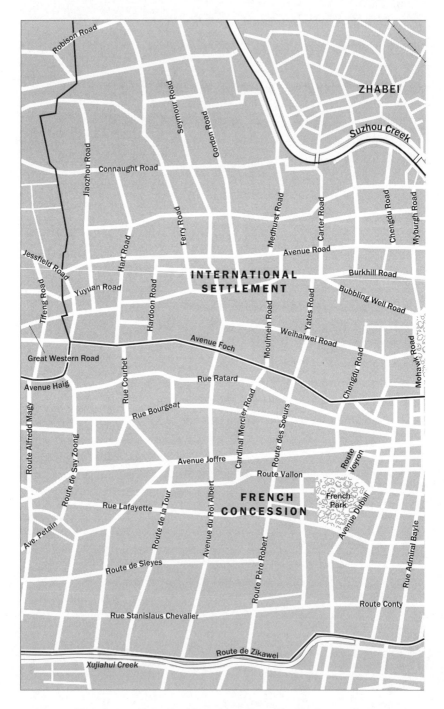

Map 1. Shanghai. SOURCE: Based on a map from Harriet Sergeant, *Shanghai* (New York, 1990).

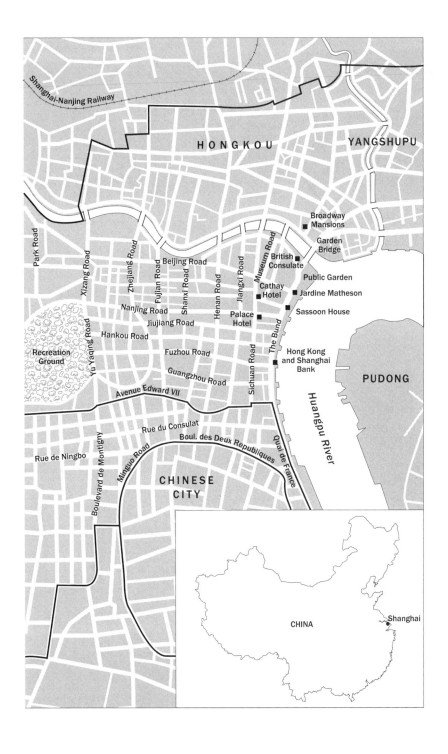

Shanghai-Nanjing Railway

HONGKOU   YANGSHUPU

Broadway
Mansions

Park Road

Xizang Road

Zhejiang Road

Museum Road

Beijing Road   British
                     Consulate

Garden
Bridge

Public Garden

Fujian Road

Shanxi Road

Henan Road

Jiangxi Road

Cathay
Hotel   Jardine Matheson

Nanjing Road

Jiujiang Road

Palace
Hotel

Sassoon House

Hankou Road

Yu Yaqing Road

Recreation
Ground

Fuzhou Road

Guangzhou Road

Sichuan Road

The Bund

Hong Kong
and Shanghai
Bank

PUDONG

Avenue Edward VII

Huangpu River

Rue du Consulat

Boul. des Deux Republiques

Quai de France

Rue de Ningbo

Boulevard de Montigny

Minguo Road

CHINESE
CITY

CHINA   Shanghai

ONE

Introduction

Omnia juncta in uno.

— Motto of the Shanghai Municipal Council

For centuries, China had experienced population movements across a land plagued by warfare, peasant uprisings, famines, and natural disasters. In the twentieth century, however, China witnessed a new phenomenon: Europeans forced out of their countries by religious persecution, war, or civil strife seeking sanctuary there. These "involuntary migrants," to use John Hope Simpson's term, were the rejects of their own societies, and, most surprising of all to the Chinese, they were white.[1]

Several events precipitated their arrival in China and, specifically, Shanghai. The most important among them were pogroms (some of them during World War I) in the Pale of Settlement, to which Jews in Russia were largely restricted until 1917; the Russian October Revolution and subsequent Civil War, which dispersed victims both east and west; the Japanese occupation of northern Chinese cities; and, finally, the persecution of Austrian and German Jews that culminated in the maelstrom of World War II in Europe. Those uprooted and alienated by these upheavals found the search for security rendered more difficult because they had lost the protection ordinarily afforded nationals of their countries. Denationalized, most refugees lacked travel documentation and other protective services normally provided to citizens by their governments. Lacking any supported claim to long-term residence, they were vulnerable to expulsion under Chinese law. They differed from both the Westerners and the Chinese sojourners who temporarily migrated to Shanghai for economic reasons or personal advancement.[2] Finding themselves in an alien country, populated by people seemingly of a totally different kind, they were outcasts, facing challenges to their personal identities and the fabric of their communities that they could scarcely have dreamed of in their previous lives. The disconnection, loss, and estrangement from which they suffered were made all the worse by their strange surroundings. *whites in China.*

The Diasporas

These arrivals in Shanghai were part of a major category of diaspora. The term "diaspora" has been most closely associated, if not specifically identified, with the Jewish diaspora, rooted in a catastrophic tradition. In recent years, however, seeking to understand migrations by various other groups, which apparently dispersed for different reasons, scholars have carefully reexamined the diaspora concept and the experiences that can legitimately be associated with it. Robin Cohen's important work on diasporas provides useful qualifications of this broad concept by identifying five categories that highlight the most meaningful characteristics of diaspora groups: "victim, labour, trade, imperial, and cultural."[3] Victim diasporas are typified by the Jewish experience of traumatic dispersal from a homeland and the sense of co-ethnicity shared by the persecuted and scattered Jews. Labor and trade diasporas focus respectively on the search for work or trade. The next category relates to the realization of colonial ambitions, combining commerce, empire, and military conquest. Finally, cultural diasporas illustrate how culture is transmitted, borne and transformed by migration.

This study deals with two victim diasporas. One consisted of Jewish refugees fleeing Nazi regimes in Europe; the other was the massive influx into Shanghai of Slavic refugees from persecution in eastern Europe, imperial Russia, and the USSR. Many of the "common features of a diaspora" that Cohen lists are clearly displayed in the behavior and experiences of both of these groups.[4] Summarized, Cohen's nine features are (1) traumatic dispersal from an original homeland; or (2) expansion in the search of work or trade or to further colonial ambitions; (3) a collective memory and myth about the homeland; (4) a collective commitment to the homeland's maintenance and safety; (5) the development of a return movement; (6) strong ethnic group consciousness based on sense of distinctiveness; (7) a troubled relationship with host societies, suggesting a lack of acceptance; (8) empathy with members of the same ethnic group(s) in diaspora settlements; and (9) the possibility of a creative, enriching life in a tolerant host country. Most of these features can be found in the Slavic and Jewish refugees who came to Shanghai.

Trade and imperial diasporas are, of course, also clearly evident in Shanghai: the first in the form of Baghdadi Jewish trading communities; the second in the shape of the British, French, American, and Japanese presence. These are examined where relevant, but the main focus of this study is on the two victim diasporas and how they played out in Shanghai.

Victim diaspora refugees of middle- and upper-middle-class backgrounds and those claiming an aristocratic heritage lost everything. They left behind their life savings, thriving businesses, comfortable homes, social position — in short, a stable and satisfying life and a promising future for their children. Most did not speak English, the language of business and, in effect, survival in the foreign settlements of Shanghai. The refugees had to begin life anew with scant or no resources. Those from more modest backgrounds and means, and particularly the younger refugees, had less of an adjustment to make, but given the extent of the challenge to all of the refugees, they, too, found it difficult to cope.

Recognizing the numbers and the diversity of social, economic, cultural, and national backgrounds of the refugees included in these two diasporas, there is no simple or collective way to describe the refugee experience. Rather, each refugee group considered in this study must be given separate attention. Who were these groups? Why did they become refugees? How did they fare after they arrived in Shanghai?

Russians suffering from nostalgia for their homeland and its traditions made it their special mission to ensure the preservation of Russian culture by building churches, opening schools, and establishing newspapers and journals. They sponsored and participated in literary and musical societies, theater groups, and other cultural events. Russian Jews, although much fewer in number, did not lag behind. They established numerous successful businesses, operated schools and clubs, and supported synagogues with active community programs. When Orthodox Polish Jews arrived in Shanghai during World War II, help from the Russian Jewish community to these Talmudic students and scholars, who barely escaped the Holocaust, made Shanghai one of the world's leading centers of Jewish studies.

These were some of the positive developments. In such a mixed community, often under severe stress, there were, however, bound to be negative side currents. Examples of these can be found in the various brands of anti-Semitism that emerged over the years. The Americans and, especially, the British, who dominated the foreign community's institutions and set the social tone, displayed a subtle but recognizable variety of anti-Semitism in their social and community contacts with most Shanghai Jews. Former White Russian troops, a large segment of the Shanghai Russian refugee community, continued at times to exhibit the tradition of anti-Semitism bred into the Russian military. The Japanese, taking their cue from the White Russians, displayed a unique version of anti-Jewish expression, combining a desire to exploit the Jews with a sense of admiration for them.

The Chinese, for their part, often found themselves in economic competition with Jewish and other refugees, and, seeing Chinese laws and courts bypassed by Jewish refugee codes and courts in Shanghai, they also expressed anti-Jewish sentiments. These were not true expressions of anti-Semitism, however, because the Chinese did not readily distinguish between Jews and foreigners in general. Chinese reaction to the Jewish and other European refugees was closely intertwined with their overall growing negative reaction to the Western presence in China. When Nazi representatives of the Third Reich arrived during the war years, the truest and most virulent statement of anti-Semitism made its appearance. It is important to see how each of these versions of anti-Jewish sentiment evolved.

In the end, anti-Semitism was mainly undercut by the diversity and mix of the more than fifty nationalities and traditions present in Shanghai. Almost as important, the great distraction of making money and building useful business and social relationships caused the various strains of anti-Semitism to remain undeveloped, so that they never achieved a full or coordinated stature. In many ways, Shanghai actually provided a positive environment especially for Jewish refugee youths, who, for the most part, would be spared the experience of overt anti-Semitism during their formative years.

Refugees of the victim diasporas came at different time intervals, from many countries. There were "White" Russians, meaning Russians who for political reasons opposed the "Reds," and those who supported the October Revolution. In this study, the term "Russian" usually refers to the "White" Russians, except in discussions where it is necessary to distinguish them from Russian Jews. Then the term "White Russian" is used. Russian Jewish refugees maintained a separate identity apart from the so-called White Russian community in Shanghai, which belonged to the Russian Orthodox faith. In addition, there were Poles, Byelorussians, Ukrainians, Czechs, Lithuanians, and Latvians. Together these refugee groups numbered about 30,000 people by the mid 1930s. More than 6,000 in these communities were Jewish. When the World War II Jewish diaspora reached Shanghai, the number of its participants coming from central and eastern Europe exceeded 18,000.

Refugee figures are inherently unreliable, however, for at least two reasons. Many who came to Shanghai were counted but then left the city for new destinations; some of these returned and were counted again. Others for various reasons preferred not to register with authorities and therefore escaped enumeration. Nevertheless, there is no doubt that the refugee populations described above came to far outnumber the British, American, and French establishments, which, according to the more reliable census data of 1934 and 1935, included 9,225, 3,809, 1,430 persons respectively, and these numbers declined in the years ahead.[5]

Despite their size and origins, refugee communities and their leaders went unrepresented in the city's power structures and remained socially apart. While the Americans and British enjoyed the convivial atmosphere of exclusive clubs, the various refugee groups each had their own enclaves, where they maintained cultural and religious connections and exchanged the information and support necessary to their survival. Altogether, they comprised what may be viewed as the "other Shanghai." Certainly, the British and American communities both had recognizable rungs on their social ladders and should not be seen as homogeneous, without an "other" element. But what is impressive is the meaningful, if modest, life that came to flourish in these "other side of the tracks" refugee communities.

The foreign population of Shanghai, including the Japanese, who by 1935 were the second most numerous, with 20,242 persons, was dwarfed by the size of the Chinese refugee communities. From the time the Western powers established their presence in Shanghai, Chinese refugees had poured into the city to escape Small Swords and Taiping rebels, warlord armies, and, later, Japanese invasion. Many of these were landlords, displaced gentry, and merchant families who could afford to relocate, while others less fortunate fled poverty and famine in the countryside.[6] The level of Chinese migrant population ebbed and flowed in response to each changing crisis. Beginning in 1895, Japanese and Western enterprises, by the terms of the Treaty of Shimonoseki, gained permission to locate manufacturing enterprises in Shanghai and other treaty ports. Thereafter, impoverished Chinese refugees became a definite boon to Chinese, Western, and Japanese manufacturing in the city, providing cheap labor and supplying prosperous Chinese and foreigners with servants and amahs, or nursemaids. Eventually, as their numbers soared, these Chinese refugees, for the most part, became the "lumpenproletariat," numbering at times as many as 150,000 and crowded into the lanes and alleys of the foreign settlements, especially in the Hongkou (Hongkew) and Yangshupu (Yangtsepoo) areas of the Japanese-dominated sector of the International Settlement.[7] How and to what extent they interacted is another part of the mosaic of the refugee experience in Shanghai.

With so many refugee groups descending on Shanghai, the question arises as to what they expected to find in this city that did not exist elsewhere. In other words, why did they come to Shanghai? How did they contribute to the internationalization of the city? What was the basis for their perception of the city as offering security and refuge? What foundation was there to the British, American, and French authorities' claim to exercise administrative, police, and security powers within the major parts of the city where the refugee communities congregated? What did it mean to the refugees that one of the two major foreign settlements was run by a multinational council? How did the eventual decline in power and authority of the Western ruling elite affect the fortunes of the refugee communities? How did members of the two diaspora communities respond to the wartime Japanese authorities? Did they resist, accommodate, or collaborate with them? These questions give us the key to understanding the substance and context of Shanghai refugee life, and in so doing, what do they tell us about the history of Shanghai? Responding to them requires first delving briefly into the historical context of the foreign presence in Shanghai, or what Cohen might refer to as the imperial diasporas. How and upon what basis the Western powers built their communities in Shanghai is key to understanding what kind of reception and society the refugees would find upon their arrival.

The Treaty Port Context

> Shanghai, not a colony, not even a concession, but a fortuitous aggregate of self-governing English Merchants.
>
> — A British Officer, *1884*

Westerners arriving in Shanghai around the middle of the nineteenth century had but one purpose in mind: to build a thriving port for international trade and commerce at the mouth of the rich Yangzi Valley, the gateway to China's interior provinces and its vast markets. They found that a flourishing system of domestic commerce already existed that could serve as a foundation for further expansion inland and abroad.[8] Applying military force to achieve these trade goals, they defeated China during the Opium Wars (1839–42, 1857–60). The outcome was the signing of the Nanjing and Bogue treaties with Britain in 1842 and 1843, the Wangxia treaty with the United States, and the Whampoa treaty with France in 1844, followed by still another round of treaty settlements completed in 1860. Under these treaties, later commonly referred to as the "unequal treaties" because of the extent to which they came to be seen as benefiting the Western powers, Chinese ports were forcibly opened to trade, including Shanghai.

This "unequal treaty" arrangement was neither an innovation, however, nor perceived as wholly disadvantageous by the Chinese government, which in 1835 had made a similar arrangement with Muslim traders on China's Inner Asian frontier. Because of the success of this earlier settlement, it became the model for arriving at settlements with the encroaching Western maritime powers.[9] In that context, the Qing authorities found it possible to represent the recent treaty settlements as a practical means of obtaining certain real benefits from a rapprochement with the West, to bring about a restored sense of tranquility, and at the same time, to pacify the aggressive Western traders.[10]

On the other hand, the treaties offered the Western powers certain unmistakable dividends. Besides gaining an expanded foothold for trade in China through the treaty system, the foreign powers gained legal exemption from Chinese laws and courts. This privilege came with the right of extraterritoriality, which guaranteed that merchants, their staffs, and their families would be able to live and function in Shanghai outside Chinese legal jurisdiction and in accordance with Western laws and practices.[11] Still another important advantage was the treaties' most-favored-nation clause: any gain won by one Western power in negotiations with the Chinese automatically applied to the other treaty signers. Qing officials viewed this, to them again a familiar policy, as offering opportunities for playing off one power against another and thus preventing any one of them from becoming predominant. Finally, and very important to the foreign merchant community, China gave up all tariff autonomy by permitting fixed, regular, low tariff rates to be established by Western powers, an obvious boon to the development of foreign trade and commerce.

The British were the first of the powers to make their presence felt in Shanghai. Their early negotiations with local Chinese authorities focused on developing the port for international trade and commerce and winning the best anchorages. The Chinese allowed Great Britain twenty-three acres of land for purchase and residence by its subjects. A Committee for Roads and Jetties dealt with improving conditions for the loading and unloading of ships. Up to this point, British behavior still more or less conformed with the terms of the abovementioned Nanjing Treaty: "His Majesty the Emperor of China agrees that British subjects, with their families and establishments, shall be allowed to reside, for the purpose of carrying on their mercantile pursuits without molestation or restraints, in the cities and towns of Canton, Amoy, Foochow, Ningpo and Shanghai."[12]

Certain pressures and events soon followed that gave the Western powers the opportunity to take a broader interpretation of the original treaty system. One pressure came from competing foreign interests in the Shanghai trade. The early American merchant consuls, not wanting to lose out in any future negotiations, and having less of a presence and much weaker military backup, pressed and won recognition for the concept of no exclusive concessions in Shanghai. The British, appreciating their own predominant status, resisted the American proposal initially, but they eventually recognized the utility of coordinating and supervising the growing and diverse foreign commercial concerns in Shanghai. The French authorities, on the other hand, unimpressed by the British and American proposals, refused this multilateral arrangement and set about establishing their own exclusive concession, giving direct authority to their chief diplomat, the French consul. Eventually, in 1863, the British and American settlements merged into one, the so-called International Settlement. Shanghai thereafter consisted of three parts: the International Settlement; the French Concession; and the area under Chinese jurisdiction, which included Nandao and the walled city, a region to the north called Zhabei (Chapei), and Pudong (Pootong) to the east. Gradually, other Western powers joined the International Settlement.

A Western Municipal Government

Earlier, in 1853, a branch of the Chinese Taiping rebels had attacked Shanghai and succeeded in taking possession of a portion of the native city. This violent intrusion galvanized the foreign interests in the International Settlement into making the decision to form a municipal government, independent of Chinese authority, to manage their own affairs. Acting in concert, the foreign powers claimed that the rebel attack proved the Chinese government's inability to provide adequate protection to the foreign communities and their pursuit of commercial activity, as promised under the Nanjing Treaty system. Taking a step further, the powers formed a multinational defense corps known as the Shanghai Volunteer Corps, probably the first of its kind in the world. As still further protection, the foreign powers demanded formal recognition by the Chinese government of their assumed position of immunity from armed conflict within the Settlement boundaries.[13] This last measure was meant to preclude Chinese military or police forces from having any basis for invading the sanctity of the new foreign enclaves. All these demands having been formulated, the time seemed propitious for the International Settlement authorities to set down, clearly and anew, the rights of foreign residents and their communities in Shanghai, putting aside the terms of the original treaties signed with the Chinese authorities.

The new Western terms, spelled out in new Land Regulations, replaced the old Committee for Roads and Jetties with a Municipal Council, elected annually by representatives of ratepayers qualified to vote by ownership of land valued at over five hundred taels of silver, with taxes on this land paid up, or by paying household rent of five hundred taels or more per annum.[14] British interests, being dominant within the settlement community, held five of the nine positions on the new council. Before World War I, the other four seats were divided at different times among Americans, Germans, Austrians, and Italians. With the changes precipitated by the end of war, Germany and Austria lost their extraterritorial rights in China. The new communist government in the Soviet Union voluntarily relinquished its claims to the unequal rights. Eventually, the four additional seats were shared equally by American and Japanese ratepayers.

An obvious omission in the formulation of this body involved the Chinese. Chinese ratepayers, under the arrangement, could reside in the International Settlement and enjoy its protection, but had no voting rights as to the composition of the presiding Municipal Council, even though most of the settlement's revenue came from taxes collected from this largest population segment. Chinese ratepayers did enjoy the security and profits to be gained from the settlement's booming trade and commerce, and the protection afforded by residing in the foreign-managed settlement operating under the privilege of extraterritoriality.

As is apparent, the scope of Chinese sovereignty diminished as the foreign powers assumed greater jurisdiction. What began as calculated Chinese policies meant only to accommodate the Western powers, and thereby permit some amount of control over their presence and activities, were gradually undermined in the face of new and increased pressures, both foreign and domestic.[15] The early success at creating and maintaining a harmonious, balanced relationship was coming undone. Subsequent revisions of the Land Regulations afforded still greater authority to the powers, without receiving official approval from the Chinese Ministry of Foreign Affairs.

The foreign powers, through their representatives on the Municipal Council, continued independently to build basic institutions for the protection and strengthening of their settlements. Besides forming an international defense force, the Municipal Council established the Shanghai Municipal Police Force to guarantee internal civilian security and control. A so-called Mixed Court system ensured the predominance of Western laws and procedures over the "backward" Chinese laws, especially in cases in which foreigners were charged.[16] The local authorities were not willing to allow Chinese sovereignty within the International Settlement by permitting the establishment of separate Chinese courts of law. An expedient solution to the problem was found in a special tribunal operating under the direction of the foreign consuls. When cases involved foreign interests, a consular official called an assessor sat with the Chinese judge and held the power to stay the proceedings or appeal the outcome, in both civil and criminal cases, if the case did not appear to support Western concepts of justice. The system allowed a Chinese judge to work independently only in cases brought before him by the municipal police that exclusively involved Chinese interests. Because the police forces in the International Settlement operated in the employ of the Municipal Council, as did the penal system, foreign interests were well protected by this judicial system.[17]

Clearly, the foreign powers, led by the British, were able to protect their status, security, and privileges by assuming the highest powers of government: defense, taxation, courts, and police. The Municipal Council set up its own postal system and fire brigade.[18] These operated under the Municipal Council's twelve departments, which among other services handled public works, police, public health, education, and legal affairs. The revenue to support the costs of this comprehensive administration came from a variety of rates, taxes, and license fees levied on its customers.

The Shanghai Municipal Council, whose membership always reflected the powerful commercial and landed interests in the city, was able to operate quite independently of the foreign consular representatives in Shanghai. Its executive powers were not bounded by treaty arrangements in the way diplomatic behavior was. Rather, Municipal Council officials could act relatively freely. This was not the case with the Conseil municipal français established in the French Concession under the *Règlements* of 1866, which gave the French consul absolute veto power over all decisions arrived at by the elected Conseil. In actual practice, however, the French consul could hardly overlook or overrule the interests of local French business interests affected by his decisions.

The Nanjing Treaty system, negotiated with Chinese officials and aimed at providing the powerful Western interests with opportunities for residence and trade, never authorized establishing foreign municipalities that would usurp the powers of government, but that was what evolved.[19] In the years to come, superior foreign power, as expressed in finance, commerce, invention, and military strength, would further diminish Chinese sovereignty. Even more important, the Chinese government, finding so much domestic or local Chinese support and complicity with the existing local arrangements, realized that the potential for containing or, certainly, for expelling the avaricious foreigners was very limited. To the original rights of trade and residence negotiated by treaty, powerful Westerners in Shanghai gradually added the right to govern, thereby denying Chinese sovereignty over key parts of the city. Their ability to do so stemmed in part from the vague threat of force, mainly from Great Britain. British local authorities reinterpreted the treaty limits and extended rights and privileges, as desired, to increase profit and privileges and safeguard life and property. The other powers quickly and automatically picked up these benefits. The Land Regulations, although described by some as a valid constitution conferring legality on the Shanghai municipal government, did not have a clear legal basis conferred by treaty. The Chinese government, as it comprehended the eroding situation, denounced each step in the usurpation of its sovereign powers. And in the last decade of Qing rule, the government did achieve some substantial gains in its drive to maintain China's territorial integrity in the face of the foreign powers. The successful containment of German imperialism in Shandong Province has been carefully examined by John Schrecker.[20]

A prime example of Western encroachment in Shanghai was expansion of the foreign-controlled areas. Through pressure on their diplomats and use of local influence, Westerners in Shanghai took advantage of China's defeat in the Sino-Japanese War of 1895 and the chaos of the Chinese Revolution of 1911 to enlarge both the International Settlement and the French Concession to many times their original sizes. The International Settlement grew from the original 183 acres to 5,583, and the French Concession from 164 acres to 2,525.[21] It took World War I to stop further Western expansion.

The vague legal basis for local foreign power and privilege, linked to military predominance, is a key background element to this study. It meant that Chinese national sovereignty in major parts of Shanghai was significantly diminished, at least as the local foreigners perceived and understood it. The city functioned as a free and open port, to which people could come with or without a passport or a visa, lacking financial guarantees, certificates of character or prearranged jobs, and still be able to live in protected enclaves guaranteed by special arrangements. The government that received them in the International Settlement included representatives of several countries, seemingly balanced carefully through annual elections to consider all foreign interests. The balanced façade, however, could not conceal the fact that for much of the Shanghai Municipal Council's existence, British interests and participation dominated its policies and functioning, even though American officials served as chairmen of the Shanghai Municipal Council during several key years. For refugees arriving at different stages, these unusual governing circumstances and the peculiar status of the city made Shanghai a unique haven and island of security for the unwanted from many quarters of the globe.

The Chinese Presence

In the early decades of the twentieth century, new factors would emerge to make the Western justification of exclusive privileges and governmental powers difficult to maintain and defend. The enfeebled and increasingly fractured Chinese government in Beijing was being bypassed by local organizations and movements committed to necessary and beneficial change. By at least the 1920s, Shanghai emerged as a key center for Chinese nationalistic sentiments and movements. The defining events in this process were the famous incident of May 30, 1925 (see p. 45 below), and the burgeoning anti-imperialism movement. In the course of the latter, raising the slogan "No taxation without representation," Chinese challenged the right of the Municipal Council to keep Chinese representatives off its executive body. Chinese raised demands both for representation on the Municipal Council itself and a thorough readjustment of Sino-foreign relations, including return to China of foreign settlements and concessions in port cities. Retrieval and defense of full sovereignty for China was part of the new nationalism, which dated from as early as 1900 among some members of China's elite.[22] Displaying a shift in sentiment inspired largely by the need to preserve the all-important stability and civil peace essential to conducting business, the Shanghai Municipal Council decided on a practical compromise. Its leaders agreed to allow a committee of respected Chinese residents with business involvements similar to their own to advise the council on Chinese affairs and interests.[23]

Chinese confidence and the articulation of Chinese demands were significantly enhanced by the successful formation of a unified Chinese Nationalist Government at Nanjing in 1928. During the previous year, on July 7, the City Government of Greater Shanghai had been established and a mayor appointed to manage the Chinese sector of Shanghai. This new Western-inspired government for the Chinese areas surrounding both the International Settlement and the French Concession presided over the old Chinese districts of Zhabei and Nandao, including the old walled city. Increasingly, the Chinese government was able to involve the Chinese bourgeoisie, which had grown in wealth and influence, in making political demands, especially concerning the local power arrangements within the foreign settlements.[24] While governing a population of more than two million, the new Chinese government of Shanghai succeeded in regaining judicial administration over Chinese nationals in the International Settlement with a system of Chinese courts, thus bringing to an end the Mixed Court system. In addition, Chinese ratepayers assumed three municipal councillor seats, elected by the Chinese Ratepayers Association and organizations representing the major Chinese commercial interests in Shanghai. In 1930, the number of Chinese seats on the Shanghai Municipal Council increased to five, giving the Chinese an equal share of the total representation with even the British.[25]

Over time, the rise of Chinese nationalism and its drive to regain national sovereignty, together with an emerging and aggressive Japan and the enormous distractions of world events elsewhere during the 1930s, helped weaken the Western position. Another key factor was the failure of the Western authorities in Shanghai to meet local challenges and manage them effectively. Lack of foresight and discernment gradually undermined their ability to exercise sovereignty over foreign Shanghai and defend its privileged status.[26]

The Refugee Challenge

In the 1920s, before all these elements came into play, and when large numbers of Russian and Russian Jewish refugees arrived in Shanghai, the Western powers were enjoying a golden age of power and privilege in

China. In addition to the business and consular communities, Shanghai had become the administrative and publishing center for Western missions. Ordinary businessmen and the missionary personnel and their families lived extraordinary lives, often with fine homes and numerous servants to take care of cooking, household work, child raising, tailoring, transportation, and every other chore. Life was quite comfortable for the foreign expatriate elites and even for the common settlers among them. Their lifestyles would stand in sharp contrast to those of the wave of Slavic refugees.

The incoming refugees, many impoverished, quickly became an under-class in the foreign community. While the refugee presence did not seriously threaten the livelihoods of the Western elite, they were a source of embar-rassment for the Westerners, in that these impoverished refugees were white and yet willing to do menial labor alongside Chinese. Their presence seemed to put a substantial dent in the social armor of the white Westerners and threatened to undermine what was widely perceived as their racial superiority.

The arrival in the late 1930s of more than eighteen thousand mainly German and Austrian refugees, escaping the persecution that led eventually to the Holocaust, happened over a short span of years. They arrived at a time of transition, when real power had shifted to the Japanese civilian and military authorities. The 1937 invasion of north China by Japanese forces eventually led to the three-month-long Battle of Shanghai, which decimated the Guomindang (GMD) forces. Japan assumed effective control over the Chinese-run Municipality of Greater Shanghai, surrounding both the Inter-national Settlement and French Concession. Presiding over what had become an isolated foreign island, the Western authorities found themselves in a significantly weakened state and vulnerable to those who might question the legal basis for deciding questions of sovereignty, such as who could or could not come to or reside in Shanghai. The old problem of having based their rule on the vague legal framework of the Land Regulations, enhanced only by ref-erence to examples of precedence, custom, and expediency, resurfaced.

Sensing the ambiguity over the sovereignty issue, some refugee officials questioned and even challenged official policy relating to refugees in Shanghai. The uneasy ambiguity regarding authority and power relation-ships seemed to offer some advantages to the incoming refugees. They found themselves in circumstances in which the Chinese national government did not determine their status, the local Chinese puppet government responded largely to Japanese direction, and the foreign powers often worked at cross-purposes. As early as 1931, Richard Feetham, a South African jurist advising the Shanghai Municipal Council, identified one of the key problems when he observed in his extensive report: "There is no national body to exercise the control to which an ordinary municipal body is subject in the exercise of its administrative as well as its legislative functions, or to give the assistance which an ordinary municipal body receives from a central national government."[27] In many ways, the situation appeared rather nebulous, and even advantageous to refugees hoping to slip through the system. But before refugee leaders could sort out the situation and perhaps initiate plans to accommodate even more refugees coming to Shanghai, the matter was taken out of their hands.

World War II eventually closed off the sea and land routes by which additional refugees might have entered Shanghai. In December 1941, Japanese occupation of the Shanghai International Settlement made the propriety and legality of Western municipal officials deciding the fate of refugees academic. Ironically, rather than continuing to manage the fate of refugees, British and American nationals were instead interned by the Japanese, officially by March 1943, while the Slavic and European refugees who had gained entry to Shanghai went free or relatively free. The Chinese, of course, continued to be the paramount victims of the war, brutality, and abject poverty. In response to Japanese pressure, the Shanghai Municipal Council was replaced in April 1941 by a Provisional Council, but it continued to function until 1943, when the French Concession and the International Settlement technically disappeared, with the return of both territories to China. By treaties signed in early January with Chiang Kai-shek's Nationalist Government in Chongqing (Chungking), the governments of Great Britain and the United States formally relinquished foreign extraterritorial rights, and the International Settlement came under the sovereignty and protection of the Chongqing government. The Vichy French regime returned the French Concession in July 1943 in accordance with treaty arrangements with the Chinese puppet government in Nanjing. After Japan signed a similar treaty, relinquishing rights to concessions in China and the extraterritoriality of Japanese nationals, with the Chinese puppet government, the latter declared war on the United States and Great Britain.

The Shanghai Municipal Council was abolished and replaced by a puppet body. The newly united Shanghai had a Chinese mayor, but one operating under close Japanese control.

After Pearl Harbor, the pressing issues for the diaspora refugees were the attitude of the Japanese authorities toward their continued presence in Shanghai and the fate of a few still trying to enter the city. How much might Japanese military and civilian authorities be influenced in their treatment of the refugees by their previous associations with right-wing White Russian groups in Harbin? Did that experience shape their attitudes and treatment of Slavic and European Jewish refugees in Shanghai? Would Japan's relationship with its Axis partner Germany determine in any large measure Japanese policies toward the Jewish refugees? In short, what policies would the Japanese, the new power in Shanghai, adopt toward the refugees, their communities, and their survival? How should refugee leaders respond?

With this necessarily brief and general historical framework as a preliminary background, we can turn to key questions such as who the diaspora refugees were, where they came from, what kind of life they made for their respective groups in China, and what became of them during and after World War II. What will emerge is the story of a collection of refugee communities, each consumed by the daily struggle to survive under often overwhelming economic, social, and cultural disadvantages. The daily toll on individual energies and spirits was great. Nevertheless, each community managed to preserve its separate ethnic and cultural identity, one of the key priorities of the victim diaspora tradition.

Refugee Arrivals Break the Calm

The city of Shanghai is located at the mouth of the Yangzi River or, as the Chinese know it, the Changjiang, or "long river." The city's most famous street, the Bund, remains as striking to visitors today as it was in the era of the International Settlement. Along its course were the powerful institutions that defined the character of the city, among them the major commercial houses, such as Jardine, Matheson & Co., several leading banks, including the Hongkong and Shanghai Banking Corporation, the Customs House, the offices of the authoritative *North China Daily News* (also known as the Old Lady of the Bund), and, a general favorite of the Shanghai establishment, the Cathay Hotel (now the Peace Hotel). At the end of the string, standing at Number Two the Bund, was a redoubtable pillared stone building, the all-male Shanghai Club, with its renowned Long Bar. Between these massive structures and the open waters of the Huangpu (Whangpoo) River lay grassy lawns and walkways forming a "public" park, but frequented only by foreign strollers and picnickers. Before 1928, a municipal regulation excluded Chinese from the parks, except for Chinese amahs caring for foreign children.[1] Enhanced by this open space, the Bund's imposing architecture spelled out who controlled the city and set its mores.

River traffic on the Huangpu clearly displayed the contrasts between East and West. Huge wooden junks, with their high sterns adorned with colorful painted dragons, phoenixes, and other symbols calling for prosperity, good health, long life, and other blessings, passed alongside large ocean liners and freighters coming to dock near the waterfront. Lumber ships, tankers, tramp steamers, and warships lay in midstream. An ever-active caravan of smaller craft — launches, lighters, and sampans — maneuvered around the heavier vessels, along with the ferries and large flat-bottomed river boats that transported Chinese passengers up the Yangzi.

Just minutes away from the Bund were the old Chinese walled city to the south and the Zhabei (Chapei) district bordering on Suzhou (Soochow) Creek to the north. In their narrow streets and alleyways, often described by Westerners as smelly, dirty, and chaotic, the sensual disparities between the two worlds were greatest. The life they observed, especially in the old city, seemed to newcomers to follow a course it had followed for centuries, since long before the arrival of the Westerners. The narrow, strangely alluring streets had open shops on either side. Densely populated and made restive by the transience of refugees and migrant workers, the old city appeared absolutely alien and somewhat frightening to Western settlement dwellers and foreign refugees alike. The existence of these Chinese neighborhoods, and foreign exposure to them, although always very limited, helped contribute to the Western picture of the city as the epitome of exoticism, adventure, color, and excitement.

In the International Settlement, on Nanking Road, the main shopping street, or on the Bund itself, one could observe a lively procession that, at the turn of the century, involved a curious mix of the old, new, and different. Customers and officials were transported in sedan chairs borne on shoulder poles; later these were replaced by rickshaws, pulled by laborers for ten cents a mile, and then by cars. Turbaned Sikh policemen ordered the daily parade of life in Shanghai: rickshaws, cars, trucks, electric trams, wheelbarrows trundling along with tremendous loads, huge two-wheeled trucking carts with as many as eight perspiring laborers straining at the ropes, pedestrians, bicycles, and carriages, the old and new, privilege and poverty.[2]

Shanghai had a prosperous Chinese middle class, some of whose members

Figure 1. The Garden Bridge crossing Suzhou Creek, with the Astor Hotel and Soviet consulate on the left and the Central District on the right. These were all part of the Shanghai International Settlement. SOURCE: Zhiganov, *Russkie v Shankhaie.*

owned department stores and famous restaurants, while others acted as middlemen for foreign businesses, but the wages of most Chinese were so low that Westerners of almost every station in life could easily afford a houseful of servants. One American mission family's Hongkou house, for example, had four bedrooms, a large living room, a dining room, a sleeping porch for when the Shanghai weather became unbearably hot, an office for the father's missionary work, a kitchen with a back porch and laundry room, opening onto a small concrete yard with a cook room for the servants and a coal storage room. Tiny bedrooms above the kitchen housed the Chinese servants. Coal stoves heated the main living quarters. Bathroom commodes consisted of a square wooden box with a hole in the top and an earthen chamber pot below, and hot water had to be bought from the hot water shop in the adjoining Chinese neighborhood.

The family employed a cook and a "boy" who cleaned, served meals, and answered the door. The latter was also responsible for seeing that the commodes were emptied, the contents being picked up daily by laborers. The International Settlement had no modern sewage disposal system, so the waste was sold to contractors, who made considerable profits reselling it to farmers in the surrounding countryside. The house also employed an amah, who assumed some responsibility for the children, a second amah for a child needing special attention, a washwoman, and a chauffeur, the latter being the only servant who lived away from the house. These were the principal servants; others would be engaged as needed for making clothing or for helping on special occasions, such as parties or celebrations.[3] Overseeing the household services, a so-called number one boy collected cumshaw, a commission from shopkeepers for bringing them his household's business, and took part of the other household servants' earnings.

Such was life for the privileged Westerners in Shanghai during the first few decades of the twentieth century. It was also the life of the established Jewish communities in Shanghai, except that some of their members far exceeded this typical lifestyle.

Early Jewish Communities in Shanghai

Shanghai became home to both Sephardi and Ashkenazi Jews. The two communities existed side by side, each with its own set of institutions and congregations. The Sephardi, who originated in Baghdad, belonged to the Baghdadi branch of Oriental Jewry, although they classified themselves as Sephardim. They arrived in China in the first half of the nineteenth century, part of a Baghdadi trade diaspora that extended from London to Shanghai.[4] Baghdadi Jews had first migrated to India, especially Bombay, where they became associated with British trading firms dealing in cotton and opium. In search of new markets, some of these Baghdadis subsequently settled in Singapore and Hong Kong. Eventually, Shanghai became the center of Jewish entrepreneurial activity in the East.

Working in Shanghai by mid-century, these talented and ambitious merchants soon established a solid presence, nurtured at first by the brilliant Sassoon family, which had already amassed a fortune in Bombay before opening a branch of the family firm in Shanghai in 1845. After some years of working for the Sassoons, promising Baghdadis left to establish independent enterprises. Eventually, their names would become familiar to anyone engaged in trade or business in the Far East. Besides the Sassoons, there were the Kadoories, Abrahams, Gubbays, Toegs, Ezras, Nissims, and Hardoon, to name only a few. They made their fortunes initially by trading in opium, tea, silk, wool, and cotton. Success in these areas led to expansion into public tramways, breweries, banking, finance, insurance, construction, and real estate. Others were retailers, import-exporters, and money changers. The Sephardim became major Shanghai landowners, especially the Sassoon firms, Silas A. Hardoon, and E. Ezra, and contributed significantly to the growth and development of the city. Some of their splendid mansions still stand in Shanghai today, housing various contemporary Chinese government functions. Sephardi leaders also served as councillors on the presiding Shanghai Municipal Council. One, Silas Hardoon, had the rare distinction of serving on both the Municipal Council and the Conseil municipal français, for a while concurrently.[5]

Clearly, the Sephardim were not refugees. They are considered in this study because, as an established Jewish community in Shanghai, they responded to the needs of Jewish refugees. Until 1918, most of the Sephardim had been born in the Ottoman empire and enjoyed protection from Great Britain or France; after the establishment of Iraq, they either accepted Iraqi citizenship or remained British subjects. Following the British lead, society at first sniffed at these "Oriental Jews" in its midst. Their different customs, appearance, and manners seemed too foreign to be acceptable. But as Sephardi wealth and influence swelled to enormous size, Shanghai society found it could not resist their sumptuous dinner parties and costume balls. After all, Shanghai was becoming a city built on trade and amassed wealth, and attending Sassoon and Hardoon parties at their mansions, complete with lantern-lit gardens, a multitude of attentive servants, and gay entertainment, sent a signal of success. Probably the pinnacle of Sephardi social success was reached when Sir Victor Sassoon, spectacular in talent and colorful in manners, was admitted to the most exclusive of clubs, the British Shanghai Club. Silas Hardoon also gained admission to the Shanghai Club and Race Club, but unlike most of Shanghai society, the eccentric Hardoon remained interested in building his status and ties among influential Chinese as well as in Western circles.

Certainly, not all of the Sephardim were wealthy. In their early days in Shanghai, many resided in the less expensive Hongkou (Hongkew) or northern region of the International Settlement. They worked in the Sephardi firms of David Sassoon, Sons & Co. and Elias David Sassoon & Co. as office clerks or in some support capacity. Two synagogues, Beth-El on Peking Road, whose congregation dated back to 1887, and Shearith Israel, which opened on Seward Road in 1900, served the small community's religious, social, and educational needs. It was customary for a Jewish community numbering ten families or more to establish a synagogue, a school, an old age home, a relief association, and a burial brotherhood. In the early days, a Talmud Torah class, "study [of the] law," or religious school, met at the Shearith Synagogue, which also housed a *mikveh*, or ritual bath.[6] In addition, the small community had established the Schehita Cemetery.[7]

In the early 1900s, the Shanghai Jewish community numbered fewer than one hundred families, including European Ashkenazi Jews and Russian Jews who belonged to the Ashkenazi branch. Ashkenazi Jews differed from the Sephardim in religious ritual, cultural traditions, and customs.[8] The widespread use of the Yiddish language, a German dialect infused with Hebrew and Russian or Polish elements, among the Ashkenazim, and, especially, the differences in synagogue liturgy and cantillation created a natural divide between the two communities. The order and wording of prayers in the Ashkenazi service differed from those Baghdadi Jews used, which derived from Babylonian rituals diffused through North Africa, Spain, and Portugal, whereas Palestinian rituals, transmitted via Italy, were observed by the Ashkenazim. The two traditions also have different wedding, circumcision, death, and festival customs. A prime example is during Passover, when the Sephardim eat rice, which is forbidden to observant Ashkenazim.

Along with refugees from Siberia and the Russian Far Eastern Maritime Province, the Shanghai Ashkenazi community included merchant, banking, and trading families. In the 1870s and later, Ashkenazim from Poland and Russia made a living running small hotels and inns in Shanghai, while others, whether in search of adventure or more desperate, became involved in less respectable activities. The Ohel Moishe Synagogue on Seward Road served the Hongkou-based Ashkenazi congregation,[9] and also housed the first Shanghai Jewish School. This school was attended by both Ashkenazi and Sephardi students, except for wealthy Sephardi students who boarded at elite British public schools. Started in 1903 by D. E. J. Abraham, the Jewish school by 1909 had 70 students and received financial support from the Hong Kong branch of the Kadoorie family. Its cosmopolitan student body spoke a mixture of languages, including Judeo-Arabic, Russian, Yiddish, and English. English instruction became a key part of the curriculum, because many students never spoke the language at home, and a mastery of English was, of course, essential for making one's way in the business world of Shanghai. Students received both a secular and religious education at the school, as well as sports training and a hot lunch. By 1924, the school had moved to the premises of the old American School in Shanghai at 146 N. Szechuen Road. It grew to 140 students and had a faculty of ten teachers and an appointed principal. Students who could paid $50 per month to attend the school; the Hebrew Relief Association covered the costs of those who could not pay and managed the collection of donations to support the school's operation.[10]

With such diversity of backgrounds, languages, customs, and religious traditions, it is not surprising that frictions existed within the Shanghai Jewish communities. Several attempts were made to bridge the differences. In 1906, the Association of the Jewish Community of Shanghai, chaired by A. E. Moses, and with a governing committee composed of representatives of the subscribing synagogues, with representation proportional to the amount subscribed by each, was formed to link the congregations of the Beth-El, Shearith Israel, and Ohel Moishe synagogues.[11] The committee had four Sephardi members and three from the Ashkenazi synagogue, and the aims of the association were to improve Jewish education and help care for the old, the poor, and refugees. Almost four years passed without much success in uniting the Jewish communities for these purposes, however, and in 1909, the Shanghai Jewish Communal Association was created to replace the earlier body and assume its key functions. Among other things, it kept a registry of births, marriages, and deaths.

This and subsequent efforts succumbed to social tensions and ingrained cultural differences. In the small Jewish community, Ashkenazim often expressed resentment of wealthy and socially prominent Sephardim, who, they claimed, often kept aloof at religious and social gatherings and had little interest in the Ashkenazi welfare. Given what is known about Sephardi philanthropy, these charges seem to reflect more than a little unfair bias, and it was said, too, that in fact the Ashkenazi Jews "were not very anxious to associate with the Sephardim."[12] Conrad Levy, a Jewish observer in Hankou, equated the conflict to "a cock fight" between the Ashkenazim, "who enjoyed superiority by [reason of] their white color," and the Sephardim, who claimed to possess greater moral fiber and practice stricter ethics, grounded in their more traditional Judaism.[13] The specious elements in these comments again reflect the distinct differences inherent in the two separate Jewish cultures and traditions. *Really? Or d. they reflect an urban setting!*

The recurring disputes might be explained at least in part by the fact that during the first decade of the century, neither community had a rabbi. A respected religious leader might have helped mediate disputes and differences, as well as focus community energies on more constructive pursuits. As it happened, the two communities, numbering about 3,000 by 1924, continued to emphasize their own issues.[14] The Ashkenazi Jews opened a new Ohel Moishe Synagogue on Ward Road in 1928. At least the location was new; the existing building there was to be renovated for temporary use until enough money could be gathered to erect a new structure on the premises.[15] The opening ceremonies were officiated over by the congregation's first rabbi, Rabbi Meir Ashkenazi, who had come to Shanghai from Vladivostok via Harbin. Being of the Lubavitcher Hasidim tradition, the new rabbi followed a more Orthodox strain of Judaism than did most in his congregation, but his presence as a teacher and community leader was greatly welcomed. As one congregant exclaimed, with a synagogue and rabbi of their own, the Ashkenazim finally "stood on their own soil."[16]

A new and splendid Sephardi synagogue, Ohel Rachel, designed by the Shanghai architectural firm of Moorehead & Halse, and dedicated in 1921, opened on Seymour Road in the Western District of the International Settlement, outside Hongkou.[17] Inscribed in Hebrew over the Holy Ark that housed the sacred scrolls were the words: "Know before whom thou stand, before the King of Kings the Holy One, Blessed be He." Its dedication was presided over by the recently arrived Rabbi W. Hirsch. The elaborate services included a choir and even organ music. The Sephardi congregants, recognizing that a choir and organ were somewhat radical in their tradition, explained that these unusual additions were necessary to attract the young to services, who otherwise were known to describe the religious proceedings as "deadly boring." Another magnificent Sephardi synagogue, Beth Aharon, financed by Silas A. Hardoon, and under the leadership of the Reverend Mendel Brown, began services on Museum Road in 1927.

Opportunities for community social occasions were enhanced by the opening in 1921 of the Jewish Club Ahduth, situated on the Ohel Rachel Synagogue compound on Seymour Road, which became known as the "Jewish Country Club." It was to accommodate both Sephardi and Ashkenazi Jewish social events, although items in the local society pages reporting parties and club gatherings suggest that most of the sponsored events catered to the Sephardim.[18] In its early years, the club did not do well. The Ashkenazi community, still located for the most part in Hongkou, was the fastest-growing of the two Jewish communities. The club's inconvenient location and Ashkenazi hesitations about Sephardi associations limited Ashkenazi use of the club. This situation continued at least until the mid and late 1920s, when a dearth of good housing in Hongkou drove many Jewish residents to seek residence in the Western District of Shanghai, bringing them closer to the Jewish Club. With the increased interest and demands, the club began to draw up ambitious plans for finding a more spacious location and improved amenities.[19] Another club, popular with the Ashkenazim, was the Jewish Recreation Club, founded in 1911. In addition to sponsoring well-attended sporting events, this club boasted a dramatics section, which entertained packed audiences at local theaters with performances of favorite Yiddish plays.[20] Finally, the Maccabean Club, a social club for men, opened in new premises in 1928, underscoring once again the expansion of Jewish social and cultural life in Shanghai.[21]

Russian Official Interests

In addition to the Russian Jews, who were active mainly in business and trade, there were a number of Orthodox Christians officially representing imperial Russia in Shanghai. The two groups were complementary in furthering Russian interests, but most of the Russian Jews belonged to the Ashkenazi Jewish community described above, while Russian officials gravitated toward the rest of Shanghai's foreign community.

The first generation of Russian officials in Shanghai dated from the 1860s, when the city was a transhipment point for tea from Russian tea factories in Hankou (Hankow), further up the Yangzi River.[22] This trade was quasi-governmental, in that, although privately financed, it enjoyed Russian imperial protection. Russian tea magnates, or "tea kings," as they were popularly called, managed the lucrative trade between Hankou and Shanghai, often spending part of the year in Shanghai to oversee the transhipment of tea via the Odessa Volunteer Fleet Line to Russia, and to enjoy the comforts and amenities of the port city. Russians preferred the red tea that was grown in several provinces near Hankou especially for export to Russia.[23] As the trade developed, Russian tea exporters, such as the Litvinovs, Mochanovs, Gubkins, and others, built themselves spacious villas at Hankou. After her tea magnate husband died, Mrs. E. N. Litvinov became one of the leading Russian philanthropists in Shanghai, playing a key role in construction of the magnificent Russian Orthodox cathedral on Rue Paul Henri.

Russian interests received a boost in 1860 with the opening of a Russian consulate general in Shanghai, initially headed by an American merchant consul. In the early years of foreign involvement, Great Britain and the United States, the predominant and earliest foreign powers to establish an official presence in the city, usually handled consular affairs for other distant Western countries. This arrangement lasted until at least 1870, when Russian functionaries began to serve national and commercial interests in Shanghai. In 1880, the Russian government appointed a Russian, J. E. Reding, to take charge of the Shanghai consulate and to manage the affairs of the few Russians residing in the city.[24] By 1900, Russians in Shanghai numbered only 47. Most of these held official positions in the Russian consulate or were employed by the Russo-Chinese Bank, which opened in 1896 and was renamed the Russo-Asiatic Bank in 1910. Others in this small community worked for the Volunteer Fleet Line, and a few unaffiliated with official or commercial circles might be considered freelancers.[25]

There was always some overlap between Russian official and commercial circles and the Ashkenazi Jewish community, some of whose members earned their livings as export-import agents and tradesmen. Russian plans for railroad expansion, promising greater access to eastern markets, stimulated the growth of both communities. Russia did not want to be left out of the developing exploitation of China's growing weakness by the great powers. China's decisive defeat by Japan in the Sino-Japanese War of 1894–95 encouraged Russia's ambitious plans for expansion into China's northeast and Manchuria. It also raised fears of expanding Japanese influence in Manchuria, where Russia had long planned to establish a foothold, ever since it had acquired the Far Eastern Maritime Province, including the valuable port of Vladivostok, under the terms of the Treaty of Beijing (1860). The initial focus was on building and financing an extension of the Trans-Siberian Railroad, to be known as the Chinese Eastern Railroad, reaching from Chita in the west across Manchuria to Vladivostok, a concession awarded to Russia by the Chinese under a secret arrangement in 1896, in exchange for a defensive treaty aimed at Japan. The Russo-Chinese Bank was to play a major role in financing and administering this railroad expansion, designed to advance Russian trade and industry. Its chief instrument was the Chinese Eastern Railroad Company, incorporated in early 1897, which was assigned a fifteen-mile-wide extraterritorial zone bordering the line, together with some broader areas to accommodate station settlements.

As a participant in "carving the Chinese melon," Russia also had plans to expand southward, but the Treaty of Shimonoseki ending the Sino-Japanese war ceded territories, including the rich Liaodong Peninsula, to Japan, complicating Russia's agenda. France and Germany supported the Russians in forcing Japan to relinquish this territory, however, and, in 1898, Russia obtained a 25-year lease to the Liaodong Peninsula and Port Arthur (Lüshun). A branch of the Chinese Eastern Railroad through Manchuria completed by 1903 gave access to Port Arthur and the port of Dalian (Dairen, or Lüda).

At the hub linking the Chinese Eastern Railroad with the line to Port Arthur and Dalian was the new Russian town of Harbin, established in 1898 by a Russian survey team on the site of a small Chinese fishing village.[26] With the extensive railroad construction centered around Harbin, northern Manchuria came to be referred to as a "railroad state," which accurately described its main focus. From March 1917 until March 1920, this "state" came under the official rule of the Russian General Dmitrii Leonidovich Horvat, general manager of the Russian railway system in Manchuria since 1902, and a member of the Russian imperial family.[27]

This expansion of Russian interests in the north and on the Liaodong Peninsula helped bring Shanghai closer to the sphere of Russian influence.

Construction of Russian fortifications at Port Arthur and the development of Dalian as a port created a strong demand for imported building supplies, war matériel, and other goods and equipment, which could best be provided from Shanghai. Russian officials and entrepreneurs consequently streamed into Shanghai. Contractors and suppliers for the Russian army arrived to set up shop. Russian military, banking, and commercial interests hoped to capitalize on the newly acquired ports to develop the Russian fleet and to launch commercial ventures that would send Russian goods through the port of Shanghai to countries around the world.

By the turn of the century, prospects for the Russian and Russian Jewish communities in Shanghai appeared promising. Imperial Russian officials and their commercial colleagues and families shared in the pleasures and benefits of the diplomatic and community life of multinational Shanghai. In a matter of a few years, however, these communities would be challenged in terms both of resources and integrity by waves of refugees.

The First Wave of Refugees

> There is a rumor that the czar is going to the front. The longer he waits, the less distance there will be for him to go.
> — A Russian soldier, *1904*

In the early 1900s, pogroms in the Russian Pale of Settlement and a particularly vicious pogrom in Ukraine drove large numbers of Jews toward the east and Manchuria, where they had heard of the economic opportunities afforded by the new railroad construction and administration. The new frontier settlements enjoyed a less restrictive political and social environment, especially attracting Jewish professionals and laborers alike. As David Wolff has pointed out, Harbin sorely needed urban commercial, technical, and labor skills to support provisioning and development.[28] In addition to persecuted Jews, the opportunities in Manchurian cities such as Manzhouli and Harbin attracted Georgians, Latvians, Ukrainians, and Poles. In 1902, seven thousand Polish laborers followed on the heels of the Polish engineers, technicians, and administrators who had helped construct and run the railroads centered around Harbin. A Polish source even identifies one of the key

members of the Russian survey team that selected the site for the town of
Harbin, A. Shidlovsky (or Szydlowski) as a Pole.[29]

Russian expansionism in Manchuria, backed up by several hundred thousand Russian troops who remained in the region in the aftermath of the
Boxer Rebellion, fueled tensions with Japan, the other major player. These
tensions reached a boiling point when Russia began to seek economic and
strategic concessions on the Korean peninsula. Recognizing the impotence
of the Chinese to deal with any incursions, both Russia and Japan planned to
exploit the mineral, timber, and fishing resources of Manchuria and the
Amur and Ussuri regions. But the Japanese regarded Russian designs on
Korea, considered by Japan to be vital to its own strategic security, as sur-
passing tolerable limits, and in February 1904, after a failed round of negotiations, Japan launched a surprise attack on the Russian Fleet at Port
Arthur, beginning the Russo-Japanese War.[30]

A string of Russian defeats followed. Operating from bases in Korea,
Japanese forces took Dalian and besieged Port Arthur. Three months later,
the Russian forces at Mukden (Shenyang) withdrew. More than 175,000
Russian soldiers died, were wounded, or were taken prisoner, and the
Japanese suffered even greater losses. The war came to a devastating con-
clusion after Japan annihilated a Russian fleet that had come all the way from
the Baltic to assist the crippled Russian navy in the Far East. This pivotal
battle took place in the Tsushima Straits, which separate Korea and Japan. By
the Treaty of Portsmouth, mediated by President Theodore Roosevelt in
September 1905, Japan once again gained control over the Liaodong
Peninsula, including Port Arthur, and the southern part of the Russian-built
South Manchurian railway.[31] Russia did manage to retain a substantial presence in northern Manchuria, particularly in Harbin.

Anti-Semitism Makes Its Appearance

The Russo-Japanese war also involved some 30,000 Jewish conscripts in the
Russian army,[32] with significant repercussions for the Jewish community of
Shanghai. The Ohel Moishe Philanthropic Society organized medical and
hospital care for wounded Russian Jewish soldiers arriving on ships from the

bloody battle of Port Arthur who were met on the docks by welcoming crowds carrying banners and placards. A charity ball helped raise funds for the disabled. Before returning north or to the front, one group was fêted at a picnic, where pictures were taken with local officials and favorite foods provided.[33]

Besides recounting the terrible defeats the Russians had suffered at the hands of the Japanese, the soldiers told of the tribulations of Jews in the Russian Army. Although numerous at the battlefront, Russian Jews could not expect promotion to the ranks of officer or noncommissioned officer in the Russian imperial army or navy. The Russian military authorities refused to cover travel expenses for family members of Jewish troops intending to stay in the Russian Far East after their demobilization, a service offered to families of non-Jewish troops. Furthermore, when on furlough, Jewish soldiers were not free to travel to destinations of their choice. Rather, they had to spend their time in the Pale of Settlement. Even special military units received discriminatory treatment. Regulations specified that no more than one-third of a military band could be composed of Jewish musicians.[34] It is not surprising, then, that after the war, many demobilized Jewish troops sought to remain in Harbin or made their way to the open port of Shanghai in search of a freer life.

Financing the war effort became an issue for both sides. The Japanese cause greatly benefited from substantial loans arranged by the American Jewish banker and financier Jacob H. Schiff, a senior partner in the New York banking firm of Kuhn, Loeb & Co. With Schiff's assistance, the Japanese government negotiated four foreign loans, totaling $410 million, $180 million of which was the U.S. share.[35] Japan's total war expenditure was $860 million, indicating that the American share was a significant percentage of the cost. The imperial Russian finance minister, S. I. Witte, had also approached Jacob Schiff for funding, but failed to win acceptable terms. The Kishinev pogrom of 1903, the most famous of czarist times, had focused Schiff's attention on the suffering of Jews in Russia and aroused his determination somehow to respond. Schiff believed that by aiding Japan, he might help to undermine the government that was oppressing Russian Jewry.[36] His actions angered Russian imperial officers but evoked much goodwill from the Japanese. When Japan emerged from the war victorious, its prestige at a *weird 30,000 Jews were fighting them while at the same time*

zenith, still another loan was arranged with its foreign supporters.[37] In an unusual display of gratitude, the Japanese granted Schiff an audience with their
emperor in recognition of his contributions to Japan's war effort. Shanghai
again came to the aid of Japan, beginning in 1906, by initiating a subscription fund to collect donations for the relief of severe food shortages in Japan.
The Schiff loans and other generous acts by the Shanghai Jewish community
would not be forgotten by Japan in later years.[38]

Russian dissatisfaction with Jacob Schiff's largesse toward Japan's war effort was only one factor in the anti-Semitism that emerged in the course of
the Russian defeat by Japan. Russian anti-Jewish outbursts and excesses had
an additional clear political purpose. The Jews were a handy scapegoat for
diverting public attention away from the Russian government's powerless-
ness, corruption, and incompetence. Jews were held responsible for the be-
trayal of Port Arthur and the destruction of the Russian fleet, as well as for
the disastrous defeat at Mukden. A Russian soldier who fought at the battle
of Port Arthur wrote in his diary, "we know you sold us to the Japanese."[39]
More pogroms followed, causing an exodus of Jews seeking refuge in Harbin
and Shanghai. The Ashkenazi Philanthropic Society of Shanghai again engaged in efforts to care for refugees from Russian persecution.

Russian defeats in World War I provided another opportunity to single
out the Jews for blame and punishment. Thousands of Russian Jews had
been conscripted to serve in the armed forces. After demobilization, some
were arrested and tried for espionage; countless others were evacuated from
Estonia, Latvia, Lithuania, Poland, and Byelorussia to be resettled in the
Russian Pale.[40] Many of those who had fought on the eastern front sought
refuge in Harbin or made their way to Shanghai.

The loss of economic opportunity after the withdrawal of Russian military forces at the end of the war was another factor that drove Russian Jews
to Shanghai and elsewhere in China. Feeding, housing, and supplying the
huge numbers of troops on the eastern front required a host of service industries. Once these forces departed, however, the economic recession and
especially the acts of retribution against Jews compelled them to seek security and a living elsewhere.

In contrast, World War I had been good for Shanghai. Wartime conditions in Russia had disrupted the transport system and created a great demand for foreign goods to supply the Russian people and especially to pro-

vision the Russian military. Russian military procurement officials, traders, and agents representing different organizations poured into Shanghai.[41] Shanghai-built icebreakers, designed for use in Vladivostok, were in heavy demand, as were other types of machinery, pharmaceuticals, and chemicals. The Russian population in Shanghai reached 700–800 by 1917, and discussions began for the establishment of a Russian Chamber of Commerce to assist in handling the increased volume of commercial activity inspired by the war.[42]

Word of the improving economic climate in Shanghai spread to the north and acted as a magnet for Jews recently relieved of military service and unwelcome in Russia. Those arriving in Shanghai found an established Jewish community able to assist them in navigating through the challenges of a society dominated by a foreign language and customs. The familiar Ashkenazi institutions of relief, a synagogue, schools, a cemetery, and old age assistance were well established, and even the affluent Sephardi Jews displayed a sympathetic attitude toward the arriving refugees. The wartime commercial demands and the influx of Russian commercial agents provided many opportunities to this established Jewish community, which it reaped with considerable success. And the gains helped to diminish somewhat the inequalities in wealth between the Ashkenazi and Sephardi communities. In addition, the growing number of Russian and eastern European Jews being added to the Jewish community further enlivened the institutions and activities of the Ashkenazi community.

Revolution and Flight

Russian history entered a tumultuous period near the end of World War I. The "Red" forces had seized power during the October Revolution of 1917, and the following year, the Bolsheviks concluded a separate peace with Germany. The Bolshevik seizure of power set off the bloody Civil War, lasting from 1918 until 1923. In the Russian Far East, major cities and territories changed hands several times in the course of the war, causing turmoil and devastation for the population. The murky military and political situation was complicated by the fact that the anti-Bolshevik "White" forces included various Cossack groups acting under orders from their own leaders, some of whom also enjoyed Japanese protection. As the struggles wore on, the Japanese found the Russian internecine struggle quite useful for their own expansion plans. The famous Cossack leader, or ataman, Grigorii Mikhailovich Semenov, enjoyed close ties with the Japanese. Relationships between the anti-Bolshevik White Russians and the Japanese continued after the war ended, and leaders of the defeated White forces would later become prominent figures in the Shanghai Russian refugee community.

By the summer of 1919, the Bolsheviks had consolidated their position in the Far Eastern Maritime Province and had effective political organizations in Siberia and Manchuria. White governments in Khabarovsk, Vladivostok, and other cities fell in early 1920, but during the spring and winter of 1921–22, White forces launched several successful campaigns, even seizing back Khabarovsk in December 1921. This high-water mark of White fortunes was short-lived. The leaders of the White forces were deeply divided among themselves and failed to produce a clear and effective program for mobilizing the Russian populace. Their armies suffered from a severe shortage of weapons and matériel.[43] In early 1922, Bolshevik forces repulsed the White drive back toward Vladivostok to areas protected by the Japanese.

Prospects for the White forces dimmed daily. They had been defeated in all other areas of the country except in the Far East. To make matters worse, Japan had come under heavy diplomatic and domestic pressure to end its intervention in the Russian Far East. Accordingly, the Japanese government decided to withdraw Japanese troops by the end of October 1922. White leaders, stunned by this announcement, failed to devise a successful plan for their own evacuation. Still convinced that Red rule in the rest of the country would crumble, they launched a final major campaign, which ended in a bloody rout.[44] Thereafter began the great exodus of White forces, fleeing the country in panic, most through the port of Vladivostok, never again to threaten Soviet dominance. Persecution and probable death were almost certainly the lot of White troops and their sympathizers if they remained. Not wanting to leave without one last foray, however, one famous White general marshaled his beleaguered forces. Two days before his departure in October 1922, General F. L. Glebov, a leading "Semenovite," who would become one of the most prominent leaders in the White Russian community in Shanghai, led his Cossacks on a final rampage, terrorizing and looting from the population in Vladivostok.[45]

The Defeated White Forces Arrive

> The Lithuanians want their own czar, the Jews want Solomon, but for us,
> Orthodox Russian Nicholas II is good enough.
>
> — White Russian officer, *1917*

Refugees had been arriving in Shanghai from the north by train, on foot, by
mule, or by ship since the Russian revolution had begun, most of them destitute. In September 1921, the League of Nations had set up a commission
for Russian refugees, headed by Dr. Fridtjof Nansen, especially to deal with
war refugees and to manage the money donated in support of relief work.[46]
A report developed by the commission specifically concerning conditions in
the Far East made a recommendation aimed at finding a "solution" for the
Russian refugee situation in China, calling for Russian repatriation and emigration. Obviously, the refugees could not safely return to their homeland,
and no other country would willingly accept these impoverished people, who
could not even afford their transportation costs. The Russians, it was thus
implied, would have to work out their own salvation with the help available
to them in Shanghai. So-called "Nansen passports" were made available to
the refugees, serving as identification certificates and meant mainly to aid in
their finding employment.[47] But rather than providing any solution to the
refugee predicament, these certificates, by their very superficiality, often only
underlined to the Shanghai authorities the rootless, unattached status of
Russians and helped create suspicion about the purpose of their extended
presence in Shanghai. The existing Russian community there, numbering
probably 2,000–3,000 by 1920, took on the responsibility of caring for the
refugees through organizations such as its Russian Aid Society.[48] Housing
and two meals a day were provided at the old Kelly & Walsh building in central Shanghai. Clothing and milk for the children were made available, the
new arrivals registered, and facts about their families and status recorded.
Fortunately, the central location of these services provided opportunities for
local employers to interview and hire at least some of the generally desperate refugees.[49] The American Community Church set up a Community Soup
Kitchen to serve meals to 420 refugees daily. In a letter expressing their appreciation to the Americans, the Russian refugee leaders remarked: "Nobody
looked at us as beggars, those people saw in us men who wished to work,

even for a loaf of bread, and they do all that is possible to let us earn our living honorably, hiring us for jobs or temporary work."[50]

Curiosity and gossip also surrounded the newcomers. "See that man over there, he had his father shot by one side in Siberia and his mother by the other," one onlooker remarked, pointing out a respectable-looking young man.[51] Recounting his story to reporters, a refugee noted that he was an Austrian who, during World War I, had been imprisoned by the Russian Army. When the revolution began in 1917, his status changed, and he was turned out of a Russian internment camp and left to fend for himself. Eventually, he married a Russian woman, and to escape further persecution and poverty, husband and wife fled to Shanghai, arriving in the city with 24 cents between them for food and lodging. A pledge from the Russian Aid Society allowed for their survival.   *Russians f.k. in r.n. it their own.*

Ingenuity was part of survival. One young teenager made his way out of Russia buried under furs in the sleigh of an Englishman who had married the sister of his Russian actress mother. The mother and his aunt had standing permission from the Soviet authorities to cross over the border in order to perform in operettas staged in certain Chinese border cities with Russian populations. On one of these occasions, the two decided not to return. Fortunately, the aunt's English husband could cross back to Russia unquestioned and retrieve the son, who eventually joined his mother in Shanghai.[52]

Other parts of the varied Shanghai community responded to the refugees' plight as well. Foreign shipping companies hired some of them as wharf and cargo hands when vacancies occurred. But even with the considerable response from charitable organizations and businesses, concern mounted that Shanghai would soon be overrun with the victims of political and religious oppression arriving from the north. Others worried about the Chinese reaction if Chinese common laborers were replaced by Russians.[53] Shanghai officials expressed serious concern about the possibility that some of the newcomers might harbor dangerous Bolshevik sympathies.[54] Edward Ezra, a leading Sephardi official who presided over a meeting to discuss the refugee "problem," emphasized that Shanghai could not continue to be a dumping ground for all the people in the different ports seeking safety and refuge.[55] The consensus was somehow to get the Russians away from Shanghai.

The steady influx of Russian refugees taxed the resources and threatened

overtix the associations made by Russians

to upset the stability of the small but well-established and cultured Russian community, composed mainly of officials and prospering businessmen. The shabby dress and dejected manner of these uninvited Russian newcomers greatly embarrassed members of this comfortable community. Soon press reports linked the refugees with crimes, creating a wave of belligerent propaganda against Shanghai Russians.[56] To make matters worse for all Shanghai Russians, in 1920, the Chinese government in Peking, after negotiations with the new Soviet government, issued a decree closing the imperial Russian consulate general in Shanghai. In its place, a Bureau of Russian Affairs was established, operating under the supervision of the commissioner for foreign affairs for Jiangsu Province. The new bureau, located in the old consulate building, continued to perform official consular duties, issuing identity certificates and birth certificates and providing visas and passports, but it had only quasi-official status.[57] Viktor Fedorovich Grosse, who had been imperial consul general since 1911 and was a founder of both the respected Russian Aid Society and the Russian Juridical Society, became deputy commissioner of the new bureau.[58]

The new Soviet government deepened the pervasive sense of statelessness when, in 1921, it deprived Russians living abroad of their citizenship. The official change in status was momentous and intensified the already tragic dimension of the Russian refugees' plight. It meant that the Russian community and refugees no longer had either independent legal jurisdiction within their community or the protection of representatives of a home government. The plaintive phrase repeatedly used by spokesmen for the Russian refugee community to describe their predicament was "we have no country, no government, no consular officials."[59] These uninvited and unwanted refugees had already suffered the emotional traumas of having lost homes, personal connections, and loved ones; now, in this unwelcoming city, along with official status, they lost a sense of personal identity and belonging.

ADMIRAL STARK'S IMPERIAL SIBERIAN FLEET

Of almost equal consequence for Russian officials in Shanghai still trying to cope with the significance of their changed status was the arrival of White Russian military forces fleeing the wrath of Bolsheviks. They came still

Figure 2. V. F. Grosse, the first chairman of the Russian Emigrants
Committee and former imperial Russian consul general in Shanghai.
SOURCE: Zhiganov, *Russkie v Shankhaie.*

armed and in considerable numbers, docking at Wusong, just north of the
port of Shanghai. Some of the arriving White Russian refugees from
Vladivostok and other cities along the Russian-Chinese border had fled to
Manchuria, while greater numbers had simply boarded any available ships,
eventually landing in Shanghai. Most of the civilian refugees did not have
funds to pay their passage out of the country. In desperation, they boarded

naval ships, large and small, assigned to carry the remains of the White military forces. White officers commandeered every type of vessel available to evacuate their men, and received help from the Japanese authorities, who supplied some of the ships for their passage. Despite severe storms, the overcrowded and overloaded ships managed to carry over three thousand refugees from Vladivostok to Shanghai. In the treacherous crossing, however, a number of the refugee ships sank.

A local Russian official reported some fifteen ships moored at Wusong.[60] The "fleet" included mail carriers, a variety of warships, harbor tugs, and even powerful icebreakers. But most of the ships were small, poorly furnished, not very seaworthy, and very overcrowded. The commander of this flotilla was none other than Admiral Iurii Karlovich Stark, who had replaced General Glebov as commander of the White armed forces at one point during the Civil War. One observer who managed to board one of the larger warships described the sight as follows: "The deck of the ship was literally jammed with household equipment, ranging from pots and pans to baby cribs. I noticed, not without amusement, that one Russian mother had hung out her babies' wash on one of the five-inch guns. I also noticed one almost new American automobile, a relic of the ill-fated American Siberian expedition."[61]

Admiral Stark's fleet had first sailed to Genzan (now Wonsan, on the east coast of North Korea), where it spent three weeks. (Japan had annexed Korea in 1910, which facilitated the stopover.) Some of the ships were sold and others simply abandoned there. On the way to Shanghai, the fleet encountered a severe storm, and two ships were lost. Stark reported that all on board his ships were destitute, including a number of officer cadets. The ships carried 1,688 passengers, including women and children and students from two cadet schools.[62] Having departed in such haste from Vladivostok, they badly needed supplies, mainly food. He explained that most of the women and children on board belonged to the families of Russian navy men. Others had clambered aboard the ships to escape the wrath of the Bolsheviks.

Admiral Stark wanted to place his party ashore, but encountered strong opposition both from the Chinese authorities, who refused him landing rights, and from foreign authorities, including local Russian officials. All expressed alarm at the size of the group, which included more than 200 marines and officer cadets from the two academies. And there was the additional worrisome fact that many on board still carried their weapons. Deputy

Figure 3. Fleeing White Russian military forces stopping in Genzan (now Wonsan, on the east coast of North Korea), on their way to Shanghai. They are receiving a meal from a makeshift soup kitchen. SOURCE: Zhiganov, *Russkie v Shankhaie.*

Commissioner Grosse, in a statement to the Shanghai Municipal Police, promised to make arrangements somehow to disarm the military refugees, and to find employment for as many as possible. Having learned that the Cossack officers from Stark's fleet liked to take their meals at a Russian home near the Yangshupu (Yangtsepoo) wharf, Grosse even suggested to the police that they might want to pay a surprise visit there and disarm them.[63] Grosse's long-term planning for ridding Shanghai of the refugees included sending some to work on sugar plantations in Hawaii. Others he planned to ship back north to find employment in the Russian community in Harbin.

Grosse did issue disembarkation certificates to ninety adults whom he judged acceptable for integration into the Shanghai Russian community and to more than a hundred of the young officer cadets.[64] Beyond this service, Grosse complained that his organizations and resources were already overtaxed and overwhelmed trying to feed and find employment for the Russian refugees who had already come to Shanghai, many of whom were penniless and lacked the necessary English. French authorities assisted the Stark party by raising sufficient funds to pay for the emigration costs of most of the officer cadets under Admiral Stark's command. After the United States turned down the French request to accept these cadets, the French made arrangements for them to settle in Serbia.[65]

Lacking adequate assistance ashore and unwelcomed by both foreign and Russian officials, Admiral Stark's remaining crew and passengers managed to obtain some coal and provisions, mainly from Shanghai charitable organizations, and set sail southward for Taiwan and then for Bolinao, Luzon, in the Philippines.[66] After reaching its destination, the hodgepodge fleet was sold. Some of the refugees on board took up residence in Manila, others reportedly managed to gain entry to the United States on board a U.S. Army transport, and still others found their way back to Shanghai.[67]

GENERAL GLEBOV AND HIS COSSACKS

Just as Deputy Commissioner Grosse was about to gain some control over the refugee settlement issues, another flotilla of three small ships arrived at Wusong, off Shanghai, this one carrying what remained of the Russian Far Eastern Army. Lieutenant General Fedor Lvovich Glebov, former commander of the Siberian Cossack units in Chita serving under Ataman Semenov, arrived with his troops in September 1923. This party, which had left the Far Eastern Maritime Province in December 1922, had stopped off at Genzan in Japanese-occupied Korea for about nine months. It included almost 1,000 armed Cossack officers, soldiers, and sailors. Understandably, the fears of the previous December reappeared in the minds of the Shanghai authorities. This was clearly a military force, and, once again, the Chinese refused to grant landing rights. This party's extensive munitions included rifles, machine guns, bombs, grenades, and two million rounds of ammunition.[68]

Shanghai Municipal Council officials and Russian authorities conjectured that given the milieu of strained and uncertain Chinese political and military rivalries, letting this armed force ashore might produce a dangerous threat to the well-being of Shanghai. Many reports circulated about Cossacks fleeing

Figure 4. Lieutenant General F. L. Glebov, a former commander of White Russian forces who became a prominent leader of the Shanghai Russian community. He was elected chairman of the Russian Emigrants Committee in 1942 and reelected to this post in 1944. SOURCE: Zhiganov, *Russkie v Shankhaie.*

Russia joining Chinese warlord armies. It was well known that Cossack forces were already in the employ of Marshal Zhang Zuolin, the military governor of Manchuria.[69] Another northern warlord, Zhang Zongchang, commanded a small army of White Russian mercenaries, known as the Russian Brigade, and included White Russian women in his circle of concubines. The concerns of the Shanghai authorities deepened when Glebov's party refused to surrender their weapons, the only remaining assets they possessed to support their existence.

In September 1924, Glebov moved his ships up to Shanghai, entering the Huangpu River to a position alongside the official Quarantine Station. There he commandeered an adjacent warehouse to serve as a hospital for his many sick officers. The terrible conditions aboard ship had given rise to a mutiny, which had involved a firefight between three vessels in the flotilla, one of which had decided in despair to return to Vladivostok.[70] Glebov reasserted control over the fleet, but the Russians remained confined to ship for almost forty months, living off the occasional sale of arms, adding to the widespread perception that Glebov's party was a clear threat to peace.[71] Gradually, members did make their way into Shanghai, often at night, and some went to join warlord armies.[72]

The next serious involvement of this armed party in local affairs came when the Chinese government signed the first Sino-Soviet Treaty, recognizing the Soviet government and closing the Bureau of Russian Affairs. The bureau's buildings and all former Russian imperial government property in China were turned over to representatives of the new Soviet government. Gradually, other foreign states recognized the new Soviet government too, with the result that the White Russians were now clearly refugees, deprived of any nationality status, even if they did have Nansen passports. As former commander of the White forces, General Glebov did not take this development lightly. Rather, acting in the name of those who still honored their allegiance to the Romanovs, he dispatched an armed party to occupy premises of the former Russian consulate. The incident required intensive negotiations by officials of the Shanghai Municipal Council, working through the Shanghai Municipal Police, to avoid an armed clash.[73]

Another ship arrived and joined General Glebov's flotilla, this one carrying 700 former soldiers known as the Ural-Siberian Group. While stopping en route in Genzan, the group's commander had signed an agreement with an American firm that had promised those on board employment in Zhejiang Province south of Shanghai. The agreement turned out to be worthless, and no work was forthcoming. The group stayed confined to ship for months, with very little food and a shortage of drinking water, until in desperation, it set sail for Shanghai. Again, only the sale of arms in the brisk

Shanghai weapons market, and the eventual disposal of the ship itself, allowed the desperate party to survive.[74]

More Refugees Come

Perhaps the most remarkable account of refugee arrivals involved those fleeing the Bolsheviks into China's remote northwest province of Xinjiang, former Chinese Turkestan. Estimates of the number of refugees fluctuate between 4,000 and 25,000, owing mostly to the constantly changing refugee population, which swelled in response to military aggression, famine, political opposition, and influxes of peasants escaping collectivization of Russian farms.[75] In the autumn of 1923, after surviving for a few years among this substantial community of Russian refugees, many of whom chose to settle permanently in Xinjiang, a group of three hundred men, women, and children, many of them Jewish, decided to set out for Shanghai. They traveled on foot, using oxcarts to transport women and children. Ill-clad and ill-nourished, but helped by local missionaries along the route and an occasional sympathetic Chinese official, the group reportedly made the 2,000-mile journey to Shanghai without a casualty.[76]

The Russian Jewish community welcomed the newcomers, providing care through the Hebrew Relief Society. A considerable amount of money was raised through the annual Purim Ball and its artistic variety program. Held every March, this festive event attracted well-to-do men and women in the Jewish community, who came in their best evening clothes or in costume. It raised enough funds to help send some of the less skilled recent arrivals to America, where they would be aided by Jewish organizations and not have to compete with Chinese in the Shanghai labor market. By 1924, the Jewish population in Shanghai had reached 3,000.[77]

A different kind of expansion of the Shanghai Russian community happened in 1925 as the result of an agreement by which the Chinese government acknowledged the Soviet Union's control of the Chinese Eastern Railway. The new Soviet supervisors thereupon began to fire White Russian railroadmen, and other railroad employees decided on their own that they no longer wanted to live under Bolshevik authority, choosing instead to migrate south. Many of them had suffered persecution under the new Soviet authorities, but at least they had not experienced the miseries of the Civil War, unlike recent military arrivals. They brought to Shanghai not only some severance pay but technical and professional skills.

Fortunately for them, their arrival in Shanghai happened to coincide with the local turmoil surrounding the famous May 30 incident of 1925.[78] This cataclysmic event in modern Chinese history centered on the intolerable working conditions and harsh treatment of Chinese at foreign-owned factories. Shanghai had become a major manufacturing center involving industries such as silk reeling and spinning, cotton spinning and weaving, tobacco, foundries, and breweries. Working in these industries became the livelihood of thousands of Chinese peasants who flocked to Shanghai from the nearby countryside. When a new round of strikes broke out in one of their mills, Japanese supervisors opened fire, wounding several Chinese workers, one mortally. This led to citywide demonstrations, culminating in a furious outburst on May 30, 1925, involving a crowd of mostly student demonstrators gathered on Shanghai's main commercial street. When the growing number of demonstrators became unruly, and it seemed as though the Louza (Laozha) Police Station was about to be overrun, the Shanghai Municipal Police opened fire, killing eleven and wounding many more. This set off a movement that had the effect of focusing Chinese public attention, until then still undefined, on the injustices and wrongs done China by the treaty system and extraterritoriality. Imperialism's disregard for Chinese worth and sovereignty became the target, and Chinese Communist Party and other leftist organizers found fertile soil in the emerging revolutionary sentiment, which spread beyond Shanghai.

A massive general strike, involving 150,000 workers by mid June, followed, closing shops and practically paralyzing the commercial and economic life of the city, including shipping. Shanghai industries and businesses suddenly found themselves without workers in every category. Ignorant and insensitive to the larger implications of what was happening, Russian leaders viewed these defining events as an unexpected boon. Deputy Commissioner Grosse seized the opportunity to supply Shanghai with Russian labor replacements. He found Russian workers to supply electric power stations with stokers, fitters, and foremen; waterworks and gas companies with laborers; shipping companies with crews; cars with chauffeurs; and so on.[79] By August 1, 1925, 953 Russians had been placed, 25 percent of them in municipal enterprises.

Another 45 percent were employed by shipping companies; 17 percent by local business firms (including 100 by the British-American Tobacco Co.); and 13 percent as seamen on tugs and lighters or as wharf workers.[80]

Word of the economic opportunities quickly spread north, causing many of those continuing to suffer under Soviet management of the Chinese Eastern Railway to try their luck in Shanghai. Some 2,000 Russians, Poles, and Ukrainians departed Harbin in search of work and security in Shanghai.[81] The availability of Russian workers to replace Chinese laborers in strikes against the power, bus, and trolley companies, to name a key few, diminished the leverage that Chinese strike leaders could apply in seeking higher wages, even causing some strikes to fail. Chinese officials began to view these developments as direct interference in Shanghai's labor market, even calling for the banning of Russian immigration. The Chinese Ministry of Communications issued instructions to Chinese shipping companies, notably the China Merchant Steamship Navigation Co., to fire Russian officers and engineers and hire only Chinese replacements.[82]

A specific demand of the trolley company strikers was that managers not fire Chinese workers and hire Russian replacements, most of whom would accept the same level of salary as the striking Chinese workers. This hiring and replacement trend, which began with the May 30 Movement of 1925, continued into the 1930s and 1940s, adding fuel to Chinese antiforeign sentiments.[83] An example of the building Chinese resentment against the Western and, in this case, Russian presence, was the 1927 seizure of the Russian church located in the Chinese neighborhood of Zhabei. A Chinese sentry on the scene reportedly told the evicted Russians: "You are White: there is an order to give nothing to Whites."[84]

Once the strikes and demonstrations petered out, most of the Chinese workers were rehired, but the strike leaders tended to be replaced permanently by new refugee hires. Subsequently, these refugee workers found opportunities to hire other refugees, so that the prospects for refugee employment brightened somewhat.[85] And as the refugee colony expanded, as a direct result of the influx, so did the need for additional people to work in service capacities, as waiters and cooks in the new restaurants and cafés, as shopkeepers, as drivers, and in other jobs. By 1927, the mainly Russian refugee population of Shanghai had reached over 8,000, at the same time contributing to further growth of the Ashkenazi Jewish community.

Figure 5. Russian seamen hired to replace striking Chinese seamen in the mid 1920s. SOURCE: Zhiganov, *Russkie v Shankhaie*.

A New Brand of Anti-Semitism

Once again, internal Russian political and military events took their toll on the Russian Jews. Just as Russia's defeats during the Russo-Japanese War had set off a wave of anti-Jewish sentiment and pogroms, the October Revolution and downfall of the Russian monarchy fueled a furious outbreak of violence against the Jews. A particularly vicious pogrom in Biisk, Siberia, led to an appeal by Jewish organizations in Shanghai to the Japanese foreign minister, Viscount Uchida Kōsai. In view of Japanese strength and interests in the region, Jewish leaders pleaded with Uchida to intervene and stop the violence against Jews. A similar appeal was made to the Chinese government to condemn the bloody pogrom led by Baron von Ungern-Sternberg and his Cossacks in the north at Urga, territory under Chinese control. Perhaps in the hope of goading the Japanese into taking firm diplomatic action on behalf of their co-religionists, the Jewish press evinced an outpouring of gratitude, expressing "love and respect for the Land of the Rising Sun" for the efforts of Japanese authorities in "giving protection of life and property to our co-religionists in Vladivostok."[86]

Even leaders of the official Shanghai Russian community blamed the Jews for Russia's troubles. During an interview with the Shanghai police in January 1922, reflecting the anti-Semitism prevalent among czarist officials, Deputy Assistant Commissioner for Russian Affairs Ch. E. Metzler, who worked directly with V. F. Grosse, blamed the October Revolution on Jews in the Bolshevik leadership and held them responsible for "strikes and other unrest."[87]

A more notable source of anti-Semitism came from the White Russian military forces, who made up a sizable proportion of the participants in the great exodus from Russia. During the winter of 1919–20, when White military campaigns were going badly, the infamous *Protocols of the Elders of Zion* circulated in Russian military circles. This document, composed of lectures allegedly drafted by a member of a secret Jewish government, described a plot on the part of these Elders of Zion to achieve world domination.[88] By this account, the Bolshevik revolution represented the "age old strivings of the Jewish people" to overthrow world civilization.[89] Excerpts of these forgeries circulated among the White officer corps, who subsequently read and explained their contents to illiterate Russian and Ukrainian troops. The documents received wide circulation in the 1920s and 1930s, with one edition of the *Protocols* published by White Russians in Japan. By 1928, rumors circulated that the Jews had had a hand in the murder of former Czar Nicholas II and his family in 1918.

Jewish organizations, trying to display an open and fair-minded response to these sensational charges, called for a thorough investigation, expressly so that the myth would not become gospel.[90] They responded to criticism that many Jews had become prominent in the Bolshevik leadership with the claim that as merchants, traders, artisans, and workers, Jews were natural enemies of the Bolsheviks.[91] They had the most to lose and suffered the most under the Reds, being especially exposed to violence by reason of their living in urban enclaves in major Russian and Ukrainian cities.

These anti-Semitic attitudes were the somber backdrop to community relations and attitudes in Shanghai. Their influence was even more pronounced in Harbin. Fortunately, several factors kept anti-Semitic expressions and actions subdued in Shanghai. Unlike Harbin, where Russian anti-Semitic elements were more prominent and gaining in strength, Shanghai was not a Russian city. Rather, it was a city with a great mix of nationalities, and Russians were clearly not in the forefront. Other restraining influences included the overriding concern of the dominant Western powers in Shanghai to preserve the peace and stability in the city; the challenges Russians faced coping with everyday life; and the proximity of real Russian adversaries in the form of the Soviet officials and Communist International (Comintern) agents, who operated extensively in Shanghai. These factors served to restrain anti-Semitic outbursts in Shanghai during the 1920s and early 1930s. As long as Russian consular officials and White Russian military personnel kept their anti-Semitic prejudices largely in check, the large Russian and Jewish communities continued to show tolerance. For the most part, the two communities in Shanghai coexisted peacefully, but separately, which was their wish.

New Challenges

With the Soviet government receiving official recognition from Chinese authorities, the local Russian community functioned with only quasi-official representation. V. F. Grosse organized the Committee for Defense of Rights and Interests of Russian Emigrants to speak to the many issues confronting the large refugee community and represent their interests. His leadership did not go unquestioned, however, and if there was one key weakness in the operation of refugee affairs, it was the constant quarreling and petty infighting that plagued refugee leaders, organizations, and members. Part of this can be attributed to the diversity of the refugee community. There were monarchists of many different factional allegiances, former followers of the several political parties that had preceded the Russian revolution, members of the former aristocracy, former wealthy businessmen, professionals, technicians, artists, and journalists, as well as peasants from different parts of the Russian empire, all caught up in the great exodus. Most preferred to remain outside of politics, but those who joined the fray came in with sharp opinions and differences, including a resentment of Grosse and his claim to represent all local Russian and Slavic interests.

Grosse met the challenge to his leadership, drawing upon substantial support from within the community, by forming the Russian Emigrants Committee in July 1926. In June 1925, in the context of the general strike, he had been commissioned by the Shanghai Municipal Council to establish a Russian Branch of the Controller of Voluntary Services, an office that afforded him a subsidy and an official voice.[92] The new Russian Emigrants Committee was headquartered at 118/1 Moulmein Road in the International Settlement, just north of Avenue Foch in the French Concession, where most of the Russian refugees eventually came to reside. The committee became the administrative center of the Shanghai Russian community, responsible for some fifty-two affiliated organizations and having to coordinate the major social and benevolent activities of the Russian community, both Orthodox and Jewish.[93] Grosse was the logical choice for this daunting assignment, having come from the former established and recognized official Russian community in Shanghai. Still, the requirement to place the interests of the established Russian community, plus the wave of new arrivals and the Russian Jewish communities, old and new, under one umbrella organization, added up to an enormous burden. It would sorely test Grosse's leadership skills and the cooperation of those working with him. The committee, occupying a quasi-diplomatic position, provided official documentation required

by the municipal government and police in connection with registration of
the refugee population and the issuance of travel documents.

Russian attempts at organization and survival did not, of course, occur in
a vacuum. At the same time, the larger Shanghai community faced many
challenges from the emerging strength of labor organizers, demonstrators
against foreign and Chinese exploitation of cheap Chinese labor, and those
wanting to reclaim China's sovereignty over the treaty ports. Organizers,
some with Comintern support and advice, infiltrated labor unions and carried out numerous strikes, which often brought major sectors of the
Shanghai economy to a standstill. The Chinese Communist Party (CCP),
born in the French Concession of Shanghai in 1921, was one key player in
these events, and its growing strength made the organization and its leaders
a priority target for competing Chinese political forces, especially those allied with the rising Generalissimo Chiang Kai-shek.[94] Chiang struck out at
the various communist-inspired labor unions in Shanghai on April 12, 1927,
devastating their urban organizations and severing the united front ties between the Guomindang and CCP in Shanghai. Several thousand leftists were
executed, while those labor union members or cells that survived were
forced underground or to other bases inland. In the succeeding years, the
Shanghai Communist Party set about strengthening discipline and began to
adopt policies more realistically attuned to a changed Shanghai milieu.[95]
Nevertheless, by ravaging Shanghai's labor organizations, Chiang's brutal
measures had the unforeseen benefit to the refugee community of once again
opening employment opportunities to refugees in factories and businesses, as
skilled replacements for Chinese workers and laborers were needed. The
Russian Emigrants Committee once again worked closely with local businesses to provide details about the backgrounds and skills of refugees to
prospective employers.

The anticommunist events of 1927 had another unforeseen and fortuitous
outcome for the refugees, particularly the White Russian military forces, unemployed and under constant surveillance and suspicion within the Shanghai
community. The need for protection from approaching Chinese armies,
viewed as communist and a major threat to the safety and stability of the
Shanghai business and commercial community, caused Shanghai authorities
to take a new and different look at the virulently anticommunist Russian military forces in their midst. The Shanghai Municipal Council and officers of

TABLE I

Russian Refugee Arrivals in Shanghai, 1922–1929

Year	Arrivals	Year	Arrivals
1922	1,268	1926	1,266
1923	1,968	1927	1,036
1924	877	1928	1,122
1925	1,535	1929	1,382

SOURCES: Simpson, *Refugees: Preliminary Report of a Problem*, p. 157; Wang Zhicheng, *Shanghai E qiaoshi*, p. 57.

the British-run Shanghai Volunteer Corps (SVC) decided to approve inclusion of more than one hundred of General Glebov's men, forming them into a Russian unit of the SVC.[96] The professional gloss the new unit gave to the SVC helped steady some badly rattled foreign nerves.

Foreign apprehensions subsided somewhat after the establishment of Chiang's national government at Nanjing in 1928. Having won recognition abroad, Chiang made additional substantial efforts to calm the fears of Shanghai's business establishment, upon whom he depended for income and support. As a friendly gesture particularly to the Shanghai Jewish community, Chiang's minister of railways, Sun Fo, expressed support for the plans of Jewish nationalists to rebuild their ancient homeland, making comparisons to China's efforts to restore sovereignty over lost Chinese territory.[97] Other Chinese in Shanghai, the most westernized Chinese city, expressed recognition of a special bond between the Chinese and the Jews. These were mainly members of Shanghai's Chinese elite who especially admired the Sephardi Jews, who had originated in the Orient but had become westernized. The Chinese saw these Oriental Jews as both recipients of Western civilization's benefits and contributors to its development.[98]

Shanghai's refugee organizations faced still another challenge in the spring of 1929, when a dispute emerged in the north between the Manchurian warlord Zhang Xueliang and the Special Far Eastern Army over control of the coveted Chinese Eastern Railroad. The ensuing skirmishes and arrest of railroad officials sent another wave of refugees fleeing south, reinforcing a common pattern by which the growing instability in the north directly affected the size, composition, and character of the refugee community in Shanghai. By 1929, the Russian community had grown to more than 13,000 persons.[99] The Chinese government kept no statistics on the arrival of Russian refugees, but the new Russian Emigrants Committee recorded the steady arrival, year after year, of refugees in Shanghai. Table 1 shows arrivals in the years 1922–29, reflecting many of the events discussed above. Most Russian Jews are not counted in these figures, because they preferred to register separately at the Registration Office of the Chinese Bureau of Foreign Affairs.[100] The committee counted 10,454 over the period from 1922 through 1929, as shown in Table 1.[101]

As the refugee communities grew, so did the need for stable leadership and organizations to provide direction and purpose to refugee life in Shanghai. During the decade of the 1930s, much effort would be given to fulfilling these objectives, not without considerable pain and friction both within and between the distinct Russian communities.

THREE

Refugee Communities Take Shape

The devastating worldwide depression of the early 1930s also affected busi-ness and commerce in Shanghai, the center of China's foreign trade, ship-ping, and manufacturing, and added to the growing uncertainty about the city's future. Some banks failed, and individuals, including missionaries and even some refugee investors, lost their life savings overnight. Added to this were the increasing Japanese pressures. If the foreign community was pre-occupied with labor unrest, warlords, and Nationalist Chinese armies in the 1920s, by the early 1930s, the specter of being overrun by Chinese forces had been supplanted by the proximity of hostilities between the Japanese and Chinese. Beginning in January 1932, fierce fighting between the two sides took place in Zhabei, sometimes spilling over into the French Concession or International Settlement. This Shanghai Incident, as it was called, brought death and destruction to Chinese and Japanese alike and fostered a pervasive sense of insecurity in the foreign settlements.

The growing insecurities, augmented by waves of refugees arriving from the north, particularly from Harbin, further prompted the Russian, Polish, Ukrainian, and Russian Jewish refugee communities to take more decisive

54

from what?

steps to shape administrative, social, and cultural organizations to protect their members. As the largest group, the Russians would succeed in gaining official recognition as speaking for the Slavs overall, but Ukrainian and Jewish groups seeking to establish their autonomy stubbornly resisted this outcome. The result was a strong undercurrent of tension among the separate enclaves making up the Slavic community.

The only organization that both dealt with security threats and was inclusive enough to potentially bridge the gulfs separating the various foreign enclaves was the Shanghai Volunteer Corps (SVC). In its organizational structure, the SVC provided a role for many of the nationalities represented in the city, but, like so much about Shanghai, the appearance was not the reality. The SVC was, first and foremost, British. Its multinational nature gave it only the veneer of equality and cooperation among the many nationalities that filled its ranks. During the early 1930s, Western refugee communities were proud to be represented in the SVC. At the same time, the nature of that participation is illuminating about the station and expectations of the refugee groups within the Shanghai foreign community.

The Shanghai Volunteer Corps

> Let us sing of that old Tavern, where dark Louis used to dwell
> Where the Olgas and the Sonyas cast their spell
> Of Whitey Smith, Bo Diddley, and the little Carlton girl
> Of Joe Farren and his own sweet Russky Nell.
> — "Maloo Memories," a pastiche of an old Shanghai Volunteer Corps song[1]

In April 1853, the British and American authorities in Shanghai formed committees to consider establishing defense forces. The British came up with the idea of a volunteer corps, and a general meeting of the American, British, and French consular and naval representatives followed, leading to the creation of a militia to protect the infant Shanghai International Settlement.[2] The new force received its "baptism by fire" in 1854 when it mustered for the first of its very few firefights, the legendary "Battle of Muddy Flat," provoked by sporadic attacks on foreign residents in Shanghai by troops from Chinese military camps adjacent to the Settlement. The ensuing battle lasted less than two hours, during which the new foreign militia corps succeeded in forcing a Chinese retreat (with the support of marines from American and British warships). Although hardly more than a skirmish, the Battle of Muddy Flat was nevertheless the stuff of song and legend throughout the SVC's history. It was seen as the first proud moment, the first battle honor of the Shanghai Volunteer Corps.

In its early days, the SVC was funded by private subscription. It received a more stable basis when, in 1870, the Shanghai Municipal Council, through its chairman and members, assumed control of the SVC and prepared a budget for its operations. An appointed Defence Committee divided the "Shanghai Municipal Volunteer Corps" into three parts: artillery, mounted rangers, and infantry.[3] These and other measures provided the population of the foreign settlements with at least a sense of adequate protection. The SVC's many marches, drills, and parades, in neatly worn uniforms, with weapons displayed, made a strong impression on a community increasingly fearful of first Chinese and later Japanese military threats. But in actual fact, when the foreign settlements were seriously threatened, as in 1927 by the advancing Chinese armies, or in the 1930s during Japanese military landings in the city, the authorities called in regular military forces to handle the situation. From about 1903 until the start of World War II, a British lieutenant colonel or colonel served as commandant of the SVC, and it trained under British officers.

The composition of the SVC clearly reflected the cosmopolitan character of Shanghai's foreign community. Over the course of its existence, it came to include volunteers and units from the following twenty-seven countries (listed here according to the strength of each nationality's representation): British, Russian, Chinese, American, Portuguese, Japanese, Filipino, German, Danish, Polish, Norwegian, Dutch, Italian, French, Latvian, Romanian, Greek, Swedish, Swiss, Estonian, Austrian, Lithuanian, Spanish, Iranian, Egyptian, Chilean, and Yugoslavian.[4] Formation of the Chinese unit in 1907 was received with ambivalence by the leaders of the Shanghai Municipal Council, who were hesitant to train and arm Chinese troops. The council had been lobbied by prosperous members of the Chinese business community who were keen to establish a unit and serve in its ranks. After some rounds of negotiations between the Chinese and the council, the two sides agreed to establish a Chinese company as a unit of the SVC "under cer-

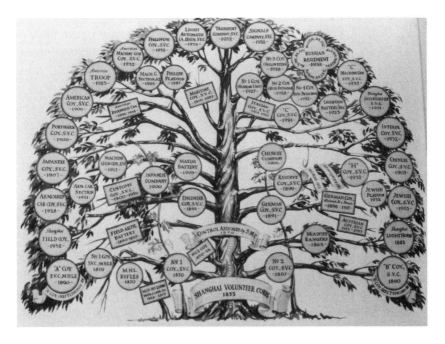

Figure 6. This depiction shows the various units of the Shanghai Volunteer Corps. Russian and Jewish units are located on the right side of the tree.
SOURCE: Kounin, *Eighty-Five Years of the Shanghai Volunteer Corps.*

tain conditions."[5] One of the original conditions was that British officers command the unit. This held until 1915, when, after much resistance from the council, a Chinese officer was commissioned as lieutenant (eventually rising to company commander). In 1932, the council also approved formation of the Interpreters Company, which drew heavily on carefully selected Chinese volunteers. Foreign troops arriving in Shanghai to meet the Japanese threat needed assistance with the language and topography of the city. To provide these services, parties of the Interpreters Company dispersed to various posts in the Settlement manned by foreign troops and units of the SVC.

The SVC also brought together prominent residents of many nationalities, playing a social role in Shanghai's foreign communities that was at least as significant as its security functions. Most of the leading merchants, officials, businessmen, and even missionaries served as volunteers in the SVC unless they were too old to take part in its more strenuous activities. As one observer noted: "Everyone enjoys the work and the uniforms and marching to the Band, very much indeed."[6] The SVC also worked closely with the foreign military personnel assigned to Shanghai, and its social events occupied a prominent role in the overall life of the community. Billeted at the Race Course, the SVC sponsored mess nights, chukkas of polo, amateur horse races, paper chases, point-to-point steeplechases, annual dinners, and balls.

One noteworthy outcome of the daily proximity, collegiality, and joint militia activity was the way in which certain national units responded to international developments. For example, the German and Austrian companies cooperated closely with the rest of the SVC in handling civil disturbances even after the outbreak of World War I. The German and Austrian units continued to drill alongside British and other companies of the SVC up until 1917, when China entered the war on the side of the Allies and against Germany and Austria. Then the two companies had to be disbanded, never again to form units of the SVC. A similar situation occurred with the Chinese and Japanese companies of the SVC. In the early stages of conflict between the two countries, the two units served with discipline, if not without tensions, and cooperated in fulfilling their assigned militia tasks of preserving order.[7] The good life that many shared, including the affluent Chinese, softened the sharp national divisions that emerged elsewhere in the world outside Shanghai.

RUSSIAN UNITS

The White Russian military refugees benefited most from their association with the SVC. Needless to say, it was difficult for men used to respect and honors to arrive in a community that often viewed them with disdain and suspicion, and for members of an intact military force to suffer the humiliations and indignities of having become indigent refugees. In the early days, their search for employment was seriously hampered by their having only a military background to offer as experience in a city that valued business acumen. The situation turned around for these former soldiers, however, when domestic turmoil threatening civil war reached Shanghai, with Chinese military and police forces attempting to rid the city of left-wing and communist influence. To protect the settlements during these "troubles," foreign troops arrived in Shanghai, the Volunteer Corps was mobilized, and the experienced Cossacks led by the famous General F. L. Glebov were mustered to form a unit of the SVC in January 1927.

This first Russian unit, 150 strong, was under the command of Captain N. I. Fomin, former chief of staff to Admiral Stark. No training was necessary to bring the unit into service, and General Glebov played an active role in its organization. Captain Fomin commanded the unit for only three months, after which Captain H. H. Thieme of the former Russian Guards took over command. The unit had been divided into two companies, supported by a platoon equipped with four Lewis machine guns. Their first military mission was to guard the Municipal Power Station. In 1928, the two Russian companies combined into what became designated as the Russian Detachment of the SVC, with 250 officers and men. During the same year, an all-volunteer unit was formed, which became the Number 3 Company of the Russian Detachment. Unlike the other units of the detachment, this company found its recruits from within the Russian Young Men's Association, most of whom had no military background.[8]

For the next few years, Shanghai enjoyed relative calm, and the Russian units served in a peacetime capacity as support for the Shanghai Municipal Police. Russian staff guarded the Ward Road Jail, Rifle Range, and Alcock Road Barracks. They formed colorful and impressive guards of honor for the Shanghai Municipal Council when council officials received visiting foreign dignitaries. When the Japanese attacked Chinese Shanghai in 1932, the three Russian companies mobilized as the SVC's Russian Detachment.[9] Numbering 19 officers and 435 other ranks, the units served under the command of Captain Thieme.[10] Adding a fourth company, the combined units became the "C Battalion, Russian."

The Russian units did not operate with the same autonomy as other national units in the SVC, however, but worked under the supervision of an "advisor." A major's billet existed for a regular British officer to serve as "Advisor to the Russian Regiment (C Battalion, Russian)." In addition, the Russian units were alone in being paid for their services in the SVC. This placed them in the category of paid help rather than volunteers. Still, without this salary, many would have become destitute or would have had to compete with other Russians for scarce positions as bodyguards for rich Chinese or foreigners, bank guards, watchmen, night club bouncers, and in other similar forms of employment. Thus, the arrangement amounted to a trade-off: the Russians performed duties for which they were qualified and compensated, and the Shanghai authorities, particularly the British, were able to employ refugees with military backgrounds in useful and largely civilian tasks. Maintaining the experienced Russian Regiment was costly, however. In 1931, the cost of upkeep for the other unpaid all-volunteer units amounted to 212,170 taels, but expenses for the Russian Regiment alone were 228,680.[11]

Whatever the special requirement, Russian members of the SVC were able to wear a uniform again and to perform duties at which they had real experience. The constant praise and frequent honors that the Russian units received for their drill formations and other military skills must have helped salve the wounds to their pride inflicted in Shanghai.

Suggestive of the confusion that the meld of nationalities and complex political allegiances in Shanghai often evoked, a British military dignitary visiting from Hong Kong, after reviewing the Russian troops, congratulated the Soviet consul in Shanghai on the fine turnout and polished military style of the Russian Regiment of the SVC.[12]

Gratitude, pride, and honor all found clear expression in the pledge that the Russian officers developed for their regiment:

> Under the National Three-Coloured Standard, be a Great Russian Soldier, observe the foreign law that protects you, respect the authorities that care for you and serve faithfully for the glory of your regiment and for the good of the community that you are called upon to protect. Develop a sacred love for your Colours, pay them their due respect, and forever guard their inviolability.[13]

The colors referred to were those awarded by "Special Order" of Colonel N. W. Thoms, the British commandant of the Shanghai Volunteer Corps from 1931 to 1934, which stated: "A Regimental Colour is hereby authorized to be carried by the Shanghai Russian Regiment . . . consisting of horizontal stripes of even width of White, Blue and Red, superimposed by a Badge bearing an eight-pointed Star in gold within which is . . . inscribed the words: 'Shanghai Russian Regiment.'"[14] These colors were consecrated in what was described as a moving ceremony involving the Trooping of the Colors of the

Figure 7. One Russian unit of the Shanghai Volunteer Corps. SOURCE: Kounin, *Eighty-Five Years of the Shanghai Volunteer Corps.*

Russian Regiment on April 3, 1932. This granting of colors to the Russian regiment constituted an unprecedented honor in its members' experiences in Shanghai as stateless refugee soldiers. Rather than suffering the embarrassment of serving in public military formations and drills flying the old Russian flag, with the image of defeat it conveyed to onlookers, the regiment could now display a banner that it had helped design.

In addition to new colors, the Russian Regiment had its own chapel, complete with richly decorated wall panels, icons, and other sacred objects. Occasionally, religious services were held outside on the parade ground, with Bishop Ioann (Mikhail Maksimovich), vicar of the Russian Orthodox Mission in Shanghai (later canonized as Saint John of Shanghai and San Francisco), giving his blessing to the troops and conducting services.[15] Because so many of the Russian refugees came from military backgrounds, service in the SVC was much sought after, and life as a member offered a sense of belonging and purpose. The regiment had its own museum, where memorable objects from days in Russia were placed on view. A library brought members together for periods of relaxation, as did the canteen, where they gathered for meals. The regiment formed an active sporting association, whose athletes became prominent in several sports. Finally, the regiment even had its own string band, which entertained nostalgic Russians with its renditions of traditional Russian folk songs and music.

Throughout its existence, members of the SVC's Russian Regiment often performed police duties. Some joined the Shanghai Municipal Police, in which a few eventually rose to become officers. The Police Reserve Unit, a specially created riot squad, initially recruited men of proven reliability from the Russian Regiment, although it later relied upon direct hires. Many others worked at more pedestrian tasks, as drivers, cooks, telephone operators, orderlies, and storemen. Fortunately for them, their overall early military training had provided them with skills applicable to both military and police work. Inasmuch as these Russians were often regarded with disdain, not only by senior British officers, but even by the British rank and file, perhaps the most important thing about service in the regiment was that it provided comradeship and a sense of purpose.

The Jewish Unit

> No advance without security.
> — Motto of the SVC's Jewish Company

As early as 1922, there had been talk in the Jewish community, and especially among Jews in the Shanghai Volunteer Corps, of forming a separate Jewish unit of the SVC. The impetus for doing so came as the conflicts between China and Japan worsened. On September 18, 1931, Japanese military leaders, disregarding the advice of Japan's civilian leadership, began a drive that quickly brought key cities in southern Manchuria under Japanese control. Military victories were followed by formation on March 1, 1932, of the new Japanese state Manchukuo (Manzhouguo), headed by the puppet emperor Pu Yi, the last ruler of the Qing dynasty. Manchukuo encompassed the former Chinese territory of northeast China, serving as an effective base for additional Japanese aggression in China.

Figure 8. Bishop Ioann, vicar of the Russian Orthodox Mission in Shanghai, who became archbishop in 1946 and was canonized in San Francisco in 1994. SOURCE: Zhiganov, *Russkie v Shankhaie*.

Shanghai became a center of Chinese resistance. An economic boycott of Japanese goods began, with widespread popular support in Shanghai among business associations, students, workers, women's groups, and others. The sale and movement of Japanese goods in the city came to a standstill, and a Chinese attack on Japanese monks claimed the life of one. The Japanese civilian community, as well as the military, was quick to respond to the escalating threat. They assumed a militant and uncompromising stand, demanding the suppression of all forms of anti-Japanese activity. By January 1932, the situation had reached crisis proportions, and fighting broke out between regular Japanese and Chinese forces in the Chinese sector, Zhabei, in what became known as the Shanghai Incident.

The settlement authorities had developed a new defense plan for the city in October 1931, which included protective sectors to be manned by units of the police, the Shanghai Volunteer Corps, and foreign regular forces already stationed in Shanghai.[16] The SVC, fully mobilized on January 28 and increased in strength from 1,500 to 2,300 through hasty recruiting, joined regular forces in defensive operations in the northern Defence Sector "B," which included the main business district and extended to the north railway station and Zhabei. The Hongkou district, already heavily Japanese in population, became the Japanese defense sector and a powerful base for Japanese operations against Chinese forces in neighboring Zhabei.[17] Brutal fighting and severe damage to Zhabei and adjacent areas in Hongkou occurred, with military casualties on both the Japanese and Chinese sides mounting in this undeclared war in Shanghai. As one witness to the events reported: "The Japanese began going into the Chinese city Thursday evening at midnight. Since then they have bombed Chapei [Zhabei] and began bombing and burning the Hongkew [Hongkou] section of the city. All the foreigners have been brought out of these areas."[18]

During the fighting, Japanese marines suffered more than 3,000 casualties, while Chinese casualties rose to about 14,000. Civilian losses may have been as high as 20,000.[19] Chinese refugees poured out of Zhabei into the International Settlement, where they resettled in camps until more permanent accommodations could be arranged for them. Finally, after stiff resistance from the Chinese forces, facing overwhelming Japanese firepower, a truce was worked out between the two sides in May 1932. Notwithstanding an end to the fighting, resentment over terms of the peace agreement and

widespread bitterness over the casualties and devastation lingered on. Chinese military leaders chafed over the fact that the Nineteenth Route Army had had to fight the Japanese alone, because no national mobilization call had been ordered. Viewing the Japanese threat, they warned: "We only hope the people of our nation will not forget [the battles of] Zhabei and Jiangwan . . ." and the fate of other dismembered nations.[20]

Faith in the security of the foreign communities was deeply eroded by the events of 1931 and 1932. Foreign military units, together with the SVC, had maintained the integrity of the settlements, but this time they had stood by and witnessed one of their treaty partners wage frightening warfare against Chinese forces, and from the proclaimed neutrality of settlement territory. In effect, Japan's behavior and the mild responses it engendered from the Western powers signaled a new course, and one that raised serious questions about the existing power relationships in Shanghai. The events of early 1932 clearly undermined the accepted modus vivendi that had for decades defined the foreign settlements' accepted neutral status and behavior. The settlement powers seemed unable or unwilling to grasp the outcome, but Japan emerged from the events of 1932 militarily and politically more influential than ever before.[21] As proof, the Japanese military erected large, strongly fortified permanent barracks for the Special Naval Landing Party near Hongkou Park, turning the Hongkou district into almost an exclusive Japanese concession.

These security concerns and the strong desire to play a significant role in promoting community welfare prompted civic-minded Jewish leaders to advance plans to contribute a separate Jewish unit to the Shanghai Volunteer Corps. Colonel Thoms sanctioned the proposal and started the unit off in September 1932 as a platoon in the existing "H" Company. Commanding the new unit, with the rank of second lieutenant, was N. S. Jacobs, for many years scoutmaster of the Jewish Boy Scouts. Jacobs was English by birth but had grown up in Hong Kong, where he served with the Hong Kong Defence Force. Later he moved to Shanghai to accept a position with the British-American Tobacco Co. He met and married a Russian Jewish woman after converting to Judaism. He never practiced his faith, but he did become very active in Jewish community affairs. Some of the recruits to the Jewish platoon had been active in scouting activities, and others were members of the Shanghai branch of the Zionist Brit Trumpeldor organization.[22]

Within a few months, another platoon formed under Second Lieutenant

Figure 9. A Jewish unit of the Shanghai Volunteer Corps being led by Robert Bitker, a prominent figure in the Shanghai Jewish Betar or revisionist Zionist youth movement. SOURCE: Courtesy of the Jabotinsky Institute.

R. B. Bitker, a former member of American units of the SVC, who, typical of the mix of loyalties in Shanghai, had also once served in the Russian Army. Bitker had been one of Jacobs's sergeants. Witnessing the extent of enthusiasm for service in the SVC being shown particularly by younger Jews, Colonel Thoms agreed to grant the wishes of the community and approved the formation of a separate Jewish Company. On May 22, 1933, non-Jewish personnel from the original "H" Company accepted transfer to "B" Company, leaving "H" an entirely Jewish unit of the SVC, under the command of the newly promoted Lieutenant Jacobs. The uniformed ranks of "H" Company wore on their collars metal *Magen David* badges, superimposed on which were the letters "SVC." At a celebration dinner at the Shanghai Jewish Club, Colonel Thoms praised the new company of the SVC, suggesting the solid military motto "No advance without security" for its use.[23] Mendel Brown, rabbi of the Sephardi Jewish community of Shanghai, became the first chaplain of the new Jewish Company.

Ashkenazi Jews Organize

Sephardim and Ashkenazim served together in the Jewish Company, but with the rising influx into Shanghai of Ashkenazi Jews, the impetus to form a representative Russian Jewish body gained strength. In June 1931, Ashkenazi leaders established the Shanghai Ashkenazi Jewish Communal Association, with a chairman and nine-member executive committee, to represent the Ashkenazi Jews in all official contacts and with Jewish organizations elsewhere.[24] Actually, the idea of forming an association dated back to 1925, but it did not materialize until the arrival of additional refugees made formation a necessity.

The severe damage done to the Hongkou and Zhabei districts during the 1932 Sino-Japanese hostilities had sent many residents westward to set up new family dwellings. It also inspired Ashkenazi leaders to consider moving the Ohel Moishe Synagogue from its location on Ward Road in Hongkou to a site closer to these new settlements. After considerable debate, however, they decided instead to establish two new synagogue branches, one first in 1934 in a building next to the Sephardi Ohel Rachel Synagogue on Seymour Road and a second in 1937 on Rue Bourgeat. These places of worship served a growing community until they were completely superseded in 1941 by the opening of the grand New Synagogue on Rue Tenant de la Tour.[25]

Having formed an active association and synagogue, the Ashkenazi Community in 1932 established a Jewish Club, with Morris S. Bloch, a Pole and senior partner in the Bloch Manufacturing Lumber Co., as its first president. The club became a major center of local Jewish cultural, intellectual, social, and charitable life, particularly for local Russian Jewish merchants. It hosted local Zionist meetings of both the Kadimah movement and the active Brit Trumpeldor (*Betar*) youth organization. By 1934, the club had some 200 members, and its library boasted a collection of over 600 books, many of them in Russian and some in Hebrew and Yiddish.[26] The Shanghai Jewish School, under the guidance of Headmistress Perry, adopted the Cambridge syllabus in order to prepare students for education in elite British universities. This school educated both Ashkenazi and Sephardi students. Mendel Brown, rabbi at the Ohel Rachel Synagogue, directed the school's program in Hebrew and Religion.

The Russians Form a Community

The undeclared war in Shanghai drove many Russians from their homes in Hongkou, but it did not diminish the internecine fighting and quarreling between factions in the large Russian community. The stressful condition for many Russians of feeling like unwanted guests in an elite community bent on maintaining its privileged lifestyle helped fuel the tensions.[27] These internal frictions greatly complicated the provision and coordination of desperately needed services both for the many indigent local Russians and for those refugees still coming in from the north.

At least five separate relief organizations claimed responsibility for handling the influx of refugees and those needing help locally. The challenge was severe, because the steady flow of refugee arrivals at Shanghai led to a twelvefold increase in the Russian population during the period from 1918 until 1930, whereas the whole foreign community only doubled itself within the same period.[28] By 1930, the majority of newcomers consisted of men in their twenties who had lost their jobs with the Chinese Eastern Railroad to Soviet replacements. Table 2 shows refugee arrivals for 1930–36, as recorded by the Russian Emigrants Committee.[29]

The Russian Military Union, also known as the Union of Russian Army and Navy Ex-Servicemen, operated soup kitchens, provided housing in shelters, and tried to supply information about employment opportunities and business leads to the refugees. The Russian Orthodox Confraternity was another active relief organization that attempted to promote a sense of Russian unity and a communal spirit by sponsoring discussion groups, religious meetings, and debates on issues and subjects known to be of interest to Russians. With a grant from the American Red Cross, the Russian Orthodox Confraternity opened a much-needed medical dispensary, which later became a large Russian hospital. It also operated a school for poor Russian children. Two banking institutions, one Russian and one American, facilitated credit opportunities for new enterprises.[30] In addition to subscriptions from the Russian community, support came from the French Municipality and the International Settlement.

As might be expected, the most severe rivalries took place in the administrative sphere, among groups claiming to exercise authority over the Russian refugee community. Because of the interest of the Shanghai Muni-

TABLE 2
Russian Arrivals in Shanghai, 1930–1936

Year	Arrivals	Year	Arrivals
1930	1,599	1934	1,635
1931	2,025	1935	1,240
1932	1,590	1936	1,094
1933	1,389		

SOURCE: Simpson, *Refugees: Preliminary Report of a Problem*, p. 156.

cipal Council in maintaining peace and stability for the sake of trade and business, and given the size of the Russian community, the council authorized its police force to keep a watchful eye on the divisions and political leanings among the Russians. These crucial services were performed by the Special Branch of the police, whose responsibilities included gathering information on political figures, groups, organizations, and movements in Shanghai. The suppression of communism was the Special Branch's top priority during the 1920s and 1930s, making the Shanghai Russian community a special target.[31] The Special Branch had access to British intelligence information through its relationship with the British Secret Intelligence Service representative attached to the British consulate, Harry Steptoe. This included access to information from the various British colonial police forces, particularly those in Singapore and Hong Kong. The equivalent French organization, the Service politique, maintained contact too, sharing relevant information. The important point for this study is that police inspectors, some of them members of the Russian refugee community, stayed apprised of any potentially disruptive activities, reporting back in detailed memoranda to their superiors.

Russian Emigrants Committee Chairman V. F. Grosse's death in October 1931 helped set off fierce competition for recognized leadership status by individuals and organizations in the Russian community. Grosse had been widely respected in all quarters of the Shanghai foreign community. The

Russian Orthodox Archbishop Simon officiated over the elaborate funeral services for him, attended by almost 1,000 mourners, at the Bubbling Well cemetery. The flag of the Shanghai Municipal Council was lowered for the occasion, and more than fifty wreaths decorated the grave.[32] A lengthy Shanghai Municipal Police memorandum reports that even before Chairman Grosse's death, an opposition group calling itself the Russian National Community formed under the chairmanship of a former White Russian naval captain, N. Y. Fomin. The influence of this new body reached beyond Shanghai, with branches in several Asian cities, formed by supporters of General D. L. Horvat, whom the late Grand Duke Nicholas had reportedly appointed head of Russian emigrants in Asia.[33] Attempts to reconcile the differences between this new organization and the Russian Emigrants Committee proved unsuccessful. Meanwhile, the new chairman of the Russian Emigrants Committee, Ch. E. Metzler, who had been sent to Shanghai from the imperial Russian Mission in Beijing in September 1917 to serve under Grosse as vice-consul, made his own bid for the leadership.[34] With this lengthy service to the established Russian community, Metzler refused to abdicate leadership to the more recent military arrivals.

The situation revealed the intense rivalries between the former imperial Russian career diplomats and those who had served in the White Russian military forces. In January 1932, the Russian National Community attempted to broaden its scope by joining with still a third group of organizations to form an umbrella organization, the Council of United Russian Public Organizations at Shanghai (SORO). The Russian Emigrants Committee now faced a large and substantial rival. Adding to a perception of its strong credentials, SORO members elected A. M. Kotenev, who was attached to the Secretariat, or central administrative body, of the Shanghai Municipal Council, as its new chairman.[35] Other prominent members of the organizing committee included Captain Fomin and General Glebov.

The regulations and bylaws of SORO provide intriguing insight into the complex loyalties of refugee organizations trying to operate successfully in the foreign settlements of Shanghai. Despite their numbers, lacking recognized official status as stateless refugees, and having no representation on the Shanghai Municipal Council, SORO members pledged, as revealed in their official documents, to obey the laws of the Republic of China, the various regulations imposed by the International Settlement, where many worked,

Figure 10. Ch. E. Metzler, who became chairman of the Russian Emigrants Committee after the death of V. F. Grosse in 1931. SOURCE: Zhiganov, *Russkie v Shankhaie.*

e French Concession, where most of these Russian refugees

ler's leadership,[37] the Russian Emigrants Committee still
..... its position as the predominant refugee organization in
Shanghai, but hoping to replace the committee, SORO sought official
recognition from the Chinese authorities as the body best able to represent
the Russian refugee community. The plan succeeded. SORO won official
registration as a public organization from the local Guomindang headquarters.[38] Using this recognition to good advantage, SORO's leaders, including
one representative of the Jewish community, immediately declared that as
the only registered public organization, SORO possessed an officially sanctioned legal status that the Russian Emigrants Committee did not have.
SORO's leaders averred that the Russian community finally had one official
institution that could effectively represent genuine and legitimate Russian
interests in Shanghai. Their position, of course, came under heavy attack
from the Russian Emigrants Committee, which apparently had never
thought to inquire about receiving official recognition from the Chinese authorities. The committee had approached the Municipal Council to request
that Metzler be accorded the same commission and prestige that had been
accorded to Grosse, but without success.[39] It appears that the council did not
want to make a choice between two competing Russian organizations. The
French authorities concurred in that decision.[40]

These and other similar instances of interorganizational rivalries continued to divide and disrupt the Russian emigrant community, which, by
January 1933, had come to number 15,768, the second-largest number of
foreign nationals in Shanghai, after the Japanese.[41] The situation worsened
with the further influx of refugees entering Shanghai after Japan established
the new puppet state of Manchukuo. The Soviet government, recognizing
that it could no longer protect its economic interests, sold the Chinese
Eastern Railroad to Japan in March 1935, a move tantamount to recognizing Japan's predominant role in East Asia.[42] Manchukuo became the base for
launching further incursions into China, driving still more out-of-work railroad employees south to the open port of Shanghai. Other Russians chose to
become citizens of Manchukuo so that they could continue to work on the
railroad.[43] The narrowing of economic opportunities created a breeding
ground for extreme political groups, and under continued Japanese pressure,

the flow of refugees intensified. Some came as citizens of the Soviet Union who had refused repatriation; others chose to become stateless, arriving without passports as refugees; and still others had become naturalized as Chinese citizens. For political benefits, many assumed technically Red affiliation but maintained White allegiances, causing them to be commonly referred to as "Radishes" — red-skinned but white inside.[44]

Behind all these tensions, local members of the Russian refugee community failed to bring pressure to bear on their leaders to stop their destructive bickering and divisive actions. They feared retaliation from Shanghai authorities for becoming involved in any form of political expression or association, even that which might force their leaders to cooperate. As stateless refugees, most felt particularly vulnerable and avoided conflict, preferring to remain apolitical in their daily lives. Instead, they focused on meeting the daily challenges, adjusting, and surviving as stateless refugees in Shanghai.

The police kept records of the dozens of Russian organizations and their allegiances to the Russian Emigrants Committee and to SORO, noting as well the chairmen and memberships of these organizations.[45] Seeking to preserve his committee's predominant role in the face of SORO's challenge, the Russian Emigrants Committee's Chairman Metzler applied for recognition from Chinese authorities in August 1935. At a general meeting of his organization in April, Metzler also "accepted" appointment as "official representative of the Russian Community in Shanghai" in all dealings with Chinese, foreign, and municipal authorities. In an additional move to broaden its base and appeal, the Russian Emigrants Committee set up an umbrella organization not dissimilar in structure to SORO, calling itself the General Committee of Russian Emigrants Associations. The newly elected chairman, Captain N. I. Fomin, was, in fact, well known for his previous association with SORO. In case these efforts fell short, Metzler also managed to enlist Bishop Ioann as honorary chairman of the new body.[46] This combination of prestige and balanced leadership, and the respect associated with this organization of long service in Shanghai, seemed bound to draw broader appeal and wider support from the community.

The local Guomindang authorities, to whom the appeal was made, now had to cope with two competing organizations within the same administrative district, both fulfilling similar functions. The situation precipitated an appeal to the Nanjing government for guidance as to which of the two organizations should be granted official backing. Nanjing's judicious response was to instruct local Chinese authorities in Shanghai to register the new body as another "official organ" for the affairs of the Russian community in Shanghai.[47] SORO's failure to prevail in this struggle to win and maintain singular recognition led to dwindling memberships and organizational affiliations, and SORO's fortunes were not helped by the support of the leading Russian newspaper in Shanghai, *Shankhaiskaia Zaria*, for the Russian Emigrants Committee. The newspaper ran numerous derogatory cartoons criticizing SORO leadership. In what became almost a formula approach for expressing opposition, the newspaper accused Kotenev of being "a paid Soviet agent" and the new chairman, General Glebov, of "having a dictatorial attitude."[48]

The Ukrainians Seek Independence

The most vocal dissent against Russian dominance of the Shanghai Slavic community came from the local Ukrainians. Repudiating the contemporary status of Ukraine as merely one republic of the Soviet Union, Shanghai Ukrainians instead pledged their loyalty to the Ukrainian National Democratic Republic, formed in 1918 and recognized at Brest-Litovsk by numerous countries, including Russia, Germany, Austria, Turkey, and Bulgaria. Unfortunately, this independent Ukrainian republic, which consisted of Bukovina, Galicia, and the Carpathic and Kniepr Ukrainian territories, was short-lived.[49] The Soviet Army quickly occupied the greater part of Ukraine, which was incorporated into the USSR, and the new Polish state took over the remainder. As a result of the fighting, Ukrainians ended up in the Russian Far East in substantial numbers, subsequently moving to Harbin, and eventually to Shanghai. In the meantime, the independent Ukrainian republican government fled west, setting up a headquarters bureau in London.[50]

Ukrainian refugees came to Shanghai mainly in the exodus associated with the Japanese establishment of Manchukuo. They settled in the French Concession, where their leaders began immediately to organize as a separate community, distinct and apart from the larger Russian-dominated Slavic community. Their plans included the establishment of separate Ukrainian schools, orphanages, and a hospital. In September 1932, Ukrainian leaders registered their newly formed association with the French authorities.[51] After several lively meetings at the Kavkaz Restaurant at 1260 Rue Lafayette, the association finalized arrangements for opening its offices on Rue Bourgeat. A large celebration to commemorate this event took place on these premises, complete with raising the Ukrainian national flag over the office entrance.[52]

The political preoccupations of the Ukrainian Association in Shanghai, and its use of the new premises in the French Concession as a Ukrainian club, provoked opposition from the French authorities. There were numerous complaints to the French police about loud parties accompanied by heavy drinking and dancing from the neighborhood adjoining the Ukrainian House where the club was located. The French authorities responded with warnings, and, when these were not heeded, the Ukrainian Association was notified that it could no longer function in the Concession, owing mainly to its political activities — certainly the most appropriate and convenient basis for expelling the Ukrainians. The French authorities forbade political expression on the grounds that it was disruptive and against the statutes of the French Concession. The Ukrainian Association, with a membership of eighty-five, thereupon moved to the International Settlement and opened modest new offices, including a reading room, at 450 Taku Road in November 1933.[53] The association's president, H. E. Boutenko-Brown, an employee of the Public Works Department of the Shanghai Municipal Council, promised settlement authorities that there would be no gambling or sale of alcoholic beverages on the new premises.[54]

The "Regulations of the Ukrainian Association of Shanghai" state that the organization's purpose was to "unite Ukrainian residents of Shanghai in order to meet their social and cultural requirements." More important, its leaders were to "represent Ukrainian residents before municipal governments and all other local public organizations."[55] Implied in these words was Boutenko-Brown's intention to act as spokesman for Ukrainian national independence. The British authorities frowned on the political coloration of the Ukrainian Association and its new leaders, however. Not surprisingly, too, the Russian Emigrants Committee spokesmen emphatically argued the falseness of the association's claim.

Nevertheless, the Ukrainian leaders remained committed to their political goal of representing an independent and sovereign Ukraine to the Shanghai authorities, taking considerable risk with the bluntness of their statements. In a letter to the Shanghai Municipal Police dated November 11, 1937, attached to a new registration form to authorize relocating their offices to Avenue Edward VII, they explained that their purpose was to "unite all the Ukrainian emigrants who are conscious of the national interests of their Fatherland which has been in constant struggle against the foreign invader — Red Muscovites."[56]

Their principal resentment in Shanghai was over the constant lumping together of Ukrainians with Russians in the periodic registrations of the refugee populations. Especially irritating was the fact that the official census forms did not even include a category for Ukrainians, causing many to register themselves under the category "Other" or as "stateless." When it was decided in 1938 to carry out compulsory registration of all Russian emigrants residing in the French Concession, the Ukrainian Association requested that in registration certificates issued by the French authorities to Ukrainians, the words "of Russian origin," offensive to the nationalistic sentiments of the Ukrainians, be replaced by "of Ukrainian origin." In a letter stating their case, the leaders claimed that in 1930, when the Nansen Office closed, the decision had been made to leave to the discretion of the government concerned determinations of refugee nationality when providing identification cards. Having this as a form of international sanction for their request, and pointing to the existing Ukrainian headquarters in London, the Ukrainian leaders were confident of the merit and persuasiveness of their arguments.[57]

The French and International Settlement authorities failed to pay great attention to the Ukrainian pleas, however, probably because so many Russians served in their police forces and fire brigades, as well as in other municipal capacities. The Ukrainian leaders stressed that their community was substantial, numbering more than five thousand persons. Nevertheless, this number, even if valid, paled beside the huge Russian community, whose leaders intended to represent both Russians and Ukrainians officially.[58] It was the Japanese who would realize Ukrainian hopes, at least temporarily.

The outbreak of Sino-Japanese hostilities in July 1937, beginning with the Marco Polo Bridge incident just west of Beiping, was quickly followed by the Battle of Shanghai, which started in Zhabei, then spread to Jiangwan, Hongkou, Yangshupu, and Pudong. By November, following three months of heavy fighting, during which there was enormous damage to Shanghai factories and countless Chinese died, the Chinese portions of the city had fallen to the Japanese, who celebrated by holding a victory parade down the main thoroughfare, Nanking Road. Chinese schoolchildren were issued Japanese victory flags and forced to attend the victory parade, while Chinese refugees once again streamed into the settlement areas. The entire economy of Shanghai came to a standstill. The Guomindang authorities evacuated to Hankou, and the Japanese-backed Da Dao (Great Way) municipal government took over Chinese portions of Shanghai in December 1937.[59]

Shortly after assuming power, the new Chinese puppet government recognized the Russian Emigrants Committee as the key administrative and representative organ of the Russian and Slavic refugee communities. Once again, the Ukrainian leadership presented the argument to the new authorities that only their leaders could speak for the Ukrainian community. But this time they could be more persuasive, in that the soon-to-be leader of the Ukrainian community spoke fluent Japanese. The Ukrainian Association submitted a memorandum to the municipal government requesting that a status equal to that of the Russian Emigrants Committee be granted to it.[60] Organizations representing refugees of Georgian and Turco-Tartar origin joined in the request, presenting a joint petition to the new authorities. To bolster their case, in November 1938, the leaders implemented a registration drive so as to have numbers to back up their petition. Speaking in fluent Japanese, the Ukrainian leader B. I. Voblyi laid out his arguments, accompanied by the registration figures, to the chief of the Japanese Special Military Mission in Shanghai, General Takeshita Yoshiharu.

Voblyi had graduated from the Japanese Language Department of the Oriental Institute at Vladivostok in 1910. He went to Japan in 1919, and from 1924 to 1934, he taught in various Japanese government schools. In 1936, he became professor of Japanese at the Institute of St. Vladimir in Harbin, which he left for Shanghai in 1938.[61] Voblyi's representations to the Japanese were successful. In a letter dated April 8, 1939, General Takeshita informed the mayor of the Municipality of Greater Shanghai that recognition had been granted by the Japanese Special Military Mission to the Ukrainian Emigrants Committee and the Georgian and Turco-Tartar Associations, with the Ukrainian Emigrants Committee authorized to serve as their common representative organ.[62] The mayor conveyed the approval to the Ukrainian Association on June 24, 1939, while *Shankhaiskaia Zaria* carried a notification for these nationalities residing in Shanghai to register with the police through the offices of the Ukrainian Association of Shanghai.[63]

In a boisterous ceremony held the same month, the Ukrainian community met at the premises of the Ukrainian Association to accomplish the official reorganization of the Ukrainian community. The meeting approved the dissolution of the Ukrainian Association and validated the election of the new Ukrainian Emigrants Committee, with Voblyi serving as president.[64] The new committee, having the same functions as the Russian Emigrants Committee, was the authorized body to attend to registering Ukrainian nationals and issuing passports, visas, and other official documents. The committee relocated to new offices in room 347 of Hamilton House.

The Ukrainian community was not immune to the sort of internal conflict that had always plagued the Russian community. After the announcement of the committee's formation, H. E. Butenko-Brown, identifying himself as chairman of the Ukrainian Association, sent a letter to the Shanghai Municipal Police and one to the editor of *Shankhaiskaia Zaria* denying the validity of the reorganization and new leadership of the Ukrainian community, reaffirming instead the continued authority of the old association, which he still headed. Butenko-Brown's correspondence drew an immediate rebuttal from President Voblyi of the new committee, charging that Butenko-Brown had severely complicated the daily workings of the committee by refusing to hand over the official seal and stationery belonging to the Ukrainian community.[65]

Butenko-Brown, the proprietor of the popular Broadway Café, had broken away from the association once before, setting up the Ukrainian Benevolent Committee, which had lasted from June 1937 until May 1938. According to his information, the association's then chairman, N. T. Kvashenko, a former soldier in the White Russian army and an unemployed painter, had engaged in political activities "incompatible" with Ukrainian national interests. In return, Kvashenko accused Butenko-Brown of "faulty bookkeeping" of his organization's finances and revealed his having been called before the First Special District Court on North Chekiang Road because of the back rent owed on his office space.

Whatever the nature and accuracy of their leaders' charges, life was very difficult for the Ukrainian refugees in Shanghai. Many, even some of the community leaders, were apprehended for petty crimes such as shoplifting and picking pockets. To aid those most in need, the association maintained a hostel, which provided hot meals and some lodging. An annual ball and raffle held at the fashionable Astor House became a principal fund-raising event. To attract affluent guests, tickets to the ball bore numbers corresponding to those appearing on certain prizes to be distributed at an appointed time. The association raised additional funds through mahjong parties held every Sunday at the Ukrainian Club, with a percentage of the proceeds to go to the most destitute Ukrainian refugees. The club also sponsored lectures, enter-tainment, and religious services.

The Ukrainian Club frequently held social events in common with the Georgian Club in Shanghai. Together, the communities enjoyed chamber concerts, tea parties, and religious services at the Russian Cathedral, presided over by Bishop Ioann. N. I. Makharadze, chairman of the Georgian Society of Shanghai, was a frequent guest at the annual festival celebrating the Ukrainian independence day held on January 22 and honoring Symon Petliura, the famed independence leader and commander in chief of the Ukrainian Army (and notorious anti-Semite).[66] On these occasions, partici-pants mourned what they saw as Ukraine's tragic history of becoming a "vas-sal state" after Germany's defeat in World War I, with the Russian part of the country being taken over by the Soviet Union and the Austrian part going to Poland.

The Polish Presence

The small Polish community in Shanghai for the most part kept to itself. There being so few of them, the Poles went unrepresented in the governing of the settlements, although they had a national association, the Polish Union. Census data collected in the French Concession, where most Poles lived, indicate that in 1931, there were only 262 Polish residents, most of whom were connected with companies such as the Polish Import and Export Co. and the Far Eastern Textile Co.[67]

Polish Catholic missionaries often stopped in Shanghai on their way to various missions around China, such as the Urumqi Catholic Mission in western Xinjiang, where there was a large Slavic community. Other Poles came to take up positions at Shanghai's St. Mary's Hospital or to join the teaching staff at the Russian-attended Thomas Hanbury School.[68]

On the whole, Poles in Shanghai lived a stable and comfortable life. They did work that was not overly taxing and could afford household servants. There were a few Polish restaurants, and the Polish Club sponsored dances, lectures, political discussions, poetry readings, and other social gatherings. Poles could choose among numerous Catholic and Orthodox religious services. The small staff of the Polish consulate mingled easily in Shanghai's international community. As was true for the established or nonrefugee Russian Orthodox and Jewish communities, the Polish experience in Shanghai was rich with variety, entertainment, and a sense of community.

Events in the north began to change this pleasant picture. First, there was the establishment of Manchukuo. The Japanese takeover of the railroad and other Russian economic interests in Manchuria, especially in Harbin, threatened the livelihoods of the thousands of Polish professionals and laborers who had helped to build, supply, and maintain the rail network.[69] These began to make contact with other Poles in Tianjin (Tientsin) and Shanghai for information about planning a move to a new life. Finally, the outbreak of Sino-Japanese hostilities motivated most of the remaining Harbin Poles to search for safety and employment away from Harbin. Shanghai, where there was an established Polish community, was a natural choice for them. The number of Poles in Shanghai expanded from a mere 200 in the early years to more than 2,000 when the exodus of mainly Polish Jews arrived during the course of World War II.[70]

The Hebrew Immigrant Aid Society (HIAS) maintained an office in Harbin to keep its center in Paris and Hilfsverein in Berlin informed of employment opportunities for European Jews in China.[71] The World War II exodus of Orthodox Polish Jews to Shanghai, who helped make up the vast majority of 1,185 Polish registrations between 1934 and 1941, is discussed in Chapter 5.[72] Two peaks in the waves of incoming refugees occurred during the years 1934 and 1937 and reflect the events occurring in the north. In 1934, 75 refugees arrived in Shanghai, most registering with the authorities as tradesmen, mechanics, merchants, and shopkeepers, all essential to the maintenance and servicing of a rail network. Some in their twenties even gave their place of birth as Harbin. The group of 262 that arrived and registered in 1937, many with expired travel documents, contained a different mix of backgrounds. In addition to tradesmen, merchants, and shopkeepers, this group included doctors, professors, journalists, musicians, students, and engineers. These were people who had a substantial career stake in continuing to stay on in the northeast, but Japanese pressure and the outbreak of hostilities made their residence in Harbin no longer tenable.[73] To aid these incoming refugees, the Shanghai Polish Union newspaper *Echo Szanghajskie* published a supplement containing employment opportunities, community information, and other news.[74]

The Polish community enjoyed close ties to the large Russian community in Shanghai, some even considering themselves part of that community. This was another factor that helped considerably to ease the transition for Polish refugees to a new life in Shanghai. Like a number of Russian Jewish refugees who had left Harbin after long residence and much hard work, many Polish refugees had done well there in lumber, grain, furs, and diamonds, but were forced to move on after the Japanese takeover. Like the Russians, too, the Polish refugees found an already established national presence in Shanghai.

Shanghai Poles initially had an advantage not shared by the Russians, in that they enjoyed official representation in the shape of a Polish consulate. Unfortunately, this was to be short-lived, owing to the outbreak of World War II and the Polish government's flight into exile in London. Members of the Shanghai Polish community resisted any reference to themselves as stateless refugees, however, firmly rejecting the stigma of being without a national identity.

Russian Cultural and Social Life in Shanghai in the 1930s

Shanghai housed the largest Russian refugee colony outside of Paris and Harbin. The established Russian community that preceded the several waves of destitute Russian refugees flooding Shanghai viewed the newcomers negatively, fearing that the refugees' desperate conditions might turn them to crime and thus give all Russians in Shanghai a bad name.[75] Indeed, some did just that, but overall, the decade of the 1930s became a rich period in the Russian community's existence. Surrounded by the alien Chinese culture, and excluded from close association with elite Western society in Shanghai,

Russians looked inward, nourishing and preserving their own cultural heritage through an array of religious organizations, schools, libraries, newspapers, journals and publications, clubs, and theater and arts groups. The widely shared hope was that one day soon, the refugees might return to Russia victorious, after the overthrow of the communist government. The prospect of counterrevolution weighed heavily on their minds, but in the meanwhile, Russian culture had to be preserved and developed, especially among Russian schoolchildren and young people. Russian culture was celebrated with a holiday each June 8, following festivities to mark the birthday of the beloved poet Aleksandr Pushkin on June 6.

Talented Russian musicians and artists, both Orthodox and Jewish, made substantial and widely acclaimed contributions to the cultural life of the city. Russian-staged operas, ballets, and plays enjoyed wide popularity. There were a light opera society, a ballet company, and a Russian musical society. The latter, for example, gave performances of Modest Mussorgsky's opera *Boris Godunov* to packed audiences. Russian musicians made up 60 percent of the Shanghai Municipal Orchestra.[76] The Siberian-born Russian Jewish musician and composer Aaron Avshalomov, composed works using Chinese subjects and themes. His Piano Concerto in G, written in 1935, was first performed by the Shanghai Municipal Orchestra in January 1936.[77] He did the first orchestration of Nie Er's "The Song of the Volunteers," which later became the national anthem of the People's Republic of China.[78] An unforgettable musical event always recalled by those who lived these times in Shanghai was the 1936 visit and performance by the beloved Russian bass singer F. I. Chaliapin. Several Russian musicians made a living giving music lessons to both Chinese and Western students. On a less elevated level, a popular Russian jazz band entertained regularly at the fashionable Majestic Hotel, and there were many other Russian bands entertaining Shanghai's brisk nightly trade.

One of the most popular Russian clubs went by the acronym Kh.L.A.M., which humorously translates from the Russian as "trash."[79] Kh.L.A.M. had as members writers, artists, actors, and musicians, who often held their gatherings at popular local Russian restaurants and cafés in the French Concession. There were specialized clubs for philatelists and chess players, as well as professional clubs for Russian doctors, dentists, accountants, lawyers, and engineers. Of course, the large Russian military presence had

Figure 11. Annual ball sponsored by the Union of Russian Army and Navy Ex-Servicemen held at the Majestic Ballroom to celebrate Russian New Year's Eve. The Majestic Ballroom was demolished that summer of 1931. SOURCE: Zhiganov, *Russikie v Shankhaie.*

clubs representing various military services, as well as regiments of the former White army, cadet academies, former naval officers, other military units, and ex-servicemen. Members of the local Russian sporting association SOKOL performed well in sports ranging from fencing and volleyball to football and boxing. "Big Boy Semenoff" was a leading contender in the well-attended boxing matches at the Canidrome. In the spring of 1935, with cooperation from the Russian Society of Merchants and Russian Chamber of Commerce, the Shanghai Russian Club was founded under the chairmanship of A. A. Reier.[80] This club became the hub of Russian social life, and a meeting place used by many of the clubs mentioned above.

Shanghai became a major publishing center for Russian books, magazines, works of literature and poetry, religious works, educational material, and patriotic writings. A popular newspaper column, "In the Russian Colony," claimed that Shanghai Russians published more books than communities in Paris, Berlin, or Riga, owing to the cheap local labor and modern printing methods.[81] The stimulus came in part from the many active poets and writers, formerly resident in Harbin, who had fled to Shanghai. Literary life in the city became very animated, and almanacs, literary journals, and newspapers were published.[82] The community supported at least six daily newspapers, the most prominent of which were the informative *Shankhaiskaia Zaria*, the popular *Slovo* (The Word), and the conservative *Novosti Dnia* (Russian Daily News). The most visited bookstore was "Russkoe Delo," on Avenue Joffre in the French Concession, which had more than fifteen thousand volumes in stock by 1937. Close by was the lending library owned by A. P. Malyk and V. P. Kamkin Co. This company was also the leading Russian publishing firm in Shanghai. After World War II, Victor Kamkin emigrated to Washington, D.C., and, with an inventory of 200 books, opened a bookstore on Harvard Street. By an agreement reached in 1957, the Victor Kamkin Bookstore became a major official distributor of Soviet publications in the United States.[83] The Russian community also operated a radio station in Shanghai (XRVN).

Russian shops and the Russian language were a prominent feature of the French Concession, adding to the cosmopolitan façade of this part of the city. Restaurants, millineries, furriers, repair shops, and salons gave employment to Russian labor, technical skill, management initiative, and creativity. The range of Russian enterprises ran from provisioning stores to small kiosks, from distinguished restaurants and cabarets to small cafés and eateries. Refugees also found economic salvation in running small businesses and managing hat and dress shops, pharmacies, bakeries, vodka distilleries, fur and leather companies, jewelry stores, and auto service and supply companies.[84] The Russians with the best professional opportunities were those who could serve their own large community as doctors, lawyers, dentists, teachers in Russian schools, and journalists.[85]

Education was not slighted by the Russian community. At the popular Commercial School, started in 1924 as the School for Poor Russian Children, students received a practical education, preparing them for advancement in the Shanghai business world, including instruction in the French and Chinese languages. Other Russian students attended the First Russian School, founded in 1921. Referred to as a "real" school, it placed emphasis on the sciences rather than offering a classical education in the arts and literature. The Ecole Remi, a French municipal school directed by

P. Guillemont, which offered a nine-form program as opposed to the usual seven-form academic schedule, was another well-attended school, with 350 Russian students in 1936.[86] In addition, 100 Russian students attended the French Municipal College, which provided more than one-third of the Russian students with financial assistance to cover tuition costs. The Thomas Hanbury Schools, one for boys and one for girls, also enrolled Russian students, as did the Kaiser Wilhelm School. Two Catholic-run schools that educated Russian students were St. Francis Xavier College and St. Jeanne d'Arc College.[87] For advanced education, Russian students attended the respected Jesuit Aurora University and St. John's University.

During the 1930s, the Russian Orthodox community founded two major churches, greatly enhancing the availability of religious services, previously held in private chapels and at the small church in Zhabei.[88] The grand Russian Orthodox Cathedral on Rue Paul Henri, with planned seating for 2,000 worshipers, began construction in 1932, supported by funding from local Russian subscriptions.[89] St. Nicholas Church, located on Rue Corneille and built in the same year, was a memorial to Czar Nicholas II and his family, serving mainly Russian ex-officers and their families.[90] Both became major centers of Russian religious life.

The small Russian church on Henan Road in Zhabei, which had existed as early as 1905, was destroyed by Japanese shells in 1932.[91] The Russian churches provided the refugees with a vital link to tradition and culture, serving as the principal factor in preserving a sense of cultural independence and identity. The elaborate Russian Easter services, often with full illumination of the imposing new edifices, drew broad attendance as well by Poles, Ukrainians, Georgians, and other nationalities. There was even a small community of "Old Believers" practicing their religion according to rituals and canons widespread before the reform of the Orthodox Church.[92]

Life in the Shanghai community also had its somber side. The language, manners, and customs of the foreign community were unfamiliar. The refugees had to merge into the whirlpool of the Shanghai business world without getting lost or perishing in it. Generally, Russian refugees were not accepted in the socially elite circles of white Shanghai society. They or their children might participate together in the many athletic activities, but refugee Russians did not receive invitations to visit the homes of Shanghai's white elite. The most fortunate Russians served in departments of the

Shanghai Municipal Council, such as on the Orchestra or Food Committees, which offered paid leave and excellent pensions. The Municipal Council, the British Defence Force, and the utility services employed 721 Russians, while 49 persons served the council and utilities in the French Concession.[93] Collectively, they represented the aristocracy of Russian labor in Shanghai. Still, Russians never achieved prominent positions in ruling circles and were not invited to many official social functions. Even in the case of receptions sponsored by the Shanghai municipal or French police, in which Russians served in considerable numbers, they tended to be excluded from guest lists; or, if they were invited, Russians were "not seen" by the other guests.[94]

British, American, and French trading houses and export-import businesses offered employment opportunities to the refugees as accountants, clerks, bank guards, night watchmen, or factory guards. Russians worked as watchmen and workmen at both the Shanghai Race Club and Shanghai Telephone Company and as mechanics for the Shanghai Omnibus Company. The Shanghai Gas Company hired Russian workers to replace Chinese staff when the latter went out on strike.[95] Still, many of those Russians lacking the essential foreign-language skills (especially English), and those who were no longer particularly young, were forced into hard labor on the docks or in construction. They reported seeing themselves as unwanted in their homeland and regarded as cheap labor in Shanghai. For those more fortunate who found office work, compensation in foreign firms was considerably lower for Russians than that for other foreign staff in equivalent positions. Russians fell midway between foreign employees and Chinese staff.

Another prospering industry in Shanghai involved working as bodyguards for rich Chinese, who were potential victims of kidnappers after heavy ransom payments. With so many of the refugees coming from military backgrounds, this was a promising field of at least temporary employment. Still, by 1938, the unemployment rate in the Russian community ran as high as 40 percent.[96] The Sino-Japanese hostilities had taken a heavy toll on the entire Russian community. Military operations destroyed Russian boarding houses, workshops, restaurants, cabarets, and shops in Hongkou, many of them owned or managed by Russian Jews.[97] Numerous firms and factories employing Russians either closed or minimized their operations. In addition, the Shanghai market, having been cut off from the interior of China, expe-

Figure 12. Russian guards protecting armored car shipments of bank money in specie and bullion. Many Russians, especially those with military background, found employment as guards, bodyguards, and watchmen. SOURCE: Zhiganov, *Russkie v Shankhaie.*

rienced an immediate general business decline, which caused increased unemployment among all nationalities, including the Russians.[98] Table 3 gives statistics on Russian employment in 1937, which show a deterioration, particularly, in business and luxury occupations (e.g., bookkeepers, chauffeurs, and furriers). As sometimes happens, certain kinds of workers actually benefited from the hostilities. Russian taxi drivers, truckers, and mechanics replaced Chinese counterparts who were unwilling to transport people or goods across Suzhou Creek to the Japanese-controlled Hongkou and Zhabei wharves and districts.[99]

Many Russians simply could not adjust to the lowered social status and lack of employment opportunity. Poverty, loneliness, overcrowding, and lack of privacy drove some to despair. After a bout of heavy drinking, for example, two idle young officer cadets took poison to end their unhappy lives.[100]

TABLE 3
Russian Employment Statistics, 1937

Profession	Employed	Unemployed
Bookkeepers– 186	51	135
Chauffeurs – 566	155	411
Clerks (female) – 165	88	77
Clerks (male) – 553	339	214
Dressmakers – 346	124	222
Electricians – 218	85	133
Engineers – 271	120	151
Furriers – 38	12	26
Manicurists – 90	46	44
Nurses – 136	91	45
Saleswomen – 89	42	47
Stenographers – 225	110	115
Teachers – 140	41	99

SOURCE: Simpson, *Refugee Problem*, p. 502, based on a
survey of employment statistics for 6,564 males and 3,360
females.

As further indication of the Russian plight, survey results indicate that marriages and childbearing among Russians were on the decline. Table 4 reveals
the difficult domestic conditions of Russian refugees in Shanghai.

Russian refugee women held the most precarious position in the Russian
community. In an age when the general pattern was that respectable women
did not work for pay outside the home, most refugee women had to work,
and many could find employment only as waitresses, taxi dancers, or cabaret
girls in the numerous Shanghai cafés, bars, and dance halls. Hongkou housed
a number of honky-tonk bars: the Venus Café was one of the most popular,
but there were many, including the Red Rose, made popular by its nightly
offerings of Russian gypsy music. Given Shanghai's active nightlife, Russian
refugee men were able to find work as guides to patrons in search of the
liveliest and sometimes the most bizarre entertainment. One particularly no-

TABLE 4
Domestic Conditions of Russian Refugees

Literacy rate	9,811 literate; 113 illiterate
Married persons	3,335
Single	6,598
Childless families	1,409
One child	1,304
Two children	443
Three children	126
More than three children	57
Children under age 21*	2,827
males	1,415
females	1,412
Housing	1,033 cases
Refugee camps	114
Barracks	71
Residences	2
Rented apartments	65
Boarding houses	781

SOURCE: Simpson, *Refugee Problem*, pp. 506–7, based on a sample of 9,924 adults taken in 1938.
*A decline in fertility is indicated by the fact that only 505 children fell into the age group 6 and under.

torious nightclub, the Black Bed, boasted an undulating cushioned dance floor covered in black velvet. On all sides of the dance floor were dressing rooms where patrons could be outfitted in exotic costumes or don their own creations. Still another in the neighborhood was the Black Cat, famous for its Korean hostesses, whose backsides were tattooed with a small black cat.[101] Among the best and busiest cabarets, the Casanova Ballroom also ran gambling parlors on its upper floors, and for a while it was reputed to be the center of a spy ring involving both the French and Japanese police. For the late-night crowd, the Del Monte Café, like the Casanova, was known for its attractive and popular Russian hostesses, whose task was to sit, converse, and dance with the male guests, encourage them to buy drinks, and generally add to the glamour of the establishment.[102] Stirling Fessenden, former chairman of the Shanghai Municipal Council and later its paid secretary-general, a bachelor, made regular visits to the Majestic and Paramount ballrooms. A short, pudgy man, he was remembered for his almost nightly circling of the dance floor with his tall, slim Russian dancing partners.

Many Russian women, unable to speak English or Chinese and lacking other employment prospects, were drawn into prostitution to survive. The respected Russian Orthodox Confraternity enumerated several key reasons for Russian females taking up prostitution:

> We know the main cause of the evil of which our women are the victims: dire poverty with no prospect of better days. Shanghai has become a center where Russian emigrants seek refuge, as conditions of life in the North are becoming more and more difficult. Upon arrival in Shanghai they are lost in this city, as they do not possess a knowledge of languages or any professional qualifications and therefore are unable to earn a living. Their children are affected by these conditions even to a greater degree, as they remain without proper education.[103]

Dancing partners in the better Shanghai clubs, like their Chinese counterparts in high-class courtesan houses, did not engage in a straightforward trade in sexual favors for payment but instead had some freedom in the selection of sexual partners.[104] Russian prostitutes at an optimum position in the loose and often fluid system of commercialized sexual relationships in Shanghai, such as those who worked at establishments like the Casanova, could earn from $200 to $1,000 (U.S.$10–52 in December 1941) a night.[105] Comparing this to the typical earnings of shop girls, which were $120–125 (U.S.$33–34 in 1930) a month, made the allure of the business to those refugees without office skills or professional training substantial.[106]

Taxi dancers who operated in the numerous nightclubs in both the International Settlement and French Concession earned a commission on the drinks sold to customers, as well as a percentage of the dance ticket price. Most also received a small monthly stipend or salary set by the terms of their contract. Dance hostesses at more typical establishments earned approximately $250–$300 a month, an amount that reportedly did not doom them

Figure 13. One of the many busy centers of Shanghai nightlife.
SOURCE: Courtesy of the Library of Congress Prints and Photographs
Division.

Figure 14. Mrs. A. Bologovsky, a dancing partner at the upscale Del Monte Café. SOURCE: SMPD 6460.

to a life of prostitution. However, some probably did engage in prostitution to supplement their incomes.[107] Because of the nature of the work and environment, many hostesses succumbed to alcoholism, drug addiction, and debt. A small Russian Women's Hostel, containing fifteen beds, opened to provide help and counseling to these women, with financial support from the local Russian and Jewish communities.[108] The Sephardi philanthropist Sir Victor Sassoon was a major contributor.

Other Russian women found it possible to work under a thin cloak of respectability as masseuses or manicurists while engaging in prostitution.[109] And still others worked for escort or guide services. By 1937, the International Settlement had 100 travel agencies, employing 700 women as travel guides, some of them no doubt Russian.[110] Russian-owned boarding houses often prospered by the trade in prostitution. The most dire circumstances involved the wives of unemployed and untrained husbands who were themselves unable to find work. Russian "hostesses" supported whole families of relatives through their liaisons with wealthy benefactors, who were often married. Some Russians even had to sell their children in order to survive. The famous and wealthy Hardoon family, recognizing the problem, included impoverished Russian young among their many adopted children. St. Tikhon's and St. Olga's orphanages took in the most destitute Russian children. There were some success stories involving incidences of refugee women marrying well, even dance hall girls. Between 1925 and 1938, 305 Russian women married British subjects in the Shanghai consular district.[111] News of these happy liaisons encouraged others to follow the same path, usually with less fortunate results.

The record is still unclear, at least concerning Russian prostitutes, as to whether an active white slave trade played a major role. As noted above, a steady flow of White Russians arrived in Shanghai throughout the 1920s and 1930s. Given the widely circulating and enticing stories about the glamorous life in Shanghai and the demographics, it seems most likely that an active and extensive white slave trade aimed at providing women who would eventually serve as prostitutes in Shanghai probably was unnecessary. Nevertheless, there was a system of what might be termed a managed supply of Russian women to Shanghai. A key point was that these young women from North China already were intent on making a new life there. Russian women from Harbin, tempted by the bright lights of Shanghai, did not have to be kidnapped; rather, they were willing partners. What their Harbin "managers" or agents did was to make the travel and settlement arrangements easy for their charges to handle. Naive, inexperienced, and many of them impoverished, these eager young women, most between 18 and 21 years, accepted the travel offers and contracts without carefully reading the fine print about their future obligations.[112] Once in the new and unfamiliar place, they discovered that finding the glamorous work they had envisioned was beyond reach. Because they were deeply in debt because of the costs of the journey, clothing, and other expenses, the options available to them were few. Adding to their vulnerability was the fact that most had left all the arrangements regarding identity papers and essential travel documents to their agent-managers, who continued to hold them. Feeling helpless under these circumstances and ignorant about their rights and what measures might be taken to challenge the demands of the agent-managers, the young women believed they had no recourse but to submit to their proposals.[113] To work off their debt, they became obliged to accept one of the forms of prostitution described earlier.

The situation became so acute that the League of Nations commissioned a study to consider the situation of Russian women in Shanghai as a key part of its effort to understand the situation of women and children in the Far East. A "League of Nations Travelling Commission of Enquiry into Traffic in Women and Children in the East" arrived in Shanghai in 1930 armed with questionnaires and a list of officials to be interviewed that covered the entire range of authorities in both the foreign and Chinese sectors. The questionnaires asked for statistics on prostitution; identification of countries involved in trafficking; specifics on laws forbidding trafficking and their effectiveness; and so on. The League's official report on the Russian situation in Shanghai, issued in 1935, following the survey by the commission, was that there were 755 professional prostitutes working in Shanghai and 890 casual or occasional prostitutes, for a total of 1,645.[114] At the same time, the League estimated that the female Russian population between the ages of 16 and 45 was approximately 7,200, meaning that at least 22.5 percent of Russian women in Shanghai in that age group probably engaged in prostitution.[115] Put differently, this number meant that almost one in four women in this age category were involved.

Those local Russian officials who had helped gather the information and prepare the record strongly supported the findings, although not without sadness. Other Russians condemned the reports as groundless and humiliating to all Russian emigrants. The Russian refugee community at large deeply regretted the negative results, believing that the ensuing publicity cast an undeserved pall on the image of the Russian woman.[116] Still another distressing study found that 75 percent of Russian schoolchildren needed more rest and better nutrition.[117]

The League of Nations's response to the plight of Russian women was less than expected, given the amount of time and public attention it had focused on the problem. As noted above, the League had made a concerted effort to study and document Russian prostitution, but once this work was complete, it failed to make available any League financial support. Instead, the burden of caring fell on local religious and service organizations already heavily taxed by relief activities. While the League's decision was a disappointment to many who had expected funding to support shelters, workshops, educational institutions, and other relief efforts, its response followed closely established League policies, which were to develop a working framework within which private agencies could provide the effective assistance. League officials appealed to the "social conscience of right-thinking people" to fund the office of an agent of the League, who could then coordinate the measures necessary "to secure the future of these women of Russian origin." The League's recommendation clearly states that these services by its agent "should not involve in the present circumstances any financial charge upon the League," not even the administrative costs of maintaining the agent's office.[118]

The Approaching War and Jewish Survival

These deep concerns of Shanghai Russians existed alongside growing apprehensions in the Shanghai Jewish community. During the 1930s, Russian and Slavic Ashkenazi Jews began significantly to outnumber the Sephardim, of whom there were never more than about 1,000. Anti-Semitism in Manchukuo and the rise of National Socialism in Germany caused a new influx of Ashkenazi Jews to Shanghai. The first Jews fleeing Germany arrived aboard the Italian liner SS *Conte Verde* in late 1933.[119] This group included German physicians, scientists, and professors. Their arrival came on the heels of a sensational ransom case in Harbin involving Simeon Kaspe, a talented pianist and the son of a wealthy Jewish businessman, owner of Harbin's famous Hotel Moderne. The Kaspe case had special importance to Shanghai Jews, because the elder Kaspe had been educated at the Shanghai Public

School for Boys.[120] The brutal murder of the 24-year-old son and subsequent lenient court treatment of his murderers sent a message to Jews that anti-Semitism had the support of the Manchukuo authorities. This despite the fact that Prince Takamatsu, brother of the Japanese emperor, had stressed repeatedly that the Japanese did not discriminate between the races, as long as residents obeyed the laws of the country. Jewish leaders also had taken some comfort in the fact that the Japanese delegation at the Versailles Conference had called for the insertion of a declaration of racial equality into the League of Nations Charter.[121]

As evidence of growing anti-Semitism accumulated both in the north and in Shanghai, the Jewish community began to look for ways to defuse the situation. They used their contacts with official Japanese in Shanghai to plead their case with the Manchukuo authorities, often reminding them of Jewish wartime generosity in the shape of the Schiff loans. Former residents reported that Jews in Harbin were being accused of blood-ritual murders, Jewish schoolchildren charged with being "Christ killers," and adult Jews with being Bolshevik spies and saboteurs. One repercussion of their actions was that Shanghai Orthodox Russians, feeling drawn into the problem and resenting a perceived guilt by association, often criticized Shanghai Jewish leaders for not always making a clearer distinction between the cruel behavior of White Russians in Harbin and the stance taken by Russians in Shanghai.

Even though they were aware of conditions in the north, Shanghai Jewish leaders initiated a series of negotiations with the Japanese to resettle Jewish refugees in Manchukuo. The situation in Europe was becoming increasingly threatening to Jews, making it seem imperative to find places of refuge for the expected tide of desperate refugees. A mass meeting of all Jewish organizations and their leaders in Shanghai, the first of its kind, gathered in April 1934 to learn about the threatening situation for Jews in central Europe. Rabbis Ashkenazi and Brown both served on the mass meeting committee. Four months later, N. E. B. Ezra, editor of *Israel's Messenger*, traveled to Japan and met with Shigemitsu Mamoru, vice-minister of foreign affairs, to raise the idea of Jewish immigration, "on a grand scale" (50,000 was the number mentioned) to Manchukuo, where they might participate in its development. The Japanese official replied with hesitation, claiming that Manchukuo faced many problems and that the proposed movement was "too big for the present." Shigemitsu stressed, however, that no restrictions would be placed on individuals wishing to settle in Manchukuo.[122] In effect, Shigemitsu had turned down the request to settle large numbers of European Jews in Manchukuo. Undaunted, Jewish leaders continued to speak to the potential role Jews could play in the development of Asia, if only given the opportunity.[123]

In the meantime, the Shanghai German community began to show the effects of developments in Central Europe. As early as 1932, the Nazi Party had established a branch in Shanghai and party leaders delivered anti-Semitic speeches, blaming the fate of Russia during the Revolution on Jewish plots. Nazi visitors came to Shanghai, exclaiming about the great promise of the new regime in Germany.[124] A Dr. F. W. Mohr, speaking at the Shanghai Rotary Club and responding to local questions, challenged members of the audience to go to Germany and see for themselves how distorted local rumors about Hitler's aims and programs were. But proof to the contrary continued to inform the Shanghai Jewish community, such as the case of renowned Polish conductor Josef Rosenstock, barred from creative work by Nazi restrictions against non-Aryan musicians. Fortunately, Rosenstock received an appointment as conductor of a new symphony orchestra in Tokyo.[125]

By the late 1930s, there were from 4,000 to 8,000 Ashkenazi Jews living in Shanghai.[126] Troubled by the growing uncertainties and spreading rumors, the Ashkenazi Jewish Communal Association, under Morris Bloch's leadership, saw a need to establish a unique and more protected identity within the large Shanghai Russian community. In 1937, the association therefore applied for and received recognition by a registration charter from the Chinese government in Nanjing, just as had the Russian Emigrants Committee and its arch competitor, the Council of United Russian Public Organizations at Shanghai. This new status did not preclude members from having to rely upon the Russian Emigrants Committee for identity certificates, visas, "certificates of character,"[127] and other official services, but the association nonetheless gained credibility as a Jewish institution in Shanghai. It was, however, about to face a challenge that would at least temporarily overwhelm both its leaders and resources.

Nazi Victims Find Refuge

In every generation tyrants have sought to destroy us, but the Holy One, blessed be He, has delivered us from their hands.

— The Passover Haggada

The second victim diaspora to find refuge in Shanghai came with the rise of Nazism. Those victimized were the Jews, against whom Adolf Hitler's anti-Semitic policies began to unfold soon after his rise to power. Plans for eliminating Jewish participation in German professional and economic life developed incrementally. Initially, only government service was off-limits to Jews, and even in this case, veterans of World War I were excepted. Soon, however, the screws tightened. The various sectors of German society were organized to exclude Jews. The legal and medical professions, the press, and even schools and universities refused to admit Jews into their respective organizations. Next, by denying Jews membership in newly organized business and economic organizations, they were deprived of a means of livelihood.

In September 1935, the so-called Nuremberg Laws deprived Jews and persons with Jewish blood of German citizenship, prohibited marriages or sexual contact between Germans and those with Jewish blood, and forbade Jews to employ female servants of non-Jewish origin. As an added humiliation, Jews were required to wear a yellow Star of David on their clothing when in public.

Jews who had served the country in World War I and could proudly display their war medals believed these honors would still protect them from harm. They soon learned otherwise. Jews were forced into ghettos, their businesses were closed or put up for sale to German interests, and their children were expelled from public schools. Those without "Jewish" first names suffered the added indignity of having "Sarah" or "Israel" added to their first names on official documents. In July 1938, the German government mandated that Jews apply for special identification cards marked with a large red "J," to be carried at all times. Within three months, that red "J" also appeared on all German passports issued to Jews.[1]

Outside help to ease or halt the growing Nazi threat to Jewish life and security never really materialized. A conference at Évian, France, in July 1938 called by President Franklin D. Roosevelt to find ways to accommodate the large-scale emigration of political refugees after the Anschluss, or incorporation of Austria into the German Reich in mid March 1938, proved ineffectual. The participant countries at Évian, still beleaguered by the miseries of the depression years, recognized the refugees' plight but offered little in the way of tangible solutions. The French and Italian governments, observing refugees disembarking from their domestic ports, made no offers to house the arrivals. The United States continued to maintain a firm position regarding its immigration quotas. Even British-controlled Palestine, the likely destination for most Jewish refugees, remained closed to anything resembling substantial emigration. This evidence of weakness and reluctance, and the divisions among the Western democracies over how to deal with Nazism, only fueled Hitler's ambitions.

On November 9–10, 1938, the so-called *Kristallnacht*, or night of (broken) glass, Nazis broke into and destroyed Jewish businesses, set fire to synagogues, beat and murdered Jews, and desecrated or demolished Jewish schools, hospitals, and cemeteries. The regime justified its terror by claiming retribution for the assassination of a German diplomat in Paris by a distraught young Jew, Herschel Grynszpan, whose parents had been detained and abused by the Nazis. During the aftermath, more than 25,000 Jews were rounded up, arrested, and sent to concentration camps. The *Kristallnacht* was a defining moment for the Jews of Europe, making it clear to those who still had hopes of holding on to the familiar, or to what little remained of their largely middle-class lives, that attempting to do so was hopeless and dangerous. Instead, they began their desperate search for a way out.[2]

The Escape to Shanghai

Nazi policy aimed to rid the Third Reich of its Jewish populations. Even those in concentration camps could gain their freedom if they or their relatives could show possession of a visa or even just the means of transportation that would allow them to exit the country.[3] The main obstacle was lack of places to go, given the tight quota restrictions existing in the more desirable countries. One popular choice was South America, but success was uncommon, and the tragic story of the German liner SS *St. Louis*, which became stranded when entry was repeatedly denied its passengers and eventually turned back to Europe, clearly confirmed the grim outlook for those attempting to flee. Only in a few areas were prospects brighter. Jewish organizations succeeded in organizing a *Kindertransport* program that allowed more than 10,000 Jewish children to travel on sealed trains to foster families or supervised and protected communities in England and the Netherlands.[4] Jews learned, too, that Shanghai was one place that, owing to its peculiar situation, required no visa, affidavit, or certificate of guarantee to enter.

Shanghai was an unknown entity to most refugees. To a few, it had a notorious reputation for being both exotic and the home of gangsters, intrigue, and swindles, but in their current circumstances, the refugees had few other viable options. The first step was to book passage on one of the Italian, Japanese, German, or Greek liners serving East Asia.[5] Demand was so great and pressure to leave so intense that bribes to reserve a berth were common. Others stood in long lines at the shipping office to get the coveted tickets.[6] Once these had been obtained, an itemized list had to be compiled for the Nazi emigration authorities of all possessions being taken on the journey.

Exit taxes effectively depleted Jews of their remaining resources, further diminishing their chances of finding another country to accept them. Those departing could take with them only ten marks (about U.S.$4.00) in cash. A few wealthier refugees found ways to shelter funds through friends or in foreign bank accounts prior to the enforcement of strict currency regulations by the Third Reich.[7] But most middle-class families had to rely on the personal belongings and household items, such as linens, china, and silver, that they were able to crate and ship out of the country. Besides lending a touch of home in their new environment, such items were insurance against total penury. So-called "board money" was provided by Jewish relief organizations upon purchase of the steamship ticket. These funds were put to good use by refugees on board ship to buy cameras, binoculars, and similar expensive items at duty free shops, which could later be resold in Shanghai.

The trip to Shanghai took anywhere from 23 to 72 days, depending on the ship, its route, and the weather. To avoid the heavy tolls required for passage through the Suez Canal, so-called "Cape ships" took the lengthy route around the Cape of Good Hope.[8] The more common route began in an Italian port, crossed the Mediterranean to Port Said, and passed through the Suez Canal to Aden, Bombay, Colombo (Sri Lanka), Singapore, Hong Kong, and finally Shanghai. After Italy entered the war in June 1940, refugees reached Shanghai via Portugal or Marseilles.[9] Travel was comfortable, usually in first- or second-class accommodations, and passengers had numerous opportunities along the route to disembark for brief periods at the various exotic ports. Still, no matter what the nature or extent of shipboard pleasures or portside adventures, there remained the haunting and exceedingly painful memory of the relatives, friends, and homes left behind. An overland route by train through the Soviet Union crossed Siberia to Harbin, Mukden, and Dalian in North China, with passengers then traveling on to Shanghai by Japanese ships of the Dairen Kisen Kaisha (DKK) Line. This route was used in late 1940, but closed in mid 1941 when hostilities broke out between the Soviet Union and the Third Reich.

Nearing their destination, the deep blue waters of the ocean voyage turned muddy brown and choppy as their ships entered the Yangzi River approaching Shanghai. The first eye-catching sight was the parade of massive Western-style buildings making up the famous Bund and curling along the Huangpu River's bank. Behind that impressive façade lay a whole new world, one that would challenge the refugees' endurance, provoke their ingenuity and imagination, and for some, prove too much to bear. The tension on board the refugee ships was eased somewhat by the appearance on deck of members of established Jewish refugee committees, who came to greet the newcomers and orient them to life in Shanghai. Still, as these necessary preliminaries were taking place, some of the new arrivals obviously struggled to cope with the surrounding scene and the sudden realization of how drastically their lives had changed: "Chinese coolies busily unloaded the ship. Their rhythmic but distorted 'ay-ho, hah-ho' cries as they carried the heavy cargo on bamboo shoulder posts filled the air with more noise than a circus could. Not the wildest imagination could paint a picture like the one I was confronted with. I glanced with longing back at my ship," Horst Wartenberger recalled.[10]

Those fortunate refugees with family or friends in Shanghai could expect to be greeted at the ship and then taken to private homes to live temporarily or permanently. The lucky ones with available funds could begin immediately to find private housing and make plans for their future. One estimate of the number of refugees able to support themselves in Shanghai counted roughly 33 percent.[11] In the earliest stages of refugee resettlement, newcomers lacking local contacts or independent funds were placed in houses or rooms rented by the local Jewish relief committees. As time went on and their numbers grew, however, most refugees found themselves loaded onto open trucks at the harbor's edge for transport to temporary housing centers after going through customs. The trucks rolled across Garden Bridge spanning Suzhou Creek and leading into the Japanese-controlled Hongkou section of Shanghai. This introductory trip gave the passengers their first views of Chinese street life, a world that by its drama and assault of the senses appeared to them unreal, strange, and altogether incredible.

Sir Victor Sassoon had made the first floor of his Embankment Building available to register the newcomers, give them something to eat, and temporarily house them. Considering that each passenger ship arrived with approximately 700 refugees, the demands on such makeshift facilities were great. In addition to the Embankment Building, early arrivals also stayed temporarily at the Beth Aharon Synagogue on Museum Road, across from the Embankment Building, or at the former British Women's Association Home at 708 Whashing Road. The Salvation Army Shelter also took in a few of the new arrivals.

In the Embankment Building, large rooms had been furnished with cots for as many as seventy people each, placed so close together that there was room only to pass between them. Men and women were housed in separate dormitories. Keeping the floor clean both under and next to the cot was the responsibility of each occupant.[12] Long lines formed in the hallways for the

Figure 15. Newly arrived Jews from Germany and Austria boarding an open truck for transport to a Shanghai refugee center. SOURCE: YIVO Institute for Jewish Research.

limited washing and bathroom facilities, which were inconveniently located in the same room. Refugees who only the day before had enjoyed the elegant cuisine of first-class service on a German liner might find themselves served a tin bowl of burned rice, with a little sugar and a sprinkling of cinnamon, at long tables covered with waxed paper in the dining hall or soup kitchen.[13]

Assistance Breeds Ambivalence

The flow of refugees from Germany and Austria reached a high tide in fall 1939.[14] In 1938, 1,374 Jewish refugees arrived in Shanghai; in 1939, 12,089; and in 1940, 1,955; but in 1941, only 33 came.[15] Some White Russians who had lived in Germany and Austria since the Bolshevik Revolution also arrived in Shanghai with the waves of Jewish refugees, many of them traveling on Nansen passports. The first thing all of them needed was housing. The existing local committees, one serving the Austrian and another the German community, could not cope with the sudden influx, and the Ashkenazi and Sephardi communities responded, setting aside their differences. Michel Speelman, a prominent local Dutch businessman with strong connections in Shanghai official circles, headed up a committee known as the Committee for Assistance of European Refugees in Shanghai, with offices in the Embankment Building. He received assistance in the handling of immigration affairs from another local notable, Eduard Kann.

Speelman's high profile in refugee assistance was such that the committee he headed soon became known as the Speelman Committee. Speelman was particularly effective and creative in fund-raising, successfully soliciting generous contributions from the local Russian and Sephardi communities. He sponsored a relief lottery at two dollars a ticket and staged a gala variety show at the Lyceum Theater, which featured American amateurs performing in its many theatrical skits. The money raised went to a Children's Milk Fund, as did admission fees to concerts, dance recitals, and comic routines performed at the Embankment Shelter. In May 1939, Speelman broadened the reach of his fund-raising strategy by taking an extended trip abroad to explain the Shanghai situation to the Council for German Jewry, the American Jewish Joint Distribution Committee, and similar Jewish organizations in London, Paris, and Amsterdam.[16] Preoccupied with his fund-raising, Speelman left the routine handling of immigration affairs to Kann, who worked closely with the Special Branch of the Shanghai Municipal Police in overseeing Jewish immigration into Shanghai.

In late 1938, as the temporary housing facilities began to exceed capacity, the Speelman Committee rented rooms for refugee families and provided a monthly stipend of $55.00 (about U.S.$3.30) per person.[17] As the refugee flow grew, additional assistance was forthcoming from the International Committee for Granting Relief to European Refugees, headed by the Hungarian Paul Komor, established on August 7, 1938.[18] Beginning in October 1938, the Komor Committee, as it came to be known, worked in cooperation with the Shanghai Municipal Police by maintaining a central registry of all immigrants, keeping individual records containing biographical information and issuing identity cards complete with photographs. Partly to help deal with the widespread sentiments of homelessness and statelessness, the committee added to its record-keeping functions by forming a Passport Division, which issued passports, or "Komorpasses," certified by the Shanghai Muni-

Figure 16. Prominent leaders of the refugee community, including, from the left, Rabbi Meir Ashkenazi, who was chief rabbi of Shanghai; Michel Speelman, chairman of the Committee for the Assistance of European Jewish Refugees in Shanghai; and A. Herzberg, an executive of that committee. SOURCE: American Jewish Joint Distribution Committee.

cipal Police as valid travel documents. Operating with a staff of ten refugees from premises at 190 Kiukiang Road, the committee when necessary negotiated on behalf of German Jews with the German consulate general.[19] It also supplied birth and death certificates, a service previously provided by the German consulate general.[20]

The Relief Society for German-Austrian Jews, led by Dr. Kurt Marx, had a somewhat different focus. It kept in regular contact with European relief agencies, and its representatives in Singapore met refugee ships in order to provide information, as well as cabling ahead to Shanghai with news of incoming refugees.[21] The Relief Society also assumed some of the workload of the Komor Committee, helping out with the practical work of provisioning, locating housing, disbursing allowances, and distributing meal tickets for use at the refugee feeding centers.

Like the Russians before them, most of the Jewish refugees settled in the Hongkou area, which had been heavily damaged during the recent Battle of

Figure 17. The staff of the International Committee for Granting Relief to European Refugees, also known as the Komor Committee after its founder Paul Komor, who is seated second from the right. SOURCE: United States Holocaust Memorial Museum.

Shanghai. The housing that still existed or had been hastily reconstructed there was cheap and thus affordable by refugees. In a very short time, a settlement that became known to some as Jewish Town grew up in the area bordered by Ward Road, Wayside, Yangtsepoo, Pingliang, and Whashing roads in Hongkou, with a population of about 10,000 by August 1939.[22] Cafés, beer taverns, bakeries, and small specialty shops sprang up, especially along Chusan Road, which began to take on an Old World character in the midst of this Japanese-dominated sector of the International Settlement.[23]

At least initially, the Japanese viewed the Jewish arrivals in Hongkou as industrious, productive, and cooperative. Because so many of them came from professional backgrounds as doctors, lawyers, engineers, architects, journalists, scholars, bankers, and business leaders, their potential contributions to the community seemed promising. The Japanese were especially pleased by the efforts immediately made by Jewish leaders and their colleagues to repair damaged buildings and other structures in order to make them habitable or useable for small businesses. In their midst were representatives of several trades, including mechanics, plumbers, carpenters, merchants, and shoe-makers.[24] Taken together, they had the skills and willingness to build a thriv-ing community in Hongkou, and in just a few years, the area took on the character of a little Vienna or slice of central Europe, with shops and cafés with names familiar in Europe.

Jewish leaders, having the survival and protection of their new community much at heart (and few other options), purposefully cultivated a favorable at-titude among the Japanese. Jewish willingness to work and their establish-ment of cottage industries and service-oriented businesses benefited the Japanese, especially the sizable Japanese military forces in what became known as the Japanese Defence Sector, occupying Hongkou, Yangshupu, Zhabei, Jiangwan, and Hongqiao.[25] But by August 1939, the swelling num-bers of Jewish immigrants placed heavy demands on the limited housing and facilities, bringing the refugees more and more into competition with the Japanese military and civilians for these resources. Jewish work teams at-tempted to alleviate the problem by continuing to repair and restore dam-aged buildings, but the numbers became intolerable to the Japanese. The Japanese authorities estimated that the Jewish population had reached about one-tenth of the Japanese population residing in their districts and declared that increases at the current rate could not be permitted to continue.[26] Japanese arrivals in the city found it increasingly difficult to find suitable housing, and the demands on available accommodation caused rents to rise sharply. One estimate is that 10,000–15,000 Japanese civilian residents of Hongkou who had fled to Japan during the Battle of Shanghai returned to the city in early 1938, just as the incoming wave of refugees from Europe started to swell.[27]

Added to these pressures was the free return of Chinese residents to Hongkou, estimated at 40,000 a month, as well as the horrendous Chinese refugee problem, which affected all parts of Shanghai.[28] In November 1937, the Japanese Shanghai Expeditionary Force had seized control of the city, aside from the foreign areas, and Mayor Fu Xiaoan's Japanese puppet ad-minstration subsequently took over the Chinese sectors. Faced with the Chinese refugee challenge, it oversaw the establishment of the Shanghai Refugee Relief Association, set up to help manage and control altogether 154 camps for Chinese refugees, housing 90,484 victims of the hostilities, with an additional 3,000 of them living in alleyways.[29]

During the Battle of Shanghai, owing to their declared neutrality in the Sino-Japanese hostilities, the foreign areas of Shanghai became a haven for fleeing Chinese refugees, just as they would for the European Jews. Housing and food were in acutely short supply. Chinese refugees found shelter in temples, guilds, empty offices, warehouses, or anything else available. The Salvation Army and International Refugee Committee took an active role in this Chinese refugee crisis, constructing housing out of mats for the hastily built camps. A mat-shed encampment sheltering 2,300 refugees sprang up on the campus of Aurora University. Jiaotong University provided facilities for another of the largest refugee camps, and a surcharge of 5 percent was placed on meals served in Chinese restaurants to help defray the cost of maintaining these refugee camps.[30] The Jesuit Father Robert Jacquinot de Besange, vice-chairman of the Shanghai International Committee of the Red Cross Society of China, played a key role in these programs by working out an agreement between Chinese and Japanese military leaders authorizing a safe zone in Nandao in the southern part of the city.[31] This protected zone housed and provided refuge for thousands of refugees who had escaped the fighting south of the city and on the outskirts of Shanghai. The dire condition of Chinese refugees was described in one account as follows: "There are tens of thousands in Nantao [Nandao] who are entirely destitute . . . the very poor live in tiny rooms tucked away in the huddle of dark houses, a family together, with their bedding on the floor and virtually nothing else. In the same room is generally a sick man, sometimes two; the air has been unchanged for the past few months."[32]

December 1938 was the peak period for the Chinese refugee crisis in Shanghai, with camps scattered all over. In fact, the numbers of Chinese refugees would diminish substantially over the succeeding months owing to various stringent resettlement and repatriation programs.[33] Still, there is no question that the refugee crisis at this time in all quarters of the Shanghai community was clearly a serious one.

The Authorities Draw the Line

At the suggestion of K. M. Bourne, commissioner of the Shanghai Municipal Police, the Shanghai Municipal Council approved the formation of a committee to study the local effects of the Jewish refugee situation. Those serving on the committee included Michel Speelman, Ellis Hayim, Paul Komor, and representatives of the departments of health, police, and public works.[34] The real purpose of the new body was to find ways to control both the influx of refugees and their movements and activities after they arrived in Shanghai. The Japanese authorities found these measures inadequate and unlikely to stem the tide of refugees coming mainly to their districts. And because no formal institutional machinery existed in the free port of Shanghai to deal authoritatively with the foreign refugee problem, the Japanese Naval Landing Party Headquarters in Hongkou decided to take independent action and call for a halt, at least temporarily, to further Jewish settlements in the Hongkou, Wayside, Yangshupu, and Zhabei districts.

To carry out this control measure, on August 9, the Japanese instructed Jewish refugee authorities that in order to receive the required official residence status in these designated areas, Jewish refugees had to register with Japanese authorities through the offices of the Committee for the Assistance of European Jewish Refugees in Shanghai, and to do so before August 22, 1939. To support the implementation of the registration process, refugees were required to complete questionnaires in duplicate and to forward them to the Japanese authorities, who would have them compiled into a directory of Jewish refugees.[35] After reviewing these questionnaires, those whose papers passed scrutiny received back one of the two copies, which was to serve as documentation of their permission to remain in Hongkou. Incoming refugees still could disembark at the Hongkou, Wayside, or Yangshupu docks, but they would need to take up residence south of Suzhou Creek, in compliance with this Japanese decision.[36] In addition, the Japanese gave permission to incoming refugees to settle in Japanese-controlled Hongqiao in the far western suburbs.[37]

The Japanese measures provoked almost immediate action from the International Settlement and French Concession authorities, who feared an onslaught of destitute Jews into their communities, aggravating the Chinese refugee crisis, and with some Russian refugees still arriving from the north. On August 14, the Shanghai Municipal Council, which had hoped eventually to confine all incoming Jewish refugees to districts north of Suzhou Creek, decided that no more Jewish refugees could enter Shanghai, given the Japanese restrictions on their residing in Hongkou. Press reports two days later indicated the depth of the council's concerns. Reportedly, Jewish refugees en route would be permitted to land only if the Japanese were to lift their ban on new immigration north of the creek. If the Japanese did not cooperate, the Shanghai Municipal Council would forbid the landing of additional refugees "whether they are already en route here or still in Europe."[38] The French response to the crisis, as announced by the French consul general, Marcel Baudez, came only hours after the council stated its position, supposedly allowing France to maintain "a uniform policy with the International Settlement and the Japanese."[39] This initial French decision amounted to closing the door to new refugee settlements in the French Concession altogether.[40]

To build its case, the council focused attention on the Shanghai consular body, whose members, including the (acting) German consul general, were known to have complained immediately to the Japanese about the new Jewish refugee restrictions. Responding to these admonitions, the Japanese consul general, Miura Yoshiaki, advised these consuls to ask their home governments to do something about the large numbers of Italian and German vessels bringing the refugees to Shanghai.[41] Actually, there was no effective way to limit immigration through the shipping companies, because acceptance of passengers was based simply on their ability to pay the fare.

Under the circumstances, the consular body, claiming to respond to council appeals, sent urgent messages back to the various home governments calling upon them to use their powers to try and dissuade Jewish refugees from coming to Shanghai. In fact, feeling their turf invaded, members of the consular body had expressed resentment at not having been consulted by the council in formulating the hasty August 14, 1939, decision, even though they fully agreed to the cessation of further refugee immigration. The German consul emphasized his hesitation to implement a decision that, he claimed, had not been made by the "competent authorities" in Shanghai. Nevertheless, he said, he was disposed to acquiesce in the council's decision "on the condition that" refugees who had already embarked for Shanghai would still be admitted and that provisions be made for entry of relatives of resident refugees and persons with independent means.[42]

To dissuade refugees from coming, posters and circulars emphasizing the lack of employment opportunities in Shanghai and its undesirability as a place to live were to be distributed to European travel agencies and railroad stations.[43] Refugees themselves contributed by writing letters to relatives in Europe telling of their own hard experiences and the poor conditions of life in Shanghai. None of them yet knew, or could even have imagined, of course, that the alternative for most of those left behind would be Hitler's "Final Solution."

Whereas Russian refugees had been arriving in Shanghai over a period of fifteen years, and thus could more easily be assimilated into the local community, the European Jewish refugees had poured in over the space of a few months, settlement authorities noted. Moreover, they charged, the Japanese decision to ban new settlements in Hongkou had been taken unilaterally and without informing or consulting with the other Shanghai authorities.[44] The Japanese countered that they had not been informed officially of the council's decision regarding the refugees and stressed that their consul had followed the accepted procedure by first informing the Shanghai consular body of the Japanese decision.[45] When asked at a press conference by what right the Japanese had adopted this policy of limiting residence in areas north of Suzhou Creek, a Japanese naval spokesman left no doubts about the position of the Japanese military. He replied that that portion (Hongkou) of the International Settlement was under control of the Japanese, who could legislate as they pleased, "by reason of military conquest."[46] This response did not sit well with the Shanghai Municipal Council, whose other members regarded Hongkou as an integral part of the International Settlement, and not as a separate and conquered entity, vulnerable to any independent Japanese actions, particularly military ones.

Nevertheless, the Japanese did in fact have real power in Shanghai "by reason of military conquest." By 1939, in addition to its puppet state, Manchukuo, Japan had established an intimidating presence both in Shanghai and elsewhere in China. It forced its wartime agenda on the Chinese population through additional puppet governments established in Beiping on December 14, 1937, and in Nanjing on March 28, 1938. And even if the Western authorities were not anxious to acknowledge these facts, neither the Municipal Council nor the consular body could effectively negate the Japanese policies, certainly not regarding Hongkou, Wayside, Yangshupu, and Zhabei. So the settlement authorities offered what they hoped would result in compromise. The British proposed that if the Japanese authorities would lift the restrictions and allow at least the 3,000 refugees currently processing into Shanghai and needing settlement to enter Hongkou, the Shanghai Municipal Council would try to place those already booked and en route to Shanghai elsewhere.[47] Japanese Consul General Miura agreed to this proposal and approved Japanese participation in a special committee composed of Japanese, International Settlement, and French Concession officials meeting to review special refugee cases for admittance to Shanghai. In addition, this Special Committee was to enforce the overall policy that incoming refugees must be able to guarantee that they would not become a burden on the community.[48]

Foreign residents, particularly the Russians, feared economic competition from Jewish refugees who were willing to labor in Shanghai factories for low wages and who were known to be good businessmen. They angrily pointed to the alleged wealth of a few Jewish immigrants, who, they claimed, could take the best apartments and dine in Shanghai's finest restaurants.[49] The British press focused on the possibility that desperate refugees might replace other Shanghai workers, even those in the professions, which in turn might incite anti-Semitic feelings and actions. Both American and British residents displayed the garden variety of country-club anti-Semitism by wanting to exclude these poor and "foreign" persons from their neighborhoods. It was common to see advertisements in the prestigious *North China Daily News* that blatantly refused rentals to refugees. For example, a want ad in this newspaper offered employment only to "Aryans" of German birth.[50] Also, the editors questioned why the refugees chose to come to Shanghai, which was "hard up," lacking sufficient fuel and other basics, which the already resident and "deserving" refugees desperately needed.[51] Another respondent questioned why Shanghai should be called upon "to save the world" and received editorial agreement that "beyond a certain point, Shanghai resources do not reach."

The established Jewish community leaders reacted to the emergency situation along lines similar to those of the International Settlement and French authorities. It appeared that they, too, were committed to preserving the calm and stability conducive to a flourishing community and favorable business atmosphere. They privately recommended to the Shanghai Municipal Police that further immigration to Shanghai be limited to "only a few desirables from time to time."[52] The Jewish leaders, police officials, and Western consular representatives agreed that a delicate system of relationships had to be protected in order to maintain the stability required by the established commercial and trade interests in Shanghai, especially given the powerful Japanese presence. All agreed that the refugee question had to be handled skillfully, with the interests of all parties being considered.

The U.S. consulate asked the outspoken American journalist J. B. Powell, editor of the *China Weekly Review*, not to publish material that might embarrass or "cause unpleasantness" for either the Speelman Committee or the Komor Committee. Powell had criticized the level of support for the incoming refugees, claiming that the early expressions of humanitarian sentiment were quickly fading in the face of fears that such aid might cost something. He also exposed some of the Nazis' calculatedly brutal treatment of Jews in Europe.[53] Addressing Powell's criticisms, the Shanghai Municipal Police described the German consulate's position in Shanghai as "cooperative" and instructed Jewish refugees upon their arrival not to give any interviews revealing conditions back home, as well as to refrain from all political expression in Shanghai.[54]

These police instructions conformed with the joint proclamation on neutrality issued by the French Concession and International Settlement authorities in May 1939, forbidding the organization of either political bodies or political activities, in order to maintain the neutrality and security of the foreign areas of Shanghai. Going against these restrictions, which were meant to preserve law and order, would bring loss of individual protection and even expulsion from the settlement areas.[55]

To ensure that no political activities occurred, Jewish organizations had to be licensed by the police in order to exist, to request police permission to hold meetings, and to inform the police about any changes in their organizational leadership.[56] The official position was that the business of Shanghai was business, not patriotism or social justice. To guarantee "acceptable" behavior, police representatives, some of them Jewish themselves, with relevant language competence, attended meetings of Jewish organizations in order to report on and curtail any forms of political expression. These same restrictions extended to the Russian and Slavic communities, not to mention the Chinese, who suffered extensively from Japanese censorship and repression.[57]

For all of these efforts to contain the disruption and fears that the refugee onslaught provoked, dealing with the problem continued to create dissension among the foreign consular representatives in Shanghai and to arouse criticism in various circles, especially on humanitarian grounds. To respond to these growing concerns, on October 22, 1939, the Shanghai Municipal Council formally issued new regulations applicable to the International Settlement south of Suzhou Creek. The Japanese authorities still remained committed to maintaining the policies they had enunciated during the summer. However, Japanese Consul General Miura did respond favorably to a query from the Committee for Assistance of European Jewish Refugees in Shanghai by agreeing to allow established residents north of the creek to send for their relatives in Europe, who might enter the Japanese-controlled area "in limited numbers."[58]

The new Municipal Council regulations rescinded the previous summer's blanket prohibition of the entry of European Jewish refugees and identified certain categories of refugees who were now eligible for immigration. Eligible refugees included those of "certified financial competency" or adults with U.S.$400 available for their use in Shanghai (U.S.$100 in the case of children under thirteen years of age). Restrictions on immigration did not apply to immediate family members (parents, husbands, wives, or children) of resident Shanghai Jewish refugees or to those with a contract of employment or a marriage contract with a Shanghai resident. Verification of the possession of funds was to be made by the shipping or railroad company when passage was booked to Shanghai.[59] The French authorities issued similar regulations regarding admission to the French Concession on December 30, 1939. Again, the main concern of the council and consuls was that newcomers be financially independent and that "persons of little or no means" be discouraged.[60] Possession of independent funds was essential. As early as February 1939, the council revealed that "it had not committed itself to any expenditures in respect to the Jewish refugees."[61]

Travel agents had to certify with the Committee for Assistance of European Refugees in Shanghai that the requisite funds did exist. And immigration certificates had to pass inspection by the Special Branch of the Shanghai Municipal Police. Without an immigration certificate, stamped by the police, entry was prohibited.[62] Abuses of this system were bound to occur, given the desperation of those seeking escape and refuge. A common ruse involved the recycling of deposit money. Once certified as the means of support for the arriving refugee, it was returned, all or in part, to European relief bodies for use as deposit money by another prospective refugee passenger. In Hongkou, rumors circulated widely that certain Japanese officials, whose identities were known to relief leaders, would supply immigration permits for the right price. Other infractions involved falsified employment agreements and even marriage contracts. Certainly, the motivation was strong: receipt of a permit won some men and women release from Nazi concentration camps.

These actions still did not satisfy local authorities. Shanghai Municipal Council officials continued to emphasize to the consular body the threat that still more refugees en route to Shanghai posed to the well-being of the community.[63] And finding a receptive response to their arguments, in June 1940, the Council further tightened the restrictions by emphasizing the necessity of a police-certified entry permit and by requiring that monetary deposits be made directly with the Committee for Assistance of European Refugees in Shanghai, rather than through travel agents. That way, the money would be available for immediate use by the emigrants when they arrived in Shanghai, thus relieving the community of any immediate financial burdens.

One of the most stringent new requirements was a time limit of four months on the validity of entry permits issued by the Shanghai Municipal Police.[64] With the difficulties of communications, irregularity of the international mail services, difficulty in getting transit visas for the overland route, uncertainty of making a successful booking, and expense of the trip (to be paid in foreign currency), this time limitation became a very serious and often insurmountable obstacle for prospective Jewish immigrants. Only 20 percent of the total number of those issued landing permits actually arrived in Shanghai, even though only two-thirds of those who applied received permits.[65]

The effectiveness of these rules and regulations at limiting immigration, as well as the extent of the Japanese share in accommodating the incoming refugees, are reflected in the following figures provided by the International Committee. They describe the dispersion of the Jewish refugees by January 1941 as follows: Hongkou and north of Suzhou Creek, 12,154; French Concession, 2,085; and the International Settlement and extra-settlement roads areas, 1,230.[66] Obviously, the course of the war in Europe also had a devastating effect on immigration possibilities.

Certainly, not everyone in the Shanghai community viewed the council restrictions without criticism or complaint. Letters to the editor pointed out the blatant discrimination against Jewish refugees, using arguments that the new restrictions did not apply to the non-Jewish nationals of the countries involved who were entering Shanghai.[67] Individual letter writers reported that regular German passports were not inspected by the police, but those with the red "J" were. Criticism from the same and different quarters chastised the established local Jewish community, and particularly its leaders, for failing to do more to provide substantial support to the refugees, and, especially, for assisting in the Municipal Council's efforts to limit immigration. They insisted that monetary support for refugees coming from abroad was more important than contributions generated locally. By 1940, the inflow of foreign currency to Shanghai in connection with refugee relief amounted to U.S.$551,300, not counting the monthly remittances some received from relatives abroad.[68]

One of the most damning incidents involved a group of 300 Polish Jews who in the summer of 1941 had booked passage with Japanese shipping companies that permitted entry into Shanghai without the necessary permits. The chairman of the Ashkenazi Communal Association of Shanghai, after unsuccessful discussions with the Japanese authorities about housing the group in Hongkou, decided to refuse this soon-to-arrive group housing south of Suzhou Creek — the only other place of residence possible — on the grounds that no accommodations could be found for them in the Central and Western Districts. A cable was sent to Kobe, Japan, where the refugees awaited clearance to proceed to Shanghai, instructing the group not to pursue their plans to seek refuge there.[69]

Plans to Settle the Refugees Elsewhere

Another option considered for handling the "refugee problem" involved finding other places suitable for their resettlement. During 1939 and 1940, both the Chinese government in Chongqing and the Shanghai Municipal Council considered several alternatives for settling incoming refugees. The Chinese proposed establishing a Jewish settlement on Hainan Island, southwest of Hong Kong, off China's southern coast, but the idea had to be dropped because the island had become an important center for Japanese military operations. Another proposal recommended by American officials that initially looked promising involved settling 10,000 Jews in the Polillo

Islands or on Mindanao Island, both in the Philippine archipelago. The Philippine government initially saw a Jewish settlement of young specialists and technical experts as a good way to support local agricultural development.[70] But the strong expression of local resistance from Filipino farmers fearing the expected competition from Jews in agriculture caused the government to stall the proposal. And in the meantime, the Jewish community centered in Manila expressed resistance and concern to Philippine government officials over the competition that an influx of new refugee doctors and lawyers likely would impose on their established professional community.[71]

One of the most ambitious plans came from a local Jewish businessman, Jacob Berglas, who in 1939 developed a plan to settle 100,000 refugees in China's southwestern Yunnan Province.[72] He presented his plan to the Chinese government, buttressing his case with claims that the Jewish settlement would benefit China by attracting foreign exchange and aiding the development of this backward and impoverished area of the country. His request received support from Sun Fo, the son of Sun Yat-sen, who had frequently endorsed Jewish desires to establish a national homeland in Palestine. Sun Fo, as president of the Legislative Yuan, was able to marshal serious attention for the Yunnan proposal from various government ministries, using arguments that British policy toward China was shaped largely by Jewish merchants and bankers in the Far East, and American interests in China were in many ways contingent on the Jewish issue. The great wealth and perceived influence of Shanghai's Sephardi Jews, such as Sir Victor Sassoon, gave some credence to these views. And like Japanese officials who held similar ideas for different reasons (to be explained at length in Chapter 5), Sun and others believed that China might receive substantial benefits from favorable treatment of Jews, in this case by working out a resettlement plan.[73]

Berglas traveled to the United States to build his case among Jewish organizations and with the U.S. State Department, but to no avail. The Chinese government, while conducting a confidential internal review of the plan, found inhibiting problems with the proposal over the difficulties of maintaining Chinese territorial sovereignty and exercising administrative control over such a large community. Although it decided to reject the proposal, the government did approve official assistance in the form of easing the entry of Jewish refugees into the country, offering guarantees against racial or religious discrimination, and providing the Jewish refugees with help in finding employment. Chongqing's lack of authority and influence in Shanghai, however, where the Chinese sectors of the city operated under a Japanese collaborationist government, made these liberal concessions in effect quite meaningless there.

Chongqing government spokesmen publicly phrased the rejection of the Berglas resettlement plan in terms of it being too large in scale, making it impractical and "premature" for implementation under existing conditions.[74] Several foreign governments, including those of the United States and Great Britain, raised additional suggestions for ways to relocate the Jews remaining in Europe, including a plan for a settlement in Alaska. But for reasons that included the costs and the distractions of the war in Europe, as well as the lack of responsiveness from key officials, none of these proposals ever came to fruition.

Room and Board North of the Creek

The temporary housing and processing facilities in the Embankment Building and on Whashing Road soon reached capacity, causing the refugee committees to look for new locations. The Shanghai Municipal Council, while still electing not to offer funding for the Jewish refugee programs, did lease available school buildings, barracks, and warehouses to their organizations for conversion into refugee camps. One such facility was the school for training customs officials located at 138 Ward Road, across from the Ward Road Jail. A large Ward Road camp able to house and feed 1,200 people opened in February 1939. It became one of altogether six refugee camps, or *Heime*, north of Suzhou Creek in the Japanese sector of the International Settlement.[75]

The Ward Road complex eventually included three sleeping halls with bunk beds, a dining hall capable of serving 200 people per shift, a day room for social gatherings, and space for workshops. The latter, operated by the refugees themselves, accommodated needs such as tailoring, shoemaking, and carpentry. The intention was to make the complex as self-sustaining as possible and, by including these skilled and craft facilities, to provide opportunities for work and productive activity to fill the long hours ahead. The home received two sewing machines, used effectively by refugee women, who seamed 2,400 bed sheets from bales of cotton cloth donated by Sir Victor Sassoon.[76] Eventually, there was also a hospital on the grounds, which included a special isolation ward and later added x-ray, dental, optical, and maternity facilities. The lands adjoining the Ward Road camp served as playgrounds for refugee children and areas where residents might work their own vegetable gardens.

An additional gift of $150,000 from Sir Victor enabled the refugee committees to loan money to arriving refugees in order to help them get started in a small business or private practice. Some went into business together, pooling their money to buy houses, which they then rented to arriving refugees. Others set up bakeries, cafés, and similar small enterprises. Successful businessmen repaid the loans, managed by the International Committee, in monthly installments, enabling others to have a similar opportunity. These rehabilitation programs also kept refugees from taking the jobs of established workers in Shanghai. Setting them up in new enterprises added an element of competition to local business, but at least it did not supplant existing employees, which is what many in the foreign community feared most. And as the refugees themselves observed, with their lack of English and the overwhelming supply of cheap Chinese labor, no one was likely to hire them anyway, so the best option was to start their own businesses. By the end of March 1939, these loans established 313 persons in some form of business, thus taking 660 off the refugee committee relief rolls when family and relatives are taken into account.[77]

As ocean liners crowded with refugees continued to reach port, refugee officials stepped up their search for additional facilities. The nature, quality, and extent of the housing found varied considerably. The London Mission Society turned over to the relief committees its huge compound at 680 Chaoufoong Road, composed of several three-storied buildings, which was chiefly used for housing married couples and families. The Whashing Road building, the former site of the British Women's Association, became another refugee hospital, at least until 1940, when the owners reclaimed the building and the hospital moved to the Ward Road camp. Sassoon donated the site of the former Aerocrete Company on Pingliang Road for use mainly by bachelor refugees, but with a few units set aside for married couples. The committee installed a model teaching workshop at this camp to help retrain men who could not follow their previous trades and professions, and to keep the new residents busy. For reasons not stated in the record, this Pingliang Road camp had to be vacated in August 1941, and the residents moved to a new facility located at 961 East Seward Road.[78]

Various other facilities, each with its clinic, included the large former municipal primary school complex at 100 Kinchow Road, the Wayside Camp at 150 Wayside Road, the Seward Road camp noted above, and the camp established at 60 Alcock Road. The latter camp, which was the former barracks of the Russian Detachment of the Shanghai Volunteer Corps, included the Emigrant bookstore. The council agreed to lease the Alcock Road camp to the Jewish relief committees for a nominal rent on condition that they provide a hospital for infectious diseases. An outbreak of scarlet fever in the camp community in May 1939 had alarmed the city officials. In fact, the council stipulated that no further council properties would be offered to the relief committees until that condition was met.[79] All of these refugee facilities, with the addition of the isolation hospital required by the Municipal Council and located at Chaoufoong Camp, were up and running by August 1939, housing 2,594 refugees and providing meals for 6,830.[80]

With concern rising over the size of the camp population and the extent of idleness among its residents, the International Committee took action to quell public anxieties by organizing a special police force responsible for maintaining peace and order inside the six refugee camps. Altogether, thirty-six refugees found employment in the special police force. Other services in the camp administration involved work in the administrative offices, in the kitchens, and in the butchery. Construction work installing latrines and bathing facilities and repairing camp structures and equipment provided additional much-needed work for the many idle and bored refugee workers.

Most of the money for the upkeep of the camp facilities came from contributions from the American Jewish Joint Distribution Committee. To manage those funds and raise more, in 1939, the International Committee combined with the Hilfsfond für Deutsche Juden and formed an executive committee, with Sir Victor Sassoon as chairman. Paul Komor became the committee's secretary, charged with its day-to-day operations. Sassoon's role was obviously key for fund-raising and lending local authority to the committee's activities.[81] A Finance Committee handled the Sassoon loan fund and money contributed by local and outside supporters. Sassoon made an ad-

TABLE 5
Jewish Refugee Facilities and Their Populations

Institutions	Males	Females	Children	TOTAL
Wayside Camp, 150 Wayside Road	144	118	22	284
Ward Road Camp, 138 Ward Road	584	80	7	671
Chaoufoong Road Camp, 680 Chaoufoong Road	359	288	44	691
Kinchow Road Camp, 100 Kinchow Road	504	162	38	704
Aerocrete Camp, Pingliang Road	40	1	0	41
Alcock Road Camp, 66 Alcock Road	50	40	0	90
Isolation Hospital	24	10	3	37
Immigrants Hospital, 708 Whashing Road	28	17	1	46
Hospital Staffs	20	10	0	30
TOTAL	1,753	726	115	2,594

SOURCE: U.S. National Archives and Records Administration, Military Records Branch, Shanghai Municipal Police Dossier 5422A, Divisional Officer Report, "D" Division, Apr. 8, 1939.

ditional contribution by putting at the disposal of the International Committee, rent free, a shop at 55 Nanking Road, which became a thrift shop, giving refugees a central location from which to sell goods brought with them from Europe directly to buyers or to borrow money on the security of their valuables. The thrift shop was also, of course, a place where refugees could buy things they needed cheaply. Any profit made by the thrift shop went to the committee's Milk Fund, which supplied milk to refugee children, pregnant women, the sick and the elderly. As noted above, the Milk Fund also received donations from charities.

The new committee's work was extensive, including disbursing rent subsidies and food allowances, providing meal tickets for use at the camp kitchens, helping to establish and supervise these kitchens, and seeing that the medical needs arising at the camps received proper attention. All of the arriving refugees, regardless of their financial status, faced the serious challenge of mastering the English language. To meet that demand, at least for the needy, the committee established a night school that provided instruction free of charge.[82] The committee also maintained a small library and administered scholarships.

Refugee families needed to plan for the future of their children, so education was a primary concern for them. Once again, the Shanghai Jewish community responded. Leadership and funds for the establishment of the Shanghai Jewish Youth Association (SJYA) were provided by Horace Kadoorie of the Sephardi community, whose family had already made major contributions in the field of education (having established the Ellis Kadoorie Public School, for 550 Chinese students, in 1934, for example). In November 1939, the SJYA school, which could accommodate 600 students, who paid minimal tutition costs, opened at 100 Kinchow Road, adjoining the Kinchow Road camp, under Headmistress Lucy Hartwich.[83] English was the only language of instruction at this school, but Hebrew and German were also in the curriculum. The SJYA school was respected not only for its high educational standards, but also for its leadership in sports, cultural, and social activities. It was not unusual for Horace Kadoorie to visit the school to check on its progress, and on at least one such occasion, some of the students on hand were treated to a ride in his Rolls Royce.[84]

Another area in which the SJYA school excelled was in its meal program. Family and committee concerns about the proper nutrition for growing children resulted in a school lunch that was far superior to that received in the camps. Even students who found school attendance less than appealing reported enjoying the lunch. However, while the meal program was more than adequate, the heating facilities were not and required occasional closing of the school during the coldest months, especially when the cost of coal and wood exceeded its tight budget.

Hongkou attracted refugees because goods and services of all kinds were cheaper north of the creek. Both food and rent were at least approachable on the limited incomes of individual refugees and relief committees. All six of the refugee camps were close together in the Japanese-controlled area, creating a spirit of enterprise in the formerly bleak and deserted, war-damaged streets of Hongkou. Those who did not live in the camps and were practically self-supporting still found that the lower cost of living and the growing Jewish community made settling north of the creek their best choice. Among these independent refugees, there were many who, although they could afford their own housing, relied on the camp kitchens for their meals.

Many questions remain to be addressed with respect to the workings and dynamics of this struggling Jewish refugee community. How did its members cope with their new life, in what was to them such an alien environment? How did they meet their personal and spiritual needs? How did they relate to the Japanese? What contributions did they make? The picture that emerges is that of a thriving, if severely challenged, society, characterized by endurance, ingenuity, and a sense of purpose.

The Jewish Presence and the Japanese Response

Who works for a living is greater than he who fears God.

— *The Talmud: Berakoth*

Until the Japanese attack on Pearl Harbor, European Jewish refugees in Shanghai enjoyed a reliable stream of financial support mainly from the American Jewish Joint Distribution Committee (AJJDC). This support allowed them to settle into their new world and begin to reconstruct their lives. From its very beginning, the European Jewish community in Shanghai lived in a kind of bubble, with little regular contact with the other foreign communities in the city. Even contacts with the Russian and Slavic Jewish communities were somewhat limited. Nowhere in the writings or memoirs of the European Jewish refugees does one find much comment on events in China. They have little to say about the plight of the tens of thousands of Chinese refugees, aside from remarking their diseases, abject poverty, and strange behavior and customs.

To be sure, much of this can be explained by the European Jews' own traumatic circumstances. Some, especially the elderly, who ended up in refugee camps were ready to declare with resignation, as they sat on their metal cots in a filthy room, that they had lost just about everything that was worth living for. The world around them was no longer of interest, because they had in fact given up, seeing themselves marooned in an alien culture. Others, usually younger, who still had hope of building a life in Shanghai, found themselves preoccupied with survival. They had little time or interest to investigate what had happened in Shanghai or China before their arrival, the politics of the ruling municipal bodies, or the prevailing social life of the Shanghai foreign community. Indeed, they were discouraged from becoming involved in any political activities. The world around them was for the most part beyond their reach, if not interest. They narrowed their contacts with the other foreign communities, including the Japanese, to focus almost exclusively on acquiring food and shelter and developing job and business prospects.

Refugees Living Independently

There were several ways in which European Jewish refugees could find their own housing in crowded Shanghai. Some had brought enough money, or possessions of sufficient value, with them from Europe, or were able to find jobs in the city that paid enough, to rent accommodations. Many chose to use the checks provided by the international Jewish migration agency HICEM to cover housing costs, often by joining together and pooling their funds in order to buy or rent property. As noted previously, the bombed-out housing lining lanes in Hongkou was within reach even of meager refugee budgets. Not a few of those wanting to rent fell victim to schemes requiring "key money" for cheap housing to be paid in advance, amounting to a levy exercised merely for the privilege of renting a property and not returnable.

A typical refugee housing situation was a nine-room house owned by German refugees who rented out its rooms to families. Such rooms usually contained a bed, a table and chairs, a wardrobe, a shelf for books and papers, and the necessary crockery, so that each became home to an entire refugee family.[1] Each family had to share the facilities of a Chinese-style kitchen on the main floor. Bathroom facilities consisted of a common toilet or a large, covered "honey bucket," emptied daily by the Chinese laborers, a wash basin, and a shower.[2] Usually, hot water had to be purchased from the Chinese hot water shop in the neighborhood, and its use was carefully planned. Part would first be used for cooking; then that same water might serve to bathe

the babies, next to wash the adults' feet, and finally to clean the floor.[3] An occasional treat enjoyed by one refugee family was to save some of the purchased hot water to mix with coffee grounds brought home from the café where a family member worked.[4] Those who used their funds to build stores out of the ruins in Hongkou often constructed family housing over the shop.

It was not uncommon for a refugee family to move about several times in the city, depending upon its economic circumstances. The most successful settled in the French Concession, which was heavily residential and had fashionable shops, sidewalk cafés, and private clubs. Those with the least income found housing in Hongkou or Wayside. Again, depending upon income and to some extent location, refugee children attended the SJYA or Kadoorie School in Hongkou or the more expensive Seymour Road school located at the exclusive western end of the International Settlement. Most students at the Seymour Road school came from the Sephardi and Russian Jewish communities. This school boasted a Boy Scout troop that enjoyed a degree of social status in Shanghai. Unsurprisingly, the British Cathedral School Boy Scout troop topped the hierarchical troop system. The Jewish troop fell last in the pecking order, but still enjoyed a certain cachet in Shanghai social circles. The SJYA school also had scouting activities for both girls and boys, and a "fresh air" camp took place on the campus of Shanghai University during Shanghai's hot and humid summers.[5]

Even for those of limited means, there was no lack of entertainment in Shanghai. Parks equipped with swings and seesaws offered free recreation and were available for family picnics. Refugees could improve their English at cinemas showing American films.[6] Statistics compiled in 1933 report thirty-seven movie theaters in Shanghai, of which nineteen showed mainly American films, while the remainder screened a mix of American and Chinese films. The trend continued, and by the late 1930s, Shanghai had more than fifty movie theaters.[7] An absolute favorite among the refugees was *The Merry Widow*, starring Jeanette MacDonald and Maurice Chevalier. In addition to moviegoing, young refugees often developed a taste for Chinese ices, buns, and dumplings, sold by sidewalk vendors, even though their parents forbade eating this fare because of concern over health and sanitation.[8] There were also the usual parades, band concerts, and municipal concerts, which were open to the public, and the pleasure of promenading along the Bund or simply observing the feverish commercial activity along Nanking Road on a weekend.

It is impossible to describe all of the circumstances of Jewish living conditions in Shanghai, given the diversity of the community. One simple estimate reported that 10 percent of the community were well off, 70 percent were able to make ends meet, and the remaining 20 percent were living in poverty.[9] This last group populated the refugee camps, which, as noted in Chapter 4, housed 2,594 people by August 1939.[10]

Life in the Refugee Camps

Conditions in the camps were hard, threatening human dignity and undermining self-confidence. Thirty to fifty people had to sleep in the same dormitory, some with blankets or sheets hung on clotheslines dividing off areas and providing the only privacy. Parents who had never undressed in front of their children were now undressing in front of strangers. Where walls did exist, they were paper-thin, and children were exposed to sounds and happenings not commonly experienced at a young age.[11] The Seward Road camp crowded several families into small single rooms. Of course, some of the camps were better than others, but all were spartan. At the Ward Road camp, men and women lived separately. The camp had a row of toilets, but no showers. It also had a large soup kitchen and hall, where diners sat on wooden benches pulled up to long tables. Describing life in the Chaoufoong camp, Horst Wartenberger later wrote:

> When we woke in the morning, we went down to the general washroom, and if we were lucky there was water running; sometimes we did not even have this. In winter it was very cold as the rooms, not being heated, felt like ice barracks. Summer brought diseases, sleepless nights, 120 degree tropical sun by day, bugs, and lice, which occasionally required "debuggissation." This procedure meant taking our bunks down to the garden, pouring lysol over them and scrubbing them until our fingers bled.[12]

Camp residents elected their own leaders, who in turn appointed the camp staff. Residents received food tickets from their camp administrators overseeing the meal programs. The menu typically consisted of tea and

Figure 18. Refugees enjoying afternoon tea in their Quonset hut at the Seward Road refugee camp. SOURCE: YIVO Institute for Jewish Research.

bread in the morning; meat, a vegetable, and bread at noon; and coffee and bread spread with margarine at night.[13] At the Seward Road camp, refugees carried their pots to the camp kitchen, where they typically received white beans, lentils, or occasionally rice, and a small piece of meat. Before conditions worsened after Pearl Harbor, this kitchen sometimes served broth with rice and meat, rice with a fatty sauce over it, or even some cold cuts of meat. When the menu was this good, long rows of refugees formed for dinner, and fights occasionally broke out when some in line tried to push ahead of others. With food so limited, jobs in the camp kitchen were in great demand in order to get served first and best.[14] By July 1940, 8,143 refugees received daily meals from the public kitchens, with the bulk of the funds supplied by the AJJDC and a relatively small portion from local donations.[15] In general, during this early period, the food was adequate, if meager and monotonous in its sameness.

Young refugees, especially those between the ages of eight and eighteen, were nonetheless able to find some pleasure living in the Hongkou camps, enjoying the sense of camaraderie that developed among them and exploring adjoining neighborhoods. A typical outing might involve visiting second-hand shops, most selling goods brought by the refugees themselves, or food stalls. The young Horst Wartenberger relished evenings spent listening to the "room chief" in charge of the boys' quarters in the Chaoufoong camp perform famous songs and dialogue from familiar operettas such as *Countess Maritza*. The boys would gather around the performer's bunk or, weather permitting, meet with him in the garden, and "everything else seemed to disappear when he [recited from] 'The Town Without Bells,' 'The Merry Widow' or the loveliest of them all: *Die Csárdásfürstin*. Those days were like heaven and with every line and explanation, it would take at least as long as the original performance."[16]

For the less musically inclined, there were games of cards and chess. And there was no lack of interest in and socialization with the opposite sex. At the Chaoufoong camp, the girls' quarters were in close proximity, "visible from our window."[17] Although young men and women were so closely associated on a daily basis, romantic liaisons were often fast and fleeting, with little privacy and much gossip about the parties involved. The rather steady changing of partners was usually harmless, helped break the daily boredom, and certainly fed the voracious rumor mills in the camps.

At least for the adult refugees, lack of privacy, monotony, boredom, stifling summer heat and bone-chilling winter dampness, filth, and bugs were even greater miseries than poor housing and the bland diet. Bedbugs, mice, roaches, rats, mosquitoes, and mold came from nowhere and everywhere, and it seemed that no amount of scrubbing or cleaning defeated these enemies. Reportedly, it was shocking at night to turn on lights and see the zoological park in the midst of which one found oneself. Acquiring cats at least took care of the rat and mouse problem. Boredom came from lack of work or lack of interest in finding work. Among the adults, the big question asked daily was, "Have you found a job already?"[18] The usual negative reply undermined self-confidence and sent a message of despair.

Work, Enterprise, and Culture

For those whose skills and background were culture-specific, starting anew was very difficult. These included professors, journalists, lawyers, and intellectuals. Within this group, a tendency developed to avoid the humiliations of being unable to find work suitable to one's credentials, and to become dependent on the available relief. These individuals became some of the saddest cases in the refugee camps, well respected in their European communities but cast adrift and even resented or pitied by their contemporaries in Shanghai. In addition, among the new arrivals, there were those who came to view a life based on charity from the relief committees as quite convenient, providing food, shelter, and a small allowance for luxuries such as cigarettes.[19]

These so-called idlers were in a small minority. Most of the refugees exhibited amazing resilience and resourcefulness in finding work and rebuilding their lives. They were motivated by the simple desire to get out of the camps and follow a more dignified life of their own making. By the summer of 1939, just months after many had arrived, their advertisements for goods and services could be found in local publications or decorating the walls of the cafés and beer taverns. Besides the notices of doctors, lawyers, dentists, and druggists, there were others offering the services of watchmakers, tailors, shoemakers, dressmakers, beauticians, grocers, machinists, electricians, packers, cabinetmakers, beauticians, liquor and wine sellers, photographers, musicians, financial advisors, and advertisers. The list was already long, varied, and impressive. A somewhat vague category advertised middlemen or agents who claimed ability to arrange business transactions for clients. Others had set themselves up in essential businesses, producing coal briquets, soap, or candles. In addition, there were many advertisements for restaurants, bars, and bakeries.[20]

One woman ran a "tie clinic," repairing and restoring old or damaged ties. Someone else ran a bicycle rental and repair shop.[21] Lighting in the camps and rooms was always dim and insufficient, so one enterprising refugee manufactured lampshades with mirrors mounted on the inner surfaces to enhance illumination. And there was at least one refugee renting a corner space in a butcher shop or grocery store for his business of sharpening used razor blades for clients. After washing dishes all day in a Wayside restaurant in exchange for a meal, with soup, main dish, and dessert, one young man sold coffee door-to-door in the evenings. Because refugees frequently changed housing, commensurate with their economic fortunes, running a moving company was a popular business, provided one could acquire a truck or wagon.

For those living in independent housing, cooking was done on small stoves about the size of a standard flowerpot, requiring constant fanning to keep them going. These stoves burned briquets made of a mixture of coal dust and mud, which refugees either manufactured themselves or bought from shops that turned them out. Wherever there was a need, refugees stepped in with a constructive and often ingenious response — some, for example, welded tin cans together for sale as exhaust pipes to those fortunate enough to have pot-bellied stoves to heat their rooms.[22]

The industriousness of the refugee community extended to intellectual endeavors. Journalists, writers, and professors living in the camps published their writings in the local press. One of the oldest and most sophisticated Jewish periodicals in China, edited by the Sephardi Jew N. E. B. Ezra, was the English-language *Israel's Messenger*, which appeared (fortnightly and later monthly) from 1904 until 1941. Although assertedly Zionist, it also reported on the growing Jewish community in Shanghai, on Jewish activities in China, and on events of interest in other parts of the world.[23] Another substantial publication, *Die Gelbe Post*, began circulation in 1931 as a monthly, edited by A. J. Storfer, but later became a weekly and then a daily. It provided learned articles on cultural subjects and politics, commentaries, and local news of interest to the Jewish community. The German-language (but English-titled)

Figure 19. A refugee family preparing a meal using the "flower pot" stove in their Hongkou refugee residence. SOURCE: United Nations Archives and Records Center.

Shanghai Jewish Chronicle, beginning publication in May 1939, became the community's journal of record under the editorship of Ossie Lewin. Its primary role was to publish proclamations, orders, local and foreign news, interviews, and other useful information essential to the daily life of the community. As one of the few publications sanctioned by the Japanese, and in many ways useful to them as a conduit for instructions and information, the *Shanghai Jewish Chronicle* continued to publish throughout the war years. After the war, it transformed itself into a daily called the *Shanghai Echo*, which continued publication until 1948. Altogether, there were at least twelve substantial Jewish periodicals being published in Shanghai by 1939. Many others came and went after a few issues.[24] The Jewish bookstores, the Lion and the Paragon, made most of these popular publications readily available.

Jewish theatrical productions were staged at the Broadway and Lyceum theaters, often with refugee casts of professional actors familiar even in sophisticated Berlin and Vienna cultural circles. As interest grew, refugees opened clubs that put on live performances, which were very well received. Amateurs also put on plays—some of them original works by refugee playwrights—in the dining hall after the camp's evening meal.[25] But it was as composers, performers, and teachers of music that refugees perhaps made their greatest and most lasting mark.

The Jewish musician Arrigo Foa came to China in 1921 to become concertmaster and soloist, and, eventually, conductor of the Shanghai Municipal Orchestra. Later, he became one of the first professors of the National Conservatory of Music in Shanghai, founded in 1927 under its president, and China's minister of education, Cai Yuanpei.[26] This prestigious institution trained many Chinese who subsequently became central to music education in China. With the diaspora from Nazi Europe, other talented refugee composers and artists came to perform at the Municipal Orchestra's weekly concerts at the Lyceum Theater and to instruct Chinese students in Western musical traditions. Some of their best students went on in later years to become the foremost musicians and composers in China. When not teaching or performing, refugee musicians had to support themselves by playing in nightclubs or dance halls. The Jewish refugee cellist Otto Joachim organized a Jewish orchestra that performed both synagogue and secular music for appreciative refugee gatherings as well as general audiences.[27] Jewish folk music was especially popular with young and old alike. Refugee light music programs, as well as ones featuring classical music and American jazz, went on the air with the opening of the American-run radio station XMHA in 1939. The refugees also formed chamber music groups, musical ensembles, a band, and a light opera company.

Austrian and German Jews Organize

Jewish refugees in Shanghai came chiefly from Germany, Austria, and Czechoslovakia, and had various economic and cultural backgrounds. Adding to the diversity of the refugee community, members followed dissimilar branches of Judaism. This inherently complex community met with additional challenges in Shanghai by reason of the great mix of nationalities in the city, the scarcity of resources, and the general adversity of the refugees' circumstances. Many among the new arrivals came to realize the need to work together, find a spokesman, and organize their own communities to deal with these enormous challenges.

The Jews arriving from Europe belonged mainly to the Conservative or Reform branches of Judaism. In fact, however, religion did not play a prominent role in the lives of most of the new arrivals, except for observance of the Jewish High Holidays, when Conservative and Reform rabbis held services in refugee camps or in rented meeting halls, school auditoriums, or even movie theaters. The few Orthodox Jews made use of a small Russian temple in Hongkou for their services.[28] Whether from lack of religious zeal or poverty, the central European Jews never made a major effort to gather the funds and support necessary to establish a large, permanent, independent synagogue to serve their community.[29] Also, there were many non-Jewish spouses and quite a few fully assimilated Jews in this recent group, which clearly set them apart from their more traditional and devout predecessors. Although religious fervor was not a principal motivator for the new refugee group, it appears that most of their leaders saw value in having a *kehillah*, or unified religious congregation, of German and Austrian Jews separate from the existing Jewish congregations that greeted them in Shanghai. The formal organization that emerged would add still another voice to the often discordant chorus resounding throughout the Shanghai Jewish community.

The new Jüdische Gemeinde (Jewish Community) was organized in November 1939, with Leopold Steinhardt as chairman, and had its offices first at 805 East Seward Road and later at 416/22 Tongshan Road in Hongkou. Its proclaimed purpose was to "maintain a good moral, spiritual, and religious standard among its members."[30] It set up departments to handle youth affairs, Jewish education, ceremonies, and statistics of births, deaths, marriages, and so on. In June 1941, it elected its leaders in the presence of the new representative from the AJJDC, Laura Margolis, Rabbi Ashkenazi, and also R. D. Abraham of the Sephardi community. Dr. Kurt Redlich became chairman of the board of directors, with Dr. Fritz Lesser and Dr. Felix Kardegg elected as vice-chairmen.[31]

The religious differences that were bound to emerge in the diverse Shanghai Jewish community received the attention of the Beth Din, or religious court, where they usually could be successfully arbitrated. A much more contentious area, which provoked complaints beyond the Jewish community, involved the settlement of civil disputes. When the International Committee, or Komor Committee, formed in 1938, provision was made for a conciliation board, or arbitration court. The following year, the Committee for Assistance of European Refugees (CFA) established a similar court, and it was the scope and definition of this that caught the attention of the Chinese and Japanese, as well as of Jewish lawyers.

During its first month of operation, the CFA's Arbitration Court for European Refugees met in seventy-six sessions, handling some sixty-two individual cases in accordance with a draft legal code developed by the committee's legal advisor, Dr. A. Grossman. These "Rules Regulating Arbitration in Disputes of European Jewish Emigrants" contained three articles that provoked a notable response. Article 1 made it clear that the committee expected "all emigrants to submit their legal disputes to arbitration" by the Arbitration Court appointed by the committee before going elsewhere. Article 6 stated that those handling the arbitration before the Arbitration Court must have their names appear on an approved list, "to the total exclusion of all outsiders." The final offending article, Article 8, took a very vague and flexible approach as to which laws would apply in the cases presented. It stated that the Arbitration Court, "while observing the laws prevailing in Shanghai, may apply such law as it may be presumed to have been the intention of the parties to apply at the time" when the act was committed. And if that failed to resolve the problem "or should same be inapplicable in Shanghai," only then would the case in dispute be settled "in accordance with Chinese law, and or prevailing local custom."[32]

Appealing to the First Special District Court on North Chekiang Road, the Chinese Lawyers Association charged that the Jewish Arbitration Court, located at the Alcock Road camp, or within the International Settlement, infringed directly on the jurisdiction of this Chinese court. Furthermore, the association argued that having relinquished its extraterritorial rights in China, Germany had lost all privileges granted to other nationalities in Shanghai with consular jurisdiction. Instead, the German refugees came under Chinese law and jurisdiction, in both civil and criminal cases. The Arbitration Court was, in effect, performing duties identical to those Chinese law assigned to a legal tribunal.[33] At a meeting of Chinese lawyers, the central issue at stake was described as a clear matter of the Jewish Arbitration

Court's infringement of Chinese sovereignty and circumvention of the judicial system. The lawyers accordingly petitioned the local Chinese Bar Association to request the Ministry of Justice of the national government and the second and third branches of the Jiangsu High Court to immediately suppress the CFA's Arbitration Court in the interests of preserving the integrity of the judicial rights of China.[34]

Chinese lawyers also bristled at language in the preamble to the code suggesting that dealing with Chinese courts somehow undermined the prestige of the refugees and was too costly and cumbersome. Joining in the debate, the Japanese naval authorities and Japanese consular police emphasized that no foreign court was recognized in Shanghai except the consular courts and promised to investigate the situation.[35]

European Jewish lawyers attacked differently, challenging the competence of the CFA's Arbitration Court, disparaging the Grossman-drafted code, and refusing to accept either that arbitration was mandatory for the refugees or that the board's decisions were to be regarded as final and binding.[36] Others lobbied against the provision that refugees who bypassed the Arbitration Court would forfeit all benefits and support provided by the CFA. Some of the most disgruntled lawyers who questioned the Arbitration Court's abilities and procedures were those angry over having been excluded from the list of lawyers recognized by the new body. One of the worst provisions in the code, in the lawyers' view, was that which excluded attorneys in cases involving less than $500. As the majority of refugee cases, most of them involving rent disputes, naturally fell into this category, the result would be loss of a considerable portion of the market for European attorneys.

Grossman attempted to defend his code and the existence of the CFA's Arbitration Court by arguing that refugee litigants knew neither the local laws nor the language and had little income with which to enforce their claims. Those who were receiving assistance from the committee could hardly be expected to spend the funds provided in paying for litigation in the Chinese courts. They must therefore, in all fairness, submit their cases to the Arbitration Court. A further benefit of handling refugee claims internally, according to Grossman, was to keep the public from knowing certain "sordid and ugly differences reflecting discredit upon the whole emigrant population."[37]

A case that came before the Chinese First Special District Court points up many of the troublesome issues involved with these overlapping legal bodies. After having lunch at the Café Louis, a German refugee couple found that a coat that had been checked was missing. The café owner advised the couple that they should have kept the coat on a chair by their table, whereupon the German couple replied that chairs in a café were not coat hangers, but were there for the use of customers as seats. They engaged a lawyer and filed for damages of $1,000, plus costs, in the Chinese court.

Subsequently, the couple's lawyer received two letters, one from Robert B. Michaelis, head of the Association of Central European Attorneys-at-Law in Shanghai, requesting that the plaintiffs withdraw their case from the Chinese court and to bring it before the Arbitration Court. The second letter summoned the couple to submit the dispute before the Arbitration Court, or "further steps will be taken against them."[38] After intense questioning, the Chinese judge in the case verified that the two letters had in fact been sent on instructions from the café owner and reprimanded him for undermining the authority of the Chinese court and bringing duress to bear on the German couple, who were attempting to follow normal court procedures to resolve their complaint. In the end, the couple prevailed.

In the face of these competitive moves for jurisdiction, the Jüdische Gemeinde became anxious to have its own voice in judicial affairs. In May 1942, it therefore established its own Arbitration Court to supervise and oversee legal issues involving German and Austrian refugees. This new court was in direct competition with the CFA's Arbitration Court, which had meanwhile assumed the arbitration responsibilities of the International Committee. (The latter had closed its court on April 1, 1942.) None of this pleased the Chinese authorities, who would have preferred to see all of these bodies suppressed. The Jüdische Gemeinde's broad membership and influence over the largest of the Jewish refugee communities offered unique opportunities for better Japanese supervision and control of a substantial segment of the foreign population, however, and the Gemeinde's Arbitration Court thus received Japanese support. The outcome was that the CFA's Arbitration Court on Alcock Road closed in April, turning over all of its pending cases to the Arbitration Court of the Jüdische Gemeinde, which thereafter was the only body of its kind serving the European Jewish community in Shanghai.[39] This simplification served Jewish interests, but a trail of resentment and ill will was left in other sectors of the Jewish community.

Rabbis and Yeshiva Students Arrive

During the summer of 1941, a new wave of refugees, renowned for their religious learning and devotion, arrived in Shanghai to challenge the limited resources of the expanded Shanghai Jewish community. They came from the yeshivas, or centers of advanced Talmudic learning, in Poland and Lithuania, recognized by many worldwide as institutions fostering "authentic Judaism" and generally eschewing secular studies. An international effort during World War II to rescue the hundreds of rabbis and their yeshiva students from the Holocaust found refuge for many of them in Shanghai.

The crisis began with the division of Poland in accordance with the German-Soviet Non-Aggression Pact of August 1939, under which eastern Poland was to come under Soviet rule. This alarmed the yeshiva students in the east, who knew that after the Russian Revolution, all the yeshivas in the Soviet Union had been closed down.[40] More encouraging news followed: the city of Vilnius (Vilna in Russian), sometimes called "The Jerusalem of Lithuania," which had been conquered and incorporated into Poland in 1922, was about to be transferred back to Lithuania by the USSR. Word quickly circulated that there was an escape route, with some means of transportation across the border still available. The young students of the Mir yeshiva and Kletsk yeshiva (yeshivas took the name of the towns where they originated), acting against the counsel of their rabbis and yeshiva administrators, decided to seize this opportunity and make their way to Vilnius. Soon they were joined there by their reluctant rabbis, making about 300 students and faculty from the Mir yeshiva, 200 from Kletsk, 200 from Baranowitz, 200 from Kamenetz, and many from Radin and Grodno.[41] Vilnius was quickly becoming a gathering place for those taking the first steps that would lead to salvation from the Holocaust.[42] The city gave refuge as well to members of the Jewish intelligentsia, including socialists, Bundist political leaders from Poland, writers, and journalists. Their window of opportunity was short-lived, however, in that the Lithuanian border closed in mid November, making it difficult, if not impossible, to reach Vilnius thereafter.

Once in Vilnius, the rabbis and students received aid from prominent rabbis with connections to worldwide support networks and to funds provided by the AJJDC. More help came from the American Orthodox community, or Agudah, which formed a special committee, eventually known as the Vaad

Hatzala (meaning "rescue committee" in Hebrew), whose sole purpose was to raise money for the Vilnius students and rabbis and see to it that the yeshivas were transferred safely abroad.[43] These efforts at relocation either to Palestine or the United States met with only mixed results; meanwhile, the Torah scholars continued their intensive studies. The momentum for emigration seemed to be subsiding, until history again intervened and necessitated firm and immediate action.

In June 1940, the Soviet Union invaded Lithuania, annexing it two months later. Once again, the pressures to leave were strong, but so were the obstacles. Where were the rabbis and yeshiva students to go? How would they get there? And how could they obtain the necessary exit permits to leave the Soviet Union? A remarkable series of events followed that saved 3,500 refugees, including the rabbis and yeshiva scholars.[44]

In the summer of 1940, a Dutch student at the Telsh yeshiva, Nathan Gutwirth, approached the honorary Dutch consul in Korvno, Jan Zwartendijk, about finding a safe refuge abroad, because it was no longer possible for him to return to Nazi-occupied Holland. It was decided he should go to the Dutch colony of Curaçao in the Caribbean. Zwartendijk checked with the Dutch consul in Riga concerning the proper procedures for issuing a visa to Curaçao and learned that no visa was necessary, but that entry through a landing permit did depend on approval from the island's governor. Subsequently, Zwartendijk agreed to provide Gutwirth with documentation confirming his right of entry into Curaçao, leaving off the stipulation that entry required confirmation from the island's governor.[45] When Polish refugee leaders in Lithuania learned from Gutwirth of this possible way out, they sought and won Zwartendijk's agreement to provide similar visas to non-Dutch refugees. The main obstacle still to be dealt with was the Soviet order that foreign diplomatic offices in Lithuania close by September 1, 1940. Time was short, but the Dutch nevertheless succeeded in issuing between 1,200 and 1,400 Curaçao visas to the Jewish refugees, many of whom were acclaimed rabbis and yeshiva students.[46]

By the summer of 1940, travel through Europe was no longer possible. The only feasible route to Curaçao was across the Soviet Union and via Japan. The next necessary step was to apply to the Japanese consulate in Kaunas for transit visas, which many of the refugees did. The Japanese vice-consul, Sugihara Chiune, had just arrived in Kaunas in the autumn of 1939.

Sugihara was aware that for issuing a transit visa, the recipient's passport was normally required to indicate a destination, in the shape of a visa to enter some country, but this did not seem to apply in the case of the Polish refugees, because their documentation indicated that no entry visa to Curaçao was needed. He therefore cabled Tokyo for further instructions.

Although Tokyo emphasized in response that each applicant had to have a firm end visa or guarantee of departure from Japan, as well as funds to support a temporary stay there, Sugihara began freely to issue 7–15-day Japanese transit visas to refugees provided they had sufficient funds to continue on their way, even if they lacked the required Curaçao documentation. When subsequently instructed by Tokyo to stop regular business and focus on shutting down the consulate, as ordered by the Soviet Union, Sugihara complied, but continued to issue visas to refugees.

Sugihara's aid to the Jewish refugees has been widely acclaimed in recent years, both in Jewish circles and in Japan, causing him to be referred to as "Japan's Schindler." He is particularly revered by Jews because he is credited with having risked his career by disobeying his government's orders. What motivated him remains uncertain. Perhaps, as many have claimed, he was moved primarily by altruistic or humanitarian impulses. But what is more likely is that Sugihara was interpreting a December 1938 Japanese ministerial-level decision on the Jewish question, to be discussed in detail below, which formulated a policy of favorable treatment of Jews. This would explain why the Japanese embassy in Moscow and Japanese consulates in Qita, Manzhouli, Qiqihar, and Vladivostok also issued documentation to fleeing Jews.[47] It would in any case have been highly unusual for a Japanese diplomat like Sugihara to repeatedly disobey official instructions.

Sugihara's career with the Foreign Ministry does not appear to have been damaged. On the contrary, he went on to hold key posts in Königsberg, Germany (now Kaliningrad in Russia), Prague, and Bucharest, with lengthy stops for consultations at the Japanese embassy in Berlin. Sugihara was fluent in both Russian and German, and the Japanese Foreign Ministry obviously viewed him as a good candidate for intelligence work on the German-Soviet border, where, in addition to performing his consular duties, he reported on German and Soviet military plans.[48] He had been active gathering intelligence from members of the Polish underground in Lithuania.

When Sugihara returned to Japan in 1947, after spending almost two years in a Soviet internment camp, the Japanese Foreign Ministry requested his resignation, saying that no position existed that suited the qualifications of the forty-seven-year-old diplomat. Subsequently, he worked for Japanese firms in Moscow.[49] Sugihara had had extensive contacts with Russians, going back to his early language training and official employment in Harbin and a first marriage to a White Russian, and he had been baptized into the Russian Orthodox faith. It seems not inconceivable that he actually left the Foreign Ministry in order to become a spy for Japan in Moscow.

Sugihara's wife, Sugihara Yukiko, provides an emotional account of the circumstances that, she claims, led to her husband's decision to disregard Tokyo's instructions and continue issuing transit visas to the refugees.[50] After repeatedly asking Tokyo for permission to issue the visas, and with crowds gathering daily at the consulate beseeching him for visas, she says, Sugihara made up his mind to issue the visas for as long as possible. On the day of their departure from Kaunas, Mrs. Sugihara writes, "Even as the train started going, he continued writing, leaning out of the window. Finally he said, 'Forgive me. I cannot write any more. I pray for your good luck.'"[51] Apparently, he then threw the blank visa forms from the train window. Surprisingly, the lucky recipients below actually found that these forms, properly filled out, were acceptable to the authorities. It has been estimated that Sugihara and his assistants issued as many as 6,000 visas to refugees in Kaunas, many of them rabbis and young yeshiva students.[52] About 2,500 of the recipients, mostly men under the age of twenty-six, but including a few families, eventually sought safety in East Asia.

With Japanese transit visas in hand, these Jewish refugees now faced a new challenge — persuading the USSR to grant exit visas. The Soviet authorities (NKVD) agreed to supply exit permits only after HIAS, the AJJDC, and Vaad Hatzala offered to cover the travel expenses of the multitude of refugees and, most important, to pay the Soviet Union in U.S. dollars ($200 per ticket). Once supplied with travel funds and documents, the refugees embarked on the 12-day rail trip to Vladivostok, where, one refugee reported, the Russians summarily relieved passengers of valuables such as gold jewelry before allowing them to board the ship for the 36-hour crossing to Tsuruga, Japan.[53]

From Tsuruga, they traveled by train to Kobe, where they were well received by the local Jewish community, made up largely of well-to-do Russian and some Sephardi Jews, many of whom worked in export-import businesses. A local Committee for Assistance to Refugees, commonly known as JEWCOM, with additional funds provided by the AJJDC and HICEM, took care of the refugees' food and shelter needs and medical care. Joseph Ganger, a member of this diaspora group, reported that most of the Lubavitcher yeshiva gained almost immediate direct entry into the United States from Japan through timely intervention by the influential Rebbe Menahem Mendel Schneerson.[54]

The exodus of refugees through Siberia continued until the end of August 1941, with the main flow finally being interrupted by the German invasion of the Soviet Union on June 22, 1941. The Japanese had attempted to limit immigration, but as more refugees arrived, some even carrying false papers, the authorities gave in and allowed them entry. Those with the limited 7–15-day transit visas found they could even extend their stays, some for as long as eight months. But official pressures increased on the community of 2,179 Polish Jewish refugees sheltered in Japan, especially after funding from American sources ended in July 1941, when, in retaliation for the freezing of Japanese assets in the United States, Japan cut off the incoming American contributions to the Jewish community in Kobe.[55] Japan, preparing for war with the United States, became anxious to expel the foreigners. With no money except what could be raised locally, the community had to take immediate measures to find new host countries that would accept the refugees.

Help came from America, and the open port of Shanghai was the chosen destination. Frank Newman, a young U.S. businessman representing the Vaad Hatzala, agreed to cover the travel and other expenses of the Orthodox rabbis and yeshiva students in Japan and the few stranded in Vladivostok, if they could gain entry to Shanghai. The Orthodox Rabbi M. Ashkenazi in Shanghai had already applied to the Shanghai Municipal Police for entry permits for members of these special groups. In his application, Rabbi Ashkenazi noted that the refugees had "special recommendations for visas" from the U.S. State Department and would therefore only be temporary guests. Aware that a main concern of the Shanghai authorities in limiting the influx of refugees was that they had often become public charges, Newman and Rabbi Ashkenazi both repeatedly emphasized the temporary nature of the stay and the planned coverage of all expenses. It was made clear that "these men are somewhat different from the ordinary type of refugee so there is no desire

Figure 20. The famous Mirrer Yeshiva conducting their studies in the sanctuary of the Beth Aharon synagogue. In the front row first from the left is Rabbi Chezkel Lewensztejn, spiritual guide; second from the right is Rabbi Chaim L. Szmuelowicz, acting dean; and first from the right is Rabbi J. D. Epstein, secretary. SOURCE: YIVO Institute for Jewish Research.

that they should be treated as inmates of refugee camps in Shanghai."[56] With these guarantees, permission was granted for the select group to enter Shanghai subject to purchase of the required entry permits from the police. The transfer took place between August and October 1941.[57]

The intention was for the Orthodox refugees to remain in Shanghai for six months and then to emigrate to the United States, where they would be able to continue their studies. As it happened, only a few of the famous rabbis reached the United States in 1941. More succeeded in gaining entry to Canada, but most of the group had their departure from Shanghai stopped by the war in the Pacific. The Orthodox group, counted among the 582 Jewish refugees registered with Polish authorities in Shanghai during 1940–41, included the famous Mirrer yeshiva, the most complete yeshiva to escape Nazi Europe, and members of the yeshivas of Kletsk (Byelorussia), Telsh (Lithuania), Lublin, and Lubavitz (Byelorussia). In Shanghai, they found housing at the Sephardi Beth Aharon Synagogue on Museum Road, where they took their meals and carried on their studies, and at the Russian Shanghai Jewish Club on Moulmein Road.[58] For a brief period, their presence in Shanghai, made possible by sponsors and outside support, made the city one of the most active centers of Jewish studies in the world. For this learned intelligentsia, Shanghai became a temporary waystation in which to survive and weather the war years.

Another consular official has been recently identified as having played a key role in saving Austrian Jews by providing exit visas from Austria with Shanghai as the destination. This was Dr. Ho Fang-shan, Chinese consul general in Vienna from May 1938 until May 1940. He is credited with issuing thousands of Shanghai exit visas to fleeing Austrian Jews against the orders of his superior, the Chinese ambassador in Berlin. Most of the recipients never reached Shanghai, however, but escaped to other destinations.[59]

Tensions among Community Leaders

Dissension caused by jealousy, cultural diversity, and religious differences was a serious problem in the Shanghai Jewish community and worked to the detriment of its well-being and survival. The wealth of Sephardi Jews and some of the Russian Jews and the special funds and housing provided for the recently arrived Polish and Baltic Jews were envied by others less fortunate.[60] Self-perceptions also differed among the various groups. Many of the German Jews had become highly assimilated into German culture, to the extent that they saw themselves first as Germans, something not uncharacteristic of Jews from western and central Europe.[61] Some even reported anti-Semitic attitudes among friends and acquaintances who regarded themselves as superior to most of the rest of the Shanghai Jewish community.[62] Sephardi Jews, especially the elite with British citizenship, tended to relate well to the German and Austrian Jews, mainly because, as a group, they included in their ranks many professionals from highly cultured backgrounds.

The mix of nationalities heading the various refugee committees and organizations added to the atmosphere of mutual suspicion and competition. It is remarkable that they were able to work together as well as they did. Paul Komor was Hungarian; Michel Speelman, Dutch; Boris Topas, Russian; Morris Bloch, Polish; add to these the key Sephardi leaders, Sir Victor

Sassoon, Horace Kadoorie, N. E. B. Ezra, R. D. Abraham, and D. E. J. Abraham, to name just a few, and the prospects for conflict are obvious. There were also different levels of religious commitment. Jews in Shanghai ranged from the nonobservant, of whom there were many among the German and Austrian Jews, to adherents of Reform Judaism, a few Conservatives, and practitioners of Orthodox Judaism. The Polish and Baltic Jews, with their yeshivas and Talmud Torah learning centers, were the most devout, a fact that impressed the Russian Jewish community, but tended to set these Jews apart within the Hongkou Jewish community. With their advanced religious training and devotion, these Orthodox Jews considered themselves guardians of "authentic Judaism" and, as such, superior to the other Jewish groups in Shanghai. The differences in their religious services and food preparation also divided the Poles from German and Austrian Jews, as did their Yiddish language and culture.

These issues were at the root of much of the tension that found expression through the several competing refugee relief committees. Together, the dissension and resulting intergroup conflict caused serious harm to refugee work, even more so than the restrictions and barriers imposed initially by the Japanese authorities. In this context, 1942 was a particularly troublesome year, especially as the means for dealing with poverty and hunger began to diminish and as new organizations formed and competed for increasingly scarce resources.

The Komor International Committee greatly reduced the scale of its operations by the spring of 1942, once immigration ceased. Handling the many aspects of immigration affairs had been its primary responsibility. A new and separate committee, known as EASTJEWCOM, was formed in March 1941 under Chairman A. Oppenheim to assist specifically with the recent arrivals from Poland, Lithuania, Latvia, and Estonia. EASTJEWCOM had a regular and reliable supply of funds from international organizations devoted to the well-being and survival of this revered group, a fact naturally resented by other Jewish groups.

Attempting to oversee and coordinate the many aspects of refugee relief work were the AJJDC representatives in Shanghai, Laura Margolis and Manuel Siegel. Unfortunately, both Margolis and Siegel found their relief work seriously impaired by local dissension over leadership issues, program goals, the nature of religious services, and the distribution of monetary contributions. Two of the leading refugee bodies, the Jüdische Gemeinde and the long-standing CFA, or Speelman Committee, engaged in heated competition for funds and services. For example, in a bid to strengthen its independent control over German and Austrian Jews and win support away from the CFA, the Jüdische Gemeinde declared through a notice in the *Shanghai Jewish Chronicle* that registration and membership in its organization was compulsory for all Jews wanting to take advantage of its various relief and social services.[63] In addition, it proclaimed that with the cessation of AJJDC direct financial aid in December 1941, its member families now must help by donating meals to the needy or by paying a monthly sum to support one needy person. Restaurants, bars, and coffeehouses were asked to charge a 10 percent surtax, and dry goods stores, 5 percent, to support relief work.[64]

Amid the rising tensions between the Jüdische Gemeinde and the CFA, Margolis and Siegel decided to resign from the CFA. Their departure caused immediate concern because of the detrimental effect it would have on fundraising at a time when the refugee camps and hospitals desperately needed support.[65] Attempting to justify her resignation at a joint meeting of the Jüdische Gemeinde and the CFA in July 1942, Margolis asserted that the CFA "had fallen to pieces" over various disputed issues; she noted that Speelman and other key members of the leadership had already resigned.[66] In the circumstances, the best course was for the CFA to shut up shop, which it did on September 15, 1942, its key relief functions of housing and feeding of refugees being taken over by the Jüdische Gemeinde and the *Kuratorium* (board of trustees) of the Kitchen Fund, yet another new organization, formed in August, under the direction of Dr. Emanuel Berglas.[67] Margolis addressed the Kitchen Fund meeting just days after it had received its new responsibilities and, in her pleas for new sponsors and donations, reproached well-to-do Jews in Shanghai, claiming that they just waited for funds from the AJJDC and neglected their own funding responsibilities.[68]

Refugee support now involved the work of the following organizations: the Jüdische Gemeinde, established by German and Austrian Jews; the new Kitchen Fund; EASTJEWCOM, representing the devout eastern European newcomers; and the Ashkenazi Committee for Assistance to the Refugees from Central Europe, or CENTREJEWCOM, established during the summer of 1942 and placed under A. Rogovin's leadership.[69] CENTREJEW-COM expressed the concern of Russian Jews about the welfare of the recent arrivals and gave Russian Jews a voice and continuing role in Jewish community affairs.

A serious dispute developed almost immediately between the Kitchen Fund, CENTREJEWCOM, and EASTJEWCOM over the distribution of funds. Laura Margolis had pleaded for the available AJJDC funds, money raised locally through donations or charity events, and funds from other sources to be used to support all needy Jews in Shanghai. EASTJEWCOM Chairman Oppenheim rejected her pleas, claiming that EASTJEWCOM had been established for the sole purpose of raising and dispensing funds to support Polish and eastern European refugees, especially Orthodox Jews, who had special dietary needs based on religious beliefs, making it impossible for them to use a communal kitchen. Oppenheim received severe criticism for his resistance, but he refused to alter his position. One particular issue that caused a considerable uproar was EASTJEWCOM's refusal to contribute from its funds to support the children of destitute German and Austrian Jewish parents. Exasperated by the quarreling and lack of cooperation, the executive committee of the Ashkenazi Jewish Communal Association attempted to force better relations between EASTJEWCOM and CENTREJEWCOM by forming a "roof committee" that combined members of the two organizations under its supervision. The end result was inconclusive, with the basic missions and behavior of both competing bodies remaining about the same. Most damaging, the dispute cut into funds, because most potential local contributors held off and waited to see how the lengthy dispute would be settled.[70]

The Japanese Court Jewish Support

As we have seen, the Japanese sector of the International Settlement housed all of the refugee camps, as well as almost all of the refugees from Nazi-controlled Europe who could live independently. The position and attitudes of the Japanese vis-à-vis the Jews were destined to have a key impact on Jewish circumstances in Shanghai. The Japanese approach shifted from official indifference to this marginal, although sizable, group of foreigners to intense interest in and study of the Jews in light of their perceived potential for supporting Japan's grandiose plans to build what was described by late 1939 as a

"New Order in East Asia" (Tōa Shinchitsujo). Certainly, early Japanese behavior displayed lingering gratitude for the Jacob Schiff loans that had underwritten the modernization of the Japanese Navy, which in turn had dealt
the decisive blow leading to Russia's defeat in the Russo-Japanese war. And
yet when N. E. B. Ezra visited Japan in 1934 with proposals to settle Jews in
Manchukuo and contribute to its overall development, the Japanese government was not interested. Moreover, a major article in *Israel's Messenger* arguing that by treating the Jews kindly and allowing them freedom and dignity,
the Japanese might attract Jewish wealth and talent, brought no immediate
Japanese response.[71]

As Japan's domestic political situation became more influenced by those
committed to an expansive political, economic, and military strategy in
China, based in Manchukuo, the Japanese authorities began to change their
views and to see an active role for Jews in their overall planning. They turned
their attention first to finding ways to centralize their influence and control
over the Jews. According to one astute observer, in 1937, the Japanese approached Dr. Abraham Kaufman, president of the Hebrew Association of
Harbin, asking him to organize an umbrella organization of Hebrew associations in China and Japan. Finding himself in a situation that the observer
described as the Jewish curse of "being reared in homelessness and fostered
in opportunism, left to shift for themselves, protected by no one," Kaufman
felt he had little choice but to comply.[72] But in so doing, he planned in return
to use this compliance to win Japanese support in diminishing the rampant
anti-Semitism inspired by White Russians in Harbin. Even more important,
Kaufman hoped to persuade the Japanese to offer protected areas for settlement by Jews fleeing Nazi Europe.

Kaufman accordingly founded the Jewish National Council of the Far
East, which held annual meetings during 1937, 1938, and 1939. This council, with Kaufman elected as chairman, included seven representatives from
Harbin, two from Mukden, two from Hailar, one from Dalian, one from
Tianjin, two from Qiqihar, and one from Kobe, Japan. Shanghai, Qingdao,
and Manzhouli had no representation originally, but representatives from
these cities reportedly joined the council later.[73] At the close of the final conference in December 1939, Chairman Kaufman signed a petition to the
Japanese prime minister, Abe Nobuyuki, expressing his gratitude for the protection without prejudice that the Japanese authorities had given Jews in East

Asia. Further, Kaufman proposed that if the Japanese were to create a special area for Jews somewhere in East Asia, all of world Jewry would be grateful. He noted that if this were at all feasible to do, the Jews in East Asia, in return, would pledge support to help the Japanese empire build its New Order.[74]

The Japanese believed they had found an effective means to get their message at least heard outside of Asia. They intended to use this organization and its annual forums to attract Jewish wealth and support, particularly from Jews in the United States, to back what became the Greater East Asia Co-Prosperity Sphere drive, a massive program designed to establish imperial Japan as the dominant power in every sphere in East and Southeast Asia. In short, Jewish leaders and their organizations were to support the goals of Japanese imperialism in Asia.[75]

An early response to the forthcoming Jewish appeals from Asia came from the president of the American Jewish Congress, Rabbi Stephen S. Wise, in November 1938. A Mr. L. Zikman, who had requested support from Wise that, he noted, might indirectly benefit the substantial Jewish communities in Harbin and Shanghai, received a decidedly negative reply and the admonition: "I think it wholly vicious for Jews to give support to Japan, as truly Fascist a nation as Germany or Italy." Wise further declared that he did "not wish to discuss the matter any further and I deeply deplore whatever your reasons may be that you are trying to secure support for Japan from Jews. I promise that everything I can do to thwart your plans I will do."[76] Clearly, the Japanese authorities had a difficult task and would need to do it in a very short time if they wished to carry out their plans to influence American and, for that matter, world Jewry to support their cause.

With their new course of action chosen, the Japanese embarked on an intensive effort to study every aspect of the "Jewish problem," as it was commonly called. They established semi-official study societies, such as the Kokusai Seikei Gakkai (Society of International Politics and Economics) and the Japanese cabinet-level Kōa-in (Asian Development Board), which published lengthy treatises examining in detail every aspect of the Jewish communities in China and their relationships with world Jewry.[77] In addition, they set up an intelligence organization in Shanghai, with operatives to gather information and the means to disseminate it to high-level Japanese authorities. In its early stages, this organization was under the direction of Navy Captain Inuzuka Koreshige, himself a serious researcher and author of studies on the Jews.[78] The South Manchurian Railway's Research Bureau, another instrument for Japan's expansion founded after the Russo-Japanese War, also produced a series of studies of Jewish matters worldwide, as well as providing detailed information on the Shanghai Jewish communities on a monthly and even a weekly basis.[79]

The outcome of the extensive research was the conviction that the so-called Jewish *zaibatsu*, or powerful web of business interests in real estate, banking, finances, gold, and the export-import trade worked directly against the Japanese government's policies in China. Even more ominous, the Jewish *zaibatsu* had close ties with the British and American governments, to the extent that Jews were able to manipulate the foreign policies of those governments in ways decidedly detrimental to Japan's interests in China.[80] Many of the studies targeted Sir Victor Sassoon as the instigator of these anti-Japanese maneuvers and policies and the key figure in providing substantial support to Generalissimo Chiang Kai-shek, to the obvious disadvantage of Japan. Sassoon was a natural subject for such close Japanese attention, given his substantial wealth, social status, and recognized expertise. To them, Sassoon's support, particularly of Chiang Kai-shek, seemed geared to keeping the Nanjing (later Chongqing) government on the side of Britain and the United States and in opposition to Japan. This Jewish stance clearly conflicted with Japanese plans to develop a policy that would utilize the Sassoon *zaibatsu* to create a self-sufficient economy supporting the broader conception of "a Japanese empire and national defense state."[81] One research study, written in quite a conspiratorial tone, pointed to the developmental loans and guarantees of export credits provided to Chiang Kai-shek from the Sassoon enterprises, calling them the means for Sassoon's "Nanking Road headquarters . . . to exploit and exercise a financial stranglehold on China."[82] It explained that Sir Victor ran the Sassoon *zaibatsu* in East Asia, although the organization had its primary headquarters on Prince Street in London, with a branch in Geneva that operated through the League of Nations, and one in New York located in the National City Bank.

The researchers mapped out all of the leading Jewish organizations and personalities in Shanghai, with biographical sketches, photographs, and detailed charts of the structures and interrelationships of the various Jewish organizations, even including their relationships with Jewish organizations worldwide.[83] No stone was left unturned in order to become thoroughly familiar with all aspects of the "Jewish problem." Why so much effort and attention? Besides the obvious desire to know this perceived rival and adversary, the Japanese researchers intended to make covert inroads into Jewish circles in hope of turning their strength and influence in support of Japan. According to them, the Jews controlled key world media channels and formed influential circles around world leaders such as President Roosevelt, and these reputed attributes and connections made it all the more necessary to recruit Jews to work for Japan.[84]

The ideas of the researchers received high-level Japanese attention and interest. Colonel Yasue Norihiro, one of the most prominent and productive of the researchers, who had also produced a translation of *The Protocols of the Elders of Zion*,[85] delivered a lecture on September 19, 1938, in the presence of Army, Navy, and Foreign Office officials. The lecture, presenting most of the ideas outlined above, attracted the interest of the minister of foreign affairs, Prince Konoe Fumimaro, who subsequently had copies circulated to the Manchukuo embassy and the Japanese consulates in China, just prior to his announcement of the concept of a "New Order in East Asia."[86] In response to the question of how Japan should treat the Jews, Yasue observed: "Obviously, we should not follow Germany's example. . . . We should protect them and let them enjoy the blessings of our imperial prestige. . . . If, as a matter of fact, the Jewish people have an actual influence over the political, economic, the press and other fields, I do not see any reason why we should have them for an enemy . . . through the Jews in the Far East, we can advertise our hospitality to [American Jews] . . . this means, I believe, will be effective also in dealing with the problem of the boycott of Japanese goods."[87]

Partly in response to the November 1938 *Kristallnacht* in Germany and the concern evoked by Japan's signing of the Agreement on Cultural Cooperation between Japan and Germany,[88] the Konoe cabinet, at a five ministers' meeting held on December 6, 1938, adopted a policy statement with three "articles" clarifying the Japanese position on the Jewish issue and incorporating the main thrust of the research done on the Jews.[89] First, Japan would not participate in the extreme German policy of anti-Semitism; rather, second, Japan would maintain a spirit of racial equality, treating Jews in Japan, Manchukuo, and China in a fair manner; and, third, Japan wished to avoid worsening relations with the United States and to stimulate the flow of foreign capital into economic construction efforts by peaceful diplomacy.[90]

This policy statement was transmitted to Japanese official installations abroad and no doubt was influential in the decisions of Sugihara and officials in Japan's Moscow embassy and Japanese consulates to interpret Tokyo's pronouncement as favoring the issuing of transit visas to fleeing Jews.

The Japanese appeal, as expressed in this policy statement and amplified by researchers like Inuzuka and Yasue, did find strong support in at least one important quarter, even if that interest eventually had to be put on hold. In June 1939, the Shanghai businessman, Morris S. Bloch, president of the Shanghai Ashkenazi Jewish Communal Association, wrote some exploratory letters to the American philanthropist David A. Brown, publisher of *The American Hebrew and Jewish Tribune*. In the correspondence, Bloch extolled Japanese respect for and study of Jewish culture, and the proclaimed Japanese policy of treating all with equal rights and privileges in both Manchukuo and Japan proper. He associated these views directly with Colonel Yasue. Bloch also claimed that the Japanese government desired to have Jewish settlers, as well as Jewish capital, come to Manchukuo. Embellishing his arguments to Brown, Bloch exclaimed that there was "not a better nor a richer country in the world" than Manchukuo. He suggested that Brown travel to Tokyo and Manchukuo, with all expenses to be paid by Japan, to see for himself the opportunities available and, upon his return to the United States, to help correct the false information reported in the American press concerning the treatment of Jews by Japan.[91]

Japan's chief interest, Bloch said, was in Brown's potential role in obtaining future American capital and loans for Japan. As further inducement to Brown's coming to Asia, Bloch pointed to the money to be made by participating in the rise of the New Japan, exclaiming that "even if we make only one percent, it will also be enough to provide even for our grandchildren."[92] In concluding his letter to Brown, Bloch qualified his ambitious proposals by explaining that his Japanese associates had not yet fully agreed to these plans; but, expecting that they would, he requested Brown's confidential agreement to garner American support.

Brown forwarded his agreement to the terms offered by Bloch in a handwritten, undated letter, confirmed by cablegram on September 6, 1939.[93] In the interim, however, the surge of incoming Jewish refugees from Nazi Europe into Hongkou and the Japanese decision to restrict their further entry derailed these plans. Apparently deciding that he had little other recourse, Bloch told Brown, in a letter dated November 12, 1939, that there had been "changes in the local situation" and expressed the hope that he would at some not too distant time still be willing "to lend us a helping hand in the proposition."[94]

Any Japanese overtures to cause American Jewry and its purported official allies to respond with more favor or even tolerance toward Japan ran up against a formidable obstacle in the form of Sir Victor Sassoon, who was vociferously pro-British and anti-Japanese. He was a British citizen of high social stature and great wealth, with much of his investment and financial interests connected with political and banking circles affiliated with Chiang Kai-shek and the Chinese Nationalist regime.[95] Navy Captain Inuzuka was particularly concerned over what he saw as Sassoon's role in helping the British arrange a loan to the Chinese government meant to finance the development of southwestern China through railroad development.

Sassoon was not to be won over by the Japanese. During a business visit to New York, which included fund-raising activities for the Hongkou Jews, he had made his views emphatically clear by declaring that the Western democracies could "cut Japan's throat" if they would only work closely together on economic policies.[96] During another visit in early 1940, Sassoon claimed that the Japanese leaders, enmeshed in corruption, lacked even the support of the Japanese people, who likely would turn against the military because of Japan's desperate economic plight.[97] These outbursts so infuriated the Japanese authorities in Shanghai that Michel Speelman and Boris Topas, leaders of the Shanghai Ashkenazi Jewish Communal Association (SAJCA), found it necessary to issue a statement emphasizing that "SAJCA, which recognizes the authority of the Jewish National Council of the Far East in Harbin, feels deep gratitude towards the Japanese Government for its just, humanitarian, and unprejudiced attitude towards us . . . Sir Victor Sassoon is not and never has been a member of the SAJCA." Having in mind the interests of the thousands of Jews living in the Japanese sector of the International Settlement, Topas stressed that no consideration should be given by the Japanese to the "irresponsible statements of private individuals."[98]

The Japanese faced another disappointment in the Jewish response to their attempts to gain greater representation on the Shanghai Municipal Council during the election held in April 1940. Directed by Captain Inuzuka, they promised to reward Jews who voted for Japanese candidates in the election with entry permits for their relatives still in Europe.[99] In response, the Jewish leaders Paul Komor and Ellis Hayim counseled Jewish voters instead to remain neutral and not engage in any such political activity, pointing out that the Jews owed gratitude both to the Japanese for their sympathetic treatment in Hongkou and to European nations and the United States for the financial support provided to their community.[100] The prospects of still more impoverished refugees joining the Hongkou Jewish community must also have given the leaders pause. Nevertheless, many Jewish residents of Hongkou did take advantage of an opportunity to obtain entry permits for family members still stranded in Europe, as evidenced by a complaint lodged by the refugee committee with the Japanese consul, Ishiguro Shirō, for allowing 1,000 new entry permits to be issued independently, without following the established procedures, which included prior scrutiny by the refugee committee.[101] Taking no chances on the possible impact of these developments on the election's outcome, the British and Americans divided their large holdings and distributed them in ways to qualify additional reliable voters.[102] The outcome of the election was preservation of the status quo on the council for another year, to the great frustration of the Japanese, who had insisted upon having a voice on the council commensurate with their increased stature and influence.

Using the detailed studies of the "Jewish Problem" developed by the various Japanese research organizations, Inuzuka helped prepare still another plan, which was to benefit the Jewish community in Shanghai by creating a settlement for 30,000–70,000 Jews, expected over the next 10–20 years, and to include those already in Hongkou. The settlement was to operate as a self-governing unit and as a satellite city of an already-developed metropolis.[103] The plan was to be financed through 200 million yen raised in U.S. Jewish circles, with 20 million yen being used to establish a leather factory, which would help solve the serious problem of Jewish unemployment. The remaining 180 million yen was to be spent on supplying scrap iron, lathes, and fuel oil, "without conditions," to Japan. To set this up, a representative of American Jewry was to visit Japan to discuss the matter. This time Inuzuka's hopes were dashed by Japan's September 27, 1940, signing of the Tripartite Pact, just days after his plan's unveiling, ending any possibilities of acquiring U.S. Jewish loans.[104]

Shanghai Jewish leaders recognized that some degree of harmony in the

Figure 21. A cartoon by the famous cartoonist, G. A. Sapojnikov — or, as he was best known, Sapajou — in the *North China Daily News*, depicting the tug-of-war for refugee votes in the 1940 Shanghai Municipal Council elections. SOURCE: Shanghai Municipal Library.

working relationship between the Japanese authorities and Jewish leaders was necessary and served the interests of their community. The opening of new facilities almost always included Japanese officials among the guests. At the ceremony marking the inauguration of the Ward Road Immigrants Hospital in June 1940, Captain Inuzuka was an honored guest and, in his opening remarks, Speelman expressed gratitude to the Japanese "for their sympathy towards the refugees."[105]

Inuzuka performed several less ambitious services that clearly benefited the Jewish community. For example, he provided the tons of cement necessary to lay the foundation for the Ashkenazi community's grand New Synagogue, at a time when cement was a precious commodity in Shanghai.[106] In addition, he played a key role in facilitating admission to Shanghai of the

Polish and Baltic rabbis and rabbinical students. Frank Newman, the man in charge of rescuing the group, gave Inuzuka a silver cigarette box engraved with a message of appreciation for his help.[107] Newman reportedly noted receiving a memorandum from Inuzuka outlining work he wanted undertaken in the United States, but without providing details. In all likelihood, the work suggested by Inuzuka, which, according to the letter, had been the subject of many unreported discussions between the two men, had the purpose of creating a favorable image of Japan, drawing support for Japanese plans, and maintaining the neutrality of the United States, as espoused in Inuzuka's research into the "Jewish question."[108]

Inuzuka's plans and work with the Jewish community in Shanghai suffered a fatal blow with the attack on Pearl Harbor. He clearly blamed the United States for precipitating the outbreak of war through its hostile "encirclement policy" toward Japan. But with the war going on, Japanese priorities had changed, and a specialist in the Jewish problem who might draw support from American and world Jewry was, of course, no longer relevant. His services in Shanghai as a kind of "friend of the Jews" were no longer needed.[109] Colonel Yasue was similarly relieved of his duties. At a farewell party given in his honor, Inuzuka lamented the fact that his three years' work in Shanghai, built around increasing understanding between Japan and the United States, had ended in complete failure, with the Americans failing to grasp the "true spirit" of Japan. Most of the prominent leaders in the Jewish community attended his send-off, including those who had worked with him and some who may even have supported many of his views.[110] For example, Boris Topas and L. Hanin had formed a "Hebrew Society for the Study of Nipponese Culture" and invited Inuzuka to serve as its honorary president.[111]

Before the end of his assignment in Shanghai, Inuzuka agreed to an important request by Laura Margolis of the American Joint Committee to give Japanese approval for the use of an AJJDC promissory note to raise funds for the refugee community locally after the outbreak of the Pacific War.[112] As Margolis tells it, she was staying at the Cathay Hotel when the takeover of Shanghai began. She could see Japanese troops moving in on the streets below and occupying the main lobby of the hotel. Refugee friends told her that Inuzuka occupied the penthouse apartment, formerly held by Sir Victor Sassoon, who, fortunately for him, was in Bombay when the takeover occurred. Under the circumstances, Margolis daringly phoned upstairs to

Inuzuka and asked for an appointment. The request was granted. "Here we were — he a Japanese and I an American, our two countries at war — and I'm sitting there sipping tea," she later recalled.[113] When the pleasantries were over, Margolis confronted Inuzuka with a bargain: "Look, you and I now represent two nations fighting each other, but we have a job to do. You have to keep the refugees quiet; you can't afford to have hunger riots on your hands when you're in the midst of occupying a big city. I have the possibility of helping you keep these refugees quiet if you'll give me permission legally to borrow money on this guarantee of the AJJDC to pay after the war."[114] Margolis had already received authorization from the AJJDC to borrow U.S.$30,000, to be repaid when possible under conditions that would not aid the enemy.[115]

Inuzuka agreed to the proposal, provided that the names of the lenders be given to him. This apparently caused consternation among many potential donors because of the large amount of black market money in circulation. People wanted to get rid of this local money but did not want to have their names associated with the funds. While waiting for contributions to come in, Margolis used the remaining money she had on hand to feed four thousand refugees for eight days, giving priority to the aged, the sick, and women and children. This arrangement had been approved by a vote taken among the eight thousand refugees needing relief. Finally, a German-Jewish businessman broke the funding logjam by providing a considerable amount of money in exchange for her IOU. His action stimulated a flow of contributions from others. These funds allowed for resumption of most of the relief activities, and life for a while began to regain a sense of near normalcy for the refugee community.[116]

SIX

A Change in Atmosphere

When birds at nightfall cease their twitter
And birches stand tall in their sleep,
How sweet it is and how bitter
To look at my homeland and weep.

—A. VERTINSKY (TRANS. B. BOGUSLAVSKY)

Wartime Shanghai (1937–45) is now receiving considerable scholarly attention, and recent publications and conferences have significantly enhanced
our understanding of Japanese wartime policies and control measures; the
responses of local groups to the Japanese authorities both before and after
December 1941; puppet government control of the city's various sectors;
transformations in the Shanghai municipal administration; and the economic
repercussions of all this.[1] Another dimension of this picture, which both con-
firms the findings of this scholarship and enriches it, can be traced in the experiences of refugees in wartime Shanghai.

When war broke out in Shanghai, the foreign concessions remained sheltered, at least until August 14, 1937, a day of carnage that became known as
"Black Saturday." The Japanese flagship *Idzumo*, anchored off the Bund, was
the paramount symbol of Japanese aggression to the Chinese, and Chinese
pilots from Longhua airfield made the ship a prime target for bombing runs.[2]
On this day, Chinese airplanes, hit by Japanese antiaircraft fire, failed in their

crippled state to strike the *Idzumo* as they had intended, dropping their bombs, instead, first on the Palace Hotel and the adjoining street, and then, a few minutes later, at the New World Amusement Center on the border between the International Settlement and the French Concession. At noon both places were jammed with rickshaws, cars, and shoppers. At the amusement center, masses of Chinese refugees had gathered to receive free bowls of rice and tea being dispensed.[3] The casualties were estimated at 1,873 wounded and 1,740 dead (26 of them foreigners), and residents of the "protected" foreign settlements of Shanghai lost for good the sense of security previously afforded by their privileged circumstances. The new reality was that the International Settlement (minus the Japanese sector) and French Concession had become an isolated island (*gudao*) surrounded by Japanese- or puppet-controlled territory.

As recent studies have shown, in addition to this isolation, the rising crime rate in all parts of Shanghai impinged upon the welfare of all. This was especially true of those who were stateless or depended upon others for their protection or well-being. Flourishing opium dens and gambling houses enriched the criminal elements in the city to the point where they began to acquire access to respectable municipal institutions. The burgeoning vice industry became a key source of revenue for both the local Chinese administration and, eventually, the national puppet regime, thus undermining their legitimacy. A new genre of crime — political assassination — also now became commonplace in the city.[4] The establishment in December 1937 in Pudong of the puppet Shanghai Municipal Government of the "Great Way" (*Dadao*) under Mayor Fu Xiaoan helped precipitate a spate of murders of people who had collaborated or even cooperated with the Japanese, something that the Russian community experienced directly.[5] As Japanese influence over the Russian community increased, Russian leaders came under heavy pressure to heed Japanese direction or be forcibly removed. Some key leaders resisted and were assassinated. Other Russians, mostly recent arrivals, who sought to supplant the presiding Russian leadership, found it advantageous and even preferable to collaborate with the Japanese. As this chapter will show, a whole spectrum of political reactions, from resistance to neutrality, to cooperation, accommodation, or collaboration, can be seen in the wartime behavior of the Shanghai Russian refugee community.

Figure 22. The Shanghai War Memorial in the foreground with the Angel of Victory on the top and clouds of smoke from Japanese bombing visible from Pudong across the river. SOURCE: Kounin, *Eighty-Five Years of the Shanghai Volunteer Corps.*

Right-Wing Pressures

The sale of the Chinese Eastern Railroad to Japan in 1935 drastically changed the living conditions and prospects of the Russian community in Harbin. Thousands headed back to Russia, and those who for obvious political reasons could not return found their economic opportunities severely narrowed. There followed a large exodus of Russians to Mukden, Tianjin, Qingdao, and Shanghai. Like the European Jews who would soon follow them, those arriving in Shanghai found life most affordable in Japanese-dominated Hongkou and Wayside. By 1938, a small community of 2,000 White Russians had formed in the Japanese districts. The Russian Orthodox Confraternity ran a hostel for the most indigent of the new White Russian arrivals, and Archimandrite Dionisii ministered to the newcomers' religious needs at a small Russian Orthodox church.[6]

Before World War II, the recently arrived Hongkou White Russians and the much larger preexisting Russian colony centered in the French Concession heatedly debated the future of the Shanghai White Russian community and of Russia itself. Russian monarchists, such as the influential Legitimist-Monarchist Party, were committed to a restored monarchy, but at the same time eschewed any involvement in local Russian political affairs. They maintained a firm link to the Shanghai Russian Emigrants Committee mainly for social and cultural reasons. Another group, known as the Russian General Military Union (ROVS), was also monarchist, but distinguished itself by advocating the unique opportunities for overthrowing the Bolshevik regime to be afforded by a war between Japan and the USSR. With Japanese backing, its leaders planned for a buffer state to be established in Russian territory east of Lake Baikal and run by a Russian National Government under the protection of Japan. Although strong in the 1920s, ROVS lost much of its appeal in the 1930s. A third group of young White Russians, the Union of Mladorossy, proposed making use of the best of Russian traditions, but adding to them certain revolutionary innovations. They saw revolution coming from within the USSR and not from without and anticipated the new system as czarist but functioning through a broadly based union of Free Soviets.[7] Finally, there was the Russian Fascist Party (RFP), with local headquarters on Avenue Joffre in the French Concession. This organization had some features in common with the ROVS, but was fiercely anti-Semitic, anti-Bolshevik, and committed to a vitriolic brand of Russian nationalism. Its domestic program envisioned construction of a "Third Russia," to be based on a new system of "Solidarism," or subordination of all personal and class interests to those of the nation-state. Internationally, RFP leaders anticipated a rapprochement between their party and Japanese and German nationalists, all united against the Communist International, whose expected defeat would lead to a union between a new Russia, Japan, Manchukuo, and National Socialist Germany. The RFP circulated its ideas through the periodical *Nash Put* and formed a meeting club at 832 Weihaiwei Road.[8] While clear in its purpose, the RFP had difficulty garnering broad support in Shanghai, where White Russians, less obsessed with counterrevolution than their compatriots in Harbin, could recognize the strong hand of the Japanese military behind this organization.[9]

A Reorganized Russian Community

In this diverse and fractious climate of opinion, Ch. E. Metzler's Russian Emigrants Committee hung on to the leading role in the White Russian community, refraining from overt political activity and concentrating on basic refugee affairs, while paying close attention to Japanese policy and direction. Nevertheless, as the committee's chairman, Metzler could not neglect the rising competition from the growing Russian community in the Yangshupu, Broadway, and Wayside districts of Japanese-controlled Hongkou.[10] In September 1938, to gain control of this community, Metzler established a special subcommittee headed by his handpicked appointee, Colonel N. K. Sereinikov. Its first mission was to handle the registration of all Russians living in Hongkou.[11]

Metzler's concern was timely. Evidence of the new Russian community's expanding influence came with the opening of a second Russian club in Hongkou at 81 Chusan Road in November 1938, under the leadership of A. A. Purin and General I. E. Tsumanenko.[12] The club was to serve as a new center of Russian culture, education, sports, and recreation. Purin and Tsumanenko had strong ties to Harbin fascist organizations and published the right-wing newspaper *Russkii Golos* (Russian Voice), but, more important, both were known to enjoy substantial Japanese military backing.[13] Along with officials of the Japanese consulate general, the Imperial Naval Landing Party, and the Shanghai Muncipal Government, Metzler attended the new Hongkou Russian club's opening party, where he made a speech to the effect that White Russians must remain united "in the active struggle against Communism in alliance with Imperial Japan."[14] Purin and a Japanese spokesman hailed the club as the center of Russian life in Wayside.[15]

Metzler's position as head of the official Russian Emigrant Committee clearly became increasingly difficult as he tried to contain any political involvement by White Russians while maintaining his leadership of the entire community. The new hardline White Russian leaders in Hongkou and Wayside had few qualms, and needed none, about expressing their political views. This was demonstrated at a meeting of 400 members of the Wayside White Russian community at the Astor House in Hongkou in November 1938, whose agenda focused on forming a united front against communism with Japan, Italy, and Germany. White Russian anticommunist organizations had already been formed in Beiping, Tianjin, and Qingdao following the Japanese occupation.[16]

The Astor meeting created quite a stir within both the White Russian and foreign communities. Russians writing letters to the editor emphasized that it did not represent the opinion of the majority of White Russians in Shanghai and said that Russians were being coerced by the so-called "White House" headquarters of the anticommunist Bureau of Russian Emigrant Affairs (BREM) in north China, which managed White Russian affairs under the direction of Japanese "advisors" from the Tokumu Kikan, or Special Services Section, the political unit of the Japanese Military Mission.[17] Another writer pointedly explained that White Russians loved Russia and had no desire to work with "selfish foreign powers against the rulers of Russia."

These protestations did not allay the anxieties of others in the foreign community. A reporter who had covered the Astor House meeting demanded that a responsible White Russian organization officially denounce it; otherwise, it would appear that belief in these radical sentiments was widespread.[18] Metzler and the moderate, established White Russians found themselves in a no-win situation. If they denounced the meeting, they would be seen as taking a political position, and one unpopular with some White Russians, not to mention the Japanese. On the other hand, reticence suggested approval and weakness. The minister of the Russian Protestant Church, A. J. Leonidov, did denounce the meeting, with the interesting justification that Shanghai White Russians would never "undermine the Russian [Soviet] government supported by 150 million people."[19]

Metzler's position was becoming more tenuous, but he still headed by far the largest segment of the White Russian community, and this fact was not lost on the Japanese. His position and strength, however, were becoming a double-edged sword. While he had decisive authority within the Russian community, this strength also made him a special target for Japanese manipulation and control, to be realized through indirect and only thinly disguised methods. The Japanese Military Mission included a Russian Affairs Division, which already had considerable experience gained from managing the Russian communities in Beiping, Tianjin, Qingdao, and Harbin. To bring this experience to bear, as they continued to improvise their establishment of control over Shanghai, the Japanese established a planning body, the Council for the Affairs of Russian Emigrant Residents in Districts Protected by

Japanese Troops, under the direction of Navy Captain K. Kuroki. Having this structure in place by August 1938, the Japanese took the additional step of having the Chinese puppet authorities issue a decree to the effect that all White Russian organizations must register with the Russian Emigrants Committee, the body selected by the Japanese as best suited for centralizing their control over the White Russian community, by June 14, 1939. The message was that groups either register with it or prepare to liquidate, because those neglecting to register would be considered "hostile to the New Order in China."[20] Moderate groups feared that after registration, the next step would be the dictation of bylaws and enforced participation in political activities, which the French authorities had warned them against, and which might be used as a basis for their expulsion from the French Concession. The theme "registration without protection" appeared in several of the leading newspapers and journals.[21]

Metzler viewed this registration drive as having some positive benefits. It might at least quell some of the many divisions within the community and facilitate better cooperation. As the officially designated body, the committee could better represent the White Russian community in Shanghai's complex political climate.[22] In addition, this new status might also provide the committee with some increased leverage, useful for procuring more charity contributions for Russian schools, hospitals, and the homeless and destitute. With this in mind, Metzler initiated a tax to be levied on committee members with income in support of Russian education and charities.[23]

As committee chairman, Metzler saw placating the many dissident factions and mediating among them as his principal role, and the one best able to maintain good relations between the White Russian and foreign communities. He believed himself to hold the pivotal position for responding to and integrating Japanese policies and demands to the best advantage of the Shanghai White Russians. In any case, Metzler must have seen that there was no other course open to him, and by maintaining control of the committee, he could at least work to keep out extremists. On June 24, 1939, he informed *Shankhaiskaia Zaria* that seventy Russian emigrant organizations had registered with the committee, representing some 25,000 refugees.[24] In addition, serving in his broadened leadership role, he hosted a farewell dinner party for Vice-Consul Takahashi Seishirō, who had served in Shanghai for seven years and been responsible for handling White Russian affairs. A short time later, the announcement came that a Japanese-language course was being started under B. I. Voblyi, who had taught in Russian schools in Harbin.[25]

Violence Against Russian Leaders

The various segments of the Shanghai Japanese establishment differed in their approaches to the Russian community, a fact that further complicated the work of the Russian Emigrants Committee. The Japanese consular authorities and the Economics Department of Mantetsu (the South Manchurian Railway) preferred to proceed cautiously, working with the moderate Metzler as the recognized community leader. On the other hand, the Special Services Section of the Japanese Military Mission, with its Bureau of Russian Affairs, advocated bringing in experienced and sympathetic outside Russian leadership from the north to run the committee. For example, the Japanese Bureau of Russian Affairs in Manchukuo and Tianjin had registered all emigrant bodies under one central organization, the Anti-Comintern Committee of Russian Emigrants in North China, which was notorious for its totalitarian leadership and methods, but very effective in exercising control over the complex Russian community.[26]

In their efforts to pacify and accommodate the various factions and Japanese pressures, Metzler and the other leaders of the Russian Emigrants Committee faced still another challenge with the unexpected establishment of a new organization parallel to their own, the Association of Russian Emigrants, at 409 East Seward Road in Hongkou. Started on August 10, 1940, it operated from the premises of the *Dal'nevostochnoe Vremia* (Far Eastern Times), a Japanese-sponsored Russian newspaper, which often carried articles showing Metzler in an unfavorable light, charging him and the committee with favoring their own interests rather than those of the Russian people.[27] The new body was staffed by the so-called "Harbin Stars," including General Tsumanenko and General V. D. Kosmin. White Russians in the French Concession derisively referred to members of this right-wing group as the "bridge people" because of their location in Hongkou, across the Garden Bridge. Most important, the association enjoyed the cooperation and support of Captain K. Kuroki, who had appointed Tsumanenko to the chairmanship.[28]

The Association of Russian Emigrants lost no time in attempting to assert its dominance. Even before its inauguration, the right-wing publication *Rus* announced the alleged dissolution, on June 15, 1940, of the Russian Emigrants Committee and its replacement by the association at the head of the White Russian refugee community, with all the rights formerly invested in the Russian Emigrant Committee bestowed upon it.[29] Reporting on the leadership of the new body included the claim that a former secretary of the Russian Emigrants Committee, M. G. Yakovkin, had defected to the new organization. As it turned out, the *Rus* story was nothing but a fabrication. Metzler responded quickly to this challenge and, hoping to defuse the situation, announced that he would shortly be convening a meeting of various Russian organizations to announce the establishment of a new Association of Russian Emigrants in Hongkou. To obviate any confusion, Metzler stressed that this new organization would function "in cooperation with and *under the control* of the Russian Emigrants Committee."[30]

This bold attempt by the opposition to dislodge the Russian Emigrants Committee from its leadership position was only a temporary setback. In early July, the Japanese announced directly their plans to reorganize the committee to resemble those already functioning in Harbin. Chairman Metzler was approached, but refused on principle the Japanese offer that he continue to lead the body during the planned reorganization period. It should be noted that Metzler had earlier annoyed Japanese civil authorities by failing to deliver a united Russian vote, including the votes of Russian Jews in Hongkou, during the April 1940 Shanghai Municipal Council elections.[31]

Obstinate and unwilling to compromise or become a full-fledged collaborator, Metzler was gunned down by a Chinese assassin outside of his residence at 208 Nanyang Road on August 2, 1940.[32] His murder shocked the Russian community, Orthodox and Jewish alike, and set off yet another round of jockeying for the position of Russian leader and primary spokesman.

Still maintaining some caution in dealing with the large Russian community, Japanese officials immediately began to search for their own candidate among the respected refugee leaders to replace Metzler. They approached N. A. Ivanov, an attorney and former imperial Russian judge.[33] A lengthy police report dated August 4, 1940, indicates that Ivanov arranged a secret interview with the Shanghai Municipal Police on August 4 to find out who the police suspected of being responsible for Metzler's assassination, what they thought the motives were, and, especially, whether the right-wing Association of Russian Emigrants in Hongkou was involved. This information, to be held in the strictest confidence, would help him decide whether to accept the Japanese offer to head the committee, he explained.[34]

In the course of the police interview, Ivanov reported that he had had a series of meetings at his residence during June and July involving the Japanese military representative Captain Kuroki, General Kosmin, General V. I. Karpov, and a Japanese interpreter named Ikeda.[35] During the sessions, Ivanov, as a former Russian vice-consul and consular judge, had briefed the parties on the history of the White Russian community in Shanghai, providing considerable detail on the subject. His thorough knowledge of and experience with Russian affairs, as demonstrated at these meetings, had convinced each member of this group that he, rather than Metzler, should have succeeded the respected V. F. Grosse as Russian Emigrants Committee chairman, Ivanov told the police.

According to Ivanov, members of the group had expressed their dissatisfaction with Metzler's leadership. Karpov, described in the police report as an advisor to the headquarters of the Kempeitai, or Japanese Military Gendarmerie, portrayed Metzler as a Freemason who had Soviet agents among his associates on the committee and reportedly found him greatly inferior to Ivanov as successor to the committee's founder, V. F. Grosse. Captain Kuroki came out in favor of Ivanov as head of "the reorganized representative body for the Russian community in Shanghai."[36] Clearly, Metzler's fate had already been sealed by July 1940.

The same police report noted that Ivanov had told the police about still another interview, arranged by Captain Kuroki and attended by Japanese Vice-Consul Matsuda, during which Matsuda informed him that the question of removing Metzler had recently been decided, and that Metzler had even agreed to tender his resignation. Matsuda had said, moreover, that Ivanov was the best person to replace Metzler. Ivanov was assured, too, that his lawyer's salary would be compensated for by his becoming a paid advisor on White Russian affairs to both the Shanghai Municipal Council and the French Conseil. Ivanov declined the financial arrangement but, still hesitant about the chairmanship, did agree to serve "for the time being" as an unpaid

Figure 23. I. N. Ivanov, the third chairman of the Russian
Emigrants Committee, who served from January 1941 until his
assassination in September 1941. SOURCE: Zhiganov, *Russkie v
Shankhaie.*

advisor to a reorganized Russian committee, operating under the chairmanship of General Tsumanenko.[37] The agreed-upon plan was to announce this change by the end of August.

Still during his police interview, Ivanov reported visiting Captain Kuroki on August 2, immediately after Metzler's assassination. Aware that rumors might connect him with the assassination, Kuroki said he was prepared to swear that he had had nothing whatsoever to do with the murder. At the same time, he insisted that Ivanov must now agree to head the committee. Ivanov consented, but shortly afterward had to request that his appointment be indefinitely postponed. Following the memorial service for Metzler at the Russian Cathedral, he explained, the widely respected Bishop Ioann, vicar of the Russian Orthodox Mission in Shanghai, had presided over an important informal conference of some twenty members of the Russian Emigrants Committee. Most of the attendees belonged to the committee's advisory body, and all had had close links to Metzler. As might be expected, the mood of the conference had been somber, and after a number of speeches of an anti-Japanese character, several of those present had been asked to succeed Metzler. All had had various reasons for declining. Finally, Bishop Ioann had agreed to act as head of the committee pending election of a new chairman.[38]

Ivanov reported the conference events the next day to Captain Kuroki, stressing his hesitancy about being made head of the committee given these new circumstances. Kuroki responded by informing Ivanov that the decision had already been made, and that he had arranged to present Ivanov to the chief of the Greater Shanghai Municipality Police and then to puppet Mayor Fu Xiaoan. He also cautioned Ivanov that as the new chairman, he had to prevent any further anti-Japanese outbursts at Russian Emigrant Committee meetings. Ivanov then told the police that he had confided his difficult situation to Bishop Ioann, including his secret approach to the Shanghai Municipal Police for information. The bishop had advised him to impress upon the Japanese the necessity of postponing the reorganization of the committee until Metzler's funeral and the mourning period were over. The bishop also explained that in addition to Ivanov, General Glebov and Captain Fomin were being suggested within the community as strong candidates for the committee chairmanship.[39] Ivanov again told the police that he would refuse the Japanese offer of the chairmanship if they had evidence that the competing Association of Russian Emigrants in Shanghai had connections, "however remote," with Metzler's assassination. He never mentioned holding the Japanese accountable.[40]

Ivanov's concerns must have been placated, or most likely, overridden by the Japanese, because in January 1941, he was announced in the press as chairman of the reorganized Russian Emigrants Committee.[41] In July 1941, he traveled with Captain Kuroki to Nanjing, where he was presented to Wang Jingwei, head of the puppet Chinese government.[42] By this time, Russian authority within the committee had become very limited. It was further curtailed on August 11, 1941, under Japanese direction, when the new mayor of the City Government of Greater Shanghai, Chen Gongbo, issued a statute explaining the newly reorganized committee.[43] It stated that the chairman and vice-chairman of the committee were to be appointed by the mayor, and that the committee was to include five departments: Registration, Economics and Finance, Schools, Cultural-Educational, and a Secretariat. Russian charitable organizations were to be unified under a Russian Charity Central Committee, with N. I. Fomin as chairman.

Ivanov's tenure as chairman of the reorganized Russian Emigrants Committee was brief. On September 9, 1941, whether by Chinese hit men paid by the Japanese, competing right-wingers supported by the Japanese, or a Chinese underground targeting Japanese collaborators, he was gunned down as he stepped from the car in which he had been riding with his wife.[44]

This second murder of the committee's top leader stunned the White Russian community. Twenty-six local Russian organizations issued an appeal for help from the broader Shanghai community to terminate incidents of terrorism against the Russian Emigrants Committee. In an emotional statement, they called upon all White Russians to cooperate in confronting "the powers who have twice 'beheaded' the Russian community and who aim to disrupt its unity, cooperation, and struggle for honor."[45] In the meantime, Mayor Chen Gongbo had appointed Colonel N. K. Sereinikov as the new head of the committee. This break in committee leadership facilitated a further centralization of the White Russian community. On November 8, 1941, a comprehensive statute was issued by the city government renaming the committee the All-Russian Emigrants Committee of Shanghai and subordinating all Russian immigrants, including Ukrainians and Russian Jews, to its authority. Previously, the registration of Russian Jews had been managed by the Shanghai Ashkenazi Communal Association, reportedly to en-able its leaders to know and stay in touch with Russian Jews and their needs.[46] A more likely explanation was that Russian Jews had strong reservations about being grouped under the authority of a broad and recognized White Russian body, whatever its purpose might be.

The appointment of heads of the five departments required approval by the mayor, upon recommendation of the committee chairman, who might only serve a one-year term. An advisory body, made up of representatives of diverse Russian emigrant organizations, was permitted to offer suggestions to the committee leadership. But even the list of advisory body members had to be submitted to local authorities for approval.[47] This organizational statute was published in the Russian press, and the new organization was registered with the municipality of Greater Shanghai.[48] The Russian refugee community finally had a legally constituted single body, but its leadership and affairs were carefully controlled from outside. On December 8, 1941, when Japanese military forces entered the International Settlement, Russian refugees, by then numbering 30,000, were told to cooperate.[49] On December 16, *Shankhaiskaia Zaria* instructed all Russian refugees immediately to acquire special certificates of identity, which they were required to show upon demand.

Colonel Sereinikov's appointment as Russian Emigrants Committee chairman was celebrated at a large dinner party held on January 31, 1942, and attended by members of the Japanese Military Mission, the Japanese embassy and consulate, the Manchukuo consulate, and the Chinese Peace Preservation Corps. In the face of such overwhelming Japanese pressure on the White Russian community, both its Church and administrative leaders counseled cooperation and support for the New Order.[50]

After mid 1940, the Russian Jewish refugee community shared the anxieties of other Russian refugees about Japanese plans to centralize all emigrant groups and pattern an organization after those already existing, and notorious in their operation, in Harbin, Tianjin, and Beiping. Russian Jews registered with the Russian Emigrants Committee in Shanghai by November 1941 included 1,366 residing in the French Concession; 391 living in the International Settlement south of Suzhou Creek; and 189 north of the Creek.[51] The entire Russian Jewish community numbered between 6,000 and 8,000, suggesting that many of the Shanghai Russian Jews preferred, if at all possible, to keep separate from the Russian Emigrants Committee.[52] This preference had already become apparent when, in October 1940,

Russian Jewish leaders, led by M. S. Bloch, filed an application to form a "separate, independent" committee under the City Government of Greater Shanghai. The objective was to conserve some measure of authority over Jewish community affairs, especially in light of persistent press stories about atrocities committed against Jews in northern cities by Russian organizations under Japanese control. Also, while Jewish leaders had worked closely with Metzler during his tenure, receiving considerable relief assistance, they were unhappy with Ivanov's appointment as the new committee leader. There were reports that Ivanov had known of an application for independent status for the Jews and let it be known to the Japanese that he saw no reason for it to be granted. In any case, the application was turned down on instructions from the Japanese Special Services Section.[53] Shanghai Russian Jews were to function under the auspices of the reorganized White Russian body.

As already noted, the All-Russian Emigrants Committee of Shanghai also included the relatively small Ukrainian population under its authority. This was a major blow to the Ukrainian community, whose leaders had spent enormous amounts of time and effort trying to establish their separate identity. In November 1941, what turned out to be a very temporary recognition of the Ukrainian Emigrants Committee as the legitimate representative body for that community was withdrawn. In the official language of the pronouncement, "all people and descendants of people previously living within the border of the former Russian Empire" must register with the All-Russian Emigrants Committee, which was thus to be considered the official organization of the Ukrainian community too.[54]

Police reporting on Ukrainian affairs was tainted by the fact that members of the force were White Russian and held the local Ukrainian community in disdain. The constant bickering and backbiting among the Ukrainian leaders did not help, especially when disturbances required action by the police. In addition, Captain Kuroki wanted to combine as many as possible of the Slavic groups in the Shanghai community, particularly those whose national identity was subject to question, into one, more manageable organization. Under these new circumstances, the Ukrainians continued to maintain their own emigrants committee for cultural and charitable purposes, but it had none of the official responsibilities and recognition that it had previously enjoyed. In fact, police reporting indicated the intention of authorities to keep a close eye on this group and its leaders, whom they regarded as disruptive and inconsonant, with the intention of closing the Ukrainian committee down if it proved at all troublesome in the future. As Chapter 8 will show, a group of Ukrainians did indeed become embroiled in serious controversy. When Nazi Germany attacked the Soviet Union, Shanghai Ukrainian nationalists characterized the Germans troops as liberators, who would help them once again realize an independent Ukraine.

Anti-Semitism and the Japanese

Jewish leaders in Shanghai feared the consequences of Japan having concluded the Tripartite Pact with Germany and Italy on September 27, 1940. They were uncertain about how Japanese military authorities might handle their large population in Hongkou. Constant rumors of impending ill-treatment and plans for solving the "Jewish problem" filled the air. A local Russian-language radio station broadcast news of the war, and local newspapers occasionally reported atrocities against Jews in Europe. Some may have seemed too sensational to comprehend, such as the account in the *North China Daily News* that 6,000 Jews had been machine-gunned by Gestapo units in a labor camp in Poland.[55]

Locally, there were sporadic incidents of violence, such as a massive fistfight in Hongkou over the appearance of a chalk-drawn swastika on the sidewalk at the corner of Chusan Road and Wayside Road. When Jews tried to erase the offensive mark, White Russian onlookers interfered. The ensuing brawl involved 150 participants and required police intervention, with some of those involved taken into custody and fined. A leading newspaper account of the event was spinelessly noncommittal, reporting that the appearance of the swastika was the "favoured version of the fight."[56] Pamphlets signed the "Aryan Union" that were found in large numbers at the Shanghai Race Course called for a war on Jewish commerce in Shanghai and urged their readers to refrain from doing business with Jews, saying that the money would only go to building bombs to be used against those "fighting for world liberation from the Jewish yoke."[57]

In early 1941, the All-Russian Fascist Union began publishing *Nash Put*, formerly based in Harbin, in Shanghai.[58] After the signing of the Soviet-Japanese Neutrality Pact on April 13, 1941, at least the anti-Soviet part of this publication's message had to be curtailed. The anti-Semitic message in the union's speeches and publications, however, continued unabated. *Nash Put*'s content was often outlandish, such as an article describing the suffering and persecution of Christians in Shanghai who had allegedly had their Russian Easter celebrations ruined by Jewish members of the Flour Department of the Shanghai Municipal Council who had diverted the best flour for use by Jews at Passover, leaving only inferior dark flour for the Christian celebrants. "Poor Christians — the history of their persecution continues," the article concluded.[59]

The editor of *Nash Put*, M. M. Spassovsky, whose pen name was M. Grott, was sharply criticized by the editor of the *Novoe Vremia* (New Times), P. A. Savintzev, for an article entitled "Can't We Dispense with the Jews?" Written in the form of a letter to the editor of *Nash Put*, it lambasted the Russian Emigrants Committee for allowing two Jewish doctors to practice at the Russian Emigrants Hospital on Rue Maresca, where "the health of Russians is controlled by Jews."[60] While disclaiming any personal affection for Jews, the pro-Japanese Russian editor of *Novoe Vremia* emphasized that White Russians had no say in Shanghai affairs, even those involving Jews, because they were "mere refugees," not even political emigrants. He went on to declare that "the Jewish problem in East Asia is a matter to be decided . . . by the powers of the New Order that is being established in accordance with the program approved by the Nipponese Empire." Moreover, the Russian Emigrants Committee was not to respond to "the wishes of Russian nationals wearing the emblem of German swastikas on their chests."[61]

Editorials in the pro-Japanese *Far Eastern Times* explained that the Japanese authorities continued to maintain respect for the All-Russian Fascist Union, particularly its anticommunist position, which had long been shared by the Japanese. However, Kuroki stressed that the Japanese alone would decide key policy questions such as those involving the Jews. Rather than delving into political questions, White Russian refugees should confine themselves to their own relief and refugee affairs. Kuroki left no doubt that all policy matters, especially those with political overtones, were to be left solely to the Japanese.[62] Press reports showed that even the Chinese National Socialist Party, which had been making headway in northern China, attracting the attention of German Nazis, could not expect Japanese support unless its programs clearly suited Japanese policies in China.[63]

The Russian fascists may in part have been inspired to publish anti-Semitic articles by news reports of an anti-Jewish rally — the first of its kind — by 1,000 people in Japan, under the auspices of the "Japanese Anti-Espionage League," which advocated the study of Jewish history in order to understand the need for an anti-Semitic national policy. Previewing this rally, the nationalistic *Hochi Shimbun* had warned that Jewish inspiration was behind the construction of air bases to be used for bombing Japan.[64]

The Nazi Presence in Shanghai

Nazi pressure on Japanese leaders to follow anti-Semitic policies had been felt for some time, and certainly there were those in Japan who shared Nazi views of the Jews. In addition, leaders of various competing factions of the Guomindang in China found aspects in National Socialism appealing, especially its emphasis on discipline and a strong organization, both believed to be essential to China's own national recovery.[65] In Shanghai, as noted, the fascist movement, motivated as it was by White Russian figures, had not fared very well. It was not until the outbreak of the Pacific War that Nazi ideas began to gain ground, largely because Nazi programs became enmeshed with the buildup of the German wartime presence in Shanghai. Still, the fact remained that Germany's Axis partner Japan continued to exercise authority within the city and to pursue the Japanese wartime agenda. The Kempeitai, the Naval Landing Party, Japanese consular authorities, and the supporting intelligence and propaganda bodies together extended the Japanese grip over every major facet of the city's life, including local administration, civilian control, economic activity, and the underworld of crime, narcotics, and espionage. In short, while the German presence and its ideological influences increased in the city, it never displaced or even played a serious role in determining Japanese policy. Nevertheless, it is essential to an understanding of the European Jewish refugees' common perceptions of the threat to them to consider briefly the nature and makeup of the German presence in Shanghai.

German nationals in Shanghai numbered about 3,000 in 1940. The loyalty of this overseas community to the new Nazi regime was a long-standing concern in Berlin.[66] Prior to the Pacific War, German business organizations with substantial interests in Shanghai began to express extreme unhappiness to the German Foreign Office over the new trends in German East Asian relations. By the mid 1930s, Germany had replaced Great Britain as the third largest trader in the China market.[67] Business spokesmen, through their Chamber of Commerce, protested against Nazi foreign policies that promoted increasingly intimate relations with Japan to the detriment of Germany's relations with China. Instead, German businessmen continued to promote the favorable development of relations with China, where they were already heavily invested. The Nazi Party's presence in Shanghai thus evoked some trepidation among Germans with commercial interests in China.[68] It might be tolerated provided moneyed interests in the German community continued to retain financial control.

A somewhat similar situation existed with the established official representation in Shanghai. As Françoise Kreissler has shown, German officials in Shanghai, particularly the diplomats, had to tread a fine line. Outwardly, they conformed to Berlin's requirements, but at the same time they took steps to protect their authority from encroachments or usurpation by the National Socialist Party.[69] Consul General Martin Fischer and Alfred Glathe, a member of the Shanghai Municipal Council and "mayor" of the German community, were both closely connected with local German business and shared its views on how best to serve German interests. The same applied to Frederich Hermann Glimpf, chief of the German news agency DNB (Deutsches Nachrichten Büro).[70] The German military mission in China had long been sympathetic to China's plight in facing Japan, supplying arms and military advisors to Chiang Kai-shek even during the initial period of the Sino-Japanese conflict.[71]

Loyalty to the Nazi Party increased among Germans in China after the outbreak of war, however. By then it paid. For the business groups, money was to be made because there was no longer strong competition from countries like the United States or Great Britain in Shanghai. Profits grew exponentially as the German government placed contracts in support of the war effort. Also, it became impossible to deal with the German government unless one was a member of the party, causing at least the most prominent German "taipans" to become party members.

Nevertheless, lingering concerns about the depth of official loyalty to the regime and wartime requirements for information and intelligence led

Berlin to establish a web of organizations in Shanghai charged with maintaining and bolstering Nazi power and influence. The Nazi Party in China, with headquarters in Shanghai, operated under the leadership of *Landesgruppenleiter* Siegfried Lahrmann, who had joined the party in 1933 and received orders directly from Berlin through the German consulate in Shanghai.[72] The main thrust of Nazi policies was to exercise firm control over German organizations, businesses, and personnel. Party officials working under Lahrmann were "to teach Germans living abroad about the New Germany and the ways and ideals of National Socialism."[73] This was one of their principal functions; another was to obtain information and build intelligence sources and methods to enhance the party's stature.

In carrying out his duties, Lahrmann occasionally found fault with consulate and later embassy officials, accusing them of lacking the "Hitler spirit." Lahrmann helped to relieve Martin Fischer, a diplomat of the old school, of his responsibilities, partly because Fischer was married to a Norwegian, an enemy national, but also because of his weak Nazi credentials. Other reports suggest that, in general, however, Lahrmann was fairly moderate in his stance toward less than enthusiastic members of the broader German community in Shanghai.[74] An analysis of the Shanghai Germans, dividing them according to the degree of their loyalty to the party, reported that 150–200 were radical Nazis, a few of whom opposed Lahrmann's moderation and reputed lack of qualifications for the post of *Landesgruppenleiter*. Some 500–700 Nazis fell into a category labeled political opportunists; 1,400–1,600 belonged to the party, but disapproved of all of its violent and radical aspects; and 60–100 were convinced anti-Nazis.[75] What at least can be inferred from this problematic survey is that clear differences of opinion did exist. This explains why it became necessary in Berlin's thinking to accelerate Nazi propaganda work.

One of the bodies formed to support Lahrmann's work was the German Information Bureau, established in 1940 and directed by the propagandist Baron Jesco von Puttkammer. Puttkammer arrived in Shanghai in May 1941 and described his mission there as follows: "The main task of the Party activity was to keep the German community in line, to give pep-speeches, whenever necessary, to strengthen the pro-Hitler feelings, to fight demoralizing rumors and defeatism, to keep the people away from fraternizing with Jewish emigres or to buy merchandise in such kind [*sic*] of shops."[76]

Puttkammer wrote propaganda books in the 1930s glorifying Nazism and its mission in the world. Operating from the sixteenth floor of the Park Hotel in Shanghai, he produced leaflets, pamphlets, photos, movies, and exhibits, many with anti-Semitic themes. He sponsored concerts and provided general information on German culture, featured on the German radio station XGRS, housed in the Kaiser Wilhelm School on Great Western Road. Puttkammer also produced a monthly magazine, *XXth Century*, two of whose most talented and effective contributors were George Sapajnikov (Sapajou), a famous cartoonist who had worked for the *North China Daily News* until the war, and Klaus Mehnert, who edited and wrote articles for the magazine. These were Puttkammer's overt activities. Covertly, he collected economic and political intelligence for the German authorities on both their Axis partner Japan and the local Jewish community.

Even more infamous than Puttkammer in the eyes of the local Jewish community was the newly appointed head of the Gestapo in the Far East, Colonel Josef Meisinger, known as the "Butcher of Warsaw," where he was said to have been responsible for the deaths of over 100,000 Jews. Subsequently appointed police attaché at the German embassy in Tokyo, Meisinger took up his post there in May 1941.[77] His authority extended to all Germans in the Far East in Japanese-occupied territory, and his job was to guarantee their loyalty to the Nazi Party and the Führer. To allow himself more authority over the disposition of those believed to be lukewarm toward the Third Reich, Meisinger acquired the additional post of embassy counselor. According to a captured Luftwaffe captain, Meisinger several times was able to arrange for Germans of questionable allegiance to be kidnapped and placed on board one of the German blockade runners that traveled from Japan to Germany between 1941 and 1943.[78]

Meisinger worked closely with Colonel Lothar Eisentraeger, better known as Ludwig Ehrhardt, of the German Abwehr, or Military Intelligence Office, in Shanghai. Ehrhardt's unusual success at gathering military intelligence and reporting on ship movements in the Shanghai harbor got his acclaimed office renamed the Ehrhardt Bureau. The bureau also specialized in procuring war matériel, rubber, leather, tea, and food supplies for shipment to Germany. Meisinger's Gestapo representative in Shanghai was Major Franz Huber, police attaché at Shanghai, who traveled frequently to Japan to report to his boss on party disciplinary matters and counterintelligence activities, especially those involving the Soviet Union. Most of the intelligence information gathered from individuals came from personnel working for German firms in Shanghai and from Chinese who were willing to assist. In addition, the numerous periodicals and newspapers in Shanghai, although censored, still made the city a more productive source of information for Meisinger and the others than Tokyo.[79]

The Jewish Response

Writing from his prison cell in September 1945, Meisinger prepared a lengthy report, required by his American captors, recounting his association with the Nazi Party and activities in the service of the Third Reich. As might be expected, given his circumstances, Meisinger did not elaborate on any anti-Semitic policies followed or carried out by him. Rather, he insisted that his principal duties concerned assisting the German ambassador within the framework of police work and fighting international crime. This work required him to make contacts with police representatives of other countries and to negotiate with Japanese police officers with whom he would exchange information and experiences.[80] While sounding rather benign, these responsibilities did give Meisinger the opportunity to pass along to the Japanese derogatory information on individuals whom he wanted blacklisted or arrested for spying for the Allies, leading to their being imprisoned or deported. On at least two occasions, the Japanese received lists of "German expatriates, anti-Axis, Jews, and persons whose political attitudes are doubtful."[81] Throughout his report, Meisinger denied ever having any policy role or involvement in shaping German foreign policies.

Regardless of the veracity of Meisinger's statements, the mere arrival of such a notorious high-level Nazi official in the Far East, who was believed to have massacred Jews, sent shock waves through the Jewish communities. In Shanghai, the recent appearances of Meisinger's colleagues Puttkammer and Ehrhardt added to fears boiling to the surface. Jewish residents of Shanghai during this period recalled the frightening rumors that began to circulate at that time that the Jews would soon be rounded up and put out to sea on unseaworthy vessels. Another had the Jews being shipped off to work in labor camps in Manchukuo. Still another left them to starve to death on an island at the mouth of the Yangzi River. These fears probably contributed to the very different versions related of what happened next.[82]

In order to contain the hysteria and sort out the situation, leaders of the Jewish community agreed to meet in an emergency session. Their sense of extreme urgency was heightened by information provided at this meeting by Shibata Mitsugu, a Japanese official who had previously worked with Captain Inuzuka of the Jewish Affairs Bureau. The Jewish officials believed Shibata to be a Japanese vice-consul, but a Japanese source identifies him as an economic consultant affiliated with the Japanese Ministry of Foreign Affairs stationed in Shanghai.[83] One version of the meeting's significance was that Shibata reported official plans, which had been discussed under prodding from the Gestapo, to take steps to "liquidate" the Jews in the various manners noted above. These plans were not yet firm as to which of the methods would be followed, but it was clear that the new Emergency Committee, composed of Dr. Felix Kardegg, Fritz Kauffmann, Ellis Hayim, Michel Speelman, Boris Topas, G. Shiffrin, and the committee's secretary, Robert Peritz, needed to respond quickly. The committee decided that members who had good Japanese contacts should use those channels to reach officials at the highest levels of the Japanese Central China Army, Naval Landing Party, Kempeitai, and Foreign Office in order to bring the plot against the Jews being developed in Shanghai to a halt.[84]

It was agreed that, if pressed as to why they were making inquiries, they would cite the flurry of anti-Semitic propaganda in the press and their fears that this might presage an attack on the Jews. Fritz Kauffmann's contact was through a German Jew named Brahn, a woman friend of whose worked as an interpreter for the Kempeitai. When Brahn approached the Japanese, however, he was intensively questioned and unfortunately broke down and went beyond the agreed-upon story, naming Shibata as the source of information that had led the committee to attempt to reach the highest levels of Japanese authority, with the intention only of putting a stop to what it believed to be a developing plot against the Jews.

Another version of this same sequence of events, reported by Robert Peritz, claimed that he had written a letter of protest, based on the information gathered at the meeting with Shibata and the others, about the threats and danger facing the Jewish community. As advised by Shibata, Peritz delivered this letter to the Japanese consul general during a luncheon at the

Cathay Hotel. What followed, almost immediately, was the arrest of the various participants in the meeting. Peritz claimed that a Mr. Inouye, the Japanese official charged with supervising the International Committee, confirmed to him that an attack on the Jews had been inspired by the Germans, particularly by Puttkammer. Inouye "begged" Peritz not to be identified as the source of this information.[85]

In mid 1942, the Kempeitai responded by denouncing the members of the committee and placing them and Shibata under arrest in Bridge House, the most feared and dangerous place of incarceration. Inside this notorious five-story building, torture and beatings were standard, and disease and vermin polluted the cells. Kauffmann tried to explain to his captors that the Jewish leaders were only trying to find out whether the Japanese would listen to the Germans and liquidate the Jews. They had no intention of doing harm to the Japanese. In response, the Japanese charged that the Jews had promoted the spreading of false rumors, thereby endangering the stability, regulations, and control so rigidly protected by the Japanese as the new ruling authority in the entire Shanghai metropolitan area. When Kauffmann finally came up with the response the Japanese wanted to hear — that he had ignored Japanese restrictions against spreading false rumors — the Kempeitai released him, after making him sign an agreement not to say that he had been badly treated during his detention.[86]

Speelman, owing to his friendship with the pro-Vichy chief of police in the French Concession, was the first to go free, after just a few days. Ellis Hayim, a Sephardi Jew, was freed by the Japanese when the British agreed to his exchange for a Japanese official on the *Gripsholm*, a special exchange ship sailing in a few days for the free port of Goa. It is likely that a darker fate awaited Shibata, whom the Kempeitai considered a traitor and ordered back to Japan.

The Jewish prisoner who suffered by far the most and longest was the Russian Boris Topas, who remained in Bridge House for at least six months. As a stateless Russian, without even a Nansen passport, Topas had no one to speak for him. But even more damning for him was his recently published book marking the twenty-fifth anniversary of the Republic of China under the leadership of the Guomindang. As a respected "Old China Hand" who had had contact with Sun Yat-sen and later Chiang Kai-shek, Topas was clearly suspect to the Japanese.[87] They got nowhere in their attempt to persuade him to sign a confession, however, and, perhaps considering him as an unnecessary burden, released him — a broken man at age fifty. One of Topas's daughters reported that a Japanese admiral, in something of a humanitarian gesture and against orders, had called her mother to report that Topas had been released and put out on the street to die. When the family arrived, they hardly recognized him because of his loss of weight and dire physical condition.[88]

The Japanese Position

As discussed previously, evidence of Japanese anti-Semitism predated the arrival of the Nazis in Shanghai. It had already been encouraged and nurtured by the close Japanese association with some of the White Russian leaders and organizations in Harbin. After 1937, and certainly after the outbreak of the Pacific War, more Japanese military officials with service exposure in the north assumed positions of leadership in Shanghai. As has already been noted, too, a number of White Russian fascists came down from the north in the late 1930s and early 1940s. The arrival of German propaganda, intelligence, and Gestapo officials could not help but augment that trend. Even a cursory review of *Yudaya kenkyū* (Jewish Research), which had previously displayed a variety of opinions on the Jewish question, shows a steady increase in anti-Semitic themes in its articles during 1941–42.[89]

Still, the question remains of what can be said about the Japanese response, as the controlling power in Shanghai, to the German presence? How much did the Japanese authorities follow German advice or guidance, and was there real trust between the two allies? Most evidence suggests that the Japanese followed their own strict wartime agenda, which was to establish the Greater East Asia Co-Prosperity Sphere (Daitōa Kyōeiken), and would brook no interference from any other authority when it appeared to challenge Japanese security and control.[90] As Bernard Wasserstein has argued, after Pearl Harbor, Japan had no interest in sharing authority in Shanghai, even with its Axis partners.[91] In the Japanese view, occupied China was part of the Co-Prosperity Sphere, and, as such, was, without any reservation whatsoever, Japan's affair. The formal Axis military agreement of January 1942 buttressed this viewpoint.[92]

On the surface, relations between the Japanese and German consular, military, police, and intelligence authorities were most cordial, but behind the scenes, there was a strong undercurrent of resentment of their Axis partners among the Japanese. German racism remained a major obstacle in the Japanese-German relationship. On the local level, the Germans were criticized for being unusually meddlesome in the workings of the Japanese Special Services offices.[93] For example, the Japanese denied Ehrhardt a visa to visit Manchukuo.[94] To some extent, the lack of cooperation and coordination was the result of geographic distance and lack of adequate communications. But as scholarship on the Axis has shown, neither Japan nor Germany was willing to sacrifice its own wartime agenda and immediate military needs for the benefit of the alliance. Rather, the common bond was aggression and maintaining territorial ambitions. These did not foster the development of trust, military cooperation, or the sharing of strategic planning.[95]

Mistrust also arose in part from the Japanese suspicion of any Caucasians, causing them to see liaisons with the Germans as an unavoidable necessity of war. Also, the Richard Sorge spy case caused significant harm to the Japanese-German relationship. Sorge was a respected Far Eastern correspondent for the *Frankfurter Zeitung* in Tokyo and member of the Nazi Party who became a personal advisor and confidant of the German ambassador, Eugen Ott. Sorge's espionage for the Red Army provided the Soviet Union with crucial information about German plans to attack the USSR and, especially, Japanese plans to advance south rather than break the Soviet-Japanese Neutrality Pact (April 1941) and join Germany in its assault on Soviet Russia.[96] According to one report, Sorge was discovered operating a radio transmitter in the company of a Japanese official of Prince Konoe's department.[97] Sorge's actions led to the replacement of Ambassador Ott. Sorge was arrested in October 1941 and admitted his former Comintern and current Red Army connections.[98] After carefully controlled trial proceedings, he was found in violation of the recent Peace Preservation Law by the Justice Ministry, sentenced to death, and hanged on November 7, 1944. The Japanese choice of this date of execution was no accident, for it marked an anniversary of the October Revolution. Colonel Meisinger, who was placed in charge of surveillance of Sorge prior to his arrest, claimed that in the aftermath of the Sorge incident, the atmosphere was fraught with mistrust and he got little cooperation from his Japanese counterparts.[99] Following the trial, the Japanese authorities strengthened their strict surveillance of all foreigners in Japan and of Japanese who had any contact with foreigners.

The German and Japanese propaganda organs in Shanghai worked efficiently, but separately. Also, the Japanese had what was almost a fetish about foreign nationals in occupied territories strictly following their rules and regulations, and they made no exceptions for Germans. A prime example involved a visit to Shanghai in 1942 by Fritz Wiedemann, the German consul in Tianjin, who tried to hold a meeting at the Kaiser Wilhelm School, a center of Nazi activity. Before he could begin his address to a packed house, Japanese officials entered the hall and interrupted the gathering to inquire what the meeting was about and ask whether the required permit for a meeting had been obtained. No permit was produced, and after an angry exchange of words and some alleged pushing of a Japanese officer by Wiedemann, the German consul was escorted away and brought before Japanese authorities. The outcome was that the meeting was canceled and Wiedemann ordered to return to Tianjin.[100] Wiedemann has been credited with saying that the Japanese policies vis-à-vis the Shanghai Jews were the result of strong German pressure. As will be shown, the Japanese authorities, increasingly sensitive to wartime exigencies, instead developed their own independent solution to the perceived "Jewish problem."[101]

SEVEN

Refugee Detention in Wartime Shanghai

> If need be, hire yourself out to flay carcasses in the market place, and say not:
> "I am a priest, a great man, and this thing is detestable to me."
>
> —*The Talmud: Pesahin*

After Pearl Harbor, the Japanese set about an orderly takeover of the sections of Shanghai that had hitherto been outside of their jurisdiction. The status of the French Concession was not an immediate problem, because Japan had recognized Marshal Pétain's Vichy government after the fall of France in June 1940, and, although officially neutral, the Vichy appointees in Shanghai had little recourse but to come to heel. Attempting to preserve a degree of local national pride, they pledged to support the Japanese in all matters where French neutrality and the statutes of the Concession were not opposed.[1]

It only remained, therefore, for the Japanese to establish control over the International Settlement, and this they did gradually, and with the cooperation of the local authorities. Meeting in a special session on the afternoon of December 8, 1941, the Shanghai Municipal Council "unanimously decided to comply with the wishes of the Japanese authorities that the Council should carry on its normal functions for the welfare of the Settlement."[2] They continued to serve for just over one year, or until late January 1943, when the American, British, and Dutch members on the council resigned their posts "at the request of the Japanese authorities."[3] Although the

Japanese refused to allow these former members to continue to serve on the council, they recognized that in the interests of an orderly transition, they would need to retain the services of some enemy nationals, at least temporarily, in government, business, and industry. The new council chairman, Okazaki Kaheida, accordingly instructed British, American, and Dutch personnel, such as those serving on the Finance Committee and in the Public Works Department, for example, that they were expected to continue their work.[4] In the meantime, Allied nationals, including Americans, British, Belgian, and Dutch citizens, were required to register with the Kempeitai at its headquarters at Hamilton House, reporting on their financial worth, debts, real estate, and movable goods.

Japanese Control Measures

Order and stability were the primary concerns of the Japanese in consolidating their control. As an initial step, a census was ordered in the French Concession. Family heads, industrial sites, and workplaces had to register their members and workers with the police, who in turn provided declaration cards, which were to be kept on hand at all times.[5] In addition, foreign residents were to register with the police and receive a photo identification card, which they were told might be needed for the likely future rationing of essential goods. To make clear their status, enemy nationals' cards had an unmistakable red border. The foreign registration was to be accomplished by July 20, 1942, with exceptions made for German, Italian, Portuguese, and Swiss nationals.

The next step was to impose the *baojia* system in both the International Settlement and the French Concession. The basis of this method of control, deriving from a traditional Chinese system dating back to the eleventh century, was the principle of public order based on mutual responsibility. During the Occupation, the *baojia* system became an effective Japanese wartime control measure designed to prevent or contain any expression of anti-Japanese sentiment and anti-Japanese activities. It was based on close collaboration between residents and the police. Households were organized into units called *jia*, which in turn constituted a larger unit, the *bao*. The *bao* corresponded to a police district and was required to maintain constant liaison with the police. *Baojia* heads kept censuses of their areas, with complete information on individuals and their families, and *jia* heads were responsible for the preservation of law and order within the *jia* unit under their direction. Males between the ages of twenty and forty-five were to be further organized into a Civilian Vigilance Corps, which was to assist and cooperate closely with the police and the Defense Corps on duty in the vicinity. Failure of a *jia* head to report anti-Japanese actions, criminal activity, or civil disturbances could bring collective punishment to those within his jurisdiction.[6] By late 1942, once the *baojia* system had begun to function south of Suzhou Creek, suggestions began to circulate for "the gradual development and expansion of the system to the area north of the Creek," including the Jewish settlements in Hongkou.[7]

The year 1942 also saw the dissolution of the much-revered Shanghai Volunteer Corps. Its demise was prefaced by the shifting of one of its prime units, the Russian Detachment. The commandant of the SVC had lost out in a power struggle with the commissioner of police over the transfer of the Russian Detachment to become the Russian Auxiliary Department of the Shanghai Municipal Police.[8] With this additional trained manpower, the police could claim to have adequate resources to implement the new and expanding civilian and criminal control measures effectively. Certainly, no one could question the fact that lawlessness and terrorism were rife in the city, and that political assassinations were increasing at an alarming rate. To the foreign community, however, the loss of the Russian unit foreshadowed the demise of the SVC.[9] The fact was that with Britain and the United States at war with Japan, a Western-dominated militia could scarcely continue to exist in Japanese-ruled Shanghai. At a regular meeting of the council on September 2, 1942, the membership, in response to the request from the Japanese consul general on behalf of "various Japanese authorities," decided that there was "no further necessity for retention of the Shanghai Volunteer Corps" and approved its disbandment. When asked to comment, Major Bartley, the SVC's staff officer, replied that he had "nothing to add to what has been said."[10] Corps members received instructions to turn in their uniforms, equipment, and "mobilization schemes," but, as solace, were given permission for the "continued use of the Corps's dining room."[11]

Enemy Nationals Interned

After consolidating their position, the Japanese began interning enemy diplomats and consular personnel. The Americans were the first to be detained and were confined in various hotels until the Swiss consulate could arrange for their departure, on June 29, 1942, aboard the SS *Conte Verdi* to be exchanged at Lourenço Marques (now Maputo), Mozambique, for Japanese coming from similar detention on the Swedish ship *Gripsholm*. British embassy and consular staff were similarly repatriated some months later. Land, buildings, vehicles, houses, and furnishings belonging to British and American families and businesses were put under seal, with notices proclaiming that any interference with them would be dealt with according to Japanese military law. Newspapers and radio stations were also sealed until negotiations could determine the willingness of the management to continue operating under Japanese direction. The stalwart *North China Daily News* had ceased publication on December 7, 1941. Two papers that did continue operating were the American-owned *Shanghai Evening Post and Mercury* and the already Japanese-leaning, but British-owned, *Shanghai Times.*[12]

The next step, after the repatriation of the diplomats, was a September 1942 proclamation requiring that all enemy nationals wear identifying armbands in public. Accordingly, the remaining Americans wore red armbands marked with an "A"; the British had armbands with the letter "B"; and Dutch citizens showed the letter "H" on their armbands. Nationalities falling into the category of protectorates or colonies of the Allies, and thus politically unreliable, wore armbands marked with the letter "X."[13] These also included citizens of countries such as Iran and Iraq, which were not formally at war with Japan. In September 1943, the last group of nationals, citizens of Japan's ex-ally, Italy, which had just surrendered unconditionally to the Allies, donned armbands hastily put together from the dark red velvet window drapes of the Shanghai Italian Club.[14]

In November 1942, the Japanese began the actual process of interning the enemy population, starting with single men, many of them former soldiers or reservists, who were sent to a civic assembly center on Haiphong Road.[15] In early 1943, the internment program began to include the civilian population. The enemy nationals supplied their own beds, bedding, canned goods, flat ware, soap, and other essentials to take with them to "civic assembly camps." They were given just ten days to pack and move to the camps. Bank accounts were frozen, with amounts available for withdrawal commensurate with what Japanese internees in the United States could withdraw on a monthly basis from otherwise frozen accounts established with Japanese banks located in the United States.[16] A subsequent proclamation ordered that all shortwave radios be turned in. Holy Trinity Cathedral became a key assembly point for the first of those having to register before being interned. After registration, the Japanese loaded the internees into trucks to be transported to the several civic assembly centers. Fortunately for them, the camps were supervised by the Japanese consular police, under the authority of the Japanese consulate, rather than by military personnel. In addition, the International Red Cross was able to deliver packages, and the internees often found other ways to get supplies into the camps too.

There were at least seven camps in the Shanghai area, with most American families housed in abandoned buildings of the Great China University in Zhabei, while single American men were taken to the Pudong camp, an old British-American Tobacco Company warehouse.[17] Laura Margolis of the AJJDC was interned at the Zhabei camp, and later remarked that she had come to China to help refugees but found herself "a refugee, standing in line for meals, spending my time between despair and hope and the hard work that brings temporary forgetfulness."[18] Morale at the Pudong camp benefited from an active program of lectures and language study. Three camps were established at Yangzhou (Yangchow), a walled town on the Grand Canal two hundred miles from Shanghai. Other camps in Shanghai included the Longhua (Lunghwa) camp and the Columbia Country Club camp, housing British families and some American missionaries.[19] Reportedly, the Longhua and Columbia Country Club camps were the best equipped of the internment camps. The former Shanghai Municipal Council and police staffs were housed at a former boys' school on Yu Yuen Road and at the Ash Camp, a former barracks for British troops, on Great Western Road. Another camp, on Lincoln Avenue, housed mainly the elderly. The very old, infirm, and sick were excused from internment, which probably explains why the American former chairman of the Shanghai Municipal Council Stirling Fessenden, "Lord Mayor of Shanghai," was able to spend his remaining months in a Chinese boarding house, where he is said to have died in the arms of his beloved Russian mistress.[20] The internment process, begun in earnest in January 1943, and affecting about 8,000 Allied nationals, was completed by late summer of that year.[21]

The Proclamation of February 18, 1943

With enemy nationals counted, registered, and either interned, scheduled for internment, or excused, the Japanese could turn their attention to the large refugee community, consisting chiefly of Jews who had fled Nazi Europe. In November 1941, the Third Reich had passed laws stripping Jews living abroad of their nationality, which took effect in January 1942, leaving the Shanghai Jews stateless. In the circumstances, noncooperation with the Japanese was not an option, and Jewish leaders strove to build a workable relationship with them for the protection of their community.

After Captain Inuzuka's departure, the Japanese Office of Stateless Refugee Affairs was headed by Navy Captain Kubota Tsutomu, who thus had the task of dealing with the Jews. Kubota's presence was reported at a major ceremonial event held in November 1942 to inaugurate the new communal steam kitchen for refugees at the East Seward camp in Hongkou. Laura Margolis had done much persuading and wire-pulling to acquire two steam boilers from the Sassoon company to improve the new kitchen's efficiency in meeting the increasing demand for refugee meals. In addition to Kubota and the chairmen of the key Jewish organizations, including prominent Russian Jews, a representative of the Imperial Japanese Navy named Sekiya attended the event. Kubota addressed the group, expressing gratitude for the well-organized support for Jewish charity organizations. He explained that with the demands of the war effort, the Japanese government could not provide the charitable funds for refugee projects that it otherwise might have done. The event ended with an auction of the key to the new kitchen. It was purchased for $5,000 by I. Kahan, a Latvian Jew. Kubota was invited to use the ceremonial key to open the new kitchen's door. In addition, fourteen large black kettles were auctioned off, one with a nameplate bearing Kubota's name and one for Sekiya.[22]

Despite all this calculated goodwill, the fate of the stateless refugees became the subject of a March 11, 1942, draft decision of another top-level Japanese ministerial liaison conference concerning measures to be taken regarding the Jews under the existing wartime conditions.[23] The substance of the new measures represented a clear change in policy, and one that canceled the "friendly" approach to the Jews emanating from the December 6, 1938, five ministers' conference. That earlier policy, based on Japanese hopes of using perceived Jewish connections and wealth to improve worsening relations with the United States and Great Britain, and to court the introduction of foreign capital into China that would aid Japan's co-prosperity agenda, had failed. The inability of Japanese officials such as Captain Inuzuka to realize those objectives prompted a turn in policy. With the Pacific War now raging, the earlier measures had lost their relevance.

Owing to their "special ethnic characteristics" (*minzoku-teki tokusei*), it was observed, the Jews required careful supervision in order to avoid disturbances in the areas where they were administered by the Japanese.[24] This anti-Semitic tone, which seemed to echo German rhetoric, was softened somewhat by the statement that the Jews, having been made stateless by Germany, were considered similar in status to the stateless White Russians. Both of these communities were to be kept under appropriate surveillance. Being stateless, Tokyo reasoned, the Jews lacked government protection and were liable to strict supervision. Their statelessness also shielded the Japanese authorities from any foreign criticism of their treatment.[25]

An interagency committee consisting of representatives of the Japanese Army, Navy, Kempeitai, Shanghai Municipal Council, and Special Municipal Government, working in consultation with the Japanese embassy in Nanjing, was established to implement the new policy. The plan decided on was to move the approximately 20,000 stateless German and European Jews into the Yangshupu area north of Suzhou Creek, making it a special district for the Jews, with surveillance and control of them as the goals.[26] The Japanese military would supervise this community.[27]

The end result of this meeting and planning was a proclamation by the Imperial Japanese Army and Navy on February 18, 1943, ordering the removal of stateless refugees to a "designated area" (*shitei chiku*). The Japanese maintained that their action was not arbitrary but "due to military necessity."[28] It was meant "to safeguard so far as possible [the stateless refugees'] place of residence as well as their livelihood in the designated area."

The Japanese proclaimed their unwillingness to follow the German lead in persecuting the Jews or rejecting them in a wholesale manner, a stance

that they stressed would be contrary to Japan's official policy of "eight cor-
ners of the world all under one roof" (*hakkō ichiu*). Their policy was, instead,
to treat the Jews as stateless, but to keep them under close observation.[29]
This "all under one roof" policy was intended as a useful propaganda initiative. It suggested that Japan viewed the various nationalities under its jurisdiction as members of a large harmonious family. The unspoken clause was
that this family was to be headed and strictly controlled by Japan. By these
veiled measures, the Japanese hoped to avoid the criticism and adverse propaganda that they believed the Allied countries could effectively employ
against them if they took more stringent measures against the Jews.[30]

As defined in the proclamation, the term "stateless refugees" applied "to
those refugees who have arrived in Shanghai since 1937 from Germany (including former Austria and Czechoslovakia), Hungary, former Poland, Latvia, Lithuania, Estonia, etc., who have no nationality at present." Nowhere
in the proclamation itself does the term "Jew" appear, but its impact clearly
affected, and was meant to affect, mainly European Jews.

In meticulous style, the document stated very specifically where the
refugees would be relocated. The Shitei chiku included the area of the
International Settlement "east of the line connecting Chaoufoong Road,
Muirhead Road, and Dent Road, West of Yangtsepoo Creek, North of the
line connecting East Seward Road, Muirhead Road and Wayside Road; and
South of the [northern] boundary of the International Settlement." The total
area has been measured as being about half a mile in length and three-quar-
ters of a mile wide, a tiny area when one considers that it was to accommodate 20,000 Jews, plus the Chinese and Japanese already there who managed
to evade relocation.[31] In addition, the document encouraged Japanese living
in the Shitei chiku to settle elsewhere in order to make room for the wave of
incoming refugees. To be sure, many Japanese residents eagerly exchanged
their modest or rundown homes for better-appointed ones owned by stateless refugees, usually on terms that heavily favored the Japanese parties.

Stateless refugees living outside the designated area were ordered to move
into the Shitei chiku by May 18, 1943. Most had to sell their property for less
than its value to meet the deadline. In addition, any affected stateless
refugees had to receive permission from the Japanese for the sale, lease, or
purchase of property or establishments outside this area before making a
move. At first, stateless Russians believed that they, too, would be required

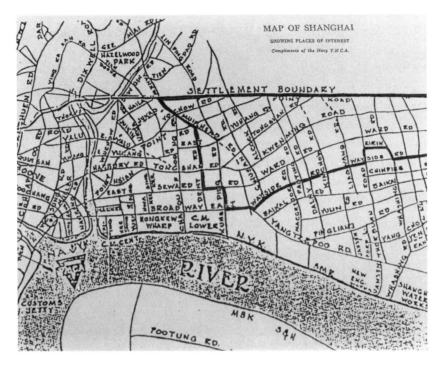

Map 2. Section of a Shanghai map showing the Hongkou and Yangshupu districts. The parameters of the Shitei chiku ("designated area"), or ghetto, are heavily outlined. SOURCE: Courtesy of Mrs. Robert Bryan.

to move north of Suzhou Creek. Some purchased houses in the new area in preparation for moving. These they later rented out to the "bona fide refugees" when it became clear that, although stateless, most of the Russians would not have to move, because they had arrived in Shanghai long before 1937. Many Russians worked in the Japanese-controlled police forces, and thus could help with the smooth transfer of stateless Jewish refugees, making them useful partners to the Japanese. The neutrality pact signed by Japan and the USSR in April 1941 may also have influenced the Japanese decision to exclude the Shanghai Russians, at least some of whom were pro-Soviet.

It is important to note that the large Russian Jewish community was not affected by the proclamation either, having also arrived before the prescribed date. Moreover, it appeared that the Japanese authorities were hesitant about the impact of the proclamation on the stability of the Shanghai multinational community, especially its established members, and may have been interested in distancing themselves from any overt anti-Semitic overtones of the proclamation by locating such sentiments firmly with the authorities in Nanjing. Just three days before publishing the proclamation, the pro-Japanese *Shanghai Times* carried a strongly anti-Semitic article written by Tang Liangli, an official of the Wang Jingwei regime. Both Wang and Tang had spent time in Nazi Germany in the 1930s, with Wang making an extended stay in 1936. They had both expressed admiration for National Socialism's advocacy of a strong nation and dictatorial government that would integrate economic development with national goals. To them and other Guomindang leaders, this emphasis on order and control was a recipe for regaining China's strength.

What matters here is that the Japanese saw Nazi anti-Semitism resonating with these Chinese leaders.[32] Tang quoted briefly in the *Shanghai Times* article from an anti-Semitic speech given by Wang Jingwei, who likened the Jews to anarchists and communists, who "take special pride in their condemnation of all things traditionally dear to China." The article went on to give a negative history of the Jewish presence in China, pointing to Jewish involvement over the years in opium dealings, yellow journalism, black market activity, and counterfeiting. The article concluded by stressing the urgent problem of "keeping Shanghai out of Jewish clutches, and keeping the financial activities in accord with the well being of the community."[33] In contrast, other reporting in this Japanese mouthpiece immediately following publication of the proclamation, and for months afterward, avoided anti-Semitic themes.

The proclamation was another major step toward bringing the civilian population of Shanghai under Japanese control, a process begun in 1937, when a Chinese government under Japanese control was established in the Chinese sections of Shanghai. Moreover, the Hongkou move was not to be the last one planned by the Japanese. The November 1942 report of the ministerial liaison conference mentioned Tokyo's intention, although vaguely stated, to tackle the issue of other Shanghai Jews and of refugees of Russian origin after the transfer of the European Jews was completed.[34] This was hardly necessary, and was never done, for as has been shown, the Russian community, including the Russian Jews and Ukrainians, was already highly responsive to Japanese direction.

Given the 1937 cutoff date, European Jews were in any case the largest group obliged to move, in that most of them had come to Shanghai from 1939 on. Of course, a great many Jewish refugees already lived in Hongkou, where the refugee camps were located. The combined population in the Hongkou camps in February 1943 included 1,729 men, 743 women, and 292 children.[35] The Japanese consular police reported that altogether 7,216 stateless Jewish refugees were already residing in the Shitei chiku.[36] For those who did not live there, the experience of having to move into crowded, dilapidated neighborhoods where the market for their businesses and enterprises was far inferior to that in areas outside was nothing short of horrific. The organization in charge of overseeing the transfer issued 6,299 permits to those moving into the area; another 1,163 moved in by July, and about 617 received approval from the authorities for extensions on the time limit for moving. Others reportedly had filed application forms with the authorities to make the move, but had not yet done so. The police reported that 617 still lived outside, but would be brought in, and noted that an unidentified number had resisted the move, and that "military discipline" would be applied to force them to move.[37] In desperation, a few Jewish refugees, especially those with established businesses outside, paid large sums of money to willing police officials to have the date of their arrival in Shanghai changed to an earlier year on their official papers.[38] Others were forced to join a community that would be severely challenged during the coming years just to survive.

The Polish Jews Resist

The term "ghetto" — in the sense of a quarter to which Jewish residence was restricted — can reasonably be used to describe the Shitei chiku in Shanghai. There were, for example, signs reading: "Stateless refugees are prohibited from passing here without permission." There was, however, no use of barbed wire to surround the area or of weapons to force submission. Moreover, the assigned area also included large populations of Japanese and Chinese, who became the Jews' neighbors. Likewise, the proclamation did not refer specifically to Jews, and Russian Jews were excepted. The Shitei chiku thus did not in any meaningful way resemble the ghettos of World War II Europe. Contrast this description of the Warsaw Ghetto in August 1942:

The entire Ghetto lives in the atmosphere of nervous strain, unimaginable horror and helpless despair, and as a result there are ever more frequent cases of insanity and suicide. Parents are known to have poisoned their children and children have poisoned their parents to save them from torture. Here and there people assisted actively. Barricades were erected inside buildings; and in certain cities, in Nieswiez for instance, armed resistance took place. These scattered cases, however, remained sporadic and rare, as the populations were being liquidated.[39]

Such was the extreme. In Shanghai, the ghetto populations did not fear for their lives on a daily basis. While some might be reduced to wearing clothing tailored out of bedsheets, or to accepting donated secondhand clothing, no one faced starvation or annihilation. Certainly, there were serious wartime shortages of many kinds and clear evidence of malnutrition. Anguish over the difficult circumstances was widespread, causing a few of the most troubled refugees to resort to suicide.[40] There was little to compare with the condition of the tens of thousands of wartime Chinese refugees crowded into makeshift housing or living on public streets or alleyways without adequate food or water. The solution the Japanese adopted to deal with this Chinese refugee problem, which they saw as putting too much pressure on urban resources, was to return the refugees to the often war-torn countryside.[41]

The Polish refugees who were being relocated, most of them the yeshiva rabbis and students, believed that they had good reason to resist the forced move to the ghetto. They argued fervently that they were not, in fact, stateless, there being an internationally recognized Polish government in exile in London.[42] The Polish embassy in Tokyo, under Ambassador Tadeusz Romer, had moreover established a Committee of Relief for Polish Citizens, with a counterpart organization in Shanghai, the Polish Aid Society.[43] When, following the pattern established by its Axis allies, Tokyo declared the Polish state nonexistent and ordered Poland's Tokyo embassy closed in the summer of 1941, its staff evacuated to Shanghai, from where they were able to proceed to Lourenço Marques on a neutral vessel. Before leaving, however, Romer set up a body called the Polish Consular Commission to represent the Polish government in exile.[44] Polish Jewish leaders petitioned the Polish Consular Commission for exemption from transfer to the ghetto, but neither these petitions nor those to the Polish Union bore fruit, and the Polish Jews felt betrayed by this lack of support from the largely gentile Shanghai Polish authorities.[45]

Poles in Shanghai occupied a curious status. The Nazis had established a new government in Poland, completely subordinate, of course, to German authorities. Therefore, Poles associated with the old Polish state who had arrived in Shanghai before 1937 might have been candidates for internment along with Allied nationals. After all, Japanese acceptance of the new German government in Poland had precipitated the evacuation of the Polish embassy from Tokyo and of Polish officials from Shanghai in 1941. So in their current status, Poles as a group were anti-Axis, but not really enemy nationals, because in Japanese circles, they were considered stateless. Taking that view, the Japanese grouped the pre-1937 Polish refugees together with the Russians and other Slavs who had arrived before 1937, who also were not made subject to internment. Thus, the pre-1937 Polish residents, including the Jewish refugees among them, escaped being moved into the ghetto and, very important, avoided having to sell their valuable properties.[46] Instead, by reason of their relative freedom, they and the Russians and Russian Jews became a valuable resource for aid and relief to those forced into the Hongkou ghetto.

There was some flexibility to the Japanese position, however. The rabbis and yeshiva students were granted repeated extensions on their move into the ghetto until such time as they could find suitable homes to rent there. This did not happen until 1944.[47] Still, of all the refugee groups, the Polish Jews put up the most resistance to the relocation. When the yeshiva students first heard that they were to be settled in the Salvation Army Shelter at 630 Muirhead Road in Hongkou, a hundred of them protested forcefully at the offices of A. Oppenheim, head of EASTJEWCOM. Order was restored only after Japanese authorities arrived at the scene.[48] Other Polish refugees who were determined to resist demanded internment as prisoners of war, or even preferred jail to moving into the ghetto. A few did go to jail, and, contracting typhus there, died because of their opposition to the move.

Their defiant attitude did not endear them to the Japanese, the Russians, or even the German-Austrian refugees, all of whom expected at least a peaceful transition. In fairness, the elite Polish Jews especially, who had come late to Shanghai and were very devout, chose not to become involved in the daily workings of the Jewish organizations and their relations with the Japanese authorities. This aloofness made them ill suited to handling their situation. Many of them continued to display an independent and superior attitude toward the various officials, relying as they often did on international organizations and Russian Jews for aid and assistance. Also, their prevailing sense of the impermanence of their stay in Shanghai contributed to their lack of connection with Shanghai politics and institutions.

The Shanghai Ashkenazi Collaborating Relief Association, or SACRA, played a role in the relocation of all of the post-1937 stateless refugees. Heavily staffed by the still free Russian Jews, SACRA worked under the direction of Kubota and his Office of Stateless Refugee Affairs, which was charged with the successful and orderly establishment of the Shitei chiku for stateless refugees in Hongkou. Together, they formed a joint administrative committee. The principal relief body, the Jüdische Gemeinde, was made subordinate to SACRA, and both were to function under the leadership of Dr. Jan Abraham Jacob Cohn, who was uniquely qualified for his post, having received his early education and medical training in Japan. Cohn, who spoke fluent Japanese, is often described as having been quite Japanese in outlook, which made him suspect in the Jewish community but highly acceptable to the Japanese.[49]

One of the first actions taken by SACRA was to dismiss the leadership of the Jüdische Gemeinde and provide a new slate of leaders from professional circles to serve as executives for this body. An article in the official *Shanghai Jewish Chronicle* proclaimed that "the reconstituted organization now represents all professional groups in the refugee community. With the introduction of a commissariat leadership, it can now be said that the motto 'Concentration of all Powers' has found its true realization."[50] The new chairman, L. M. Rogovin, a Russian, was chairman of CENTREJEWCOM. Most of the other leaders came from leading positions in the Kitchen Fund.[51] Once again, indirectly, of course, the Japanese had created a pliable and manageable official body.

Finding adequate housing was a major problem faced by SACRA. To assist in the refugee transfer, SACRA kept a list of all Japanese residing in the Shitei chiku who were willing to exchange their often less well appointed residences for those of relocated refugees. These exchanges raised many legal issues, involving removals, transfers, changes of leases, and so on, to be managed through the Stateless Refugees Affairs Office and Jewish Arbitration Court. A common problem was the practice of charging refugees exorbitant prices for ghetto real estate.[52] SACRA also purchased or renovated housing for use by incoming refugees. Two buildings that became available and required extensive renovation were a Salvation Army compound and a Chinese school. Making the necessary repairs often required extensions on the deadline for relocations. Professionals such as doctors, nurses, and teachers received extensions owing to their special circumstances.[53] Also excused were those with special skills that might benefit the Japanese military or corps of engineers, such as construction, bridge-building, or industrial experience. The sick and their caretakers sometimes received exemptions. Finally, permission for extensions might be granted to those who made additional contributions to the refugee relief fund, but with the qualification that they should prepare eventually for removal to the Shitei chiku.[54] Altogether, the Japanese granted 529 people exemptions during 1943.[55]

Inside the Shitei chiku

Kubota described the Shitei chiku as "neither a ghetto nor jail, but an area which is full of hope for the refugees and in which they may build a haven for themselves where they can carry on peacefully and with great advantage to themselves."[56] But just in case not everyone shared these views, the Japanese instituted a variety of controls over the Jewish population of the Hongkou ghetto. Of course, there was the initial requirement of filling out registration forms. But the control procedure that was considered the most onerous was the need for a pass in order to go outside the ghetto area. After August 10, 1943, all exits from the ghetto required a pass.[57] The seemingly innocuous task of obtaining a pass was made terrifying to some by the Japanese official who controlled the passes, a man named Ghoya, who has been described as in all likelihood mentally unbalanced. He called himself "King of the Jews" and took delight in intimidating applicants for passes with shouts, slaps to their faces and bodies, and, perhaps worst of all, by refusing time and again to grant some people's requests, thus requiring them to experience the humiliation of his behavior over and again.[58] It was impossible to predict his moods or reactions, which made the application process all the more frightening. Only children or young people seem to have had an easier time with him. Ghoya was backed up by another Japanese official, Okura, who was believed to be even more sadistic. These were the two main contacts that most Hongkou Jews had with the Japanese authorities, who otherwise remained aloof.

Passes were mainly granted for work outside the ghetto or to attend school. Those who received one had to wear a blue badge bearing the Chinese characters for the word "to pass." Jewish sensitivity over having to wear such identification brought a response from Kubota, who in an article published in the *Shanghai Jewish Chronicle* stressed that wearing such insignia outside of the Shitei chiku was not to be construed as discrimination or of a racial nature.[59] The refugee passes indicated the destination to be reached and the length of time permitted under the conditions of the curfew. Also, passes came in different colors, indicating the length of time for which they were valid. A blue pass had to be renewed every three months; a red pass, monthly.[60] Those who received the "special passes" (*Sonderpässen*) issued for extended periods of time learned of their good fortune by the publication of successful pass numbers printed daily in the German-language *Shanghai Jewish Chronicle*.[61] And because these passes required more investigative work, the Stateless Refugee Affairs Office came to rely upon SACRA to vouch for the reliability of their holders.[62]

Most pass holders had to cross Suzhou Creek by means of the Garden Bridge to reach their place of work or other approved destinations, and to do so required passing the Japanese sentries stationed on the bridge. Jews generally found the crossing uneventful. In contrast, Chinese bridge crossers had to give a respectful bow to the Japanese sentry on duty. It was common for Chinese passersby to be beaten severely by the sentry for the slightest misstep, or even for no reason at all.

Another control measure imposed on the Hongkou Jewish ghetto was the institution of the *baojia* system. Japanese wartime policy was to make as much use as possible of the local population in order to control and govern, and this system of mutual responsibility and accountability served that purpose well. Jewish overseers were appointed in the ghetto to keep order in specified areas, just as their counterparts did elsewhere in Shanghai and even within the foreign internment camps. *Baojia* leaders patrolled the borders of the Shitei chiku and checked the passes of those crossing. Not infrequently, Jewish refugees complained that these *baojia* heads took their responsibilities too seriously. They might report infractions of the pass system, such as surreptitious trips outside the ghetto, or even a late arrival back, bringing pun-

Figure 24. A Jewish *baojia* unit charged with maintaining order and enforcing Japanese regulations in the Hongkou ghetto community. SOURCE: United States Holocaust Memorial Museum.

ishment and hardship to the individuals involved. However, under the *baojia* system, if the Japanese authorities caught someone breaking the rules, the responsible unit chief who had failed to report the infraction was equally punished. The system thus bred close supervision and created tensions among the refugees.

Additional *baojia* duties involved promoting good conduct, enforcing the wartime blackout regulations in the ghetto, and participating in emergency rescue missions. As Head of the Office of Stateless Refugee Affairs, Kubota awarded four Jewish *baojia* members with certificates at a ceremony at the Ward Road camp for their courageous rescue of several Chinese during a typhoon.[63] These broad duties existed apart from an air defense system under which the whole Shitei chiku was divided into subdistricts, with the refugee inhabitants organized into these units. Within this configuration, each camp counted as a complete district. Servicing these subdivisions were various troops, including an alarm troop, fire brigade troop, security troop, medical troop, and so on. As air raids became more frequent, the appointed air "guards" acquired a sense of self-importance as members of this little "army" within the ghetto enclave, even though their duties were purely civilian in nature and geared toward safeguarding life and responding to emergencies in the event of an attack.[64] In contrast, the ghetto population became increasingly casual about the raids, causing the Japanese Army Air Raid Protection Command to issue proclamations warning that the refugees should take the raids and drills seriously and follow orders.[65]

All populations in Shanghai, free or not, lived under broad wartime restrictions, which included press censorship, dissemination of news only from official sources, and prohibitions on spreading rumors and participating in political activities. Obviously, anti-Japanese activity or criticism of Japanese authorities would not be permitted. No large public gathering could take place without police permission. For the most part, these restrictions, aside from the need for passes to leave the ghetto, did not seriously affect the general Jewish population in Hongkou. These Jews were recent arrivals in Shanghai and were heavily preoccupied with finding employment and surviving. And because so many viewed Shanghai as a temporary home in which to wait out the war, they did not aspire to become deeply involved in local affairs or feel the need to protect some role in the local establishment. This raises the question of what kind of life and community they did succeed in building during this period in their diaspora.

Struggles to Survive

Funds from the American Jewish Joint Distribution Committee were not forthcoming from spring 1943 until summer 1944, placing a heavy burden on local relief organizations and the local Jewish community.[66] In addition, wartime shortages led to the rationing of vital goods and foods such as cotton cloth, cooking oil, bread, rice, flour, and sugar, which in turn led to a flourishing black market in such items. With rampant inflation so prevalent during these years, it was common for households to hoard essential foods until the price rose and then unload them on the black market for a profit. Articles such as paper, leather, and soap in particular gained in value as the currency plummeted. From 1942 until August 1945, Shanghai prices increased at an average rate of 26 percent per month.[67] According to a Shanghai resident, in July–August 1943, a cake of laundry soap cost about $30; sugar, $60 a pound. In June 1944, a loaf of bread cost $24, but this increased to $530 in 1945 and to $3,700 by August that year.[68]

The practice of hoarding was not limited to hard-pressed Jewish households, but occurred throughout the city and was the subject of many Japanese proclamations and published warnings. Under such strained conditions, Japanese threats had little effect. Notices even appeared in the local newspapers offering to do the buying for those engaged in hoarding.[69] The Japanese authorities were not wholly insensitive to the plight of the Hongkou Jews living under such inflationary conditions, as is evidenced by the Kempeitai of Yangshupu Station, which made a notable attempt to lighten the refugee burden by contributing $10,000 to the Jewish Kitchen Fund in November 1943.[70]

A more lucrative aspect of the black market involved exchanges of currency such as U.S. dollars or gold bullion. Throughout the war, there was active circulation in the ghetto of U.S. dollars, which were the store of value in Shanghai currencies and had been in good supply. The U.S. dollar became the currency used for savings and by exchanging $10 at a time, perhaps U.S.$30–40.00 a month, one could get along quite well. Of course, these exchanges were not made openly, but in houses or in secluded alleys or doorways.[71] Chinese paid more for U.S. dollars that were new, clean, and crisp, so Jews with dollars to exchange took to laundering the money, literally washing, ironing, and applying a little starch to the bills to appeal to buyers.[72]

Many refugees with valuables or properties to sell made sure they were paid in gold bullion, the parallel store of value to the U.S. dollar, and adamantly refused payment in the constantly devalued local currency. As the Shanghai currency continued its downward spiral, an active market emerged in buying gold bars as a hedge against inflation, but given the poverty of most Jews in Hongkou, this was not, of course, as common as hoarding.

In addition to being illegal and dangerous, gold deals could be complicated and troublesome, so wealthy Shanghaiese hired Jewish middlemen or brokers whom they knew and trusted to handle them. It was essential that every deal be aboveboard, because as a refugee, a Jewish broker might easily be suspected of taking a cut or holding back some of the gold. This would mean the end of his trusted relationship with his patrons (many of them prosperous Russian Jews) and hence of his livelihood.

The story is told about a young refugee broker sent on an errand by a wealthy Russian Jew to an exchange shop to pick up a 10 oz. gold bar and six small gold bars, the equivalent of U.S.$14,000. The gold was in payment for the sale of the Russian's LaSalle automobile and other goods. Having received the gold, the young man returned in a waiting pedicab, which happened to belong to a Japanese-owned chain of pedicabs. It rained during his ride, and the larger gold bar slipped out of his shorts pocket en route. When he realized his predicament, after arriving home, his greatest fear was the anticipated comment from his patron and his friends, "Well, he is a refugee, maybe he took that bar." But, fortunately for him, the rickshaw driver had an even greater fear. Upon finding the gold bar while cleaning out the pedicab, he was sure the Japanese rickshaw owner would suspect him of stealing the gold and severely punish or even kill him. Acting on the advice of the chief of the rickshaw drivers, and after making several inquiries, the rickshaw driver was finally able to locate the young broker and safely return the gold bar.[73]

Jewish families having to make that additional step downward by moving into the ghetto area experienced new hardships. Few employers wanted to hire workers who had to wait in line to receive only temporary passes.[74] In addition, living conditions were far less desirable in the Shitei chiku, which was crowded and dirty, and food was in short supply there. Added to these privations were the nightly air raid drills, usually lasting two hours until the "all clear" sounded. A typical routine involved scrambling out of bed, racing for a downstairs closet or enclosed area and placing a wash basin over one's head and a mattress or protective blanket around the body. For some, the Ward Road Jail became a regular bomb shelter. The Hongkou area was not hit until late in the war, but there was always the fear that it would be, as well as the knowledge that the outskirts had been hit.

The numbers of refugees taking advantage of soup kitchen meals, meager and unappetizing though they were, increased during 1943. The Japanese reported that 4,888 refugees received meals from the Kitchen Fund, 2,105 of whom came from the camps. As conditions worsened, an additional 3,500 refugees received one meal a day from these relief services.[75] In addition, the Kitchen Fund made bread tickets available to some residents in the camps. By late February 1943, 2,243 persons had received such bread tickets.[76] Standing in the soup line displayed one's poverty, so in order to preserve

Figure 25. Jewish refugees selling their goods from stalls in the Hongkou ghetto. SOURCE: YIVO Institute for Jewish Research.

their dignity, some families paid a small sum to other refugees to receive and deliver the meals to them.[77] Jewish refugees with their gifts and belongings displayed for sale on tables were another common sight in Hongkou.

Malnutrition, congestion, cold winters without adequate heating, and hot, humid summers made for greater susceptibility to diseases. There were cases of typhus, malaria, scarlet fever, and smallpox, but thanks to the presence of good refugee doctors, these outbreaks remained limited and controlled, unlike in Chinese refugee camps, where thousands died of these diseases unattended. Those without adequate warm clothing during the cold, damp winters resorted to stuffing newspapers in their clothing. An organization of Quakers in Shanghai was able to make some clothing available to the refugees.

Those who could not stand the strains of ghetto life and wartime shortages sometimes resorted to drinking and gambling. Their further impoverishment as a result reduced some family members to begging on the street. Pride in the reputation of the community and concern for the family's well-being led the Welfare Department of the Jüdische Gemeinde to try to meet the problem by issuing "beggar tickets." These tickets, of different denominations, were bought by persons willing to provide support to desperate individuals, but anxious to know that proper use would be made of their gift. The plan called for the tickets to be exchanged at the Welfare Department for purchase vouchers good for food at certain Jewish-owned stores and groceries.[78]

The most tragic circumstances among Hongkou Jewish households involved prostitution and even the sale of newborn babies. As already discussed, White Russian women in large numbers found themselves reduced to working as bar girls, taxi dancers, and masseuses, which frequently involved prostitution. The same conditions were not unheard of among the Hongkou Jews, who, like many of the Russians, had very limited employment opportunities.[79] Jewish bar girls, some of them housewives, were required to encourage patrons to drink heavily before taking them upstairs for sex. Some refugee husbands had to leave their homes so that their wives could spend half an hour entertaining male guests, usually Japanese.[80]

Still, there were many examples of remarkable perseverance and gumption among the Hongkou refugees, especially among the youth. Operating out of a suitcase, which he transported by bicycle, one teenager sold German sausages, mainly to nonrefugee German customers.[81] Another youth found temporary work cleaning houses and selling newspapers. He had to give up a good permanent job as an apprentice at a German bakery because the work required him to report at 3:00 A.M., which meant he had to sleep during the day if he were to sleep at all. Living in a camp with fifty people to a room made it impossible to sleep during the day, and after one sleepless week, he was forced to quit. As a sideline, he bought "Palace" and "Ruby Queen" brand cigarettes from Chinese vendors, which he then sold by the pack or piece.[82]

Good fortune in the job market came and went as conditions constantly changed. A well-paying job in a Japanese-commandeered American leather factory, producing wartime goods such as belts, rucksacks, and saddles, was lost to cutbacks and downsizing, obliging Horst Wartenberger to accept back-breaking employment in a Chinese factory that produced coal briquets. Everywhere, electricity had to be conserved, and sometimes there was none, because manufacturing took priority. Electricity was generated by burning coal, and making coal briquets from coal dust took hard labor. After a ten-hour day, "when we came home from work at night, we sometimes felt we wouldn't live to see the next day," Wartenberger recalled.[83]

The Ghetto as an Economic Base

Both Kubota of the Office of Stateless Refugee Affairs and Dr. Cohn of SACRA repeatedly advocated the potential economic benefits of the Shitei chiku for the Jewish community. As Parks Coble has noted, the economy of Shanghai became increasingly important to the Japanese forces in China, and in December 1942, with its military needs in mind, Tokyo formulated a new policy aimed at reviving the Chinese economy.[84] Inasmuch as the Shitei chiku lay in the heart of Hongkou and Yangshupu, which were rich in shipping and industry, Kubota and Cohn pressed refugee leaders to promote whatever economic activity they could inside the ghetto. Addressing a meeting at the White Horse Café attended by key representatives of the economics department of the Jüdische Gemeinde, Kubota stressed the need for refugees to move their businesses inside the Shitei chiku in accordance with the February proclamation. He promised to contact the municipal authorities and make a strong case for easing the delivery of raw materials to businesses inside the Shitei chiku. Kubota maintained that Jewish businessmen should not fear the loss of business because of the recent restrictions, but rather see the situation as an economic opportunity, in that more people moving into the Shitei chiku meant more customers.[85] What he overlooked in his analysis, of course, was the fact that the incoming and potential customers had little money to spend compared with their old customers in the former French Concession and International Settlement. Furthermore, Kubota announced the availability of 400–500 jobs in Japanese and Chinese firms, which he claimed could be filled by refugees. Jüdische Gemeinde officials added that in order to help prepare refugees to become a trained workforce, courses in economics, history, technical subjects, and art were being offered at the Gemeinde's Wilhelm Teichner House at 609 Dal'ny Road.[86]

On the contentious issue of the exit passes, Kubota told the *Shanghai Jewish Chronicle* that, ideally, passes would be issued to everyone, but that the intention of the system was not to issue passes so that people could go about their private business. Rather, the system was intended to encourage productive activities inside the Shitei chiku and make it an economic and cultural base. This kind of activity would have the larger purpose, according to Kubota, of contributing to the common welfare within the Greater East Asia Co-Prosperity Sphere. By August 1943, Kubota noted, 3,000 long-term and

700 short-term passes had already been issued, with 2,000 applications still pending. In the future, he predicted, further limits on issuing passes could be expected. Stressing that the refugees should not depend too heavily on outside help, Kubota encouraged them to heed the old bromide "Hilf dir selbst, so hilft dir Gott" (God helps those who help themselves).[87]

Kubota's general remarks reflected the even more ambitious plans for the Shitei chiku that Dr. Cohn had explained in an earlier interview with the *Shanghai Jewish Chronicle*. Cohn exhorted the Jewish business community to create more industrial enterprises in the Shitei chiku and encouraged them to contact and draw upon resources from both Japanese and Chinese financiers to establish private and semi-private enterprises. He promised support from SACRA in obtaining the necessary licenses and in keeping up the pressure on the Japanese authorities to procure the necessary equipment and raw materials. In addition, Cohn encouraged factories and other Jewish businesses to sell their wares outside the Shitei chiku and to solicit orders to further develop their enterprises. Cohn promised that SACRA leaders would provide the support necessary to obtain the loans and establish the partnerships for realizing these plans. He underlined the importance of soliciting Chinese and Japanese capital.[88]

When asked during the interview by someone concerned about the food shortages whether it was feasible to farm inside the Shitei chiku, Cohn responded by stressing that an acre of land put to industrial purposes was worth ten times as much as an acre of land under cultivation. Carrying his point to rather extreme lengths, Cohn even suggested that the Shitei chiku become a "small Manchester" in China. In his closing remarks, Cohn stressed Kubota's goodwill toward the refugees and counseled that "the authorities will cooperate with us if we cooperate with them."[89]

Preserving Jewish Traditions

What made for the community's survival and even its prosperity in some respects during the difficult ghetto period was the fact that if one followed the rules set by the Japanese, one could live freely, in the sense that schools continued to function and even expanded, religious services were permitted, and refugee shops and enterprises grew, with some even prospering. Out of their meager surroundings, the Hongkou Jews constructed a whole new world. Ironically, many German nationals planned frequent outings to the Shitei chiku in order to enjoy the familiar life and entertainment in its cafés and shops. Hongkou reminded them of home, offering the kind of food and goods they liked and renewing their cherished connection with German culture and traditions.

Jews from many religious backgrounds — Orthodox, Conservative, Reform, and nonobservant — had their ties to basic Jewish traditions renewed by being thrown together in such close proximity. A branch of HICEM opened in the Shitei chiku to help refugees obtain information on the whereabouts of missing people or about people concerning whom information was wanted. HICEM received letters and inquiries from many cities abroad, some of them even coming from concentration camps such as Westerborg in the Netherlands.[90] The previously highly assimilated German Jews found themselves participating once again in Jewish institutions and events. Frictions among these diverse groups persisted, but a mutual awareness of a vital Jewish community also developed. To a large extent, this sense of community came about through new and ongoing educational programs, cultural and artistic endeavors, and sporting events.

What could be more useful to refugee youth having difficulty finding employment than learning new skills, if for no other purpose than to gainfully occupy their time? At the ORT Training School for Craftsmen, established in September 1941 and presided over by Boris Topas, one young man learned machine knitting.[91] Others learned carpentry, radio repair, practical mechanics, shoemaking, tailoring, and locksmithing, all free of charge.[92] Another very valuable training school was the Gregg School of Business, run by Wilhelm Deman. As the name implies, students there learned typing, shorthand, commercial English, commercial law, filing, bookkeeping, and general office work. Apart from these classes conducted in the daytime, classes in the Japanese and Chinese languages met five evenings of the week and were attended by students of varying ages.[93] Professor Deman ran the Shanghai Jewish Youth Association Club, where young people spent afternoons learning bookbinding, fashion, manicuring, dancing of all varieties, etiquette, and cooking. The cooking class was especially popular, because the students could eat what they prepared. The club established a savings bank, and students learned how to save and write checks and acquired the basic principles of banking.[94] A high level of regular curriculum continued at the Freisinger School and the Shanghai Jewish Youth Association School. In June 1941, the SJYA school was forced to move to East Yu Yuen Road after the Chinese reclaimed the school building. The move placed the school outside the Shitei chiku, but students succeeded in procuring a collective pass from the Japanese to attend their regularly scheduled classes.

Sports were very popular among the young, especially soccer, hockey, and football, and the active cultural and religious life of the Hongkou Jews gave the camaraderie and sense of community that grew out of these sporting activities deeper significance. Yiddish theater productions became increasingly popular, along with theater performances of favorites such as *Menschen in Weiss* (People in White) and George Bernard Shaw's *Pygmalion*. In addition, numerous concerts by various ensembles enriched the community and helped greatly to lighten the mood during the war years. When the High Holidays arrived, Jewish leaders rented school auditoriums and movie theaters, such as the Eastern Theater on Muirhead Road, to accommodate the large numbers wishing to attend. Reportedly, the Japanese financed and helped construct a small synagogue built next to a military post in Hongkou.[95] Radio station XMHA broadcast a refugee hour from 4–5:00 P.M. each day, with the news in German, lectures, and performers who sang, played instruments, and supplied a measure of humor.

In addition to their religious observances, a lasting and impressive contribution came from the Polish rabbis and yeshivas, who during the course of the war produced a new edition of the Babylonian Talmud and copies of scores of important rabbinical and devotional works, such as Maimonides' *Yad Ha-hazakah*, Danzig's *Hayye Adam, Midrash Rabba*, and other key works.[96] One who was most jubilant over this prolific scholarly output was Rabbi Ashkenazi of the Lubavitcher Hassidim. After so many years in Shanghai, Rabbi Ashkenazi finally had a devout congregation under his charge, so that Jewish religious life took on richer meaning.

Yiddish writers from Poland also were very active, publishing anthologies of the Yiddish classics as well as writing and producing plays to start the Hongkou theater season. Particularly rich and varied were the periodicals. Weeklies and monthlies appeared in Yiddish, German, Russian, and English. More than thirty German, Yiddish, and Polish newspapers and magazines appeared in Shanghai just between 1939 and 1946.[97] Shanghai had an active

Zionist movement, reaching back to 1903, when the first of many such organizations, the Shanghai Zionist Association, started and soon thereafter began publishing the official Zionist organ, *Israel's Messenger*.[98] The editor, N. E. B. Ezra, and Ellis Kadoorie were major spokesmen in the Sephardi community for Zionist aspirations.[99]

Under the conditions of 1943, with the Japanese authorities stressing the consolidation of "similar" organizations, leading Zionists held a meeting in June at the Café International on Chusan Road to discuss working out their differences and to appoint a committee composed of three members from each organization to bring about the unification of the Shanghai Zionist movement.[100] Apparently, these efforts did not succeed, because addressing a Zionist gathering in August, Rabbi Ashkenazi once again urged their leaders to form one organization. Using the metaphor of the older Zionist organizations, such as Kadimah, as the railroad track and the new revisionist organizations as the train, he argued that the train could not go forward without the tracks, so all organizations must work together to accomplish any goals.[101] These attempts to unify had only temporary and limited success. In the view of both Rabbi Ashkenazi and Dr. Cohn, the main hope of improving the Jews' situation lay in their being restricted to the Shitei chiku, where Jewish leaders could preach to their young "captives" about the need for an independent Jewish state to be recognized as a nation. A key organization working on this theme was the Brit Noar Zioni, another Zionist youth organization, led by Dr. Bernard Rosenberg.[102]

Wartime Experiences

The war touched the lives of the ghetto Jews mainly through the frequent air raids, inflation, and widespread shortages of vital goods and foods, but these influences affected all of Shanghai. More specific to their sense of fear and hostility was the occasional sighting in Hongkou of members of the German KDF (Kraft durch Freude, or "Strength Through Joy") organization. The KDF's purpose was to promote sports, healthy lifestyles, and provide monthly lectures on National Socialist ideology.[103] Still more ominous to the Jews who saw them were the uniformed members of the Hitler Youth. Leaders of this organization staged marches, organized a musical band, and

arranged workshops and camping expeditions. Members of the group are believed to have been given military training. Along with the girls' branch, the
Girl Guides, the organization produced a widely available magazine, *Hitler
Jugend in China.* The Hitler Youth formed a uniformed unit of the Kaiser
Wilhelm School.[104] Perhaps another dividend of being restricted in their
movements was that only a few refugees reported seeing or being exposed to
members of these Nazi bodies in Shanghai.

As the year 1944 drew to a close, the nights were filled with terror by the
almost constant air raids. At the same time, the refugees could take some
comfort in the realization that Germany was weakening. War news from
Soviet radio broadcasts gradually revealed the turn of fortunes. Closer to
home, an event that greatly heartened the ghetto community was news that
Ghoya, the Japanese in charge of issuing passes to leave the Shitei chiku, had
been "uncrowned," and that a new man, Harada, had taken his place. "'The
King' was gone and with him, it seemed, an entire era," Horst Wartenberger
remarked.[105] From then on, passes were freely available, and visits outside
were hampered only on occasion by safety measures, which increased almost
daily.

Perhaps the most memorable and horrifying experience of the wartime
ghetto was the air raid of July 17, 1945. The day was not unusual, with re-
connaissance aircraft taking to the air, sirens following somewhat later, and
people trying to go about their regular, accustomed duties, Wartenberger recalled. The sky was a mixture of bright blue and low hanging clouds, perfect
for planes not wanting to be spotted. Just before 2:00 in the afternoon, "a
deafening racket broke loose like a million thunders right over us."[106] Not
waiting for the "all clear" to sound, the medical troops of the air defense system raced to see what had happened. "One of our colleagues had been a
courier on his way to headquarters when it happened, and he was brought in
ripped in two, his insides hanging out, his entire body a mess of blood."[107]
The camps fortunately had many doctors, but the carnage was so great that
they were soon overwhelmed. Older camp residents helped out by assisting
the doctors and nurses as best they could.

The bombing attack on "Black Saturday," August 14, 1937, might have
produced more casualties, but this time the ghetto itself was hit, bringing the
horror and carnage to the doorstep of the Jewish refugee community. At one
crossroads, a bomb had broken through the asphalt and remained anchored

in the street, unexploded. Around it was the worst of the death and destruction. In an area of only twenty-five to thirty square yards, about fifty people lay dead. Doctors, nurses, and helpers crossed the borders of the Shitei chiku several times that day to help with the wounded and dying. At the end of the day, when most of the medical work had been accomplished, Japanese military officials visited the area and expressed their appreciation for the selfless work done by the refugees in responding to the disaster. They also reorganized one of their large school buildings to serve as a shelter and provide additional medical attention to the wounded.[108] Widespread damage had been done to property in Hongkou, which had to be repaired for adequate living conditions to be restored. Another major attack by American planes followed a few days later, but struck toward the outskirts, missing Hongkou altogether. These were the final blows launched against the Japanese in Shanghai. The war in the Pacific ended less than one month later.

EIGHT

The Slavs Remain Free

> Russia is baffling to the mind;
> Not subject to the common measure,
> Her ways — of a peculiar kind . . .
> One only can have faith in Russia.
>
> —FEDOR TYUTCHEV

The breakup of the large Russian émigré communities in Europe, such as those in Paris, Warsaw, and the Baltic countries, which were absorbed either by Hitler or Stalin, left the Russian community in China the most important group of Russians residing outside the borders of Stalin's domain. Germany's attack on the Soviet Union sent shock waves through the various refugee enclaves in China. Reactions in Shanghai were decidedly mixed. Some in the White Russian community began to consider an early return to their homeland to resume their previous lives and escape the curse of statelessness and uncertainty. Others found their passions aroused by patriotism for the motherland suffering under the Nazi blitzkrieg attack.

Russian Jews were not exempt from these anxieties, especially during the uprooting process involved with establishing the Hongkou ghetto. However, when it became clear that their group was to be excepted from the move, their future looked more promising, especially for those still in the import-export businesses. They no longer faced competition from the Americans, British, Belgians, and Dutch, who languished in internment camps. Thus,

Russian Jews in the Slavic community, some at least, actually were able to maintain a reasonable standard of living during the war years.

The high stakes that accompany any wartime scenario, as well as the mix of so many nationalities in Shanghai, together made the city a fertile breeding ground for intrigue, international espionage, and crime. The White Russians were not excepted from involvement in these and its consequences. Foreign intelligence services did not lack for ready agents, eager to enjoy the fruits of a rewarding and glamorous if somewhat dangerous business. Occasionally, their undoing came from the disturbing discovery that some of the best of their operatives served more than one master. The subject of wartime espionage in Shanghai, its effectiveness and impact on the war's progress, remains difficult to research, owing to the loss, dispersion, and continued secrecy of pertinent records. Perhaps more of a barrier were the number of countries playing the game, the incredible complexity of loyalties involved, and the frequent murkiness of operations planned or under way.

In short, during the war years, Shanghai was a city still crowded by Chinese refugees, plagued by crime and assassinations, run by a Chinese puppet government under Japanese direction, beset by heavy inflation, and the scene of multiple espionage activities. And yet, the city still maintained within its boundaries a modicum of safety and everyday routine for its inhabitants. Some of the greatest challenges were on a personal level, especially for those whose homelands were under siege.

A Divided Russian Community

Hitler's invasion of the Soviet Union had a peculiar effect on the White Russian community. It was both energized by this momentous event and, at the same time, gradually polarized between those who saw merit in the Soviet regime presiding over the motherland and those who continued to call for its defeat. These opposite sentiments, which had fired heated debates in the local Russian press, began to coalesce around committed adherents of one position or another.

The emotional undercurrents stirred by the invasion began to favor the growing number of those wanting to defend the motherland. Young Shanghai Russians volunteered to fight the Nazis, and the Soviet embassy in

London received substantial donations from White Russians, some of them in the form of old Russian gold bullion.[1] Increasing contributions from the hard-pressed community also poured into the Soviet Red Cross Fund. The Shanghai Russian press reported calls to replace the slogan "Down with Bolshevism!" with "Down with the Nazis!" Russian Prince Vsevolod, in an emotional letter to *The Times* in London, exclaimed that "we are fighting a common foe and I feel that all Slav races should now unite to rid the world of Nazism."[2]

Shanghai was flooded with Soviet propaganda in the form of books, pamphlets, records, and films brought in by ship from Vladivostok.[3] As one resident commented, the barrage of propaganda "was so thick that you were almost choking in it."[4] The prevailing theme was to extol the heroic Soviet Army (the earlier name "Red Army" still evoked the hostility of White Russians). The Soviet Club encouraged visits to its premises and participation in its film showings of both old movie favorites and new ones, including documentaries.[5] Films about Alexander Nevsky and Peter the Great were typically followed by an open bar, where visitors could drink, talk, and be given "information" about the fate of the motherland.[6] Saying that such films and similar materials posed a threat to the "preservation of peace and order," Vichy officials in the French Concession banned them, along with Soviet broadcasts of war news.[7] Letters to the local press bitterly protested this censorship.

Another powerful enticement to switching loyalties was the Soviet invitation to stateless White Russians to register for citizenship. Rumors circulated about promises to return all their property if they went back. In any case, this strategy proved successful, and the Soviet embassy in Tokyo was soon swamped with applications for Soviet passports. Some of the young, especially, took a close look at their future prospects and decided that their best chance to pursue a meaningful professional life was in the Soviet Union.[8]

Another channel of Soviet influence that became very important in Shanghai was the radio station XRVN, whose Russian-language broadcasts were astutely dubbed the "Voice of the Motherland" (whereas the English version was the "Voice of the Soviet Union"). The Russian-language broadcasts received added prestige and developed a following because of the reputation of the commentator, Vsevolod Ivanov, a poet and prose writer who had fled Japanese persecution in Harbin and eventually joined the Soviet side. His journalistic talents made him an influential figure in Shanghai, and his broad knowledge of Russian society and culture allowed him to provide interesting and substantive commentary for his Shanghai audiences.[9] Of course, much of the radio audience needed no other reason to tune in than to learn the latest on the war situation. Fortunately for the local population, the Japanese did not censor war reporting on this station, because of Japan's pact with the Soviet Union. Thus, for most English and Russian speakers in Shanghai, this was the best source for war news.

The English-language broadcast was directed by none other than the son of V. F. Grosse, the first chairman of the Russian Emigrants Committee and former czarist consul general in Shanghai. The younger Grosse epitomized the predicament of young Russians who continued to respect the sacrifice and contributions of the older White Russian generation, but had not themselves lived through the same bitter experiences. They saw many of the ideals and notions of their fathers as outworn and unrealistic. Instead, they were receptive to the patriotism of the day and desperately wanted to reclaim respect and a national identity. Even more urgent, they wanted to envision their future connected with a homeland and not with spiritual and economic degradation. In their view, the underground movement in the Soviet Union often extolled by their elders showed no signs of strength or even existence.[10] Their mix of feelings and strained loyalties often engendered what appeared on the surface at least to be states of confusion. In an open letter to the *North China Daily News*, L. V. Grosse described himself as a "pro-Soviet Russian defending the Allied cause and respecting the Japanese authorities as well as the Soviet Japanese Neutrality Act."[11]

Even before the Soviet regime could extend it an invitation to do so, the Russian Orthodox Church in the USSR displayed its allegiance to the motherland by launching an appeal to the faithful to support the war effort. Church members responded generously. Money collected from Russian Orthodox congregations in various cities and countries financed the formation of the Alexander Nevsky Air Squadron and Dmitrii Donskoi Tank Unit. Additional funds supported military hospitals and children's homes, assisted invalids, and paid for warm clothing and gifts for the troops.[12] Church services condemned the Nazis and praised the courage and strength of the Russian soldier. In Shanghai, the more that was known of the Church's role in the war, the more support it encouraged for the defense of the homeland.

With increasing evidence of rearoused Russian nationalism and patriot-ism, Colonel N. K. Sereinikov and the leaders of the All-Russian Emigrants Committee, the leading force in the White Russian community since its be-ginnings in the mid 1920s, saw their power and influence erode. The reac-tion of Sereinikov and the committee leaders reflected the different kind of committee leadership that had replaced that of Ch. E. Metzler and N. A. Ivanov. Unlike the latter, who had both been civilian professionals associated with the established and highly respected Russian diplomatic community, their successors were refugee military commanders who had risen to promi-nence during the Civil War. For example, Lieutenant General Glebov, who would follow Colonel Sereinikov as chairman, had received his high rank from the fiercely anti-Bolshevik Cossack Ataman G. M. Semenov, not from the imperial Russian military establishment.[13]

The All-Russian Emigrants Committee decided on a firm and uncom-promising approach to the problem of its eroding support. Meeting on October 17, 1941, the committee resolved that Russians who expressed sym-pathy for the Soviet government would lose the committee's protection and the right to all forms of official refugee documentation. Another meeting, on October 26, increased taxes needed to raise additional relief revenues and, in an even more provocative measure, banned committee members from giving support to the Soviet cause.[14] This later action, which identified Soviet sym-pathizers as moral and practical enemies of the committee, caused immedi-ate concern among its members about the direction being taken by their leadership. Considerable uproar accompanied information that members of both the Young Russian Party, or Mladorossy, and Union of Repatriation, or Vozvrashchentsy, had already been removed from the committee's protec-tion.[15] These actions set off a furious round of debate. Committee members opposing the decisions stressed that "there is hardly a Russian here that does not support the committee, but this does not mean we must forget the dan-ger to our country."[16] Others maintained that without a country, the loss of refugee rights did not mean much anyway and preferred blacklisting to giv-ing up support for the motherland. Whichever position was taken, certain doubts and misgivings always remained, given the uncertainties and emo-tions attached to the choices available.

The young Grosse immediately protested the committee's drastic ban-ning of all dissenting views, a position that, he reported with regret, had also been endorsed by the Shanghai diplomatic corps. He claimed that through his own contacts with the Japanese emperor [*sic*] via Japanese court officials, he had learned that the "Japanese being great patriots themselves would never compel the Russians to go against their own country unless they wish to do so freely by their own will." Grosse emphasized that the Japanese both supported the "White cause" and yet remained on good terms with the pro-Soviet Russians because of the Soviet-Japanese Neutrality Pact of April 1941. The committee's position therefore merely aided the German cause, as did Allied diplomats in supporting it. Grosse called on the foreign communities to clarify their positions toward the All-Russian Emigrants Committee and to allow Russians to speak without fear of punishment. He naively claimed that there was nothing to fear from "the Japanese who will always respect an honest enemy."[17] What Grosse and so many others in the White Russian community overlooked, of course, was the historical record, which showed that Japan had never sustained a friendly relationship with either czarist or communist Russia.

Two days later, in a reply to Grosse, J. A. Basil wrote that Russians should stop being refugees and support the Soviet government, regardless of whether the Allies desired this or not. Pointing up one of the most pervasive and strongly felt refugee issues, Basil said that by taking an independent stand, they would win the Allies' respect, "which is actually what true Russian patriots in Shanghai need."[18] He called for a collective appeal to regain lost citizenship. Responding to Basil, Grosse claimed that those wanting to become Soviet citizens must first overcome their egoistic, competitive, exploitative tendencies.[19]

Grosse continued his campaign by calling upon Russian newspapers in Shanghai to define clearly their attitude toward the Allied cause. He described *Slovo* as taking a very encouraging patriotic, although anticommunist, stand. When *Slovo* ceased publication on November 25, 1941, Grosse remarked that "we will miss it even though its ideas of nationalism are old fashioned, for it is wrong to think the USSR does not represent the interests of the Russian people."[20] Regarding *Shankhaiskaia Zaria*, which Grosse described as being neither red nor white, he challenged the editors "to choose their colours once and for all."[21] Articles appeared in this newspaper that were anti-German, he noted, while others proclaimed "Long live England!" or were pro-Japanese; some were pro-Chinese; some supported Soviet construction plans; and several were pro-czarist. "What is their stand?" he asked. Grosse described the *Russian Daily News* and *New World* as clearly Soviet in their orientation. As to the Hongkou-published *Russian World*, which he suggested was pro-Nazi, Grosse remarked, "I don't want to comment further on this because I want to live on this old planet of ours."[22] Trying to arrive at a solution, Grosse proposed that British and Russian pro-Allied journalists come together to create a strong anti-Axis front.

Still another "Young Russian" speaking through the press wrote that "all are Russians" and the committee leaders only made fools of themselves and played into Germans hands by blacklisting the pro-Soviet refugees. He predicted that the outcome would be the loss of funds for charity from those able and willing to contribute. Taking the argument a step further, he called on the local Soviet community, particularly the Shanghai Soviet Association, to give more attention to the ongoing dispute and "maybe make a small step forward to meet us."[23]

Meanwhile, the "White House" headquarters of the Bureau of Russian Emigrant Affairs (BREM) in Tianjin in north China, headed by the Cossack leader E. Pastukhin, was calling for conscription of all young Russians to join the battle against communism. ("Those not with us are against us!" Pastukhin exclaimed.) Not surprisingly, this idea proved very unpopular in White Russian communities. In Qingdao, twenty young Russians were notified that they were being called up to fight, and several who disobeyed the BREM order to register for military training, which was signed by the Japanese commissioner of police of Greater Tianjin, "were banished from Tientsin," presumably meaning that their residence permits and other official documentation had been revoked.[24]

In Shanghai, the committee had not taken such drastic action. Instead, a new challenge faced the committee once the United States entered the war and the American and British consulates and businesses in the city closed. Sereinikov and the committee leaders had to fashion a response. Not out of character, they cautioned the White Russian community to lie low, unite around their committee, hang on to whatever employment they had, stay away from political issues and large gatherings, and register with the committee before December 15, 1941, the date designated by the municipal authorities. The Russian leaders emphasized the fact that the committee was the officially endorsed body of the White Russian community, which made it imperative for members to refrain from any anti-Japanese activity. The committee's recognized official status precluded any anti-Japanese expression, and its leaders exhorted everyone to foster order and stability in the Russian community. Committee directives called for newspaper censorship of any rumors, unfounded news reporting, and anti-Japanese commentary. In addition to obtaining registration identification, members needed to acquire a special identification pass that included a Japanese translation.[25] These seemingly necessary restrictions, given the current circumstances, unfortunately only added to the existing pressures in the already tense and increasingly polarized White Russian community.

Sereinikov's one-year term had expired, but restraint and caution continued under the next committee chairman, General Glebov, whose candidacy won approval by a majority of members present at a general meeting held at the Russian Club and attended by two Japanese observers and Bishop Ioann. The selection of Glebov received the approval of the new mayor, Chen Gongbo, in December, and it was announced officially on January 1, 1943.[26] His election received endorsements from the *Shankhaiskaia Zaria* and *Novoe Vremia* (New Times), both of which described Glebov as possessing qualities necessary for the leader of the community at this crucial time.[27] Three days later, the new chairman visited Mayor Chen to pay his respects. Glebov was also guest of honor at a dinner party to celebrate his election at the Russian Club. In addressing the assembled guests, he pledged to "guide his community firmly."[28] In the weeks that followed, not the least of his congratulators, Ataman Semenov, issued an appeal to the troubled Russian refugee community to rally around Glebov and the committee.[29] Both Glebov and newly appointed committee leaders admonished the White Russian community "to maintain an irreconcilable attitude toward communism" and warned the refugees against having any relations with the local Soviet community.[30] The ban included the popular Russian theatrical groups, which were no longer to employ Soviet citizens in their productions.

Working against Glebov and the committee was war news filtering in from the Russian front. Headlines in the Japanese-backed *Shanghai Times* proclaimed German victories, raising the hopes of those counting on a quick Nazi overthrow of the Soviet regime as their ticket back to the homeland. On the other hand, the Stalingrad campaign, which had begun in July 1942 and lasted until February 2, 1943, showcased the sheer heroism of the poorly supplied Russian soldier and, at the same time, strongly suggested that the Nazis were indeed not invincible. Russian pride soared when it became known that the Germans were in retreat. Still, press accounts continued to report the costs: "Attack on Kharkov — 129 Tanks Destroyed, 4,000 killed," "3,700 Men 143 Planes Downed in 4 Days," "Since February 23, 61,460 Soviets killed in the Staraia Russa Sector."[31] The response in Shanghai was an outpouring of sympathy and support for the motherland and its troops struggling against Hitler's armies.

Shanghai Russians began to change color, blushing many shades of red, from delicate pink to bright scarlet, and registration for Soviet citizenship surged. For Russians who had expressed anti-Japanese sentiments, or were simply uncertain about what Japanese policy might be toward those who had worked for U.S. or British interests, the option of registering with the Soviet authorities had significant appeal. These developments brought a prompt response from Glebov, who formally notified Russian refugees who had obtained "other papers" or surrendered their emigrant passports issued by the Shanghai Special Municipality through the All-Russian Emigrants Committee that the protection of the committee was at stake. He gave those who had changed sides a month to reject these "other papers" by placing an official announcement to that effect in the press. If they failed to do so, Glebov promised, he himself would publish the names of those who to his knowledge had obtained or applied for "other papers."[32] Some in the community reacted to these measures by deciding to register with the Soviet authorities in order to escape the control of the increasingly repressive committee.

Captain Kuroki, still liaison officer between the Japanese authorities and White Russian community, appeared dissatisfied with the degree of control exercised by Glebov and the committee. Although Glebov's reelection in 1944 received the mayor's approval, it was criticized by the Japanese-sponsored Russian press, which called for a firmly implemented reorganization of the committee. The result was a general meeting of 143 representatives of various Russian organizations (166 in all) to elect three new committee bodies: an executive committee of 6 members, a 5- to 9-member public arbitration court, and a 12-member supervisory and control commission, charged with regulating the economic life of the community (and helping with the collection of back taxes for the years 1940–42 destined for the Chinese puppet government).[33]

What must have been a particular irritant to the general membership was the newly formed control commission,[34] which had the authority to examine the composition of the Russian organizations, exercise more control over their activities, and even to "decide the necessity" of their continued existence. The third elected body was a 5-member court of public arbitration "to consider and settle" internal disputes.[35]

The attending representatives' requests for open discussion of candidates nominated for these new bodies met with refusal. The top candidate for the executive committee in terms of votes was Colonel G. K. Bologov, and other members included three colonels, a physician, an engineer, and a merchant. Sereinikov was reelected as vice-chairman of the All-Russian Emigrants Committee. In an acceptance speech to the gathering that must have done little to console the disaffected, Glebov once again stressed the need for order and discipline, so as "to justify the confidence of the authorities which have granted to the emigrant community the right of self-administration."[36]

The position taken by the Russian Orthodox Church did little to help calm the divisiveness within the White Russian community. When the patriarch of Moscow and All Russia died in May 1944, the election that followed became a worldwide event, involving representatives of far-flung groups such as the Egyptian Coptic Church, Lebanese Orthodox Christians, and many others. In China, the Russian Orthodox Mission in Beiping was an old established institution and its head, Archbishop Viktor, a former White Army officer, publicly extended his allegiance to the Moscow patriarch. This action split Church followers in Shanghai. The most prominent local Orthodox figure, Bishop Ioann, made it clear he was against joining the Moscow Church, a position that obviously not everyone locally could adopt. The pro-Soviet Russian press in Shanghai attacked the bishop's stance and insinuated that he was taking a position favored by the Japanese. Bishop Ioann remained firm in spite of these pressures, ministering to the local non-Soviet-supporting Russians.[37] Nevertheless, this was one more important factor that divided the local Russians.

With resentment of the All-Russian Emigrants Committee's high-handed behavior increasing, Captain Kuroki took care to be highly visible at all its meetings. Refugee disaffection became clearly apparent during the December 1944 election, the published rules for which were signed by Kuroki, identified as the "Officer in Charge of Russian Affairs, Imperial Nipponese Military Mission in Shanghai." Of the 3,000 refugees qualified to vote in December in this first secret ballot election for the chairman of the committee, in which every registered refugee with taxes fully paid could participate, only 851 voters bothered to turn out. General Glebov received 616 of the votes. The least number cast for a candidate, 50 votes, went to General Tsumanenko, the Japanese favorite.[38]

Ukrainian Defiance

Hitler's attack on the Soviet Union stirred the passions of the local Ukrainian community, whose leaders saw the Nazi advance as providing Ukrainians with the long-sought-after means of regaining some form of autonomy and freedom from the Soviet Russian yoke. At an extraordinary meeting on July 7, 1942, of the Ukrainian Emigrants Committee, located at 1292/3 Avenue Edward VII, the meeting's chairman, S. A. Sobolnikov, exclaimed that the Axis Powers had liberated the Ukrainian people and rid their sacred territory of the enslavers.

The meeting adopted a number of resolutions based on a firm belief "in victory of the Axis Powers, whose victory brings to the people of Asia and Europe liberation from slavery; we are confident in the successful establishment of the New Order in Asia and Europe for the welfare of all mankind."[39] After expressing thanks to the Japanese and Chinese authorities in Shanghai, the resolution implored them to restore to the Ukrainian leaders their former rights as the only representatives of the Ukrainian community in Shanghai. It lamented that these precious rights had been improperly transferred to the All-Russian Emigrants Committee in November 1941. The meeting concluded with the election of a new slate of leaders, headed by N. T. Kvashenko as chairman.[40]

In conclusion, the meeting unanimously decided to send a telegram on behalf of the Ukrainian people, who had been "liberated by the Axis Powers from rule by the Red Devils," to Erich Koch, Reich minister of the Ukraine, expressing appreciation for his work in the restoration of Ukraine. A voluntary collection to cover costs of sending the telegram netted $500 from the attending members, described by the police as a clear indication of member support and more than enough to cover the expense.[41]

What was not known locally was that German intentions toward Ukraine were to use its land and population as key sources of food grain and forced labor. Reich Minister Koch maintained that it was Germany's "right and duty" to exploit the East and made clear his attitude to Ukrainians with statements like: "If I find a Ukrainian who is worthy of sitting at the same table with me, I must have him shot."[42] Ukrainian territory had become a vortex of exploitation and destruction, especially during the buildup for the Nazi assault on Stalingrad.

Disregarding news reports, however, local partisans of the Ukrainian Independence Movement saw only the possibility of realizing their dream of an independent Ukraine. Shanghai Ukrainians argued, moreover, that because Ukraine had recently been liberated from Soviet domination, they were no longer stateless. The leaders of the Ukrainian Emigrants Committee asserted that the time had come for it to rename itself the Ukrainian Representatives Committee.

None of these changes came without friction within the Ukrainian community. In March 1942, disagreements over policy and a dispute over finances led to a split in the governing board, four of whose members left to form still another body, the Ukrainian National Committee in East Asia. Even more devoted to Ukrainian independence than its parent, this breakaway organization worked with the local German broadcasting station on a daily one-hour broadcast in the Ukrainian language that provided news and cultural programming.[43] The local response was immediate. A respected and well-liked Russian commentator at that station resigned over the hiring of a Ukrainian German partisan, and *Nash Put*, the local Russian fascist newspaper in Shanghai, apparently not wanting another group to steal its thunder, condemned the Ukrainian broadcaster, claiming he was "financed by Jews."[44]

As required by police regulations, the new Ukrainian National Committee in East Asia submitted its proposed constitution and details of its aims and membership for official approval. J. V. Sweet, its chairman, stressed its benign aspects, listing its aims as protecting the cultural and national interests of local Ukrainians, caring for the upbringing of their youth, and supporting the Ukrainian press in East Asia. The new organization published two newspapers, *Ukrains'ky i Holos na Dalekomu Skhodi* (The Ukrainian Voice in the Far East) in Ukrainian, and *Call of Ukraine* in English.[45] The membership qualifications made it clear, however, that only those who supported the principles of the Ukrainian National Movement were eligible. Given the friction and political colorations characteristic of the Ukrainian bodies, Chief Inspector A. Prokofiev, who followed mainly Russian refugee affairs for the police, recommended withholding approval and awaiting the possible resolution of differences between the two existing bodies before recognizing a new one.[46]

Captain Kuroki, the official Japanese Russian handler, reacted sharply to Ukrainian efforts to assert a national identity and establish a presence in Shanghai separate from the local White Russians. In an article published in the Russian-language *Novoe Vremia*, Kuroki made it plain that he did not welcome any challenge to his policy of centralizing control over the Russian/Slavic community and managing it in Japan's interest. The Ukrainian radio broadcasts were promoting discord by calling for self-determination, he said. Lumping the Ukrainians together with the White Russians, he asked: "[W]hat cooperation is possible when a small group of persons with great ambitions brings sharp discord into the anti-Communist choir by means of their Ukrainian dialect[?]" This could not but be welcomed by enemies of the anticommunist front.[47] What was needed, Kuroki said, was a united front against communism. Clearly, it was to be an uphill struggle for local Ukrainian leaders to influence and change Japanese views of their proposed goal of establishing a unique identity. Also, their case was not helped by the fact that most of the reporting to authorities on their organization and its activities was done by White Russian police officials.[48]

Becoming ever more sensitive to Japanese concerns, but also refusing to give up their quest for separate recognition, Dr. M. Milko and J. Sweet of the Ukrainian National Committee in East Asia and P. A. Boiko-Sokolsy and G. Totsky of the Ukrainian Emigrants Committee together drafted a new Statute of the Ukrainian Representative Committee. This seemed to suggest that agreement had been reached between the feuding bodies, thus restoring unity to the Ukrainian community.[49] Carrying their case a step further, with the help of their German connections, the negotiators presented their petition directly to the Japanese authorities for acceptance. The Japanese remained unmoved by this or the show of unity that preceded it. They contin-

ued their commitment to the existing policy of grouping all Slavic nationalities, including Slavic Jews, under one umbrella organization, the All-
Russian Emigrants Committee.

As more news from the front in European Russia trickled through to
Shanghai, mainly through Soviet news sources, the Ukrainian leaders began
to mute and eventually severely limit, if not drop, their praise for their
German "deliverers." There were rumors, actually based on fact, that
Ukraine had become mainly a source of raw material and slave labor for the
Nazi invaders. Thus, somewhat better informed of the actual situation in
Ukraine and aware that a pro-Nazi argument was more of a hindrance to
their cause than support, even with the Japanese, the Ukrainian leaders returned to their earlier position, which focused specifically and relentlessly on
their plea for a status independent of the Russians.

In a lengthy petition to the chairman of the Shanghai Municipal Council,
Chairman Drobiazko and Secretary Pirogov of the Ukrainian National
Committee in East Asia pointed out the ongoing and insulting problem for
local Ukrainians of being identified as "Russians" by the foreign registration
officers of the Shanghai Municipal Council. Going into considerable detail
to explain the historical roots of the Ukrainian community, dating from the
downfall of the Russian czar in 1917 and the establishment of the "Ukrainian
Democratic Republic," which they insisted had received recognition from
several foreign powers, they once again tried to build a legitimate case for
separate recognition. Indeed, the "Census Table for Foreigners" available in
July 1942 listed thirty-eight nationalities, with four categories for Jews
alone. Categories existed for Syrians, Turks, Greeks, and so on, but there was
no designated category for Ukrainians, only ones for Soviet citizens, White
Russians, and "other" and "stateless" persons.[50] Dobriazko and Pirogov argued that even the Soviet authorities, "the arch enemies of the Ukrainian
people, never dared to deny the Ukrainians' right to their national name"
and that "the Russian Emigrants Committee of Shanghai, too, defines us as
Ukrainians and not Russians."[51] Taking their argument a step further, they
pointed to the existence of two Ukrainian national organizations in Shanghai, two periodical organs, and a radio broadcast, and yet "according to the
registration officers of the S.M.C., it seems as if there are no Ukrainians in
this city."[52] Moreover, they noted that the same could be said for the attitude
of the French authorities.

Even without any favorable results to show for their efforts, the Ukrainian leaders remained undaunted. As late as December 1944, they doggedly assembled additional points with which to buttress their arguments. Dr. Milko and R. Korda-Fedorov composed a lengthy letter dealing with the official Japanese position that the state of Ukraine no longer existed, if, indeed, it had ever existed in the past, and that Ukraine was currently only a province of the USSR, all of whose inhabitants were of Russian origin.

In their letter, they tried a new tack, which took them into rather perilous territory, given what they had formerly said on the subject. They rested their case firmly on authoritative Soviet documents. This time they argued that according to the Soviet Constitution, "the union of states [i.e., the USSR] is put together on the basis of a voluntary unity . . . with equal rights."[53] Furthermore, they pointed out that this same constitution stated that each of the Soviet republics had a guaranteed right to leave the USSR. They stressed the point that the USSR was not a state with only one nationality, but a union of many states of different nationalities, and that each one had its own government, or Council of the People's Commissars. Thus, their argument rested on the point that the terms of the Soviet Constitution actually refuted the position taken by the Japanese authorities that Ukraine was only a very subordinate province of the USSR.

The second major point they made, again using Soviet circumstances as prime evidence, was that citizen-inhabitants of the Soviet Union were not the subjects of Russia but of the Soviet Union. At the same time, the origin of each subject of the USSR was to be defined by his state membership within the Soviet Union. Therefore, they argued, Ukrainians were not Russian subjects, because they lived, not in the Russian Socialist Federative Soviet Republic of the Soviet Union, but in the Ukrainian Soviet Socialist Republic. In other words, origin had to be determined by the individual's citizenship of this or that separate republic, and "since a Ukrainian is descended from the Ukraine, it is only clear that being a Soviet subject, he is at the same time an Ukrainian by birth."[54] They concluded this tortured plea by asking how the Japanese could classify Ukrainians as Russian in origin, when even the Soviet Union did not.

Unfortunately, despite their admirable persistence, the Ukrainian leaders failed to move the Japanese authorities even to revise their registration forms and procedures. As a last resort, the Ukrainians asked that they be classified as "stateless, of the Ukrainian origin" or "stateless, Ukrainian emigrant."[55] Perplexed by these arguments, the Japanese were little motivated to make any of the requested changes in bureaucratic procedure. Ukrainians continued to list themselves and their families in official documents as Ukrainians, however, and were thus counted by the police as "other."[56] This was a victory of sorts, at least for those determined not to be identified officially in any way as Russian.

Fascism and the Japanese

The outbreak of the Soviet-German war led to a revival of local fascist activities after a period when the All-Russian Fascist Union and its membership had become practically defunct. The union's fortunes improved somewhat in early 1941, when M. M. Spasovsky, recently arrived from Persia, tried to energize the movement. Although he adopted the title "Chief of the Central Direction of the All-Russian Fascist Union," Spasovsky still took his cues from K. V. Rodzaevsky, the leader of the union in Harbin. He established a secretariat at 1317 Yu Yuen Road and began the work of registering members. *Nash Put* resumed publication in Shanghai as a weekly in April 1941, carefully following the editorial line emanating from its parent body in Harbin. By July, members of the union had managed to become included in the Advisory Body of the All-Russian Emigrants Committee and in the so-called "Ideological Center" established in July 1941, which set out to counter Soviet propaganda and unify and redirect nationalist thinking in the Russian community. From this inside vantage point, union leaders worked to promote their ideas for a national revolution aimed at realizing a corporate, unified state, to be governed by a federation of local, regional, and national councils. Eschewing both communism and capitalism, they took as their rallying cry the slogan "God, Nation, Work."[57] As to how their message was received in Shanghai, it is safe to assume that at least the strong anti-Bolshevik tenets of union spokesmen received close attention and support from White Russian listeners.

Another stimulant to fascist fortunes, particularly to the Harbin-based Rodzaevsky group, was the death in January 1942 of K. A. Steklov, head of the local fascist group that took direction from the other key fascist leader,

A. Vonsiatsky.[58] Like Vonsiatsky, Steklov had promoted an anti-Bolshevik movement among White Russians aimed at establishing a "Third Russia" built on new economic and social foundations, rooted in a shared commitment to building and strengthening the state through the new concept of "solidarism." This Third Russia, neither Bolshevik nor monarchist, communist nor capitalist, would integrate the best of Russian traditions and culture into suitable social, economic, and political concepts. And rather than being driven by class conflict in achieving social goals, the state would be built on the twin premises of common purpose, or solidarity, and exaltation of the national spirit.

But what Steklov did not share with the Rodzaevsky group was its blatant anti-Semitism and pro-Japanese stance. These two points became the focus of virulent attacks by the Harbin group on Vonsiatsky and, by extension, Steklov and his supporters. One particularly poisonous characterization of Steklov described him as a mere "bodyguard and mental pygmy."[59] For Steklov's faction, raising the "Jewish Question" only deflected from what was to be the main focus of the movement, which was anti-Bolshevism.

The Shanghai Municipal Police followed social get-togethers of the Shanghai fascists with representatives of the German, Italian, and Japanese press bureaus carefully and concluded that "no regular cooperation existed in the activities of their respective organizations."[60] The Russian Ex-Officers Club entertained on some occasions, and the Kaiser Wilhelm school screened German war newsreels to entertain its guests (it is hard to imagine, however, that even Russian fascists would have been thrilled by scenes of German soldiers using heavy weapons and flamethrowers on hapless Russian troops).

The stance of key fascist leaders vis-à-vis the Jews caused an uproar in the Shanghai Russian community. An article in *Nash Put* entitled "Can't We Dispense with the Jews?" (see p. 174 above), signed by M. M. Spasovsky and N. Karganov, had castigated the All-Russian Emigrants Committee and others for the fact that two Jewish doctors practiced medicine at the Russian Emigrants Hospital, warning that the health of local Russians was thus in the hands of Jews. The article drew fire from the All-Russian Emigrants Committee, which had Jewish members on its Advisory Board, from the Ideological Center, and especially from the editor and publisher of the Japanese-sponsored *Novoe Vremia*. Captain Kuroki's editor, P. A. Savintsev, stressed the by now familiar Japanese theme that it was not for the fascists, "nor for the Germans," nor "mere refugees," to determine such matters as the status of the Jews in East Asia. These were questions to be handled only by the New Order, "in accordance with the program approved by the Nipponese Empire."[61] A secondary argument employed to bolster the case against Spasovsky regarding the Jewish doctors was the revelation that even the revered Fedor Ivanovich Chaliapin, while performing in Shanghai, had purportedly entrusted his golden bass voice to these very doctors for treatment.

At least publicly, most Shanghai White Russians expressed indifference on the subject of the Jewish doctors. Spasovsky's blatant anti-Semitic sentiments did not suit the more subtle, guarded, and cautious Russian community of Shanghai. This is not to say that anti-Semitism did not exist in the White Russian community. Rather, the expression of any even quasi-political views had, over the years, become muted and subdued in multinational Shanghai, where Russian refugees were acutely aware of their vulnerable, stateless condition, especially after the Japanese occupation. Spasovsky, who had made a controversy out of this matter, was a relatively unknown quantity, and his recent arrival from Persia seemed a bit suspicious. Moreover, residents of cosmopolitan Shanghai tended to look most favorably on groups already heavily represented there.

Additional unspecified journalistic "problems" with Spasovsky had gotten him excluded from the Ideological Center and in trouble with the All-Russian Emigrants Committee, the Ex-Officers Military Union, and even with Bishop Ioann. And certainly at least part of Spasovsky's problem was that he had not yet learned to mask some of his more controversial views and refused to keep quiet about these sensitive issues.

Spasovsky's outspokenness in local circles such as the Ideological Center (before his exclusion from it) did not discredit him with the Harbin fascist leader Rodzaevsky. In a letter from Rodzaevsky to the editor of *Novoe Vremia* entitled "Leave Us Alone," Rodzaevsky accused it of having as its real target, not Spasovsky, but the Russian Fascist Union. He applauded Spasovsky's "uncompromising struggle with World Jewry," as expressed in his many publications, and accused Jewish agents in the Russian community of misleading people and diverting attention from the primary struggle against Bolshevism.[62]

In fact, articles in *Novoe Vremia* attempted to focus their criticism specifically on Spasovsky, while continuing to project respect for the All-Russian Fascist Union in general.[63] It was another case of needing to preserve an appearance of unity and order while subduing any radical opinion that might seem to challenge Japanese control in Shanghai. For all these efforts, a serious outcome of the mudslinging, name-calling, and acrimonious debates was the further weakening of the position of the White Russians, who faced growing Soviet pressure, especially in the heated competition to win the allegiance of Shanghai's Russian youth.[64]

The All-Russian Fascist Union managed to survive these contretemps, as demonstrated by a formal ceremony opening its local branch, which took place at the premises of the Cossacks' Union. The impressive array of 60 special guests, among the 160 who attended, included the Japanese consul general, Miura, representatives of the Japanese Navy, and the German consul general and three representatives of the German Information Bureau. A Mr. A. Santi of the "Italian Fascist Group" also attended the gathering.[65] The function opened with a religious service celebrated by Bishop Ioann, after which a tea party took place, studded with speeches pledging solidarity with the Axis Powers in their struggle against communism.

At additional meetings and social events held during 1943, the All-Russian Fascist Union continued to attract followers, although not in impressive numbers.[66] Bishop Ioann spoke at one gathering on the importance of religion in the new Russia that was to be constructed. Some of this success may well be attributed to the new temperance being shown by Spasovsky in his speeches. At a meeting attended by both Bishop Ioann and Archbishop Viktor, head of the Russian Orthodox Mission in China, Spasovsky gave a lecture on the "New Order," which was not the New Order in East Asia but that to be realized after working out the ideology and government structure of a new Russia. As the police reported, Spasovsky kept the Jewish issue in check, so that there was only "an undertone of subdued antisemitic feelings" in his lectures.[67]

Links to the Underworld

Espionage and intrigue were rife in wartime Shanghai and involved members of the diaspora communities. One of the most colorful villains in Shanghai for more than two decades was the Latvian-born Evgeny Mikhailovitch Kojevnikov, more commonly known under the aliases Hovans or Pick. Born in Riga in 1900, he had acquired a string of aliases reflecting his busy career, involving forgery, counterfeiting, extortion, murder, and arms dealing, which led to a string of prison sentences.[68] In addition to his criminal activities, Hovans authored a book entitled *China in the Claws of the Reds*, exposing the work of the Comintern in China, presumably after his relationship in Hankou with the famous Comintern agent in China Michael Borodin had gone sour.[69] Hovans reportedly had worked for a while in Shanghai for Soviet intelligence until the British recruited him to sell information on Soviet affairs to them, including to the British-run Shanghai Municipal Police. This was just another step in his career as a professional informer and agent provocateur willing to work for anyone prepared to pay well for his services. In 1930, he worked for the Chinese Intelligence Service. Later, he worked for the U.S. Treasury Department and American intelligence in connection with their interest in drug trafficking in East Asia. Next, he signed on with U.S. Naval Intelligence, while at the same time being in the employ of Japanese Naval Intelligence.[70] One source gives a graphic description of Hovans as being as "active as lice, jumping from one body to another."[71]

Hovans was also a popular figure in Russian theatrical circles, where he gained a reputation for his fine singing voice and acquired a resplendent theatrical wardrobe, tended to by his boy servant and mistress. Besides being an outlet for his natural talent for acting, his involvement in the theater also became a useful cloak for recruiting and working with his agents. At his peak, Hovans is credited with running some 2,000 agents from his headquarters and residence at the Cathay Hotel. Many of these fit the description of partners in crime rather than espionage agents. One of Hovans's more famous associates was the Buddhist monk and colorful international spy Trebitch Lincoln.[72] Included in his ring of Russians were a lieutenant in the Russian Regiment, SVC; a Shanghai Municipal Police official and former officer in the elite Russian Guard; and a Russian count working for the Japanese.[73]

The outbreak of hostilities between China and Japan in 1937 provided Hovans with fertile ground for cultivating both Japanese and Chinese sources, while simultaneously working for the Americans and reporting back to his new Japanese sponsors. Through his ring and connections, he was able to inform the Americans, British, Chinese, and Japanese about information received by any one of the others. Inasmuch as the Americans and British exchanged information, but did not share sources, having the same story appear from two or more sources worked to his advantage by appearing to provide confirmation.[74]

In dry periods or when funds ran low, Hovans reportedly resorted again to blackmail, extortion, and arms dealing. In a notorious case, posing as a German military advisor to the Nanking government, and bringing along one of his cronies, who posed as a high police official, Hovans attempted to procure $1.8 million in arms and ammunition, to be diverted to rebel factions in Guangzhou.[75] Wealthy Shanghai Jews also became targets for Hovans's ring of "information assistants." Such operations typically involved inviting a well-to-do Jew to a party at the Cathay Hotel, where, with Japanese present, the Jew would be politely invited to subscribe an unspecified amount of money. A refusal, which was the exception, led to certain subsequent detention on a trumped-up charge. Often a request for subscriptions to "art and the Russian theater" proved useful for extorting funds to line Hovans's pockets.[76] In another of his schemes, Hovans succeeded in using the members of the Japanese establishment as a means to extort money from wealthy Shanghai citizens. Japanese authorities, including the police and Municipal Council, permitted racketeering and economic speculation by those willing to collaborate with the Japanese.[77] Officials in high positions in the Shanghai police participated in Hovans's scheme, usually by providing useful information obtained during police work.

After the attack on Pearl Harbor, Hovans began to work much more actively for Japanese Naval Intelligence, even holding an official rank in that organization. In November 1941, a Chinese court had sentenced him to a fifteen-year term for ordering the murder of an alleged Soviet agent, S. Mamontov, but the Japanese, recognizing his talents, got him out of jail.[78] Mamontov had written an exposé on Hovans that was to be distributed widely through printed leaflets and therefore had to be stopped.[79]

Hovans was productive for the Japanese. A Chinese source, writing on the White Russian community in Shanghai, reported that Hovans had succeeded in providing the Japanese with maps and intelligence related to Pearl Harbor, as well as the same kinds of material concerning key landing sites among the islands in the South Pacific. In addition, he gathered information on Chinese forces in the middle China region for the Japanese. Still another of his many useful talents was his ability to forge passports and identification papers as they were needed.[80] Other reporting has the German ambassador to Japan, Eugene Ott, stating that Hovans provided material from U.S. Naval Intelligence archives to German authorities in Shanghai, although it is not clear how he could have obtained such material.[81]

Hovans insinuated himself artfully into overt political activities in Shanghai. He became one of the sponsors of the Ideological Center of the White Russian community discussed above, most likely at the behest of the Japanese, probably the German, and possibly the Soviet authorities, all of whom needed information about the political leanings and activities of the White Russians. In addition, Hovans collected data on pro-Allied elements and investigated and reported on anti-Japanese activities. He also appeared occasionally at Bridge House, where he helped interrogate suspected Allied spies, prisoners, and internees.

The Angel Bar became the meeting place for those connected with Hovans and working for the Japanese. Some of the most infamous included Nathan Rabin, an extortionist, a blackmailer, and "a killer when drunk"; Francisco Carneiro, a Portuguese from Macao who was active in buying military supplies for the Japanese; and Pietro Terni, an Italian citizen, who extorted money from Italian firms, ostensibly to save them from seizure after Italy had capitulated.[82] Finally, there was Paul Lojnikov, a former boxer, who served Hovans as a muscleman and bodyguard.

The Japanese dispatched Hovans and this gang and others like them to Manila around May 1944 as a counterintelligence group charged with uncovering any pro-Allied underground movement. They were to pose as pro-Allied, infiltrate the underground, and then expose its members to the Japanese. Another purpose of the trip was to extort diamonds and precious metals from wealthy Spaniards and Portuguese. Hovans and some gang members went on to Singapore after Manila on a similar mission before returning to Shanghai. Subsequent reporting indicates that at least the second part of the two-part mission was accomplished. Gang members who returned flaunted large sums of Philippine currency and made delivery of a suitcase containing ten bars of platinum.[83]

Japanese Intelligence had other groups in its employ, including a ring of Chinese female spies known as the "Hollywood Group," who collaborated in exchange for protection for their families.[84] Also, there were a number of

Jewish refugees who gave information to the Japanese. Captain Kuroki re-portedly had eighteen to twenty Jewish informers keeping him abreast of ac-tivities in the Shitei chiku ghetto.[85] A Russian Jew with connections to Hovans was active in betraying Jews to the Japanese for their anti-Japanese sentiments and activities; an Austrian Jew was able to get exempted from moving to the ghetto as a result of his work for Japanese Naval Intelligence; and one who served the Japanese Stateless Refugee Affairs Bureau as an in-terpreter was another Japanese source on Shanghai Jews.[86] Some of the other Jewish informers may well have been counted with those individuals who were able to continue their employment with the Shanghai police. In those cases, the motivation would have been to make a living, and their work would not necessarily have involved intelligence activities, but rather regu-lar police work.[87]

An intriguing incident that involved the entire panorama of espionage, drug trafficking, and other foul play in Shanghai involved the alleged mur-der in June 1944 of a German, Dr. A. von Miorini, at the Paulus Hospital, lo-cated at 415 Feng Yang Road, where Nazi doctors were employed.[88] Miorini was reportedly an intelligence agent for the British, but had also been a Gestapo agent, as well as having worked for the Japanese Special Services Section and for Chinese intelligence. In the 1930s, a place known as the "Spider Club" had organized as a rendezvous for wealthy Chinese and for-eigners to meet and drink, take drugs, and form liaisons. Miorini, as a spe-cialist in gynecology, could perform abortions for club clients and introduce new female members to the club. He also dealt privately in his offices with Chinese he had met at the club who were interested in drug trafficking. It was rumored that Miorini may have poisoned a drug trafficker named Alois Stey, who had died under mysterious circumstances after a number of arrests in the United States had led to a breakup of the ring. Stey, it turned out, had been manufacturing heroin on the fifth floor of the Paulus Hospital.[89]

Miorini became ill with what was thought to be paratyphoid, given his high fever and other typical symptoms. After he died, the autopsy, performed by none other than the infamous Dr. R. Neumann, who had allegedly treated Jews in German concentration camps, showed all the signs of the dis-ease except for the germs that cause it. Rumors spread that Miorini had been poisoned, and that Neumann was responsible for his death.[90]

Daily Life in "Free" Shanghai

The sometimes glamorous life and lavish parties enjoyed by those involved in activities such as espionage certainly did not describe the dark and threatening regimen of the refugees who were still "free" and struggling to cope with daily life in wartime Shanghai. Besides being plagued by poverty, unemployment, accompanying social ills such as alcoholism, and even hunger, like others in the city, the Russians were subjected to close supervision. The Japanese authorities in 1943 had implemented the *baojia* system to secure order and maintain control over the distressed Russian community. On the positive side, culture and the arts continued to flourish. The Russian community enjoyed good amateur theater, dramatic societies, concerts, dancing schools, and ballet performances throughout the war. The Lyceum Theater was the center of most of these cultural activities, and favorite programs included *Hussar Love* and star performances by the *Ballets russes* ballerinas E. Bobinina and N. Koevnikova. As a young girl living in Shanghai with her British parents, the future Dame Margot Fonteyn studied dance under an elderly Russian teacher, Mme Tarakanova, and later under George Goncharov, who had trained and danced at the Bolshoi Theater in Moscow. Goncharov joined with Vera Volkova from Leningrad and George Toropoc from Moscow to form an acclaimed Shanghai dance trio. Vera Volkova eventually returned to the West to become a renowned dance teacher.[91]

Before the war years, Chaliapin had given two sold-out performances in Shanghai, held at the Grand Theater, which seated an audience of more than 2,000.[92] Another great local favorite was the crooner, bard, and poet Alexander Vertinsky who, although normally based in Paris, had become stranded in Shanghai for three years because of the war. He sang his own compositions, often dressed as the clown figure Pierrot. His music expressed malaise and protest, while extolling individual value, sentiments that resonated well with the local Russian community. The Soviet authorities regarded Vertinsky as a prize to be enticed to return to the Soviet Union, which he did. He subsequently embarked on a second career as a motion picture actor playing famous persons from prerevolutionary days. Soviet propaganda publicized his considerable success as an enticement for others to follow his path home.[93]

During the months after the Nazi attack on the Soviet Union, the Polish and Russian communities together organized variety shows, known as Moonlight Follies, featuring Russian and Polish performers and aimed at raising money for the British War Fund. These events demonstrated the peculiar unifying effect that World War II had on the disparate communities of Shanghai. Divisions became surmountable in the high context of the motherland under attack, but not on a daily basis, when this temporary common identity became lost in more immediate issues and differences. The Follies were held in the garden at the home of Ellis Hayim, a prominent Jew, and besides local White Russians, Russian Jews, and Poles, guests sometimes included local Soviet officials. After the well-attended performances, numbering more than ten evenings, the groups auctioned off the costumes, props, and sets to maximize their profits for the cause.[94] Jewish Girl Guides of the Shanghai Jewish School organized fairs to raise money for the same purpose. While the Moonlight Follies were being enjoyed in Hayim's garden, similar events were apt to be held at the German compound, raising funds for the Third Reich.[95]

At the Russian social events, conversation often turned to discussions of whether to apply for Soviet citizenship and return to the motherland. For some whose personal experiences in Russia had been traumatic, even this casual talk was too much. One such woman recalled to the guests how she had managed to annoy a Soviet soldier while waiting for a departing train in trying to flee the Soviet Union. The irate soldier grabbed her baby from her arms and threw him against the wall, killing him. But for others such atrocities had happened long ago, and things had now changed, so that life would certainly be better. Information circulated that some families who left Shanghai for the Soviet Union had even been separated by the Soviet authorities, wife from husband, and children from families, but such news failed to dissuade those who wanted to believe in a good return. For those of this persuasion, including professionals such as doctors, lawyers, and professors, returning seemed the best choice, even when it involved putting their children at possible risk. In one reported case, an optimistic emigrant who departed Shanghai just before the end of the war promised to write back about her experiences in the "new" Soviet Union in black ink on white paper if all went well, but in red ink if serious trouble had been encountered. The letter that finally arrived at the Shanghai friend's house was completely penned in red ink.[96]

During the Pacific War, one's personal security and privacy in Shanghai were under constant threat. The Japanese might at any time commandeer living quarters and furnishings for their own use under the pretext of "military necessity," or they might decide to settle one of their officials in an extra room (there were, however, some advantages to this, including protection from unannounced searches and in some cases perquisites such as a natural gas cooking stove). The Kempeitai affixed seals to both movable and immovable property of enemy nationals, making whatever use of it they wanted. They also often conducted searches of the households of neutrals without warning, usually without explanation and typically leaving the premises in chaos. Some foreign and Chinese residents received orders to vacate their properties, again under pretext of military necessity, so that the property could be sublet at a more favorable rent to a new tenant. Given the housing shortage, such eviction orders signaled a major catastrophe for their recipients.

Russian Jews Aid the Ghetto

As conditions in the Shitei chiku ghetto worsened, especially before the resumption of outside aid in 1944, the Russian Jewish community launched an appeal to help its population. The first efforts were not very successful, owing to friction caused by the German Jews, who reportedly continued to display a superior attitude toward the Russian Jews. The situation changed after an outbreak of tuberculosis in the ghetto, when the Russian Jews launched a new campaign to raise money, collect clothing, and provide medical supplies and services. The results were a great deal of competition within the ghetto for the limited funds and hard feelings against those unfortunate enough to be in charge of dispensing the aid.[97] Funds within the largely middle-class Russian Jewish community were far from unlimited, and the number of Jews in the ghetto greatly outnumbered the Russian Jews outside. So besides direct monetary aid, the Russian Jews made efforts to provide jobs for the ghetto inhabitants, some even making the effort, at some risk, of approaching the Japanese authorities in order to win individual exemptions from the ghetto or to procure passes for their employees.[98] Special efforts were made to buy goods when ghetto Jews came door to door selling articles such as sweaters and belts, often handmade. As one observer described these peddlers: "All of a sudden those people would come to the door. They did not speak English, they spoke German, and they all carried suitcases on their back, European style. They would put them down, open them and begin to sell their items, little things such as sweaters, ties, and hats."[99]

The mother of one Russian Jew went twice a week to the ghetto to help out by working in the soup kitchen. These visits to the ghetto were apparently not uncommon. The Japanese consular police reported issuing more than 4,000 special passes to those visiting the camps and ghetto area. In order to exercise more control over the volume of traffic into the ghetto, the police posted a sign in English stressing the necessity of having a pass in order to enter it.[100] In addition, some Russian Jewish leaders sponsored fund-raising evenings, and some managed to persuade wealthy Sephardi Jews to donate money from their overseas funds.[101]

Once again, the success of Russian Jews in fund-raising attracted the interest of the Japanese military authorities, who invited members of the fund-raising committee to expand their activities by contributing to a broader objective — the well-being of the Greater East Asian Co-Prosperity Sphere. In fact, the Japanese had in mind quite a sizable contribution from the Russian Jews, enough money to purchase at least two light tanks, close to U.S.$250,000.[102] Jewish committee members were ordered to assemble at Japanese military headquarters, where they were asked to explain their financial status and how they might fare at fund-raising over the next half year. After explaining how limited their means were, and how what funds they raised were being used to feed and clothe destitute Jews, the committee members were escorted out into the corridor, where they were invited to re-consider. After a painful five-hour wait, the Japanese invited them back and asked if they had changed their plans. Having answered politely in the negative, the group expected jail time in the dreaded Bridge House certainly to follow. But instead, and to the surprise of all, the Japanese listened carefully and then told the group to go home.[103]

The Occupation Draws to a Close

Black market activity, skyrocketing prices, and speculation increasingly impoverished not only the White Russians but also Japanese living in Shanghai.

Whereas relief and aid for the ghetto residents from the AJJDC had resumed in 1944, the "free" population continued to have to rely on their own diminishing resources. Even interned enemy nationals could at least expect to receive two meals a day. Severe shortages in housing, food, and fuel, especially coal, affected everyone else and compelled General Glebov to convene a Special Economic Council consisting of representatives from well-to-do circles, including Russian Jews, to make recommendations for improving economic assistance to the needy. Actual famine conditions existed within segments of the Russian community, requiring the establishment of a Community Kitchen, with feeding stations located around the city. This effort, sponsored by the new council, led to other organizational changes designed to strengthen charitable services to the poor. On June 22, 1945, however, in light of the rapidly declining economic situation, and frustrated by the lack of overall success of these community efforts, Glebov officially advised refugees to avail themselves of every opportunity to secure work outside of Shanghai.[104]

In waning months of the war, tattered Japanese troops could be seen pulling heavy carts and wagons loaded with equipment in order to conserve precious fuel. Utilities such as electricity and natural gas functioned for only one hour a day. Soldiers dug foxholes in the streets and occupied the lower floors of apartment buildings, bricking over the windows and stashing ammunition, food, and fuel, in preparation for a final stand against the expected Allied invasion. The invasion never came, and the end of the Pacific War was surprisingly anticlimactic in Shanghai. After hearing the imperial broadcast announcing the war's end, the Japanese capitulated without incident, withdrawing to the city's borders while airlifts brought Chinese and American troops to assume control over Shanghai.

Even with the war's end, General Glebov maintained his cautious position, characteristic of the unprotected, stateless refugee, still of necessity beholden to others. In a September 8, 1945, interview with the *Shanghai News*, Glebov advised local Russians to realize that they still played no role in the political arena and should concern themselves only with their own affairs: he exhorted them "to remain loyal to the government of the country where they have found refuge." In a final message, apparently meant to console them, Glebov stressed his belief that honest Russians need not fear political repression in the aftermath of the war. Glebov was never to know whether his convictions were well-founded. On October 10, 1945, he died.[105]

The Diasporas' End: Postwar Emigration and Uncertainty

For in and out, about, above, below

'Tis nothing but a magic

shadow-show

Play'd in a box whose

Candle is the Sun

Round which we Phantom

Figures come and go.

—OMAR KHAYYAM

Shanghai residents first heard of Hitler's suicide and the Allied victory in Europe over their shortwave radios in the spring of 1945. Throughout the summer, rumors circulated about the course of the war in the Pacific. When official word reached Shanghai that the war with Japan had come to a close, people ran into the streets to share the news, to hug perfect strangers, and dance with joy. In the Hongkou camps, they dashed to radios to listen to the "Voice of the Soviet Union" for verification of the good news and to gather details. "We were sitting around in our camp when one of our top comedians who had worked downtown came rushing through our gates and announced that the war was over," Horst Wartenberger recalled. "I remember as if it were yesterday that almost everybody jumped up and ran to the radio in the hope of finding out details."[1] Confirmation of the news came on August 20, and one of the first things Hongkou camp residents did was tear down the hated signs marking the borders of the district.[2] After this came the pleasure of being able to go about the city as one pleased, exquisite freedom after years of confinement and bureaucratic intimidation. Some, especially among the elderly, had not set foot outside the Shitei chiku ghetto for years.

Walking freely in the city was not easy, however, with the streets filled with celebrants. "Wherever we went, people were crowding and singing, swinging placards and signs; ornaments hung down from lamp posts and wires, flags of the victorious nations waved in the wind, and the entire population was in a most jubilant state," Wartenberger remembered. "I have never seen the like. Weeks later this state still persisted."[3]

In addition to freedom of movement, it was now possible to escape the crowded and often filthy conditions in the Shitei chiku and choose a new place to live. Businesses could reopen, and a normal life could again be freely anticipated. To a large extent, these developments, seen as such a blessing, especially by those living in the camps, came with the arrival of the U.S. military.

The Americans Arrive in Force

As units of the U.S. Army, Army Air Corps, Navy, and Marines arrived in Shanghai, the need for support services escalated daily, creating a job bonanza for Shanghai's refugees, with the additional and very appealing prospect of being paid in American currency. The primary mission of the U.S. forces was, of course, to help oversee the surrender, disarming, and evacuation of the sizable Japanese military and civilian contingents still in Shanghai. In addition, Americans were to assist the Chinese authorities in the essential task of identifying and transferring enemy property and records. American aircraft had airlifted U.S. and Chinese troops to Shanghai to take over the city from the Japanese, who had withdrawn to the municipal borders, giving up the city almost without incident.[4] By September 1945, Chinese authorities had assumed control over the entire metropolitan area of Shanghai. Of course, the foreign concessions and consular jurisdictions had already ended with the treaty abolishing extraterritorial rights and approving the return of the concessions signed back in November 1943.

All of these American responsibilities required an immediate pool of able workers, and the Hongkou refugee community was ready and well suited to the task. Positions became available for clerks, secretaries, PX staff, drivers, mechanics, warehouse workers, craftsmen, and watchmen, to name only the most common categories. Jiangwan Airfield, north of the city, needed everything from tire changers and drivers to mechanics, for example. Horst Wartenberger, who was one of those who got a job there, recalled: "The base commander sent trucks to our camp in the morning to pick us up and delivered us back again at night."[5] Jewish refugees trained in the ORT courses that had occupied so many free hours during the wartime years of confinement suddenly found themselves well qualified to step into these positions. Representatives of Jewish organizations, able to operate freely again, helped match the new jobs with Jewish applicants. Work was so plentiful that fears of losing a job or of having one's position abolished diminished significantly.

Russians who had experience in the police and SVC were often successful candidates for positions as watchmen, drivers, and security guards. Not all were so fortunate, however, because at least initially, owing to the wartime alliance, the U.S. military favored hiring Soviet citizens in Shanghai rather than White Russians.[6] Shanghai Jews, who had the able assistance of world Jewish organizations, benefited more directly from the U.S. presence than the White Russians or the Chinese.[7] The advantages for the latter were often indirect. Enterprising Chinese hawked old American uniforms, blankets, and canned rations, mostly pilfered, at strategic points throughout the city. Other Chinese entrepreneurs turned condoms — in little demand locally, but now available in huge quantities — into colorful balloons for children.[8]

American soldiers, sailors, and marines pouring in on leave added to the carnival atmosphere of the city. Their casual manner and dress were in sharp contrast to the formal demeanor of the Japanese occupiers, or even to the European refugees, who were reserved by comparison. "The Americans whistled and called to us in very free and friendly fashion," Betty Grebenschikoff recalled. "Obviously, they had not seen any girls for a long time. They complimented us on our looks and asked us for dates. We were enthralled and flattered."[9]

The troops' presence generated an abundance of new bars, nightclubs, and other places of entertainment, all of which meant more jobs and a lively night life for refugees. Refugee families invited servicemen into their homes, sharing meals with them and questioning their guests closely about life in America. In return, the entire family might be invited out for an evening in one of Shanghai's more expensive restaurants. A whole new side of life in the city opened up for many, especially for the Hongkou Jewish refugees. Small groups of servicemen visited the refugee camps, spending an evening entertaining an appreciative audience with songs, dances, and skits. American Jewish servicemen became regular visitors at the local synagogues. Stanley Bergman, an American officer who had recently lost a family member, found solace in being able to visit a Shanghai synagogue each day to say Kaddish, the Jewish prayer of mourning.[10]

Less positive was the high incidence of refugee involvement in prostitution. U.S. servicemen met local women in a variety of ways. One of the most common was to drive around the city in jeeps, looking for women to pick up. These "jeep girls," as they came to be called, expected to be paid in U.S. dollars.[11] Women could also be met at one of the numerous cafés, among them the appropriately named "Jeep Café." Russian women especially favored the New Ritz Café, owned by M. Yenalevicz, where they could meet American servicemen without having to turn over their earnings to the management. Rather, they functioned as "floaters," freelancers whose solicitations drew substantial business to the café.[12]

U.S. officers also formed relationships with White Russian women in Shanghai, just as British and Shanghai Municipal Police officers had before them. Most of the women were dressmakers or bar girls whose incomes did not permit a decent living. To help ease their situation, they therefore formed liaisons with foreigners, who escorted them openly and provided for their support while the men were on duty in Shanghai. The common hope was that the men would eventually marry them, and some did, but the usual scenario was for the American to turn them over to another American upon departure. These women were "young, very attractive, clean and well-dressed, good mannered, and many spoke fair English," one of the Americans, Vorda Hounold, recalled.[13]

With the refugees' new wages and freer lifestyle, certain luxuries previously only dreamed of became possible: a new suit or dress, or even just a restaurant meal, was now within reach. There was no longer the nagging sense of being a supplicant for handouts — of feeling like a beggar, as Wartenberger put it.[14] A holiday atmosphere accompanied the receipt of the first boxes and packages of surplus rations distributed by the U.S. military. As one recipient reported: "I will never forget the first day we opened a 'ten-in-one' and saw all the wonderful articles inside, including cereal. I had five portions that day and this was a true luxury and for the first time in years, I was able to get up from the table and say truthfully, I've had enough."[15] Still another recipient of goods distributed through the AJJDC organized K-ration parties to enjoy the puddings, butter, cheeses, eggs, cakes, meat, fish, and snacks included in the prized packages.[16]

The celebrating and common sense of relief that came with peace brought people out of their separate enclaves and mixed them together in ways not experienced before in Shanghai. The dissolution of the foreign concessions contributed to this shared experience. Notably, too, the Americans now replaced the British as the city's social and cultural trendsetters. "As before, the flags of the free nations were waving side by side, but the Star Spangled Banner was now predominant," Wartenberger noted.[17] The film *Naughty Marietta* staring Jeanette MacDonald and Nelson Eddy, with music by Victor Herbert, drew large audiences and enthusiastic reviews. The American presence proved to be only temporary, but while it lasted, it was a significant force in shaping the lives of city residents.

Relief Supplies Pour In

The United Nations Relief and Rehabilitation Administration (UNRRA) was another key organization that provided services to the populace in Shanghai and acted as an employer for those anxious to find jobs. It, too, paid wages in U.S. currency. Established in 1943, UNRRA's mission was to provide food, clothing, medical, and agricultural supplies, transportation, and industrial rehabilitation to war-torn countries. China was allotted the largest share of all nations receiving UNRRA assistance, amounting to U.S.$530 million.[18] Its first shipment of supplies reached Shanghai in November 1945. UNRRA personnel worked closely with the newly sovereign Chinese government through the Chinese National Relief and Rehabilitation Administration (CNRRA), under the direction of P. H. Ho. Eventually, the UNRRA/CNRRA team, with headquarters in Shanghai and a liaison office in Nanking, came to include fifteen regional offices and six main supply depots.[19]

The generosity of the program overwhelmed the ability of Shanghai to absorb and distribute the relief supplies. A total of at least 2,241,294 long tons of supplies had arrived in China by August 1947.[20] With a broken infrastructure throughout the country, a general paralysis of industrial production, and the task of transferring and rehabilitating political authority,

Figure 26. Refugees unload a shipment of UNRRA rations arriving in Shanghai after the war. SOURCE: Horst Eisfelder, courtesy of the United States Holocaust Memorial Museum.

Shanghai became overburdened by the complicated relief program. China's meager transportation system had been disrupted in key areas or destroyed. Industrial centers had been bombed and looted. Considerable areas of the country suffered from severe flooding. How to fairly distribute goods under these conditions, and with civil and military conflict spreading across the country, was a major problem, further complicated by the fact that the Guomindang diverted a good deal of the UNRRA relief unloaded in Shanghai to the Nationalist forces.

In the meantime, the inflation of the war years continued to escalate. The government only enflamed the problem by printing more money to meet its many obligations, driving prices even higher and causing massive hoarding and currency speculation. Prices between August 1945 and July 1948 increased an average of 33.7 percent per month. A U.S. dollar, worth 39,000 Chinese *yuan* in August 1947, bought 474,000 by May 17, 1949. From the end of August 1948 until the end of April 1949, the average monthly price increases in Shanghai were 300 percent.[21] A newspaper report comparing what 100 yuan could buy over a ten-year period pointed out that in 1937, it would have bought two cows; by 1946, one egg; and by 1947, one-third of a packet of matches.[22] In 1947, almost any American could easily become a multimillionaire in this local economy. Small wonder that members of the refugee communities stood in line for hours to apply for employment with the U.S. military and UNRRA.

Inflation and the inability to move the goods pouring into the port created an active black market in UNRRA relief supplies. Food and cotton became key commodities, as did almost every kind of item shipped to the American PX network throughout China. A parallel system of barter also developed. It was mainly the Chinese who suffered, and their resentment helped to weld antiforeign sentiment and patriotic feeling, making the most discontented susceptible to communist agitators. Joseph Froomkin, a young reporter for the *Shanghai Evening Post*, found little interest among his editors in statistics detailing the number of Chinese dying from hunger in famine areas in the interior of China. His investigative reporting revealed that UNRRA relief supplies in famine areas were being shipped back to Shanghai, where prices for rice and wheat were higher, even though no great shortages existed there.[23] The Chinese press refrained from reporting such information because doing so would imply criticism of the Guomindang regime. Such negative commentary could easily provoke the serious charge of being in sympathy with the communists.[24]

A potentially explosive issue that never completely surfaced involved the different standards of relief provided to European refugees and to Chinese in Shanghai. It hinged upon the "minimum basis of requirements" established by the UNRRA Council, which stated that standards of relief were to be equitable for all groups aided by UNRRA relief. No criteria equivalent to the European ones had been developed for China, however, and UNRRA officials argued that the poverty of the two populations could in any case not be compared. Europeans' standards of poverty were simply much higher than those of the Chinese, who had been "inured by generations to stoical acceptance of cold, rags, disease and hunger." [25] UNRRA thus faced a dilemma. If it treated European refugees better, as history seemed to warrant, in a Chinese city where nationalist feelings were clearly in the ascendant, intolerable Chinese criticism would likely result. On the other hand, if the available aid were uniformly distributed to both Europeans and Chinese, sponsors and patrons of the European groups in the supplying countries would be infuriated. A practical solution was worked out with consenting CNRRA officials, whereby the standards of care for Western refugees were raised to meet European standards, but the criticism this preferential treatment was likely to provoke in China was avoided by "arranging that UNRRA reports on this operation would be distributed only outside China."[26]

Jewish Relief Programs

In sharp contrast to the Russian community, Jewish refugees had a number of means of support, in addition to their greater opportunities for employment. As noted above, once the war ended, Jewish refugees could again receive speedy relief from major Jewish service organizations, which were ready to provide it and effective at speaking on their behalf. With the liberation of the foreign internment camps, Manuel Siegel once again assumed responsibility for the work of the American Jewish Joint Distribution Committee (AJJDC) in Shanghai, serving until the arrival of its new representative, Charles R. Jordan.[27] Under Jordan's direction, the AJJDC set up five departments — finance, relief, general welfare, housing, and medical — to implement its new mission. It worked closely with UNRRA and CNRRA in making food and clothing available to the refugees. With the aid of paid refugee staff, UNRRA supplied both food and thousands of articles of clothing and blankets to 9,100 people.[28] Refugee carpenters and masons became involved in the AJJDC's program to restore and renovate housing in Hongkou, including repairing refugee camps and Chinese-style "lane houses" owned by the AJJDC, all of which had fallen into disrepair. The AJJDC, which was providing U.S.$100,000 a month in relief aid to the refugees, reported that 13,475 Jewish refugees remained in Shanghai by November 1946, with about 20 percent of them still living in the camps.[29] Figures provided noted that in addition to the 2,238 living in the various AJJDC refugee camps, 1,201 persons had found shelter in the AJJDC's private lane houses in Hongkou.[30]

CNRRA cash relief provided to refugees in local currency proved inadequate in the face of local inflation. The AJJDC was able to increase this subsidy by 30 percent, so that 5,626 persons received enhanced cash assistance twice a month, making the curse of inflation easier to bear.[31] In addition, the AJJDC covered the cost of steamship tickets for those fortunate enough to have visas.[32] The AJJDC also improved refugee medical care by adding temporary extensions onto the refugee hospital and built recreational facilities and a new Jewish Community Center, which became a cultural and recreational center for Jewish youth, sponsoring sporting events, handicrafts, and social occasions. In addition, it built a home for the elderly and a library holding a collection of 2,713 books.[33]

Through its offices in many countries, the Hebrew Immigrant Aid Society helped Shanghai refugees reestablish contact with family members lost during the war years.[34] HIAS staff circulated lists of names of Jews from various parts of Europe who had survived the war, which were posted locally on the walls of Hongkou shops and cafés. Frequently, of course, the news was tragic, with reports of dead or missing relatives. HIAS was also extremely helpful in facilitating financial assistance from relatives overseas. Remuneration to 2,534 persons amounted to U.S.$119,109 by the end of 1946.[35]

ORT-Shanghai stepped up its training programs in order to qualify refugees for opportunities with the U.S. forces and to prepare them for employment after emigration. More than 1,000 persons trained in these programs in the postwar period. The scope of the program was remarkable, offering courses from the most challenging, such as engineering and mechanics, to simple gardening. Some of the most popular courses were carpentry, locksmithing, and welding. Others chose cloth cutting, dressmaking, bookkeeping, and bookbinding.[36]

Rabbi Fine, a U.S. Army chaplain, attempted to organize a teen-to-college-age chapter of B'nai B'rith. Another youth organization was the Jewish Youth Community Center, operating under the guidance of the AJJDC social welfare supervisor Geraldine Grodsky and funded largely by the Jewish Welfare Board. It published its own newspaper, *Future*. Having funds at its disposal, this youth organization was able to sponsor a variety of sports, games, handicrafts, and social activities, and it included girls as members.

The Russian Jewish community's Jewish Recreation Club made a very welcome contribution by reviving its boxing matches, suspended during the war. One local favorite contestant from the German Jewish community, Alfred "Lako" Kohn, competed at this club and in later years went on to win light heavyweight honors in the New York City Golden Gloves matches. Sports were very popular and well attended in Shanghai. Soccer matches, football games, tennis, and ping-pong attracted both enthusiastic players and supportive fans.

Time to Emigrate

> This period of unspeakable human distress is not the time for us to close or to narrow our gates.
>
> —President Harry Truman, *1945*

Unlike the Sephardim who had lived in Shanghai since the middle of the nineteenth century and considered it their home, or even the Russian refugees, who had been in the city for twenty years or more, many having been born there, refugees from Nazi-controlled Europe saw Shanghai only as a "waiting hall" where they could find refuge until a more suitable and permanent home could be arranged. China was embroiled in a civil war and in the midst of a desperate economic crisis, facts that encouraged the refugees to look elsewhere to build a future life for themselves and their families. A survey indicated that 40 percent of Shanghai Jewish refugees wanted to go to the United States, 21 percent to Palestine, which was still closed to them, 26 percent to Austria and Germany, and the rest to Australia and Latin American countries.[37]

Working through its affiliated organization, the Intergovernmental Committee for Refugees, UNRRA took charge of overseeing the repatriation of refugees to their native lands. Although for most refugees, a return to their devastated homelands was unthinkable, others found this the best if not the only choice. The new Chinese authorities initially regarded the European refugees, especially the Germans and Austrians, as "ex-enemies" and stateless, as well as a potential drain on scarce resources, both financial and administrative, at a time when Chinese so desperately needed assistance. The Chinese government issued a proclamation stating plans to intern and later deport these "aliens."[38] The proposed legislation brought immediate resistance and pressure by officials of both the UNRRA China Office and CNRRA, as well as foreign governments and Jewish organizations.[39] UNRRA, joined by the

Intergovernmental Committee and the AJJDC immediately agreed to provide formal guarantees vouching for the refugees as bona fide displaced persons. Using arguments asserting China's obligations as a member of UNRRA, the opposition managed to get the legislation canceled, largely by making pledges to the Chinese to serve as the refugees' custodians and guarantors.[40]

To avoid further inflaming Chinese resentments, UNRRA officials took additional steps to establish special funds, apart from their overall regular relief budget, to cover assistance to the Jewish refugees and to ensure that these refugees did not become public charges. In the meantime, antiforeign sentiment in Shanghai continued to gather strength. Jewish residents in Hongkou faced hostile protests from Chinese who wanted them to vacate the refugee properties and return them to Chinese desperate for housing.[41] One resentful Chinese observer described the Hongkou Jews as "idlers in ironed trousers," who lacked resources, dealt mainly in secondhand goods, and had never bothered to learn either Chinese or Japanese.[42] In short, to many Western residents, the message received was clear. It was time to leave Shanghai.

The postwar repatriation or resettlement of refugees from Shanghai became burdensome problems for the Allied governments and United Nations relief agencies, which were struggling to cope with the many war orphans and uprooted millions in Europe. The scope of the problem in Europe led to a broadening of the definition of refugee to give full attention to "displaced persons" (DPs), or those who, as a result of the war, had been forcibly removed from their countries of residence, and who required care and assistance until they could be repatriated or resettled. The term "refugee," on the other hand, remained more narrowly focused to mean those who had left their countries to escape oppression by Nazi or fascist regimes, or, as had happened with many in both the Jewish and Russian refugee communities in Shanghai, those who had become refugees for reasons of race, religion, nationality, or political opinion even before the outbreak of World War II.[43] As this study has defined them, these refugees were members of victim diasporas. The need to assist those dislocated by war placed the Shanghai refugee communities in direct competition with huge communities in Europe for the scarce resources of relief agencies. In effect, the scope of the problem in Europe became a serious distraction for those who might otherwise immediately have come to the aid of the Shanghai refugees. In addition, their statelessness complicated the Shanghai refugees' status. In order to qualify for assistance, they needed to be of a nationality with UN membership, an obvious problem for Shanghai's Russians.

The Shanghai Russian Situation and Soviet Response

The Chinese government did not view the stateless Russians as "ex-enemies," but its policy toward the Russian refugee community was initially unfavorable. The Chinese authorities refused to recognize the Russian Emigrants Committee through the standard process of registration, and ordered all non-Soviet Russian newspapers in Shanghai to be closed.[44] In response, the committee's chairman, G. K. Bologov, took action to mobilize the Russian community for the purpose of inducing the Chinese to reverse this decision. At the same time, the committee was about to hold a new election of its top leadership. Bologov gave an inspiring speech to the committee membership at a rally before the election, held at the Shanghai Canidrome, and eventually won the election. As the chosen leader of the Russian community, he was able to use his new authority and popular support to persuade the Chinese to reverse their decision and register the Russian Emigrants Committee, once again giving it official status. Most important to the Chinese, this reversal relieved them of the burden of having to supervise this large and stateless community.[45]

Just after the war ended, the Soviet Union initiated an appeal to the Slavic refugee community, even sending an envoy to Shanghai, offering a period of amnesty during which stateless refugees could easily receive Soviet passports and return, supposedly, to a warm reception in the motherland. Well-known persons who had accepted the offer and had done well by repatriation became effective advertisements for the program, which began to generate considerable enthusiasm among Shanghai Russians. Some who participated even found ways to use their newly acquired passports to obtain visas to enter other countries.[46] The disbandment of the Communist International inclined many stateless refugees to wonder whether the political climate in the USSR had really changed. There were rumors that churches were being reestablished in Russia. It was said that officers in the Soviet Army (it was no longer the hated "Red Army") once again sported epaulets. Incredibly, former imperial officers somehow construed this as credible evidence foreshadowing an eventual reinstatement of the Romanovs.[47] Their long separation from the realities of the Soviet Union, the nostalgia and misery of their state-lessness, and the effectiveness of the local Russian press in evoking patriotic sentiments, especially during the war years, had the refugees clinging to any ray of hope.

In response to the variety of favorable reactions, Soviet authorities dispatched to Shanghai a captured German transport ship, capable of carrying a volunteer group of 1,000 passengers. The ship's arrival was suitably marked by greetings from Soviet consular officers, an orchestra playing familiar Russian songs, and blessings from a local Russian Orthodox priest.[48] Several thousand persons took advantage of the Soviet offer to overcome their state-lessness and return. The first departure was in August 1947, when 1,100 persons departed for the Soviet Union, including Soviet immigrants, journalists, engineers, and athletes. A second voyage carried 1,257 persons, with engineers, technicians, students, and young people on board. In October 1947, another trip transported 1,300, and in November, a fourth voyage carried 300 persons. The last trip occurred in March 1948, carrying 1,000 White Russian passengers. The actual number of Russians who departed for the Soviet Union is estimated to have been about 4,000.[49]

Those who had departed reported back to Shanghai friends and acquaintances that conditions in the new settlements and promises of a good life in the Soviet Union had been greatly exaggerated. This news caused many still in Shanghai to reconsider their plans to return. In order to rescind one's Soviet passport, a notice had to be published in the local Shanghai press. Soon evidence of the hardship and disappointment provided by those who had returned to the Soviet Union began to mount, as shown by the growing numbers of notices of dropped passports that appeared in the local Russian émigré newspapers.[50] The tide began to turn; increasingly, Shanghai Russians chose the no-man's-land of statelessness rather than the growing uncertainty of a return to the motherland.

The Outlook for Jewish Emigration

Prospects for the German Jews at least brightened with President Truman's executive directives on immigration of December 22, 1945.[51] Although their primary focus continued to be on the situation in Europe, particularly in the American zone of occupation, they did not exclude Jews in China, and some aspects of them even benefited the Shanghai Jews. One directive specified that visas be distributed among persons of all faiths, creeds, and nationalities, by country of origin. The crucial feature was that two-thirds of the immigration quotas for all countries for one year were allotted to Germany.[52] This generous quota figure meant that German-born Jews in Shanghai could expect to emigrate to the United States without difficulty. (Immigration quotas were calculated by taking into consideration the ratio of the number of any nationality in the United States based on the population figures of 1920, with a limit of 150,000 immigrants per year.) Furthermore, Truman's order allowed for the use of corporate affidavits providing blanket financial guarantees for groups of successful applicants.[53] This feature greatly facilitated emigration procedures by giving organizations such as HIAS, working together with the United Service for New Americans, an efficient alternative to the time-consuming work of preparing individual guarantees.

Adversely, however, the spouses of many German-born Jews had been born in countries with much smaller quotas, such as Austria, Poland, Czechoslovakia, and Romania, and so if these German Jewish refugees chose to emigrate to the United States, husbands or wives would have to be left behind until their respective quotas opened, which might take years. Nevertheless, more than 5,000 refugees born in Germany and registered under corporate affidavits left Shanghai for the United States, many without even a relative in the new country. Those who left loved ones behind hoped that the quota situation would soon change so that family members would be able to follow.[54]

Austrian Jewish refugees were in particularly difficult circumstances. The annual U.S. quota for Austrian immigration was 1,413, but that figure applied as well to the numerous Austrians in DP camps in Europe. It must be kept in mind that after VE Day, there were about 770,000 Jewish DPs in Europe who did not want to repatriate.[55] Some of Shanghai's Austrian Jews had registered even before the war under the German quota, Austria having become part of Germany. Their registrations were canceled after the war, however, when Austria once again became an independent country. Truman's directive disqualified them as Germans, because the new criterion was place of birth.

The Shanghai Austrians, having to compete under very unfavorable odds, often chose repatriation. By the end of 1947, 957 Austrians had departed for their native land. One hundred and fifty of the 250 Czechs registered for repatriation, as did 512 German Jews, the latter mostly elderly, poor, and without relatives abroad.[56] To illustrate how discouraging the situation was for those from countries with small quotas, the total number of quotas allotted to Shanghai for the year 1947–48 for the issuance of visas amounted to only 220. This number was to apply to Austrians, Poles, Czechs, Romanians, and Hungarians.[57]

The independent-minded and politically assertive Polish Jews found themselves in perhaps the most difficult circumstances of all, but for reasons that had both positive and negative outcomes. Members of the famous Mir yeshiva and the Telsh, Kletzk, and Lubavitch yeshivas, who had made so many important contributions to the spiritual life of the Jewish community in Shanghai, received priority treatment for immigration visas through high-level intervention on their behalf by Jewish leaders with both the U.S. State Department and the Executive Branch. In May 1946, a Polish chargé d'affaires arrived in Shanghai along with the new secretary of the Polish consulate, Professor Jablonski, a respected sinologist. The new consulate issued valid Polish passports, which the U.S. consul then approved for visas. On July 4, 1946, more than 100 members of these yeshivas and 80 other Poles with preferred status set sail on the *General Meiggs*, 55 of them destined for Canada and the remainder for the United States. Plans existed for the rest of the rabbis and rabbinical students to follow on the next transport until all had left by the fall. In all, the authorities issued 400 visas to this elite group.[58]

The negative aspect was that these high-level departures exhausted the 1945–46 Polish quotas for laymen, with the expectation that future new quota numbers would go to DPs in Europe. These fears proved correct. Polish Jews in Shanghai received only 29 quota numbers in 1949, after not having received any in 1947–49 because of the special preference given to the Polish rabbinical groups.[59] Moreover, other Shanghai refugee groups complained that processing such a large Polish group tied up the U.S. consulate staff, thus making it unavailable to service other pressing refugee needs. Of the 1,300 Poles in Shanghai in August 1946, only six registered for repatriation, two of them Jews.

Group Tensions and Rivalries

UNRRA took responsibility for the repatriation of refugees by getting approval from military authorities and the European governments involved, arranging necessary passports and visas, and providing food, clothing, and transportation. The AJJDC provided assistance to UNRRA, often assuming administrative responsibilities, which it handled through its Joint Migration Office, opened in February 1946. The AJJDC also provided each refugee being repatriated with U.S.$15.00 in board money.[60] UNRRA did not become involved in resettlement activities, which, beginning in 1947, were handled by the new International Refugee Organization (IRO), assisted in Shanghai by the major Jewish organizations. A key challenge to all of these bodies was transportation, because the end of the war had brought an acute shortage of shipping for all purposes. Japanese shipping had been obliterated, and the expanded U.S. fleet was burdened with repatriating the Japanese from China and transporting servicemen and their dependents home. In addition, goods such as clothing were scarce, and therefore expensive, and it was difficult to find prospective staff for the relief bodies who were interested in serving far from home for another long period after wartime separations.

By the end of 1947, 6,670 Jewish refugees in Shanghai were still waiting for resettlement and some for repatriation.[61] Representatives of several major Jewish organizations were on the scene trying to deal with the problems of emigration. These included the AJJDC, under the direction of Charles Jordan, the World Jewish Congress, which had established a special China Section, reportedly to emphasize the importance of the Shanghai refugee crisis, the HIAS organizations, and the Palaestina Amt, a German Zionist agency. It was perhaps inevitable that disputes and arguments would develop among these often competing bodies, to the detriment of the refugees, as they tried to work through the feuding bureaucracies to deal with their problems. Charles Jordan frequently expressed concern to the World Jewish Congress that its funding efforts would cause UNRRA to cut its budget for Jewish refugee relief, which amounted to U.S.$2 million. He called for better coordination of efforts between the AJJDC and the World Jewish Congress.[62] On the other hand, there were those who criticized the

AJJDC's wartime functioning, even claiming that its representatives had collaborated with the Japanese and saying that its organization consisted of "anti-social elements," who mismanaged funds and programs.[63]

The World Jewish Congress claimed it was "endangered almost uninterruptedly by the preponderance of the Joint [Committee]," while at the same time suffering from chronic internal arguments among its political department, religious affairs section, and other key units.[64] Zionist organizations were at odds among their groups and with the other Jewish organizations over the arrangement of priorities and chosen agendas. The Kadimah Organization and United Zionist Revisionists pressed for all efforts to be concentrated on creation of the new state of Israel, attacking the World Jewish Congress for dissipating Jewish organizational energies by advocating instead a broad program of relief, emigration assistance, and social services.

Certainly, the overlap in responsibilities was one of the major sources of conflict between Jewish organizations. For example, the AJJDC, HIAS, and World Jewish Congress all managed programs to search for relatives of Shanghai Jews, but without any effective coordination of effort. Even the Vaad Hatzala became involved in relief assistance, providing 12,000 lbs. of used clothing for distribution among the various refugee groups. There were also charges of favoritism. William Deman, secretary of the Council of European Refugee Organizations in Shanghai, complained that the "grand Jewish organizations" always gave primary attention to the German refugees and neglected the needs of others.[65]

Discouraged by the course of events in Shanghai, refugee leaders often attempted to influence events by writing independently to the headquarters of Jewish organizations, to individual congressmen, and even to the president of the United States to explain their predicament. Their hopes came to center around the new legislation being introduced in Congress, some parts of which were favorable and some not to the future of the Shanghai Jews. Unfortunately, sentiment in Congress was becoming increasingly inhospitable to accepting more refugees and DPs, with some members displaying a particularly negative attitude toward Jewish refugees. A frequent argument, reinforced by UNRRA officials, was that the new state of Israel, established on May 14, 1948, should take care of these refugees, especially since for many years, the Jews had demanded an independent homeland. Congressional thinking overlooked the fact that many of the Shanghai Jews had immediate family members in the United States or did not feel ready or able to go to a new and in many ways primitive land, where they would have to pioneer its development. Older refugees who had experienced significant hardship surviving the war years in Shanghai especially resisted being faced once again with a difficult and challenging life. Also, the AJJDC's heavy involvement in and commitment to the support of the Shanghai Jews led many refugees simply to expect eventual resettlement in America.

U.S. Refugee Legislation and Its Effects

The Displaced Persons Act, Public Law 774, was a disaster for the Shanghai refugees.[66] Its main focus centered first on clearing Austria, Germany, and Italy of DPs. Shanghai was essentially forgotten. President Truman attacked the legislation for being "flagrantly discriminatory," especially "against displaced persons of the Jewish faith."[67] Truman agreed to sign the bill only so as not to hold up the resettlement process but stressed that new legislation should be prepared quickly to rectify the bill's injustices. The new law canceled provisions of the Truman directive allowing for the corporate affidavit system that had so facilitated the emigration process and granted Shanghai refugees preference or priority DP status. Worse yet, section 2 of the act restricted immigration eligibility to only those DPs who had entered Germany, Austria, or Italy between September 1, 1939, and December 22, 1945, and were still there and had not permanently resettled by January 1, 1948. Of course, most of the Jewish displaced persons who had entered those countries during that time had subsequently left, including the Shanghai-bound refugees. In addition, section 12 of the act reserved, for a period of two years, 50 percent of the German and Austrian quotas for what were called *Volksdeutsche*, persons of German ethnic origin born in Poland, Czechoslovakia, Hungary, or Romania and currently residing in Germany and Austria. This clause prolonged the waiting period for Shanghai refugees from these small quota countries indefinitely by mortgaging their national quotas for years to come. The Shanghai Jewish refugees would accordingly have to share the remaining 50 percent with the great numbers of prospective immigrants to the United States.

Refugee hopes were invested in a coincident bill introduced by Emanuel

Celler (D-N.Y.), chairman of the House Judiciary Committee, which specified that 5,000 Shanghai refugees be included in the overall number of DPs admitted. Unfortunately, this legislation did not pass, even though press campaigns and prominent members of Congress such as Jacob Javits (R-N.Y.) gave the issue much prominence and publicity.[68] Instead, under the new act, the German and Austrian quotas were opened for Germans and Austrians residing inside their own countries, and the State Department received immediate authorization to resume consular activities on the spot to process their applications. Thus, Shanghai DPs found themselves in competition with every German or Austrian wanting to emigrate to the United States, save those clearly identified as Nazis. In view of the oversubscribed quotas, especially for the small quota countries, many were effectively prevented by this legislation from reaching the United States for years to come.

Public Law 774 was especially hard on 350 families, 480 German members of which had gone to the United States after the Truman directive. Their relatives in Shanghai (440) who came under the small quota numbers could neither expect to join their U.S. family members nor seek visitor visas. Visitor status, according to regulations, would immediately remove them from the DP rolls, ending any chances for future immigration. And when the allotted visitation period came to an end, no longer DPs, they would by law suffer deportation. Even a temporary stay in Israel would be considered resettlement and exclusion from favorable provisions of the law.[69] To publicize their predicament, this special group established a formal organization, the Emergency Committee of Parents and Children of European DPs in Shanghai, and wrote to all the relevant and potentially helpful authorities for understanding and assistance. The disappointing, and from today's perspective shocking, outcome was that although members of this group received transit visas that allowed them to enter the United States, upon arrival in California, they were loaded onto a sealed train that took them to Ellis Island, New York, where they were allowed to spend only forty-five minutes with resident family members before having to leave the country again. Altogether 228 refugees made this trip in March 1949, with 192 passengers traveling on via Naples toward the final destination of Israel, while 36 accepted repatriation to Austria.[70]

Refugee groups attempted in various ways to make themselves particularly appealing to countries for emigration. Austrians formed an organization

Figure 27. Jewish refugees hold a religious service on board a sealed train traveling across the United States. SOURCE: U.S. National Archives and Records Administration.

of "skilled craftsmen" that succeeded in attracting the attention of Canada, which had stated a preference for skilled tradesmen, engineers, and technicians (but not doctors or lawyers). Canada accepted 280 refugees on a temporary basis, but when asked at a later date to handle still more, refused on the basis of political insecurity arising out of growing domestic unemployment.[71] During 1946, some 700 Shanghai refugees found their way to Australia, which sent representatives to select specially qualified individuals for resettlement. These hopeful developments met with resistance from the Australian consul general in Shanghai, however, who claimed that Shanghai Jews were not suitable as immigrants to Australia owing to the alleged involvement of some in criminal activities such as prostitution and drug activity. He received official support for his position, which led to authorizing a meager quota of 300 Australian landing permits annually for Jewish DPs. By setting this quota, it was possible to deflect the negative publicity likely to be generated by ordering a blanket limitation on Jewish emigration to Australia.

By early 1949, the political situation in China had become more uncertain, with the communists obviously winning, but Australia rejected a U.S. request that it provide a staging area for refugees from Shanghai. Even the Executive Committee of Australian Jewry seemed unwilling to take decisive steps to reverse that rejection.[72] It is estimated that from 1,500 to 2,500 Jews entered Australia between 1945 and 1953, depending on which Jewish record-keeping organization one heeds.[73] In desperation, the head of the Shanghai Council of European Refugee Organizations suggested that the World Jewish Congress look into setting up a U.S. camp in the Dominican Republic to handle the refugees until legislation pending before the U.S. Congress became final. If the congressional outcome was still not favorable, the refugees would be able to go to Israel.[74]

Another suggestion that raised considerable hopes in Jewish circles drew upon the precedent set in 1944 by the rescue and relocation in the United States of a group of 982 wartime refugees from Italy, including 918 Jews, by order of President Roosevelt. Arriving on a military transport, this group was housed at an Emergency Refugee Shelter at Fort Ontario in Oswego, New York, near the Canadian border, where its members were interned.

Their eventual legal immigration became possible because of the same 1945 Truman directive that had allowed for the corporate affidavit system that eased the postwar immigration of Jews from Shanghai and elsewhere. The Truman directive granted the Oswego group special permission to remain in the United States after an approved adjustment in their immigration status.[75] Shanghai Jewish leaders interpreted this previous action as a rescue without violation of the immigration laws and one pertinent to their own circumstances.[76] Unfortunately, the realities of postwar conditions, which included growing restrictionist attitudes fueled by the huge DP problem in Europe, dashed their expectations. The World Jewish Congress leaders gave firm guidance to the hopeful Shanghai Jews to drop the proposal immediately, explaining that raising it in any form would create self-defeating resentment and hostility in the U.S. Congress, where key members viewed the Oswego case as "a willful circumvention of our immigration laws."[77]

The fact that new DP legislation was on the horizon, but had yet to be taken up, caused those who might otherwise have taken action to delay and await the outcome. In the meantime, the U.S. consulate in Shanghai closed, causing further difficulties for the remaining refugees, who needed access to their files and records. Fear and frustration among those facing an imminent communist takeover of the city and an uncertain future is reflected clearly in the plea to the World Jewish Congress by one refugee official in Shanghai: "For God's sake, call in an extraordinary meeting of all organizations and explain to them the importance of exercising all possible influence with the State Department that sanctuary be given us immediately."[78]

One option available to the refugees was to emigrate to Israel. The new Israeli government sent Moshe Yuval, its consul in New York City, to Shanghai with authority to process 7,000 visas for immigration to Israel. Some gladly accepted. Others wished only a temporary stay until they could reach their desired U.S. destination. The IRO provided the necessary transportation, and in December 1948, the SS *Wooster Victory* left Shanghai for Israel with 892 passengers on board. In January 1949, another ship, the SS *Castle Bianco*, carried 900 to the same destination. Two more ships, the SS *General Gordon* and SS *Marcos*, between them transported 712 passengers to Israel in early 1949. Still others departed for Israel by plane. In all, a total of 2,676 Shanghai refugees chose to go to Israel, leaving 2,668 registered with the American AJJDC as of the beginning of February 1949.[79]

Concern in the White Russian community mounted as the Chinese communists gained victory after victory over Chiang Kai-shek's Nationalist forces. The Russian perception in Shanghai, which was shared by U.S. authorities, including some in Congress, was that a communist victory in China would put the Russian refugees in Shanghai at particular risk. IRO officers began a concentrated resettlement effort, as did Russian religious organizations and well-known Russian émigré figures. With the war's end, the government of Australia began to consider ways to recruit the young and able-bodied to contribute to the postwar development of its large and underpopulated country. Shanghai Russians responded in large numbers.

In addition, the government of Argentina willingly offered assistance and acceptance to both Shanghai Russians and Ukrainians. Damage was done to Argentina's hospitality in 1948, however, when newly arrived Russian refugees from Shanghai became embroiled in disputes with the resident Ukrainian community. The quarrels escalated to the point where the Argentine government suspended the visas of more than 1,000 persons, many who had lived in the country for more than a decade. In the hope of finding an amicable solution to the problem, Father Nicodemous of the Shanghai Russian Orthodox Church undertook a mission to make peace between the Shanghai refugees and the Argentine government. His negotiations were not entirely successful. Many of the more discontented Russian refugees decided to set aside their plans to settle in Argentina and, instead, approached the Soviet consulate in Buenos Aires for permission to proceed to the Soviet Union for permanent resettlement.[80]

The Chinese communists took Shanghai in May 1949, facing little resistance from Chinese Nationalist forces. Subsequent reports from refugee leaders stated that law enforcement improved and corruption began to diminish, but antiforeign sentiment remained strong. The prospect of new U.S. DP legislation helped buoy refugee spirits somewhat, and in May 1950, another group of 108 refugees with relatives in the United States crossed the country in a sealed train bound for Ellis Island, hoping that amendments to the Displaced Persons Act would pass during their stay and make them eligible for permanent residence.[81] This did not happen. Time ran out, after a 24-day stay, with the State Department claiming that it could not properly screen prospective immigrants because, with the consulate closed in Shanghai, the refugees' dossiers could not be located or were unavailable. In the circumstances, the group had no legal options but to leave the country and seek readmission under the clause that applied to the country of their provisional residence. Recognizing the extraordinary hardship that this provision caused, President Truman ordered that these refugees be accommodated as temporary returnees at an IRO camp in Europe, rather than a German-administered center, ensuring that they did not forfeit their rights to emigrate to the United States.[82]

The new legislation amending the Displaced Persons Act of 1948, approved in June 1950, finally gave relief to the troubled Shanghai refugees, both those in the city itself and those abroad.[83] It provided for the issuance of 4,000 non-quota immigration visas to refugees residing in China as of July 1, 1948, or who on July 16, 1950, qualified for admission into the United States and were still in China, or, having left China, had not permanently settled in another country. There was no need for affidavits of support or for housing or employment guarantees under the amended act. A new problem arose because of the lack of consular facilities in China. The only alternative was for refugees to make use of the existing consular facilities either in Hong Kong or on Taiwan. In November 1950, more than 500 refugees finished processing and departed for the United States, leaving behind a Jewish community of about 1,200.

Refuge in the Philippines

Before this new legislation passed, the International Refugee Organization opened another avenue to the Shanghai refugees, which appealed to the remaining Russian, Ukrainian, and Polish refugees, who in any case had few other options. IRO officials proposed that they go to Tubabao Island, off the island of Samar in the Philippines, where they might expect to stay for four months while awaiting processing for other destinations. With the communist threat very real by this time, at least as seen by these exiles from Bolshevism, more than 5,000 of them accepted the IRO offer.[84] Others in smaller numbers found their way to Australia, Argentina, Bolivia, Brazil, Chile, Guatemala, Peru, Uruguay, or Paraguay. Many hopeful candidates saw their chances dimmed by the results of medical tests that showed spots on their lungs. Russian poverty and malnutrition, often combined with the deprivations of the Civil War, had caused some to become infected with tuberculosis. If lung spots were detected, a probationary period followed before a candidate could be passed for emigration. The first group of 500 refugees destined for the Philippines left on the *Hwalien*, chartered by the IRO, on January 15, 1949. One member, Nikita Moravsky, reported that the entire refugee transfer, involving ships and air transports, took place between January and May 1949.[85]

IRO officials tried to persuade the remaining Shanghai Jewish leaders to accept the opportunity to go to the Philippines, at least as a temporary measure. Jewish organizations had information through their own channels, however, that conditions in Samar were anything but hospitable. U.S. Army personnel who had served in this area of the Philippines had told some about the region's harsh climate and the potential hardships. Jewish refugees also feared ingrained anti-Semitism among the large numbers of Russians and Ukrainians making up the transiting group.[86] In any case, very few Jews accepted the IRO's offer. Most of those who did were already spouses of Polish or Russian refugees. Refugees arriving in the Philippines did receive welcome support from Rabbi Josef Schwarz of the Jewish Community of the Philippines. He had recommended that the Shanghai Jews consider coming to the Philippines, where, he said, they might receive support from local Jewish organizations for permanent resettlement in that country. Still, there were few Jews who responded.

The jungle-like conditions at the abandoned Guiuan U.S. naval base on Tubabao were a rude shock to the incoming refugees. Several complained loudly to the presiding officials. After repeated requests from IRO officials, G. K. Bologov agreed to fly to Samar in early February to help calm the situation and facilitate the transition. Despite his modest educational training, reflecting his Cossack background, Bologov was a skillful and articulate leader, with recognized diplomatic talents, effective for managing the large and diverse refugee community. The need for his skills was real. The IRO had supplied the refugees with surplus U.S. Army tents, many with holes and tears in them, and a good supply of K-rations and powdered food. The newcomers lived in tents holding twelve persons or in smaller ones holding two to four. The supply of fresh water and electricity was uneven. The poor living conditions and the subtropical climate bred dysentery and malaria. As part of the security measures, initiated in the belief that subversives might have infiltrated the camp, all outgoing mail had to be written in English and was then subjected to censorship. A police force, armed only with sticks, was staffed by former Russian policemen in Shanghai. Refugee excursions outside the camp, even just to visit the town of Guiuan, required an official pass.[87] Overall, it was a very bleak picture.

What had been meant to be a temporary home soon began to take on the contours of a permanent residence. There was no choice but to make use of the best of the existing facilities, which included a Quonset hut and a few barracks, to set up schools, a hospital, and even churches. The "camp" was broken up into districts, with a typical one housing and servicing 300 people. Each district elected an administrative body, which in turn selected a member to sit on the camp's Administrative Council, presided over by the camp president. The camp's elected president, G. K. Bologov, reflected the predominance of Russians in the Samar community. As in the refugee camps in Shanghai, work in the camp kitchen, where one had better access to food, always in short supply, was much sought after. For example, 28 lbs. of meat and bones would make stew and soup for the 300 people in a district, and the lucky kitchen help had the privilege of sucking the stewed bones after every morsel of cooked meat had been scraped off them and added to the community pot.[88]

The Russians and Ukrainians in the Guiuan group included both Eastern Orthodox Christians and Uniate Catholics. In addition, there was a small community of "Xinjiang Baptists" who had made their way from China's northwest to Shanghai and then joined the exodus to the Philippines. The Xinjiang group found their services as shoemakers and general repairmen in demand. The Uniate Catholics had run a successful school in Shanghai and were able, through some of their talented leaders, such as Father Wilcox and Father Urusov, to provide both education and counseling to the numerous young people in the camp.[89] There were substantial numbers of Poles and Ukrainians, and in much smaller numbers, fifteen other nationalities in the Samar community, Latvians being the most numerous of these.[90] Most belonged to the Eastern Orthodox faith, and in one account, out of the 1,117 refugees considered, only 10 were Jews.[91] The community as a whole boasted seven churches and one mosque, all housed in tents.

Life under canvas in Samar began to seem endless. The "four-month stay" extended into two years. The government of Australia sent a "selecting" delegation to the Samar camp to find able-bodied young refugees for emigration to Australia.[92] Reportedly, 1,800 camp residents made the cut.[93] While this was an attractive opportunity to some, the requirement that those interested sign up to work for a two-year stint at a location to be designated by the Australian delegation gave pause to others. After taking a disappointing chance on the Philippine destination, they feared being committed to the hardships of an unknown place, this time without friendships or community support.

Prospects for Samar finally brightened when Shanghai's Russian Orthodox Archbishop Ioann visited the camp and, after extensive discussions, left for the United States to lobby the U.S. Congress on behalf of this refugee group.[94] With the support of California Senator William E. Knowland, who had been pressured by the Russian community in the San Francisco Bay Area, and who spent a day at the Samar community camp in November 1949, Bishop Ioann was instrumental in getting new legislation passed by the

U.S. Congress in 1950.[95] This legislation amended the 1948 Displaced Persons Act, which in addition to helping the Shanghai Jewish refugees emigrate, made it possible for the long-suffering Samar refugees to receive visas and emigrate to the United States. Legislation passed in 1953 subsequently made provision for 3,000 additional refugees in the Far East, some Russian, particularly those who had fled the communist regime in China for different destinations, to apply for and receive visas through the U.S. consular offices in Hong Kong.[96]

Russian benefactors, particularly Mrs. Alexandra Tolstoy, the daughter of Leo Tolstoy and founder of the Tolstoy Foundation, procured the necessary assurances from various religious agencies and individuals willing to guarantee a home and support for the new immigrants. The San Francisco Russian community and its affiliated charity organizations provided affidavits, as did several religious bodies, including the Methodist Committee and the World Church Service, the latter consisting of Episcopalians, Methodists, and other Protestant denominations.

At least three crossings on the *General M. L. Hersey* and the *General W. G. Haan* carried the refugees to their new home. The latter ship left on Russian Orthodox Christmas Day, January 6, 1951. Rough weather took its toll in seasickness among the passengers, but services considered essential continued to function. The seventy-five pupils of the IRO school at Tubabao received tutoring in classes established aboard the ship. When the eve of the old Russian New Year arrived on January 14, a New Year's mass was held for a congregation, followed by Thanksgiving Devotions, complete with choral support. On New Year's Day, passengers sent season's greetings by telegram to their former Russian Emigrants Committee head and Tubabao camp leader, G. K. Bologov. A shipboard newspaper, *Our Herald*, provided passengers with a steady stream of information and entertainment. Actors, musicians, and vocalists among the passengers entertained at parties and dances and helped relieve the anxieties all shared concerning their uncertain future.[97]

Upon arriving in San Francisco Bay, the refugee ships met with a warm reception by local officials and especially the resident Russian community. A brass band playing familiar songs, and a rough, hand-lettered sign reading "Welcome to America" greeted the newcomers. This was one of the largest groups of refugees ever to arrive in San Francisco. Among the broad mix of backgrounds and ages were twenty-five orphans from Shanghai's St. Tikhon's Orphanage, including members of the orphanage band, which had frequently entertained their fellow passengers on the voyage across the Pacific. The transplanted St. Tikhon's Orphanage was slated for a new location at 498 15th Avenue in San Francisco. St. Tikhon's was also revered for its service to homeless Chinese children, who, under its care, learned Russian, received Russian diplomas, and followed the Orthodox faith. Some of these from Samar went on to pursue successful professional careers in the United States.[98] After more than thirty years of rootlessness, a large portion of the Russian diaspora in Shanghai had finally found a resting place. The sense of gratitude, common endurance, and continued hopeful outlook are best expressed by one refugee who boarded the former U.S. Navy troopship *General W. G. Haan*, bound for San Francisco in 1951:

> The remnants of Old Russia, unshakable in their fundamental principles
> through hard labour have been trying for 33 years to build up their
> new lives: they have been building their own churches, schools, cultural
> and artistic institutions, thus contributing their share. . . . None of us
> is building castles in the air of having a light and easy life in the U.S.A.,
> we know that only by steady work, perseverance and belief in our own
> strength we may reach our goal which was dreamt of for so many years
> in exile. We shall roundly sacrifice everything which is in our power for
> the benefit of our newly acquired motherland. . . . Let us all be worthy
> of this, to obtain rights without obligations may destroy all that has with
> such hardships been gained and will create a wrong impression concerning the bulk of White Russian Refugees from China.[99]

The End of the Jewish Communities in China

With emigration channels now firmly in place, the AJJDC closed its offices in Shanghai in 1951, but it continued to fund the dwindling community there.[100] A new organization, the Council of the Jewish Community, established in 1949, took over all major responsibilities, including emigration, repatriation, health, and education.[101] The new council registered with the Foreign Affairs Department of the Shanghai Military Committee on September 1, 1950, as a voluntary charitable organization for the welfare of China's Jewry. Under the strained local conditions, the council immediately urged close cooperation between the Sephardi and Ashkenazi communities, which, as we have seen, had had significant difficulties working together in the past.

In 1953, two of the oldest Jewish organizations in Shanghai, the Shanghai Hebrew Relief Society and Hebrew Shelter House, amalgamated into a new Shanghai Jewish Center. In August, the Sephardi Jewish Communal Association and the Ashkenazi Communal Association took the additional step of forming a joint Sephardi and Ashkenazi committee to handle synagogue, burial, cemetery, and other community affairs. The Sephardi Jews agreed to furnish one half of the funds to support these basic services.[102] Thus, as the refugee population decreased, the two Jewish congregations, which had first met in Shanghai in the nineteenth century, moved steadily closer together, even sharing religious services at the only remaining place of worship, the New Synagogue.

In 1956, the merger of the two communities' internal affairs under the Council of the Jewish Community became final.[103] With so little participation in synagogue services, it soon became necessary for the Shanghai Jewish Center to take over the religious services and begin arrangements for the sale of the New Synagogue. The Torah Scrolls and religious books, together with 1,022 other volumes, were shipped to Israel.[104] Following disposal of the synagogue, the Shanghai Jewish Center held religious services in its newly adapted prayer hall, as well as sponsoring Hebrew classes and other functions. The Shanghai Jewish Club closed its doors, forwarding more than 3,000 selected books from its library to the Israeli Ministry of Education and Culture.[105]

The Shanghai Jewish Center, which housed the offices of the Council of the Jewish Community, carried out the key function of maintaining complete personal files and records on the nearly 20,000 Jews who had found refuge in Shanghai, including those who had resided in the Shitei chiku.[106] Council officers issued death certificates and letters to refugees' survivors. Equally important, they prepared so-called ghetto letters for use in filing claims for restitution with the German and Austrian governments for having been forced to spend the years 1943–45 restricted and deprived of liberty and individual freedom in the Shanghai ghetto.[107] By July 1957, the council had issued 771 of these letters.[108]

Putting these letters or any other documentation to good use became complicated by the fact that it was under Japanese authority that the Jews had experienced the Shanghai ghetto. Documentation was needed to show that the Jews "were deprived of liberty in a ghetto on the basis of a law or decree forced upon them by the influence of the Nazi government," as had occurred in Italy.[109] If a connection could be documented between the Japanese establishment of the ghetto and Nazi pressure, then the affected German and Austrian refugees might have an enforceable claim against those governments. In the early 1950s, several former refugees applying for restitution gave affidavits supporting the claim, which they believed, that the Japanese had given in to Nazi pressure in establishing the Jewish ghetto in Shanghai.[110] In order to explore the subject officially, the World Jewish Congress contacted the Jewish community leaders in Tokyo, who were unable to locate any conclusive evidence of Japanese responsiveness to German-instigated designs regarding the Shanghai Jews. Furthermore, research into the Nuremberg documents also failed to uncover any references to the Shanghai ghetto.[111]

Still another effort to prove German pressure on the Japanese to establish the Shanghai ghetto involved the proceedings of the Shanghai War Criminal Trial, or Ehrhardt Case, which lasted from August 1946 until January 1947. In this case, the United States charged twenty-three former German officials in Shanghai, including Jesco von Puttkammer and Lothar Ehrhardt, with "willfully and unlawfully" violating the unconditional German surrender by engaging in continuing military operations against the United States and its allies.[112] A request was forwarded to U.S. military judicial authorities for a review of the trial record, because some had recalled that testimony given at the Shanghai Nazi trial showed the Japanese responding to a German request to establish the ghetto.[113] The Office of the Judge Advocate, which had custody of the trial records, reported back: "[T]here is no evidence in the Shanghai Case concerning the establishment of the 'Shanghai Ghetto.'"[114]

Gradually, changes in legislation allowed the Hongkou detainees to receive long overdue restitution. The German Federal Republic in 1953 enacted legislation to pay compensation for personal injury to victims of Nazi persecution. This legislation was expanded in legislation enacted in June 1956 that specifically cited deprivation of liberty and restrictions on liberty, among other damages, as legal basis for restitution. It included instances where the government of a foreign state was induced by the Nazis to deprive victims of their liberty.[115] Then, in 1990 and 1992, the reunited German government made provisions under the Article 2 Fund for the award of pensions to those who could prove that they had been confined in a ghetto for a period of at least eighteen months during the war.[116] Also responding, the Austrian government implemented a pension program with a survivor benefit for Austrian Jews who had been living in Austria on March 12, 1938, the date of the Anschluss, or Nazi takeover, before being forced to flee. Under this program, a monthly stipend averaging U.S.$300 was provided by the government. In June 1995, the Austrian parliament passed new legislation providing for a one-time payment of an average of U.S.$7,000 to qualifying individuals who had escaped from Austria after the Anschluss for a variety of reasons. This broader legislation applies to those who fled for reasons of race, ethnicity, politics, sexual orientation, or other causes. The main stipulation was that affected individuals must have resided in Austria on or shortly before the key March 12, 1938, date.[117] Some former Shanghai ghetto residents qualified and received compensation.

And what of the few Jews still remaining in Shanghai during the 1950s and beyond? Most were very elderly or ill "hard-core" cases. Communist China's policies of nationalizing commerce and industry left few employment opportunities, creating a constant stream of emigration flowing to the United States and, especially, to Israel, which in the spirit of the "Law of Return" approved immigration by Jews with no age or financial restrictions. A few, having obtained the required Chinese exit permits, repatriated to Germany, the Soviet Union, or Austria, while others emigrated to Australia, Canada, or Latin American countries.

Subsequent figures report that the Shanghai Jewish community had 171 members (87 USSR citizens and 84 others) in 1956, 109 in 1957, 56 in 1961, and 20 in 1965. In 1955, 110 Jews emigrated to the Soviet Union. Many of these registered for the ill-fated opening up of "virgin-soil" regions, first announced in February 1954. The following year, only 10 Jews accepted the offer.[118] Horace Kadoorie, who had resettled in Hong Kong, and W. J. Citrin were appointed representatives of both the AJJDC and HIAS to look after the few remaining Jews.[119] Kadoorie said that only 15 Jews remained in Shanghai in 1967. In 1982, a Hong Kong newspaper reported the death of the last Shanghai refugee, a Polish Jew, leaving only one person from the Jewish refugee community in all of China, an elderly woman in Harbin.[120]

TEN

Conclusion

At first appearance, the subject of this study seems quite modest — the experiences of several thousand refugees who found themselves in a far corner of the world. The timespan of the work, covering as it does almost half of the twentieth century, is substantial, but the limited numbers of actors and the remote location would seem to preclude treatment of important historical issues and trends. Yet a closer look reveals that the stories of these diaspora communities actually unfold in ways that reflect directly upon many of the human events and dramas that trouble our contemporary world and assail our sensibilities almost daily via the media. The many victims of "ethnic cleansing" in the 1990s recall the human toll taken by the Nazis. There are also numerous recent parallels to the White Russians who found themselves on the losing side and forced to flee for political reasons. Familiar currents of religious hatred — sometimes disguised, sometimes not — led to the pogroms that drove Russian and Ukrainian Jews to flee to Shanghai.

Prewar Shanghai was a multinational city in which no one nation exercised clear control, at least not until Pearl Harbor, when the Japanese took charge. No treaty arrangement existed that awarded clear authority to one power over the others. With the city divided into three distinct parts, political and legal authority were nebulous, especially in the International Settlement, where consular authorities existed alongside the multinational Municipal Council. The importance of this peculiarity was that it ran counter to the predominant strivings of most twentieth-century societies — the creation of a nation-state and its accompanying myth of national sovereignty. Instead, we see a polyglot entity run by various councils, into which poured the remains of collapsed empires (czarist Russian, Austro-Hungarian, and German). Once again, comparisons with the recent collapse of the Soviet Union, Yugoslavia, and perhaps Indonesia come to mind. This open port, the only place in the world that required no documentation to enter, attracted adherents of fanatical movements, fascist, communist, and nationalist. In a space of less than thirteen square miles, these many disparate groups intersected, unfettered by clear-cut, accepted rules and regulations. In this society, built on commerce with many national participants, the fine points of jurisdiction and authority were never clearly addressed. Rather, the leeway built into the system allowed for better manipulation of one's position. This leeway also benefited the refugees crowding into the city.

In this unique Shanghai setting, seemingly separate — often rigidly separated — identities came to overlap and sometimes merge. Germans, for example, took comfort in spending an afternoon in the Jewish ghetto, where the bakeries, shops, and cafés reminded them of the fatherland. The loose political atmosphere and multiplicity of nationalities made such behavior seem ordinary, even acceptable. Russian Jews served on the White Russian–dominated Russian Emigrants Committee, an unusual combination in the context of this relic of the Russian empire, famous for its institutionalized anti-Semitism and episodes of rampant violence against Jews. When the ghetto was established, the Russian Jews, who were excluded from it, supplied food and other forms of support to Polish Jews and even to the other Jews of European nationalities confined there.

The dissonance of being so many things sometimes took a toll on the diaspora communities, already under great stress. Politics had driven the White Russians from their homeland, and politics infected their debate as to what kind of future was best for Russia. The monarchists imagined a Russia led once again by a Romanov; others had different visions. When the Nazi-Soviet war began, many embraced their roots in the motherland and, if they had not already done so, adopted a pro-Soviet stance. Russian youths remained responsive to the people and traditions that had formed them, but they also were the most unsettled by the multiple identities that plagued their community, often in conflict with each other. It was hardest for them to imagine their futures, make choices, and come to terms with their circumstances. From their experiences, we can learn more about the condition of exiles immersed in a metropolitan culture.

In general, the constant bickering and replaying of political scenarios centered around community leaders seemed to root the Russian community in the past, with memories of a lost world, but also to foster a determination to preserve and enhance Russian culture and traditions. Certainly, their hated statelessness was a constant reminder of their separation and defeat. In contrast, the Ukrainians remained single-minded in their determination to realize an independent Ukraine in which they would be able to express their full and complete political and cultural identity. By embracing the invention of a government in exile, they found solace in what for them was a necessary connection to a nation-state, whatever its standing. The same imagining preoccupied the Shanghai Poles.

The stateless European Jews also faced alienation in the Shanghai environment, but their ability to connect to their Jewish tradition gave them solace and often created unusual bedfellows. We find wealthy Sephardi Jews working in the same organizations for the benefit of the community alongside penniless Ashkenazi refugees. These two separate traditions in Judaism were thrown together in adversity and, while still maintaining their distinct identities, managed to serve the needs of the refugee communities. German Jews whose Jewish ties had diminished at home found their connections to Jewish traditions restored and enhanced, especially in the setting of the ghetto. There was a layering of identities: one might be a stateless German, be of the Ashkenazi tradition, have a certain level of income, skill, or education, and so forth, and each of these defining factors played a role in predicting the nature of one's life in multicultural Shanghai. But in the end, being Jews put them in touch with a tradition, networks, resources, and an encompassing identity that was sustaining even in the worst of times.

Both diaspora communities were cursed by their statelessness in an age when documented national identity seemed as essential and presumed as gender or race as the signature of a person. Both also were confronted with the multiplicity of identities that characterized their multinational beginnings. But in the rarified atmosphere of prewar and wartime Shanghai, where the modern artifact of the nation-state never really took hold, these groups were at least able to find refuge. The Jewish diaspora even succeeded in cultivating its traditions and, most important, in building vital connections across its many inherent differences. Interviews with these former refugees always include reports of hardship, but not without mentioning memories of rich relationships and positive personal experiences as well.

The same cannot be said of the Slavic experience. There, the emphasis is largely negative, with reports of self-conscious poverty and hurtful perceptions of being social and political outcasts. In the end, Judaism enabled the Jewish diaspora in Shanghai to overcome its major differences and sustain itself as a community. For the Slavic diaspora, the outcome was less positive. Japanese control eventually quelled its noisy political differences, forcing White Russians, Ukrainian nationalists, Russian Jews, and pro-Soviet Russians into one cowed organization. But rather than finding strong, sustaining connections in common Slavic roots, most remained marooned in longings for an imagined national political identity — in a city that would deny them this "privilege," but as an open port could never really require a documented national identity of any of its inhabitants.

A brief review of some of the key experiences of each of the major victim diaspora communities will help bring into focus some of these observations. The White Russian community arrived in Shanghai to a less than warm welcome, even from their own resident countrymen, who were overwhelmed by their numbers and needs and embarrassed by their poverty. And within the broader Shanghai foreign community, there was a lack of acceptance that never really subsided. Nevertheless, the newcomers set about building clubs, schools, churches, and a myriad of organizations to satisfy their need for identity and preserve and strengthen their Russian culture and traditions and collective memory of the motherland, activities identified at the beginning of this study as common to victim diasporas. These bonds of religion, language, culture, and a sense of common history were often sustaining. Their biggest challenge, which they never successfully overcame, was the daily one of finding gainful employment. Failure led to humiliating poverty, idleness, crime, alcohol abuse, and rampant prostitution, not to mention the open disdain of other European groups in Shanghai.

With their organizations for almost every conceivable purpose, the Russians succeeded in providing a sense of community and a socially diverse atmosphere. But, at the same time, their success encouraged a competitive spirit in leaders who vied to be the primary spokesman for the large community. Groups formed and reformed around those who claimed to speak for the entire Russian community. The resulting divisiveness was a key weakness, especially when outside pressures began to be felt, such as those exerted first by the Japanese, who were able to manipulate these differences, and, later, by the Soviet Union, which exploited the Shanghai Russians' stateless condition. This is not to say that the Russian leaders could have withstood, especially, the Japanese pressure to consolidate all Russians, including Russian Jews and the Ukrainians, into one easily controllable organization. But the endemic sniping, with its charges and countercharges, polluted the atmosphere and fractured the community. It also contributed to the disillusionment, particularly, of Russian youth, a fact not missed by the Soviet authorities, anxious to entice members of the diaspora to return to the motherland so that they could experience Soviet revenge. This serious but essentially political weakness within the Russian community was only relieved to some degree by the sense of ethnic unity nourished by the rich cultural institutions that the community developed and maintained.

We have seen that a return movement did emerge among the Slavic refugee communities, for a variety and often a combination of reasons. Older Russians cherished their ties to their familiar and beloved motherland. Some among them still entertained plans to overthrow the Soviet government and return the imperial family to power. The young often saw their prospects as best served in a Russian state rather than by remaining estranged in Shanghai. Others, of all ages, were deeply distressed at having no official recognized status.

Shanghai's White Russians maintained generally amicable relations with the Russian Jews. But while the leaders of the two groups maintained official contact, their communities preferred to remain separate. The Russian Ashkenazi Jews were established and more prosperous. Their thriving community had its own club and religious and social organizations. Spokesmen for the Russian Jewish community expressed resentment when Japanese policies forced their leaders and members to operate under the All-Russian Emigrants Committee and follow White Russian leaders. But their resistance was muted. Unlike in Harbin, where outbursts of verbal and physical abuse of Jews were not uncommon, anti-Semitism in Shanghai was veiled. The two communities coexisted peacefully, and even under the changed circumstances, each group continued to live, socially and substantively, in its own separate enclave.

The reaction of the relatively small Ukrainian community was much more intense. Ukrainians' time, energy, and talent were focused on educating the Shanghai authorities, and particularly the Japanese, about their own historically separate identity and the need to treat them as an independent national entity, clearly different from the Russians. Their primary point of unity involved a common commitment to a sovereign Ukrainian state free of Soviet control. Although they established their own club, organizations, and publications, Ukrainian leaders still found themselves unable to deflect the Japanese from disputing their uniqueness and obliging them to unite in structures that the Japanese could easily direct and control for their own purposes.

If diversity and division often characterized the Russian and Ukrainian diasporas, these factors were at least as intense among the groups that fled Nazi Europe. This is not surprising. They came from so many different countries and such diverse religious and cultural backgrounds. Most remained connected by a common link to Judaism and their refugee status, but intense internal differences often set them at odds, or at least apart from one another. The German Jews, many of them highly assimilated into German culture, maintained a sense of superiority vis-à-vis Slavic Jews, while enjoying the able support of Jewish world organizations. An almost similar statement might be made about the Austrian Jews. Jews from the famous yeshivas of Poland, who believed that their community alone represented "authentic" Judaism, were a case apart. This Jewish elite had the support of Shanghai Russian Jews and especially of the powerful international Orthodox Jewish community.

Friction was a constant among these groups as each attempted to maintain its own cultural and religious identity. Nevertheless, they were forced to work together owing to the circumstances of their diasporas. Relief programs and resources were not limitless, and disputes developed between leaders and organizations over planning, programs, and, especially, the dispensing of funds and services. These are the negative factors; the positive ones were the successful and vital cultural, educational, religious, and social organizations that these hard-pressed Jewish groups were still able to establish, and that prospered over a short period of time in a city with a tolerance for pluralism.

All of these interlinked groups — White Russians, Ukrainians, and Russian, German, Austrian, Baltic, and Polish Jews — became subject to the overriding presence of the Japanese military and civilian authorities in Shanghai. A main inhibiting factor for the White Russians was their statelessness, and the concomitant lack of formal government protection, circumstances that were real and deeply felt. Japanese attempts to establish control over this community and the other Slavic groups by means of an umbrella organization obedient to Japanese direction brought about resistance from two key Russian leaders. Their independent and principled stands almost certainly led to their subsequent assassinations. The outcome was a fully intimidated organization, one still holding on to its traditions and beliefs, but powerless against Japanese manipulation and control.

World War II further eroded political support for the main, long-standing White Russian organization by arousing Russian patriotism in support of Soviet troops defending the motherland. In addition, the Soviet authorities, seeing their advantage and aware of the pain of White Russian statelessness, found a powerful means to appeal to the diaspora Russians by enticing them with offers of Soviet citizenship. Such offers were welcome, especially among Russian youth, who had little or no memory of life under the Bolsheviks. Quite understandably, some chose to end their diaspora status by returning, usually with disastrous consequences. In fact, the White Russians were squeezed from all sides: by their general poverty, by the opportunities missed by their exclusion from elite Western society in Shanghai, by their statelessness, by Japanese intrusions supported by local fascist groups, by Soviet appeals, and by their own divisiveness.

The European Jews who arrived in Shanghai in the late 1930s could look to both well-established Ashkenazi leaders and organizations and the wealthy members of the Sephardi community for help. Jewish identity evoked support for the needy arriving Jews. As noted, however, the numbers and diversity of the refugees in terms of nationality and their differing degrees of religious commitment led to intense divisions and rivalries. This situation seriously impaired organized efforts to provide them with assistance. But even with these obstacles to overcome, local Jewish organizations, helped significantly by international Jewish bodies, were still able to meet the basic need of the Jewish refugees for food and shelter.

The Pacific War disrupted these efforts and also led to a momentous change in Japanese policies toward the European Jews in Shanghai. The Japanese policy toward the European Jews especially can best be characterized as highly ambivalent. On the one hand, the Japanese felt gratitude to Jews in general for the Schiff loans that had enabled Japan to win the Russo-Japanese War. Added to this was the Japanese recognition of and admiration for Jewish talent and accomplishments in many fields, as evidenced by the offer to Albert Einstein of a teaching position at one of Japan's top universities.

On the other hand, the Japanese had been exposed to the anti-Semitism of White Russians, especially in Manchuria, and, being intrigued by some of the arguments, had translated and digested the contents of the infamous *Protocols of the Elders of Zion*. These two incongruous factors, admiration of and gratitude to Jews, along with exposure to Russian anti-Semitic conspiracy theories, came together in the mid 1930s. The Japanese responded by undertaking an extensive study of the Jews, carried out by study groups that produced detailed research publications. Having in mind their own experience with the Jews in arranging loans for Japan, and buying into the White Russian theories about worldwide Jewish influence, the Japanese began to consider the Jews as powerful, potentially useful, and, for these reasons, somewhat dangerous, especially in light of Japan's grandiose plans to establish dominance in East Asia.

The Japanese planned to cultivate the Jews, believing that Jews controlled world financial markets, communications, and the press, and more specifically, had special influence on American foreign policy makers, including even President Franklin D. Roosevelt. Japanese researchers reasoned that just as Jews had engineered the Schiff loans, other Jews, including local Jewish leaders in Shanghai, might accomplish similar feats, such as helping to finance Japan's ambitious designs in China, and perhaps even influence policy makers in the United States. One of their key goals was to keep the United States out of a war in Asia or the Pacific. If the local Jews themselves could not accomplish this, perhaps their allegedly powerful contacts elsewhere in the world could.

Pearl Harbor necessarily put an end to these ambitions, and Japanese leaders had to rethink their polices toward the Jews. Still harboring lingering suspicions about Jewish power and influence, the Japanese concluded that the Jews had chosen not to support the Japanese agenda, and that they should therefore be kept under strict surveillance, given wartime conditions. The solution they arrived at was to put the Jews in a designated area where they could be closely monitored.

This ambivalent Japanese policy stance toward the Jews, which included both admiration and a degree of fear, and was rooted in an unrealistic estimation of their capabilities, was thus the reason for establishing the Hongkou ghetto, rather than Japanese responsiveness to German desires, as has been suggested. The Japanese creation of the Shanghai ghetto was self-serving and independent of Berlin's dictates. The Japanese had their own agenda in Shanghai, and by extension in China and East Asia, and the Jews were to be one important supporting element in its realization.

When the Shanghai Jews failed to live up to this — and some, such as Sir Victor Sassoon, who sided with Japan's wartime enemy Chiang Kai-shek, were candid about their lack of support — the result was resentment and a turn in Japanese behavior. Nonetheless, the Japanese continued to try to encourage Jews in the Hongkou ghetto to make it an industrial base in support of Tokyo's war effort. The Japanese also approached the Russian Jews, who were allowed to remain outside the ghetto, for help in raising funds to pay for Japanese armaments.

The post–World War II years again showed the impact of the well-organized Jewish relief organizations. Officials of these organizations arranged employment opportunities and relief supplies of all types, mainly for the European Jews. Another of their major tasks was to deflect early Chinese initiatives to deport German and Austrian Jews as enemy aliens. World Jewish organizations had also helped expedite the escape from Nazi Europe, and later, Shanghai, of revered Polish rabbinical groups and kept open channels of communication about the fate of Jews in other Nazi-occupied countries. What these key organizations could not control, however, were the nationality-based quota restrictions on immigration imposed by various countries, especially the United States.

Each refugee "nationality" presented its case for immigration to the United States, the destination of choice for most. Only the German refugees were in a favorable quota position. The Austrian Jews and remaining Polish Jews were in very difficult quota positions. The White Russians, in a twist of fate, eventually found themselves in a somewhat favorable light as Cold War thinking began to take shape and interest focused on this now interesting anticommunist group's dangerous situation vis-à-vis the Chinese communists. Even with this sudden attention, however, this previously unprotected and unspoken-for community still had to spend two years in jungle-like conditions in the Philippines before being rescued and, for the most part, brought to the United States.

As noted, some White Russians ended their diaspora status by returning to the Soviet Union. Others maintained it by settling in any of a variety of countries that would accept them. Most Jewish refugees chose not to return to Europe or the Soviet Union. Many of the Slavic Jews readily accepted the challenge of life in the new state of Israel, thus ending their diaspora status.

The Chinese themselves by and large did not impinge on the lives of most of the diaspora refugees in Shanghai, except as they encountered them on the street, as hired help, or in the marketplace. A few upper-class Chinese students attended school with affluent Russians and Jews, and there was some competition for jobs between Russians and Chinese, especially during strikes by Chinese workers. Russians who served in the police forces worked alongside Chinese constables. Chinese shared the same physical spaces as refugees, especially in the crowded neighborhoods of Hongkou. But as for social, religious, educational, organizational, and cultural life, the Chinese and diaspora communities lived very much apart. Any comparisons, especially of the wartime experiences of the victim diasporas and their Chinese refugee neighbors, would find Chinese economic conditions, housing, health, sanitation, and overall social well-being far inferior, and yet these often glaring disparities go largely unreported by members of the diaspora groups.

The overall Chinese view of the refugees reflected their own identification with the rising tide of Chinese nationalism and resentment of the foreign presence in China. The Chinese commitment to national salvation was a powerful force, which gathered strength in Shanghai beginning at least by the early 1900s. Because of its influence, the views and issues pertaining to the refugees became intertwined with the overall Chinese response to foreign imperialism. When the Chinese nationalists gained sovereignty over

Shanghai after the war, they hesitated to extend recognition or registration to any Western refugee organization. And the Shanghai Chinese responded by wanting to evict the Jews from housing formerly owned by Chinese and expressed resentment at the refugees taking any share of the UNRRA relief supplies. The diaspora communities were seen as just another group of acquisitive Westerners, less stylish perhaps and some downright destitute, but still identified in the Chinese mind with the sins of imperialism.

Even with these negative sentiments, reflective of the times, it remains a fact that it was in China's key port city that these victim diaspora groups found refuge and managed their own survival. Paradoxically, their painful statelessness often became interlaced with the Chinese quest for a strong nation-state and regained sovereignty. As we have seen, their stories lack any single comprehensive view or explanation. It is in their diversity that the complexity of these Shanghai communities and their links to our contemporary society are best understood and appreciated.

Former Name	Current Name
Alcock Road	Anguo Road
Avenue Edward VII	East Yan'an Road
Avenue Foch	Yan'an Zhang Road and West Jinling Road
Avenue Joffre	Huaihai Zhong Road
Bubbling Well Road	West Nanjing Road
The Bund	Zhongshan Dongyi Road
Chaoufoong Road	Gaoyang Road
Chusan Road	Zhoushan Road
Dal'ny Road	Dalian Road
Dixwell Road	Liyang Road
East Seward Road	Dongzhangzhi Road
Gordon Road	Jiangning Road
Great Western Road	West Yan'an Road
Kinchow Road	Jingzhou Road
Kiukiang Road	Jiujiang Road
Lincoln Avenue	Tianshan Road
Moulmein Road	North Maoming Road
Muirhead Road	Haimen Road
Museum Road	Huqiu Road
North Szechuen Road	North Sichuan Road
Peking Road	East Beijing Road
Route Pichon	Fenyang Road
Rue Bourgeat	Changle Road
Rue Cardinal Mercier	South Maoming Road
Rue Corneille	Gaolan Road
Rue Lafayette	Fuxing Zhong Road

Former Name	Current Name
Rue Maresca	Wuyuan Road
Rue Paul Henri	Xinle Road
Rue Tenant de la Tour	South Xiangyang Road
Route Vallon	Nanchang Road
Seward Road	East Changzhi Road
Seymour Road	North Shaanxi Road
Taku Road	Dagu Road
Tongshan Road	Tangshan Road
Ward Road	Changyang Road
Wayside Road	Huoshan Road
Whashing Road	Xuchang Road
Yangtzepoo Road	Yangshupu Road
Yu Yuen Road	Yu Yuan Road

SOURCES: Tess Johnston and Deke Erh, *Welcome to Shanghai!* (Hong Kong: Old China Hand Press, 1997), pp. 88–90, and various city maps.

Abbreviations Used in the Notes

AJA   American Jewish Archives
AJJDC   American Jewish Joint Distribution Committee
CWR   *China Weekly Review*
IM   *Israel's Messenger* (Shanghai, 1904–41)
WJC   World Jewish Congress
NCDN   *North China Daily News*
NCH   *North China Herald*
OSS   U.S. Office of Strategic Services
SJC   *Shanghai Jewish Chronicle*
SMP   Shanghai Municipal Police
SMPD   Shanghai Municipal Police Dossier, U.S. National Archives and
         Records Administration, Washington, D.C.
UNRRA   United Nations Rehabilitation and Relief Association

Chapter 1

1. Simpson, *Refugee Question*, p. 1.
2. For a discussion of Chinese sojourner migrants, see Wakeman and Yeh, *Shanghai Sojourners*, pp. 5–7.
3. Robin Cohen, *Global Diasporas*, p. x. This volume introduces a series (fifteen volumes planned) about the formative conditions of the diasporas and the relationships that emerge between the migrants' homelands and their places of settlement.
4. Ibid. The unabridged listing of these nine features appears on p. 26.
5. The 1935 census data report 6,595 British and 2,017 Americans in the

International Settlement; the 1934 census data report 1,430 French, 2,630 British, and 1,792 Americans in the French Concession. See Shanghai Municipal Council, *Report for the Year 1935*, p. 49, and Conseil d'Administration municipale de la Concession française, *Bulletin Municipal, 1934*, p. 204.

6. For discussion of the Chinese bourgeoisie that emerged out of these migrations, see Bergère, *Golden Age of the Chinese Bourgeoisie*. For detailed discussion of the life and circumstances of Chinese sojourners arriving in Shanghai from rural areas, see Lu, *Beyond the Neon Lights*.

7. Perry, *Shanghai on Strike*, p. 49. Perry's account differentiates Shanghai's laboring masses according to native place origins and skill levels and describes their response to labor initiatives from the left and right. To understand the importance of native place ties to sojourners forming organizations and institutions, see Goodman, *Native Place, City, and Nation*.

8. For a critique of the popular notion that Shanghai was an insignificant fishing village before becoming a Western Treaty Port in 1843, see Linda Cooke Johnson, "Shanghai: Emerging Jiangnan Port," pp. 151–81. See also id., *Shanghai: From Market Town to Treaty Port*.

9. Fletcher, "Heyday of the Ch'ing Order," pp. 375–85.

10. Fairbank, "Creation of the Treaty System," pp. 213–63.

11. Eventually, fourteen powers enjoyed the privilege of extraterritoriality: Belgium, Denmark, France, Great Britain, Italy, Japan, the Netherlands, Norway, Portugal, Russia, Spain, Sweden, Switzerland, and the United States. Germany and Austria lost this right after World War I.

12. Hsia, *Status of Shanghai*.

13. *Chinese Year Book, 1940–41*.

14. Johnstone, *Shanghai Problem*, p. 61.

15. The Foreign Inspectorate of Customs, a joint Chinese-Western institution created in 1854, simultaneously enriched the Chinese government, provided systematic administration of a key public sector, and facilitated the economic exploitation of China by Westerners. See Fairbank, *Trade and Diplomacy*.

16. Kotenev, *Shanghai: Its Mixed Court and Council*.

17. Johnstone, *Shanghai Problem*, pp. 134–35.

18. Koffsky, *Consul General's Shanghai Postal Agency*, 1972.

19. Clifford, *Spoilt Children of Empire*, pp. 16–17.

20. Schrecker, *Imperialism and Chinese Nationalism*.

21. Shanghai Municipal Council, *Report for the Year 1935*; Jones, *Shanghai and Tientsin*, p. 2.

22. Kirby, "Internationalization of China," pp. 433–57.

23. An earlier Chinese Advisory Board began functioning in 1921, but with little influence on the Shanghai Municipal Council. See Clifford, *Spoilt Children of Empire*, p. 27. See also Pott, *Short History of Shanghai*, pp. 244–45. Two

Chinese representatives functioned in a consultative role on the French Council in 1915. See Goodman, *Native Place, City, and Nation*, p. 193.

24. Henriot, *Shanghai, 1927–1937*, examines Guomindang policies channeled through the Shanghai municipal government and directed at establishing control.

25. It might appear that the new arrangements threatened the dominant Western position on the council, but such was not the case. Chinese and Japanese ratepayers (the latter with two votes) were unlikely ever to vote in unison, and the British could always count on the Americans (with two votes) to support their position in any challenge.

26. Bickers, *Britain in China*, p. 30. This work examines the formation of the British settler society and its impact on Great Britain's China policy.

27. Feetham, *Report of the Honorable Richard Feetham*, vol. 1, p. 86.

Chapter 2

1. Contrary to popular legend, there was no sign excluding Chinese and dogs at the entrance to the Public Garden, as journalists have claimed. The regulation that did exclude them from public parks was rescinded in 1928. Subsequently, entrance to the parks required buying a ticket, a system that effectively kept out the poor, especially the Chinese masses. See Bickers and Wasserstrom, "Shanghai's 'Dogs and Chinese Not Admitted' Sign."

2. Moore, "Cosmopolitan Shanghai."

3. Fulcher, *Mission to Shanghai*, pp. 38–39.

4. There is debate as to whether this group is more appropriately identified as Oriental or Baghdadi Jews rather than as Sephardim. This study adopts the designation subscribed to by this Shanghai Jewish community. For further discussion, see Meyer, "Sephardi Jewish Community of Shanghai."

5. Hardoon served as a councillor on the Conseil d'Administration municipale de la Concession française from January 1892 until January 1902; he served on the Shanghai Municipal Council from March 1900 until March 1904. See Betta, "Silas A. Hardoon (1851–1931)," p. 75.

6. Leventhal, "From Your Historical Society," p. 15.

7. The first cemetery, on Mohawk Road, was sponsored by David Sassoon. Darwent, *Shanghai: A Handbook*, p. 20. Eventually, the Jewish communities managed four cemeteries in Shanghai, including the first on Mohawk Road, followed by those on Baikal Road, Columbia Road, and Point Road. Some early tombstones are described in Brown, "Jews of Modern China," p. 161.

8. *The Encyclopedia of Judaism*, ed. Geoffrey Wigoder (New York: Macmillan, 1989), pp. 82, 635–36; Zimmels, *Ashkenazim and Sephardim*, pp. 4–5.

9. By 1906, three synagogues served the Jewish communities of Shanghai: Ohel Moishe, Beth-El, and Shearith Israel. *IM*, Apr. 6, 1906.

10. *IM*, Mar. 7 and Aug. 1, 1924.

11. *IM*, May 31, 1907.

12. *IM*, May 14 and 28, 1909.

13. Conrad Levy, letter dated Jan. 19, 1921, in *IM*, Feb. 11, 1921.

14. *IM*, Aug. 1, 1924.

15. The Ohel Moishe Synagogue at 62 Changyang Road has now become the Jewish Refugee Historical Museum. See *Shanghai Pictorial*, no. 4 (1994): 24.

16. *IM*, Nov. 2, 1928.

17. *IM*, Feb. 11, 1921. This synagogue still stands in Shanghai on what is now North Shaanxi Road. It has the original holy ark and inscription, but the scrolls are gone. It is sometimes used as a meeting place for official gatherings, as it was during President Clinton's state visit in 1998.

18. *IM*, Nov. 11, 1921.

19. *NCH*, Sept. 13, 1924.

20. *NCH*, Feb. 27 and Nov. 13, 1926.

21. *NCH*, Apr. 4 and 21, 1928.

22. Zhiganov, *Russkie v Shankhaie*, p. 33.

23. Interview with Professor Wang Zhicheng, Shanghai Academy of Social Sciences, at the International Seminar on the Jews in Shanghai, Shanghai, Apr. 21, 1994.

24. Wang, *Shanghai E qiaoshi*, pp. 4–5. In 1861, two Englishmen, Albert F. Heard and G. B Dixwell, represented Russian interests. In 1870, the Russian official in Tianjin, C. A. Skatschkov, began to handle official and commercial affairs in both Tianjin and Shanghai. He was followed in October 1873 by C. Waeber. In 1880, the Russian J. E. Reding, who had earlier served in an official capacity in the Shanghai Russian consulate general, was appointed by the Russian government to the Shanghai post.

25. Lidin, "Russkaya emigratsiya v Shankhaie," p. 309.

26. For a detailed discussion of the founding of Harbin, see Wolff, *To the Harbin Station*, pp. 21–29. See also Clausen and Thøgersen, *Making of a Chinese City*, pp. 3–4, 12–16, 22; Fogel, "Integrating into Chinese Society," p. 48.

27. Mancall, *China at the Center*, p. 237.

28. Wolff, *To the Harbin Station*, pp. 10, 78–79, 103–8.

29. Woźniakowski, "Polonia Chińska w latach," p. 98. Another source identifies M. V. Gruliov, a Russian Jew who converted to the Russian Orthodox faith, as having selected the site for Harbin. See Bresler, "Harbin's Jewish Community," p. 202.

30. Nish, *Origins of the Russo-Japanese War*, p. 256.

31. Nish, "Overview of Relations," pp. 602–4.

32. Shillony, *Jew and the Japanese*, p. 222.

33. *IM*, Mar. 24, 1905, p. 309.

34. "Rights of Jewish Soldiers in Russian Army," *IM*, p. 194.

35. Best, "Financing a Foreign War," p. 313.

36. Ibid., p. 315.

37. The five loans underwritten in the United States totaled $196,250,000. Ibid., pp. 320–21.

38. *IM*, Mar. 22, 1906, p. 14.

39. *IM*, Dec. 30, 1904, p. 223.

40. Bresler, "Harbin's Jewish Community," p. 202.

41. Simpson, *Refugees: A Preliminary Report*, p. 157.

42. Zhiganov, *Russkie v Shankhaie*, p. 34; Lidin, "Russkaya emigratsiya v Shankhaie," p. 310.

43. Smith, *Vladivostok under Red and White Rule*, p. 169.

44. Ibid., p. 173.

45. Ibid., p. 164.

46. Nansen was appointed high commissioner of the League of Nations for Russian Refugees in September 1921 and served until his death in 1930. He mobilized refugee assistance from governments and major charities. See Simpson, *Refugee Problem*, pp. 197–203.

47. In 1922, Nansen secured the agreement of fifty-one nations to adopt and recognize the identity certificates, the first international certificates of the kind ever issued. The conventions of 1933 and 1938 guaranteed additional civil rights to refugees, but China was not a signatory nation. Simpson, *Refugee Question*, pp. 12–13.

48. V. F. Grosse, spokesman for the Russian emigrant community, provided the precise figure of 1,174 Russian permanent residents in 1921. See Grosse report to the secretary, Shanghai Municipal Council, June 9, 1928, in SMC Secretariat File, U1-3-3002 (hereafter SMC Secretariat File).

49. *NCDN*, Jan. 20, 1920.

50. "Community Church, Now Campaigning for Funds, Gets Fine Testimonial," *China Press*, June 10, 1923.

51. *NCDN*, Jan. 20, 1920.

52. Interview with Boris Boguslavsky, Nov. 11, 1994.

53. "The Russian Refugee Problem," *NCH*, Jan. 13, 1923.

54. "Russians in China," *NCH*, Feb. 21, 1920.

55. *NCDN*, Jan. 20, 1921.

56. Balakshin, *Final v Kitae*, vol. 2, p. 328.

57. "Origins and Future of the Local Russian Community" (a 5-part series), *Shanghai Sunday Times*, July 26, 1936.

58. V. F. Grosse was imperial consul general in Shanghai from 1911 until 1924, when Russian diplomatic institutions in China were transferred to the Soviet authorities. He was one of the founders and permanent chairmen of the "Aid" Society. Grosse was an honorary member of many Russian and foreign organizations. He died Oct. 6, 1931. Zhiganov, *Russkie v Shankhaie*, p. 51.

59. Police report, Apr. 15, 1935, in SMPD 5002.

60. Police report, Dec. 8, 1922, in SMPD 4880. A listing of fourteen Russian ships appears in a police report dated Dec. 11, 1920, in SMPD 4880.

61. Powell, *My Twenty-Five Years in China*, p. 57. U.S. troops were in Vladivostok in 1918 to guard a huge supply of war matériel provided by Russia's allies before Russia concluded a separate peace with Germany in 1917. The American forces remained in the region for nineteen months.

62. Police report, Dec. 11, 1922, in SMPD 4880.

63. Police report, Jan. 3, 1923, in SMPD 4913.

64. Police report, Jan. 4, 1923, in SMPD 4913.

65. Ibid.; see also V. V. Fedoulenko, "Russian Émigré Life in Shanghai" (hereafter Fedoulenko interview), p. 51.

66. Stephan, *Russian Far East*, p. 154.

67. For an account of their transfer to San Francisco and other destinations, see American National Red Cross, *Annual Report* for the year ending June 30, 1923. Another account reports that Admiral Stark eventually made his way to Paris to earn a living as a self-employed truck driver. See *Shanghai Sunday Times*, July 12, 1936. A report that some made a successful residence in the Philippines appears in *NCH*, Jan. 25, 1939.

68. *Shanghai Sunday Times*, July 12, 1936. A photograph and biographic sketch of General Glebov reporting his military career is contained in SMPD 5002A. Born in 1890, Glebov served in various Siberian Cossack units between 1914 and 1918. He was commander of Admiral Kolchak's personal guard and later commander of the 10th Siberian Cossack Regiment. By 1920, he was commander of the Siberian Cossacks in Chita under Ataman Semenov and achieved the rank of major general. From 1921 to 1922, he was commander of the Grodekovo Group of the White Army and was promoted to the rank of lieutenant general by Ataman Semenov. He left Russia in December 1922.

69. This group, formed in 1923, reportedly numbered some 1,699 White Russian officers and men. The Russian Brigade became part of this force. V. F. Grosse report to the commissioner general, SMC, Oct. 23, 1926, in SMC Secretariat File.

70. *NCH*, Dec. 22, 1931, p. 416.

71. "Russian Ships and Arms," *NCH*, Jan. 19, 1924.

72. "In the Russian Colony," *NCDN*, July 29, 1940, p. 11.

73. *Shanghai Sunday Times*, July 12, 1936. Another incident occurred in 1927 when a White Russian demonstration in front of the Soviet consulate turned violent as those inside celebrated the tenth anniversary of Soviet rule. See Zhiganov, *Russkie v Shankhaie*, p. 295.

74. Ibid.

75. Simpson, *Refugee Problem*, p. 496.

76. *Shanghai Sunday Times*, July 12, 1936.

77. *IM*, Aug. 1, 1924, p. 9. Purim is the Jewish festival to commemorate the deliverance of the Jews from Haman as related in the Book of Esther. It is observed in the middle of the Jewish month of Adar.

78. For a discussion of May 30 and its background, see Clifford, *Spoilt Children of Empire*, pp. 97–112. See also Rigby, *May 30 Movement*.

79. Zhiganov, *Russkie v Shankhaie*, p. 35.

80. V. F. Grosse report, Office of the Controller of Voluntary Services, dated Aug. 10, 1925, and Grosse report dated Jan. 1, 1926, in SMC Secretariat File.

81. Zhiganov, *Russkie v Shankhaie*, p. 35.

82. *NCH*, Sept. 21, 1929, p. 447.

83. Wang, *Shanghai E qiaoshi*, pp. 55–56, 238–47.

84. *NCH*, Apr. 8, 1927, p. 77.

85. *Shanghai Sunday Times*, July 12, 1936.

86. *IM*, Oct. 2, 1921, pp. 5–6; "Jews Enter Protest at Urga Pogrom," *NCH*, June 4, 1921, p. 673.

87. Police report, Feb. 1, 1922, in SMPD 4398.

88. Cohn, *Warrant for Genocide*, p. 61.

89. *IM*, Oct. 2, 1921.

90. *IM*, Aug. 3, 1928.

91. Prominent Jews often noted among the Bolshevik leaders included Trotsky, Radek, Zinoviev, Kamenev, Bukharin, Karakhan, and Litvinov.

92. Memorandum from Ch. Metzler, chairman, Russian Emigrants Committee to secretary, SMC, Oct. 1932, in SMC Secretariat File.

93. Memorandum from the SMP, June 13, 1933, in SMPD 2882; *Shanghai Sunday Times*, July 26, 1936.

94. For a study showing the diversity in backgrounds and politics of radical Chinese workers, see Perry, *Shanghai on Strike*.

95. Stranahan, *Underground: The Shanghai Communist Party*, p. 102. See also Ristaino, *China's Art of Revolution*.

96. *NCH*, Dec. 22, 1931, p. 416.

97. *IM*, July 5, 1929.

98. *IM*, Dec. 7, 1928.

99. Zhiganov, *Russkie v Shankhaie*, p. 35.

100. V. F. Grosse report to the acting secretary, SMC, dated Sept. 10, 1926, in SMC Secretariat File.

101. Wang bases his figures on a June 19, 1930 report of arrival figures by V. F. Grosse, which lists the same figures as appear in the Simpson account, except for the year 1928, for which the Grosse account reports 854 arrivals, rather than 1,122. A June 9, 1928, report by Grosse of arrival figures uses the figure 1,635 for 1925, rather than 1,535, but in his June 19, 1928, accounting, Grosse reports 1,535 arrivals for 1930. In this listing, and all the other sources

cited above, Grosse also notes1,174 refugee arrivals between 1900 and 1921.
See V. F. Grosse report to the secretary, SMC, dated June 9 and 19, 1928, in
SMC Secretariat File.

Chapter 3

1. An excerpt from "Maloo Memories," combining words from an old
Shanghai Volunteer Corps song with those of the Whiffenpoof Song (originally written for the Yale University Whiffenpoofs, an a cappella men's singing
group, but most notably recorded by Bing Crosby in 1947) in a printed program for a dinner given in Hong Kong in April 1954 to mark the centenary
of the SVC (Frank, "Shanghai Volunteer Corps").

2. Kounin, *Eighty-Five Years*, pp. 11–13.

3. Frank, "Shanghai Volunteer Corps," p. 4.

4. Ibid., p. 9. Frank's figures give a total strength of 2,320 by the end of
1938.

5. Kounin, *Eighty-Five Years*, pp. 184–88.

6. Karns and Patterson, *Shanghai*, p. 2.

7. Frank, "Shanghai Volunteer Corps," pp. 7–8.

8. Kounin, *Eighty-Five Years*, pp. 242–47.

9. General Glebov also organized a special detachment, with two companies of twenty-five Russians apiece, for the French Concession. *NCH*,
Apr. 19, 1932, p. 103.

10. Kounin, *Eighty-Five Years*, p. 246.

11. Ibid., p. 92.

12. Davidson-Houston, *Yellow Creek*, p. 143.

13. Kounin, *Eighty-Five Years*, p. 126.

14. Ibid., p. 126.

15. The future Archbishop Ioann (1896–1966), a former member of the
Poltava Cadet Corps and student in the Juridical Faculty of Kharkov University, left Russia for Istanbul with General Wrangel's army in 1920. After com-
pleting his studies in the Theology Department of the Belgrade Royal University, he taught in a gymnasium and later entered a monastic order. See *Russkie
v Shankhaie*, p. 47. He was consecrated bishop on May 28, 1934, arrived in
Shanghai on November 21, 1934, and became archbishop of all Russians in
China in 1946. In July 1994, he was canonized in an elaborate ceremony at
the San Francisco Russian Cathedral, where he is buried in a basement chapel.
See Perekrestov, *Man of God: Saint John of Shanghai and San Francisco*, p. 11;
Rose and Herman, *Saint John the Wonderworker*; Luke, "Glorification of Saint
John of Shanghai and San Francisco."

16. Shanghai Municipal Council, *Annual Report*, 1932, p. 18. A Defense
Committee, composed of various foreign powers in Shanghai, existed as early

as 1850 and assigned defense zones. See Wakeman, *Policing Shanghai*, pp. 387–98, n. 176.

17. For a map showing principal Japanese landmarks in Hongkou, see Peattie, "Japanese Treaty Port Settlements," p. 185.

18. Fulcher, *Mission Shanghai*, p. 117.

19. Coble, *Facing Japan*, p. 48.

20. Ibid., p. 51.

21. For discussion of Western shortsightedness regarding the real threat to Western Shanghai, see Clifford, *Spoilt Children of Empire*, esp. pp. 274–75.

22. Frank, "Jewish Company of the Shanghai Volunteer Corps," p. 20; *IM*, Jan. 1933, p. 12.

23. Kounin, *Eighty-Five Years*, p. 215.

24. For the constitution and bylaws of the new association, see Shanghai Municipal Archives file Q6-5-1115, July 14, 1931.

25. *IM*, Apr. 3, 1936, p.14; *Almanac Shanghai 1946/47*, ed. Lewin, p. 49; Johnston and Gao, "Jewish Sites in Shanghai," Mar. 15, 1990.

26. *IM*, Sept. 7, 1934, reports the original site of the Jewish Club as 83 Pichon Road and speaks of 200 members in 1934.

27. Interview with former Shanghai resident Nikita Moravsky, Mar. 1995.

28. V. F. Grosse report to secretary, SMC, June 19, 1930, in SMC Secretariat File, p. 2.

29. V. F. Grosse reported arrival figures for 1930 as 1,699 rather than 1,599. See his report dated Mar. 24, 1931 to the secretary, SMC, in the SMC Secretariat File.

30. V. F. Grosse report, June 19, 1930, p. 8.

31. The SMP was headed by a British commissioner of police. The Special Branch evolved from a small intelligence office in the early 1920s to be entrusted with numerous responsibilities, including, over time, a labor section, a general inquiries section, a Chinese liaison unit, an Indian section, a film and newspaper censorship section, a translation unit, and a boarding house and licensing section, to name the most prominent. SMPD 8/9-10/1930. See also OSS China Theater declassified secret X-2 branch report Z05-831, Jan. 8, 1947, "The 'Special Branch' of the Shanghai Municipal Police."

32. Interview with Irena Tokmakova, a former resident of Shanghai, Sept. 1994.

33. "Memorandum," June 13, 1993, in SMPD 2882.

34. Charles Eduardovich Metzler finished Saint Petersburg University in 1911 and entered the Ministry of Foreign Affairs. In 1912, he was appointed to the Russian Mission in Beijing, where he remained until September 1917, at which time he was sent to Shanghai to be vice-consul, a post he held until the consulate closed. From that time until July 1924, he was secretary of the Bureau of Russian Affairs. After Grosse's death in 1931, he became chairman

of the Emigrants Committee. Metzler was also honorary chairman of the Student Union in Shanghai and one of the organizers of the "Aid" Society and the Juridical Society (of which he was chairman). See Zhiganov, *Russkie v Shankhaie*, p. 51.

35. *NCH*, Nov. 6, 1932, p. 253.

36. The regulations of the Council of United Russian Public Organizations at Shanghai, in both English and Chinese, and samples of its official seals, are preserved in SMPD 2882. SMPD 5002 contains a brief outline of SORO's constitution and a membership list. The regulations state: "The Council adheres . . . to the laws of the present Republic of China as well as to the administrative and municipal regulations in force in the International Settlement and French Concession of Shanghai."

37. In 1934, Metzler became the official representative of the Nansen Office for Refugees in China, managing contributions to aid needy and aged Russian refugees.

38. *NCH*, Oct. 19, 1932, p. 97.

39. A report "In the Russian Colony" noted that the Russian Emigrants Committee received "no moral or material support from any government." See *NCH*, Aug. 30, 1939.

40. "Result of Enquiry with Reference to the Russian Emigrants' Committee," n.d.; "Russian Emigrants Committee & Other Organizations, Item no. 3 on the Council Agenda," Jan. 20, 1932; memorandum from Ch. Metzler to secretary, SMC, Oct. 1931; and "Extract from Council minutes dated Jan. 20, 1932," all in the SMC Secretariat File. The last document shows that council authorities suspected the rival factions of coveting the paid post formerly held by Grosse. While serving as committee chairman, Metzler continued his employment with a local insurance company.

41. Police report, June 17, 1993. The *NCDN*, Jan. 22, 1932, estimated the Russian refugee community at between 15,000 and 18,000. The Union of Russian Cossacks, founded in 1925, and representing 587 men and 436 women and children, also claimed independent authority. It had a dormitory for unemployed members, a mess, a school for teaching English, and a recreation ground at 311 Rue Vallon (Nanchang Road). Police report, May 8, 1932, in SMPD 2882.

42. Mancall, *China at the Center*, p. 240.

43. Interview with Viktor Petrov, Feb. 15, 1993. Petrov said these Russians were deported to Siberia after World War II by the Soviet government.

44. Dorfman, "White Russians in the Far East," p. 167. The Japanese often viewed these refugees under a reverse color scheme: white on the surface but red at the core.

45. SMPD 2895.

46. Police report, Aug. 5, 1936, in SMPD 5002.

47. *NCDN*, July 3, 1936.

48. English translation of *Shankhaiskaia Zaria* article, Jan. 26, 1934.

49. Ibid., Jan. 17, 1939.

50. Bulletin no. 10 of the "Ukrainian Bureau" in London, dated Mar. 5, 1932, estimated the total Ukrainian population in the Far East at about 350,000 persons and includes a map showing its dispersal. SMPD 5471.

51. Police report, Nov. 29, 1933, in SMPD 5471.

52. Police reports, Nov. 29, 1933, and Sept. 18, 1939, in SMPD 5471.

53. Police report, Nov. 29, 1933, in SMPD 5471.

54. Police report, Nov. 29, 1933, in SMPD 5471. Other leaders were G. F. Totsky, secretary, and A. N. Vansovitch, treasurer.

55. Attachment to letter from the Ukrainian Association of Shanghai dated Nov. 16, 1933, and addressed to the commissioner of police, SMC, in SMPD 5471.

56. Police report, June 22, 1942, in SMPD 5471. The Ukrainian Club and Association relocated to 1292 Avenue Edward VII. English translation of *Shankhaiskaia Zaria* article, May 3, 1940.

57. Letter from the Ukrainian Association of Shanghai to M. Baudez, consul general of France, Feb. 10, 1938.

58. This estimate of the Ukrainian population appears in a police report, Mar. 31, 1942, in SMPD 5471.

59. Fu, *Passivity, Resistance, and Collaboration*, p. 32.

60. Memorandum, July 30, 1938, attachment "B" to police report, Sept. 18, 1939, in SMPD 5471, signed by N. Kvashenko, chairman; N. Voblyi, vice-chairman; and Th. Snizhny, secretary.

61. Police report, Sept. 18, 1939, in SMPD 5471.

62. Communication no. 86, Apr. 8, 1939, from General Takeshita, chief of the Special Military Mission in Shanghai, to Fu Xiaoan, mayor of the Municipality of Greater Shanghai, in SMPD 5471.

63. A registration certificate form and questionnaire produced by the Ukrainian Association of Shanghai for presentation to the Bureau of Police, Da Dao City Government of Shanghai, is contained in SMPD 5471.

64. Other members of the committee included S. A. Sobelnikov, vice-chairman; G. F. Totsky, secretary; and P. A. Sokolsky, treasurer. See "Life of the Ukrainian Community at Shanghai," English translation of *Shankhaiskaia Zaria* article, Jan. 11, 1940; *NCDN*, Jan. 20, 1940.

65. Letter to the SMP, Jan. 29, 1940; English translation of *Shankhaiskaia Zaria* article, Mar. 3, 1940.

66. "In the Russian Colony," in *NCDN*, Feb. 1, 1940, p. 12.

67. Conseil d'Administration municipale de la Concession française, *Bulletin Municipal*, Oct. 19, 1931, Shanghai Municipal Archives, bk. 38/2799.

68. Polish immigration to China during the years from 1934 through 1941

is recorded in the Polish Record Book at the Polish consulate general in Shanghai, which was loaned to the author to copy. A photocopy of the Polish Record Book is available at the Library of Congress. Another copy is located at the Sino-Judaic Institute at Menlo Park, California.

69. Some of these Poles had come to Harbin from Birobidzhan, the failed Soviet Jewish state established northeast of China by Stalin in 1930, which had been granted status in 1934 as the "Jewish Autonomous Region" of the USSR but never became a viable home for Polish Jews (*Encyclopaedia Judaica*, p. 1046). After the Soviet annexation of parts of Poland, plans were to move Jewish settlers to Birobidzhan, but the outbreak of the Soviet-German war curtailed these. Wasserstein, *Vanishing Diaspora*, p. 41, dates the origins of Birobidzhan to 1928 and notes that its Jewish population never reached more than 1 percent of Soviet Jewry.

70. Woźniakowski, "Polonia Chińska w latach," p. 99.

71. Wischnitzer, *Visas to Freedom*, pp. 150–51.

72. The Polish Record Book (see n. 68 above) lists a total of 1,476 registrants to enter China. The data include each registrant's name, date of registration, profession, religion, place and date of birth, marital status, address in Poland, address in China, documentation (passport number), names and dates of birth of family members, passport expiration date, and a note category for any additional special information. Of course, there may have been other Polish emigrants in China who never registered with Polish authorities.

73. See Polish Record Book.

74. The *Echo Szanghajskie* supplement *Wiadomosci* was published irregularly in late 1945–46 by a group of Polish Jews (Ewa Barteczko, Polish National Library, letter, Apr. 1994). Issues of the two periodicals are to be found in the New York Public Library and at the Jozef Pilsudski Institute of America in New York and the Polish Émigré Press Archive in Sunnyvale, Calif.

75. Zhiganov, *Russkie v Shankhaie*, p. 34.

76. Ibid., p. 149.

77. A recording of Aaron Avshalomov's Piano Concerto in G is available at the Library of Congress, Col 68870, set 286, and on CD under the Marco Polo label, Catalog No. 225035 (released Feb. 22, 2000). Avshalomov wrote four symphonies, a ballet, operas, and numerous other works. Ho and Feofanov, *Biographical Dictionary of Russian/Soviet Composers*.

78. Xu Buzeng, "Jews and the Musical Life of Shanghai," p. 236.

79. Kh.L.A.M. stood for "Khudozhnikov, Literatorov, Artistov i Muzykantov."

80. *NCH*, June 2, 1935, p. 342.

81. *NCH*, Mar. 24, 1937, p. 509.

82. For discussion of the Russian press, publishing, and literary activity in Shanghai, and an accounting of those individuals (translated from Zhiganov,

Russkie v Shankhaie) prominent in press and literary circles, see Polansky, "Russkaia Pechat' v Kitae," p. 5.

83. Polansky, "Russkaia Pechat' v Kitae," p. 12; interview with Viktor Petrov, Feb. 15, 1993; telephone interview with Mrs. Viktor Kamkin, Feb. 1993.

84. "In the Russian Colony," *NCDN*, Nov. 10, 1937, *Shanghai Sunday Times*, Aug. 2, 1936. Photographs of many of these establishments are contained in Zhiganov, *Russkie v Shankhaie*, pp. 163–98, including Baranovsky's Shop, Tkachenko's Cafe and Bakery, Siberian Jewelry Store, the bookstore Russkoe Delo, Sonola Radio and Music House, the First Russian Bakery, Cathay Pharmacy, Star Pharmacy, Siberian Fur Store, and others.

85. In 1930, there were 30 qualified physicians, as against 2 in 1920; 372 Russians subscribed to the local telephone system, whereas only 5 had done so in 1925. V. F. Grosse report, June 19, 1930, pp. 8–9.

86. Ch. Grosbois had been the previous director of this school. Zhiganov, *Russkie v Shankhaie*, pp. 90–91.

87. Zhiganov, *Russkie v Shankhaie*, p. 95.

88. *NCH*, Jan. 15, 1927, p. 72.

89. *NCH*, June 7, 1931, p. 374.

90. *NCH*, Mar. 7, 1934, p. 368.

91. Darwent, *Shanghai: A Handbook*, p. 107; Zhiganov, *Russkie v Shankhaie*, p. 40.

92. "In the Russian Colony," *NCDN*, Mar. 15, 1939, p. 12.

93. In 1930, 37 Russians served in various departments of the council; 54 on the Police Force; 21 in the municipal band; 251 in the Russian Detachment, SVC; 125 as police watchmen; 51 in the British Defence Force; and 182 with utilities: 135, the Shanghai Power Company; 39, the Shanghai Waterworks Co., Ltd.; and 8 with the General Omnibus Co., Ltd. See V. F. Grosse report, June 19, 1930, pp. 11–12.

94. "In the Russian Colony," *NCDN*, Jan. 23, 1939, p. 12.

95. *NCDN*, July 20, 1940, p. 8.

96. A detailed sampling of 9,924 Russian refugees in Shanghai revealed this unemployment figure. Simpson, *Refugee Problem*, p. 503.

97. *NCH*, Oct. 13, 1937, p. 66.

98. Simpson, *Refugee Problem*, p. 503.

99. "In the Russian Colony," *NCDN*, Oct. 3, 1938, and June 27, 1939.

100. *Shanghai Evening Post and Mercury*, July 6, 1940.

101. SMPD 7779.

102. For discussion of Shanghai's night life, see Karns and Patterson, *Shanghai*.

103. Letter from the Russian Orthodox Confraternity to Ch. Metzler, chairman, Russian Emigrants Committee, Jan. 22, 1935, in Department of

State Files 893.1151. See also in this collection, 511.52 D1/437: "Ch. Metzler Report on the Situation of Russian Women in China," Nov. 29, 1934.

104. For discussion of Chinese prostitution in Shanghai, see Henriot, *Belles de Shanghai*; Hershatter, *Dangerous Pleasures*. For equivalent currency rates, see Chang, *Inflationary Spiral*, p. 41.

105. Wang, *Shanghai E qiaoshi*, p. 341. For details on Russian prostitution, see Ristaino, "Russian Women as Icons in Republican Era Shanghai." On currency values ca. 1930, see Wakeman, *Policing Shanghai*, p. xi.

106. *NCH*, Aug. 31, 1938. Because of the massive inflation between 1930 and 1941, these salary estimates and comparisons can only be regarded as suggestive.

107. League of Nations, COL 115 (1928–32), interviews with the French consul general and officials of Shanghai Municipal Council offices, Mar. 1931.

108. *NCH*, Aug. 16, 1939.

109. Sergeant, *Shanghai*, p. 63.

110. Wakeman, "Licensing Leisure," p. 27.

111. Simpson, *Refugee Problem*, p. 507.

112. League of Nations, COL 115 (1928–32), interview with the French consul general, Mar. 1931; O'Callaghan, *White Slave Trade*, p. 24.

113. League of Nations, COL 115 (1928–32), interview with the French consul general, Mar. 1931.

114. League of Nations, "Situation des femmes d'origine Russe en Extrême-Orient," Aug. 14, 1935, A.12 in file R4692.

115. Ibid.

116. Lidin, "Russkaya emigratsiya v Shankhaie," p. 315.

117. "In the Russian Colony," *NCDN*, Nov. 10, 1937, p. 12.

118. League of Nations, "Traffic in Women and Children," C.476.M.318. 1937 IV, p. 66.

119. *IM*, Dec. 1, 1933.

120. *IM*, Jan. 1, 1934.

121. Presseisen, *Germany and Japan*, p. 2; *IM*, June 1, 1931.

122. *IM*, May 4, 1934, and Sept. 7, 1934.

123. Sopher and Sopher, "China and Japan's Need," pp. 7, 14.

124. *IM*, June 1, 1934.

125. *IM*, Sept. 4, 1936.

126. *IM*, Mar. 12, 1937, p. 17, asserts 4,000 Ashkenazi Jews then lived in Shanghai; *China Press*, July 3, 1940, reports 8,000. Speaking to the April 1994 Shanghai reunion, David H. Zysman of Yeshiva University referred to 5,000.

127. The police issued "certificates of character" providing biographic information about Russians, including Russian Jews, to support visa applications, etc. Box 80 of the SMP files contains a collection of these for the years 1933–40.

Chapter 4

1. Finnane, *Far From Where?* p. 32.

2. Snyder, *Encyclopedia of the Third Reich*, p. 169; Levin, *Holocaust*, 1968. On the *Kristallnacht*, discussed as "The Week of Broken Glass," see Shirer, *Rise and Fall of the Third Reich*, pp. 430–35.

3. Finnane, *Far From Where?* p. 26.

4. Interview with Susan Herlinger, conducted at the Bamboo Reunion of Shanghai Jewish refugees held in Chicago, Sept. 1992; telephone interview with Eva Hamburg, Feb. 21, 1996; Drucker, *Kindertransport*, p. 144. A *Kindertransport* was an interdenominational humanitarian effort to rescue Jewish children.

5. Refugees traveled mainly on the Italian Lloyd Triestino line, the Japanese Nippon Yusen Kaisha line, the German Norddeutsche Lloyd line, and the Greek Messageries Maritimes line. Other lines providing service were the Blue Funnel Line, Glen & Swire, Osaka Syosen Kaisya, Ltd., American President Lines, and Canadian Pacific Steamship, Ltd. Letter from Japanese Consul S. Ishiguro to heads of these companies dated Oct. 28, 1939.

6. Grebenschikoff, *Once My Name Was Sara*, p. 37; Heppner, *Shanghai Refuge*, p. 29; interview with Henry Compart, July 10, 1994.

7. Police report, Jan. 31, 1939, in SMPD 5422.

8. Ginsbourg, *Jewish Refugees in Shanghai*, p. 12.

9. Police report, July 14, 1941, in SMPD 5422A.

10. Wartenberger, "My Shanghai Memoirs," written in 1952, close to the period under study, p. 5 (hereafter Wartenberger, "Memoirs").

11. Using the figure of 4,044 refugee arrivals, 691 came with funds provided by the American Jewish Relief Society in Paris. Another 650 did not register with Shanghai refugee authorities, thus making them independent of relief funding. Police report dated Mar. 15, 1939, in SMPD 5422. *NCDN*, Feb. 1, 1939, gives a lower estimate of 16 percent for those with independent funds.

12. Leo Baeck Institute, Jerome Agel Collection, Report of Refugees, folder 1.

13. Wartenberger, "Memoirs," p. 8.

14. A list of German nationals resident in Shanghai and a listing of 875 German refugees who arrived in Shanghai after 1937, reporting names, dates of birth, professions, addresses in Shanghai, and dates of arrival (latest Oct. 1941), is found in SMPD 8263/1.

15. Figures provided to the Shanghai Municipal Council by the International Committee for Granting Relief to European Refugees, Jan. 17, 1941, in SMPD 5422A.

16. *IM*, May 5, 1939, p. 15. Between August 1938 and April 1939, the sum of $343,096.30 was collected by the American Jewish Joint Distribution Com-

mittee; the Council for German Jewry; the Jewish Refugee Relief Committee, Singapore; the Jewish Refugee Association, Hong Kong; smaller contributors in India and the United States; and by local established Jews. The latter contributed $146,676.30 of the total amount. Police report, Apr. 5, 1939, in SMPD 5422A.

17. Ginsbourg, *Jewish Refugees*, p. 19.

18. Komor, "European Refugees"; Komor, "Report of the International Committee," Feb. 28, 1939, in SMPD 5422A; and Police report entitled "International Committee for the Organization of European Immigrants in China," Nov. 29, 1941, in SMPD 5422A.

19. "Jewish Refugees in Shanghai," p. 290.

20. "Report of the 'International Committee' up to Feb. 28, 1939" by Paul Komor, in SMPD 5422A. See also police report, Nov. 29, 1941, p. 3, in SMPD 5422A. The committee had its office at 190 Kiukiang Road.

21. *Shanghai Times*, Jan. 8, 1939. David Frankel was chairman of the Singapore Jewish Relief Committee formed in Oct. 1938 to help refugees pass through Singapore.

22. *Shanghai Evening Post and Mercury*, Aug. 7, 1939.

23. Ibid., June 30, 1939.

24. See SMPD 5422, police report, Mar. 15, 1939, for a list of the trades and professions of 1,570 registered German and Austrian refugees, who included doctors, engineers, dentists, pharmacists, tailors, cutters, butchers, bakers, locksmiths, shoemakers, upholsterers, goldsmiths, leather goods workers, musicians, bookkeepers, chauffeurs, and clerks.

25. Police reports, May 22 and Sept. 18, 1940, in SMPD 5422A.

26. *NCDN*, Aug. 12, 1939.

27. *NCDN*, Feb. 15, 1938.

28. *Shanghai Times*, Aug. 14, 1939.

29. Shanghai Municipal Council, *Municipal Gazette* 31 (1938): 21, 207. U.S. State Department, Shanghai Consulate Files, RG84, 125 (1938): 842–50, contains the constitution of the Shanghai Refugee Relief Association, headed by Director Yu Yaching.

30. Shanghai Municipal Council, *Municipal Gazette* 31 (1938): 353.

31. See U.S. State Department, Shanghai Consulate Files, RG84, 125 (1938): 842–50.

32. *Story of "The Jacquinot Zone" Shanghai, China*, p. 11.

33. By November 1939, there were thirty-two camps housing 37,319 Chinese refugees, with 3,983 of them living in alleyways. Shanghai Municipal Council, *Municipal Gazette* 32 (1939): 411.

34. Police report, Apr. 4, 1939, in SMPD 5422A.

35. Mention of a directory appears in *Asahi Shimbun*, Feb. 22, 1989. A copy of a directory entitled *Emigranten Adressbuch*, compiled by a German-Jewish

refugee surnamed Klaus in 1939, and reprinted in facsimile in Hong Kong by Old China Hand Press in 1995, may be this original list compiled for the Japanese military authorities.

36. *Shanghai Evening Post and Mercury*, Aug. 7, 1939; *NCDN*, Aug. 12, 1939.

37. *China Press*, Aug. 15, 1939.

38. Ibid., Aug. 16, 1939.

39. *Shanghai Times*, Aug. 15, 1939.

40. *China Press*, Apr. 13, 1939; *Shanghai Evening Post and Mercury*, Aug. 7, 1939; *Shanghai Times*, Aug. 15, 1939.

41. Letter from Consul General Y. Miura to the acting consul general for Italy, Dott. F. Farinacci, Aug. 10, 1939. In this letter, Miura notes a similar statement of concern from the acting German consul general, Dr. E. Bracklo, regarding suspension of emigration into Hongkou.

42. Dr. E. Bracklo, acting German consul general, letter dated Aug. 19, 1939, to G. G. Phillips, secretary and commissioner general, Shanghai Municipal Council. The acting consul general for Italy sent a similar letter dated Aug. 16, 1939, to Poul Scheel, consul general for Denmark and senior consul.

43. *Shanghai Times*, Feb. 5, 1939. Letters from the Shanghai Municipal Council to Senior Consul L. Neyrone, consul general of Italy, dated Dec. 23, 1938, and Jan. 16, 1939.

44. *Shanghai Times*, Aug. 15, 1939.

45. *China Press*, Aug. 15, 1939; *Shanghai Times*, Aug. 15, 1939.

46. *NCDN*, Aug. 12, 1939.

47. *China Press*, Aug. 15, 1939.

48. Ibid., Aug. 18, 1939.

49. *Russian Voice*, Shanghai, Jan. 7, 1939, in SMPD 5422 (B).

50. *NCDN*, Jan. 1, 1939.

51. *NCDN*, Dec. 28, 1938; *Shanghai Times*, Dec. 4, 1938.

52. Police report dated May 23, 1940, in SMPD 5422.

53. Two articles by J. B. Powell, entitled "Jewish Refugees Should Be Welcomed and Assisted Here" (Apr. 2, 1939) and "Shanghai Receives More Victims of Anti-Semitism" (Oct. 6, 1939), are contained in SMPD 5422A.

54. Police report, Aug. 12, 1939, in SMPD 5422A. An interview by a German doctor revealing inhumane treatment in Germany appeared in the Chinese newspaper *Hua bao*, June 13, 1939, and brought an immediate complaint to the Komor Committee by the German consulate general. In response, the Komor Committee requested the SMP to use its influence to eliminate "sensational stories" and refugee interviews from press reporting. Letter from Paul Komor to the commissioner of police, June 16, 1939, SMPD 5422A.

55. Conseil d'Administration municipale de la Concession française, *Bulletin Municipal, 1939*, proclamation dated May 11, 1939, Shanghai Municipal Archives, bk. 38, p. 1.

56. Police reports, Apr. 9, Sept. 18, and Oct. 27, 1940, in SMPD 5422A.

57. See Fu, *Passivity, Resistance, and Collaboration*, pp. 30–38.

58. Letter from Y. Miura to Ellis Hayim, Oct. 28, 1939, in SMPD 5422.

59. Shanghai Municipal Council, *Municipal Gazette* 22 (1939): 327.

60. Shanghai Municipal Council, minute book, 1939, report of meeting on Feb. 8, 1939, p. 140.

61. Ibid., p. 139.

62. Police report, July 28, 1942, in SMPD 4749; police report, Mar. 1, 1940, in SMPD 5422; and police report, July 3, 1940, in SMPD 5422.

63. Letter to Dr. A. J. Alves, consul general for Portugal and senior consul, from Cornell S. Franklin, chairman, Shanghai Municipal Council, Dec. 23, 1938.

64. "Entry of European Refugees," in SMPD 5422. The SMP received a fee for the issuance and renewal of immigration certification. By Nov. 1941, the police had collected $106,700 for these services. See also Shanghai Municipal Council, *Municipal Gazette* 23 (1940): 136.

65. Police report, July 17, 1940, in SMPD 5422.

66. Report by P. Komor to the Shanghai Municipal Council dated Jan. 17, 1941, in SMPD 5422. Of this number, 8,490 were men and 5,855 were women and children. In addition, Komor notes that the total of 15,469 included 325 Roman Catholics, 444 Protestants, 25 who identified themselves with "other religions"; and 131 claimed "no religion." The extra-settlement roads areas developed west of the settlement border as Europeans settled along municipal council–owned roads. See Clifford, *Spoilt Children of Empire*, pp. 27–28.

67. Press reports summarized in police report dated Sept. 26, 1940, in SMPD 5422A.

68. The substantial contributions came from the American Jewish Joint Distribution Committee, the Council for German Jewry in London, and from similar organizations in Cairo and Singapore. See *NCDN*, Sept. 5, 1940.

69. *Shanghai Times*, Aug. 6, 1941, in SMPD 5422A; police report, Aug. 22, 1941, in SMPD 5422A; police report, 28 Aug. 1941, in SMPD 5422A.

70. *China Press*, May 16, 1939.

71. "Jew Settlement in Mindanao Said 'Nonsense, Impossible,'" *China Press*, in SMPD 5422.

72. *Shanghai Times*, June 24, 1939. See John Ahlers, "Proposal to Send 100 Thousand German Jewish Refugees to Yunnan Province," *CWR*, July 22, 1939, pp. 226–27.

73. A collection of five official government documents that deal with plans for a Jewish settlement in southwestern China is presented in material selected by Bi and Ma, "Plan to Settle Jewish Refugees in China," pp. 66–84. The original Chinese language documents are reportedly located in the Second Historical Archives, Nanjing, China.

74. *Shanghai Times*, June 24, 1939.

75. *NCDN*, Feb. 1, 1939; police report, Jan. 31, 1939, in SMPD 5422A. *Heime* is the German word for "homes."

76. *NCDN*, Feb. 1. 1939.

77. Police report, Apr. 5, 1939, in SMPD 5422A.

78. Letter to the commissioner of police from the Committee for Assistance of European Refugees, dated Aug. 25, 1941, in SMPD 5422A.

79. Shanghai Municipal Council, minute book, 1939, report of meeting held July 12, 1939.

80. Police report, Aug. 5, 1939, in SMPD 5422A.

81. "Jewish Refugees in Shanghai," p. 291. Other members of the committee were A. S. Jaspar, Karl Haas, J. D. E. Shotter, and Charles H. Arkwright.

82. Police report, Nov. 29, 1941, in SMPD 5422A.

83. *Almanac Shanghai 1946/47*, ed. Lewin, p. 62.

84. Interview with Henry Compart, July 10, 1994.

Chapter 5

1. Interview with Henry Compart, July 10, 1994; Leo Baeck Institute, Jerome Agel Collection, AR7269, box 1, folder 4.

2. Grebenschikoff, *Once My Name Was Sara*, pp. 49–50.

3. Leo Baeck Institute, Jerome Agel Collection, AR 7269, box 1, folder 2.

4. Interview with Margot Kahn, provided by Professor Pan Guang, Shanghai, 1992.

5. Interview with W. Michael Blumenthal, June 10, 1993.

6. Interview with Henry Compart, May 6, 1995.

7. Cambon, "Dream Palaces of Shanghai," p. 125; Leo Ou-fan Lee, *Shanghai Modern*, pp. 83–85, 356–57 n. 9.

8. Wartenberger, "Memoirs," p. 30.

9. Individuals fell in and out of the latter two categories depending on their economic fortunes. Police report, Jan. 29, 1940, in SMPD 5422A.

10. Police report, Aug. 8, 1939, in SMPD 5422A. Paul Komor reported a population of 13,463 Jewish refugees in Shanghai by 1939. Komor report, Jan. 17, 1941, in SMPD 5422A.

11. Interview with Henry Compart, May 6, 1995.

12. Wartenberger, "Memoirs," p. 52.

13. Memorandum entitled "J.D.C. Aid to Refugees in Shanghai," Mar. 6, 1940.

14. Leo Baeck Institute, Jerome Agel Collection, AR 7269, box 1, folder 4.

15. Ginsbourg, *Jewish Refugees in Shanghai*, pp. 20–21.

16. Wartenberger, "Memoirs," p. 27.

17. Ibid., p. 28.

18. Ibid., p. 11.

19. Ginsbourg, *Jewish Refugees in Shanghai*, p. 16.

20. A kind of Yellow Pages, consisting of thirty-one pages listing categories of goods and services and individuals, with their addresses, and telephone numbers, available for contact (some listing addresses in refugee camps), is contained in *Emigranten Adressbuch*, pp. 129–50.

21. Presentation by the former Shanghai refugee Herta Schriner at the Leo Baeck Institute, May 1995.

22. Interview with Henry Compart, July 10, 1994.

23. A comprehensive but not complete run of *Israel's Messenger* is housed at the Hebrew Union College Library, Cincinnati, Ohio.

24. Löwenthal, "Jewish Press in China," pp. 104–13.

25. For a discussion of plays, playwrights, and performers, see Kranzler, *Japanese, Nazis and Jews*, pp. 368–70.

26. Xu Buzeng, "Youtai yinyuejia zai Shanghai," *Yinyue yishu*, nos. 3–4 (1991).

27. Ibid., p. 6.

28. Schurtman, "Report on the Jewish Refugee Community in Shanghai," pp. 11–12.

29. A small synagogue on MacGregor Road did begin operations in late 1941. See also Finnane, *Far From Where?* p. 163.

30. Statement by the Jüdische Gemeinde to the Social Affairs Bureau, reviewing the organization and its mission, dated May 18, 1947, in SMA (Shanghai Municipal Archives), File Q6-5-1115, vol. 1, no. 16–17.

31. Kranzler, *Japanese, Nazis and Jews*, p. 415.

32. The German-language version of the code was published in the *Shanghai Jewish Chronicle*, Feb. 18, 1940. The English-language version was made available to the SMP. See SMPD 5422B.

33. *China Press*, Nov. 13, 1939, and Dec. 10, 1939.

34. *Hua bao*, Nov. 14, 1939; *Da mei bao*, Dec. 8, 1939; and *Shen bao*, Dec. 8, 1939. The situation would be further complicated when, on Nov. 8, 1940, the Nanjing Reformed Government took over the courts in the French Concession, leaving those in the International Settlement under Chiang Kai-shek's Chongqing regime. See *NCDN*, Nov. 9, 1940, p. 1.

35. *Mainichi*, Nov. 15, 1939.

36. *China Press*, Nov. 14, 1939.

37. Dr. A. Grossman, letter to the editor, *China Press*, Nov. 15, 1939.

38. *China Press*, Feb. 22, 1940.

39. Police report, Apr. 1, 1942, in SMPD 5422A.

40. *Encyclopaedia Judaica*, 16: 770.

41. Zuroff, "Rescue via the Far East," p. 157.

42. Davies and Polonsky, *Jews in Eastern Poland and the USSR*, p. 4.

43. *Disaster and Salvation*, p. 27.

44. Zuroff, "Rescue via the Far East," p. 163.

45. See ibid., pp. 162–167, on the various channels and procedures used to support the exodus of Jewish refugees from Lithuania. Zwartendijk was a businessman who served as consul for both Denmark and Holland. See Lipschitz, *Shanghai Connection*, pp. 31–32. Known as a Curaçao visa, the documentation also applied to Suriname and other Dutch possessions in the Americas.

46. Zuroff, "Rescue via the Far East," pp. 162–63.

47. Sugihara, *Visas for Life*, pp. 53, 138–39; interview with Ishiguro Kenji, Washington, D.C., Sept. 11, 1996. A refugee source reports that the Japanese consul in Prague also supplied visas to Jews. Finnane, *Far From Where?* p. 35.

48. Levine, *In Search of Sugihara*, pp. 131–32. Sugihara, *Visas for Life*, pp. 13–14.

49. Sugihara, *Visas for Life*, pp. 108–9, 117.

50. Ibid., pp. 10–19. See also "Sugihara's List," *Economist*, Sept. 24, 1994; "'Japan's Schindler' Hailed," *Japan Times*, Sept. 21, 1994; "Sugihara's List," *Washington Post*, Oct. 3, 1994; and "The Honors Come Late for a Japanese Schindler," *New York Times*, Nov. 8, 1995.

51. "Sugihara's List," *Washington Post*, Oct. 3, 1994.

52. Estimates of the numbers of visas Sugihara issued vary: Goodman and Miyazawa, *Jews in the Japanese Mind*, pp. 133, 233, say 6,000; Levine, *In Search of Sugihara*, p. 7, estimates 10,000. Levine reports (p. 7) locating a Japanese archive listing of 2,139 Sugihara visa holders; the same figure and report appear in Sakamoto, "Policy of the Japanese Ministry of Foreign Affairs Towards Jewish Refugees," pp. 15, 255.

53. Interview with Benjamin Fishoff, May 1994; Leitner, *Operation — Torah Rescue*, p. 92.

54. Interview with the former Polish refugee Joseph Ganger, 1994. For others who received immigration permits, especially through the efforts of Rabbi A. Kalmanowitz, see Lipschitz, *Shanghai Connection*, pp. 57–58.

55. This number included 79 rabbis and 341 yeshivah students. Zuroff, "Rescue via the Far East," p. 171.

56. Police report, Mar. 6, 1941, in SMPD 5422A.

57. Letter from Rabbi Ashkenazi to Frederick Pitts, Police Hqs., Mar. 6, 1941; police reports, Mar. 6 and 20, 1941, in SMPD 5422.

58. Among the 582 registered in the Polish Record Book were 22 rabbis and 149 Talmudic students. The rabbis were Leek Szafran; Wigdoz Cypersztejn; Mejez-Fajwel Żywica; Chajkie Grynberg; Benejou (Kalman) Glejzel; Szmul Warszawczyk; Aron Bokow; Salomon Szapiro; Josef Lewinson; Chaim Batglej; Lejb Abzam Markus; Abramczyk Michel Bursztyniarz; Oszez

Czeczyk; Majez Frenkel; Enach Kronzak; Aron Kopelowicz; Icchok Kalisz; Lipman Dioje Lipmanowicz; Hillel Mannes; Nuta Szajnberg; Saul Dawid Margulies; and Szymon Kalisz.

59. This recent development is discussed in Manli Ho, "Feng Shan Ho and the Rescue of Austrian Jews," in Kremer, ed., *Diplomat Rescuers*, pp. 6–20.

60. Interview with Joseph Ganger, 1994.

61. Lukas, *Forgotten Holocaust*, p. 124.

62. Interview with W. Michael Blumenthal, 1993.

63. Police report, May 5, 1943, in SMPD 5422. In 1943, the Jüdische Gemeinde had just over 6,000 members, for a total of about 10,000 people, in that usually only heads of families registered. Another 5,000 people who belonged to the Gemeinde chose not to register because of the fees charged and dissatisfaction with its leadership.

64. Proclamation, Jan. 11, 1942, in SMPD 5422A.

65. Police report, July 22, 1941, in SMPD 5422.

66. Laura Margolis reported that when she first arrived in Shanghai, the Committee for Assistance of European Refugees had been anxious to turn over management of the refugee problem to her, having apparently been worn down by dealing with its many issues and difficulties. See interview with Laura Margolis Jarblum by Menahem Kaufman, p. 19.

67. Police report, Sept. 3, 1942, in SMPD 5422A. Other resignations included those of A. Sopher, the Reverend Mendel Brown, and J. Bitker.

68. Police report, Sept. 10, 1942, in SMPD 5422.

69. Police report, Sept. 9, 1942, in SMPD 5422. Rogovin was formerly president of the Jewish Community of Dalian.

70. Police reports, Nov. 19, 1942, and Dec. 10, 1942, in SMPD 5422A.

71. Sopher and Sopher, "China and Japan's Need," p. 14.

72. Rabbi Betram W. Korn, chaplain, U.S. Navy, in AJA MS collection, 99, China (Jews), p. 2.

73. Bresler, "Harbin's Jewish Community," pp. 5–6.

74. Shanghai representatives Boris Topas and Morris Bloch attended this 1939 meeting. A Japanese version of this petition, signed by Kaufman on December 25, 1939, appears in Inuzuka Kiyoko, *Yudaya mondai to Nihon no kōsaku*, pp. 136–37.

75. One formulation of this approach appears in Goodman and Miyazawa, *Jews in the Japanese Mind*, pp. 125–26.

76. Stephen S. Wise, letter to L. Zikman, Nov. 22, 1938.

77. *Yudaya Kenkyū* (Jewish Research), the journal of the Kokusai Seikei Gakkai, printed articles ranging from anti-Semitic attacks to academic inquiry. The Kōa-in was established within the cabinet in December 1938 as a central organ to coordinate the various China policies of the Japanese ministries and was headed by the prime minister, with the ministers of foreign affairs, finance,

Army, and Navy as vice-presidents. It was formed to study China for the purpose of supporting Japan's policy goals, particularly economic expansion and the development of an independent strategy on the continent. The body was phased out in November 1942, when it was replaced by the Ministry of Greater East Asia. The Kōa-in's existence outside the Foreign Ministry had alienated those in that ministry and, over the years, offered the military a screen for maneuvering in China. See *Kokushi daijiten* [Japanese Historical Dictionary], vol. 5 (1985): 276.

78. Inuzuka Kiyoko, *Yudaya mondai to Nihon no kōsaku.* Inuzuka Koreshige also wrote under the pen name Utsunomiya Marehiro. Some other noted researchers included Colonel Yasue Norihiro, chief of Army Special Services, Dalian, who wrote under the pen name Hōkōshi; Hocho Seiichi, who wrote very anti-Semitic material; and Nakashige Kiichi.

79. Japanese Foreign Office Files, S9460-3-2075.

80. Kokusai Seikei Gakkai, *Shina o meguru seiji keizai . . .* , pp. 1–2.

81. Top Secret document, July 1, 1940, in Japanese Foreign Office Files, S9460-3-2248-2259.

82. Kokusai Seikei Gakkai, *Shina o meguru seiji keizai . . .* , p. 76.

83. Ibid.; Nakashige Kiichi, *Yudaya-jin mondai ni kansuru chōsa hōkokusho,* contains the chart showing the Jewish organizations of Shanghai and their interrelationships and relationships worldwide. A detailed outline of the enterprises controlled by E. D. Sassoon appears in Utsunomiya Marehiro, "Kokusai Yudaya zaibatsu no Shina keizai seiha masani kansei sentosu."

84. Kokusai Seikei Gakkai, *Shina o meguru seiji keizai . . .* , pp. 107–14, contains the list of Jewish figures "surrounding Roosevelt."

85. Hōkōshi [pseudonym of Colonel Yasue Norihiro], trans., *Sekai kakumei no rimen* [What is Behind the World Revolution?]. An account of Yasue's involvement with the Jewish issue, written by his son, is Yasue Hiroo, *Dairen tokumu kikan to maboroshi no Yudaya kokka.*

86. Japanese Foreign Office Files, S9460-3-750, Oct. 13, 1938.

87. Ibid. Excerpts from a lecture by Colonel Yasue Norihiro on the Jewish Problem.

88. For Japan's responses to questions at a press conference called to discuss the Japan-German cultural agreement, and for a text of the agreement, see *Shanghai Evening Post and Mercury,* Nov. 29, 1938.

89. The December 6, 1938, policy statement about the treatment of the Jews is included as a reference document in Japan, Ministry of the Army, Military Affairs Section, "Jikyoku ni tomonau Yudaya-jin no toriatsukai" [Treatment of Jews in View of the Current Situation], R118-F31256. The conference consisted of Prime Minister Konoe, Foreign Minister Arita Hachirō, Finance Minister Ikeda Shigeaki, Minister of War Itagaki Seishirō, and Minister of the Navy Yonai Mitsumasa. Translated, the document states:

Since it is the fundamental axis of the Empire's diplomacy at this time to preserve and maintain a close and friendly relationship with Germany and Italy, we should as a matter of principle avoid activities that embrace into the Empire Jews who are being rejected by our allies. Nevertheless, to take an attitude of extreme persecution or rejection as practiced by Germany would be contrary to the spirit of equality for all races that our Empire has been advocating over many years, and, because of the present needs of the Empire in facing the emergency, we need to introduce foreign capital for economic construction, and, in light of the possibility of a disadvantageous result stemming from the worsening relationship with the United States, we therefore declare that we shall handle this issue based on the following policies:

> 1. At present we shall not reject the Jews now living in Japan, Manchukuo, and China; we shall treat them equally with other foreigners and shall not take actions that would result in special persecution [of Jews].
> 2. Jews [seeking] to enter Japan, Manchukuo, and China in the future will be treated generally in accordance with and within the limits of the entry control regulations [applicable to] foreigners.
> 3. We shall avoid deliberately inviting such persons as Jews to Japan, Manchukuo, and China. However, such categories of persons as capitalists and engineers who have a special utilization value are excepted.

90. Letter from M. S. Bloch to David A. Brown, Feb. 14, 1939, in M. S. Bloch, AJA MS collection, 18, file 1/10. Brown had a long association with China through his work with the AJJDC and the famine relief. In 1933, Brown was entertained at the Jewish Club by its president, Morris Bloch. See *Israel's Messenger*, Jan. 1, 1933, p. 9.

91. Letter from M. S. Bloch to David A. Brown, June 12, 1939, p. 2, in AJA MS collection, 18.

92. Ibid.

93. Letter from M. S. Bloch to David A. Brown, Nov. 12, 1939, in AJA MS collection, 18. Japanese plans to have Bloch attract British and American Jewish support for Japan are noted in Kranzler, *Japanese, Nazis and Jews*, pp. 239–40.

94. Chinese authorities had negotiated a banking agreement with British financiers in May 1937 worth £15 million for railroad construction in southern China. See Coble, *Facing Japan*, p. 365.

95. Utsunomiya Marehiro, "Kokusai Yudaya zaibatsu no Shina kezai seiha masani kansei sentosu."

96. *NCDN*, Aug. 2, 1939.

97. *Shanghai Times*, Feb. 29, 1940.

98. *NCDN*, Feb. 24 and Mar. 10, 1940.

99. Police report, Apr. 15, 1942, in SMPD 5422A; Yamashita, "Shanghai no Doitsu Yudaya-jin," p. 175.

100. *NCDN*, Apr. 3 and 4, 1940.

101. Letter to S. Ishiguro from E. Kann, Committee for the Assistance of European Jewish Refugees, Apr. 25, 1940, in SMPD 5422A. One report states that the Jüdische Gemeinde was used by the Japanese Residence Association to obtain votes. See police report, May 31, 1940, in SMPD 5422A.

102. Bickers, "Settlers and Diplomats," pp. 16–17.

103. Top secret document, Special Report 40.4, "Yudaya hinanmin shūyō chiku," dated May 20, 1940, Japanese Foreign Office Files, S-9460-3-2146-51.

104. Yamashita, "Shanghai no Doitsu Yudaya-jin," p. 174.

105. *NCDN*, June 24, 1940, p. 6.

106. A letter of gratitude to Inuzuka from M. S. Bloch and officials of the Oheil Moishe Synagogue for this contribution appears in Inuzuka, *Yudaya mondai to Nihon no kōsaku*, p. 303.

107. Ibid. Copies of letters from Newman appear on pp. 273 and 276. A photograph of the cigarette box appears on p. 275. The *Jerusalem Post Magazine*, Mar. 12, 1982, discusses the Newman gift and provides different interpretations of the motivations for Inuzuka's benevolent actions toward the Jews.

108. Letter from Frank Newman to K. Inuzuka, Apr. 20, 1941, in *Yudaya mondai to Nihon no kōsaku*, p. 276.

109. Inuzuka's wife reports that insinuations of Inuzuka's involvement in a scandal were used to support his removal. He was later sent to sea duty in the southwestern Pacific. Inuzuka, *Yudaya mondai to Nihon no kōsaku*, p. 490.

110. *Shanghai Times*, Mar. 7, 1942; Inuzuka, *Yudaya mondai to Nihon no kōsaku*, p. 434. Guests included Inuzuka's assistant, M. Shibata, D. E. J. Abraham, R. D. Abraham, B. Topas, M. Segal, L. Weinberger, O. Lewin, H. Ezekiel, Laura Margolis, and others. The Japanese researchers regarded D. E. J. Abraham, B. Topas, and H. Ezekiel as receptive to their ideas. See Kokusai Seikei Gakkai, *Shina o meguru seiji keizai . . .* , biographic sketches.

111. U.S. National Archives and Records Administration, "Hebrew Society for the Study of Nipponese Culture," RG-182A, Shanghai, box 18, folder 134. The Hebrew Society for the Study of Nipponese Culture's address was 722 Bubbling Well Road.

112. Laura Margolis explained that her chief mission in going to Shanghai for the JDC was to help the U.S. State Department move 20,000 refugees in Shanghai out to the United States. See Laura Margolis Jarblum, interview by Menathem Kaufman, p. 13.

113. Ibid., p. 20.

114. Ibid., pp. 20–21.

115. Independent Jewish Press Service, Inc., New York, press release, Dec. 31, 1943.

116. Laura Margolis Jarblum, interview by Menathem Kaufman, p. 22.

Chapter 6

1. Treatment of most of these issues is found in Yeh Wen-hsin, ed., *Wartime Shanghai*. See also Wakeman, *Shanghai Badlands*; Wasserstein, *Secret War*; Fu Po-shek, *Passivity, Resistance, and Collaboration*.

2. It became common for observers to stand on the roofs of tall buildings and observe the deadly hostilities between the warring parties. Candlin, *Breach in the Wall*, pp. 302–3.

3. Powell, *My Twenty-Five Years in China*, pp. 298–303.

4. Boyle, *China and Japan at War*, pp. 115, 277–85. See also Martin, *Shanghai Green Gang*, p. 5; Wakeman, *Policing Shanghai*, pp. 254–59.

5. One estimate reports that more than 150 assassinations, carried out under Chiang Kai-shek's military secret police chief, Dai Li, occurred in Shanghai between August 1937 and October 1941. See Wakeman, *Shanghai Badlands*, p. 25. Police reports make frequent reference to the notorious gangster and puppet terrorist headquarters at No. 76 Jessfield Road. See also Boyle, *China and Japan at War*, pp. 282–85; Wasserstein, *Secret War*, p. 24.

6. "In the Russian Colony," *NCDN*, Jan. 27, 1940, p. 14.

7. Police report dated Jan. 30, 1935, in SMPD 6457. The first monarchist group was headed by V. Mihailov, a former naval officer and employee of the Public Health Department of the Shanghai Municipal Council. The group published *The Standard*. The second was founded by the famous White Russian General P. N. Wrangel and led in Shanghai by Lt. Gen. M. K. Dietericks; the third, with a center in Paris, operating in Shanghai under V. A. Klarin, published *Novyi Put* (New Road). The SMP file includes the program of the "Union of Young Russians." Another publication of monarchist Russian youth was *Russkii Razvedchik* (Russian Scout).

8. For discussion of the Russian Fascist movement in Shanghai, see police reports, Mar. 17, 1936, in SMPD 5835, and Mar. 17, 1937, in SMPD 7478. A prominent leader was K. A. Steklov, who along with A. N. Lenkov published *Russkii Avangard* (Russian Vanguard).

9. Stephan, *Russian Fascists*, pp. 74, 155. Their publication was *Natsiya* (Nation). Even a stop in Shanghai on a world tour by A. Vonsiatsky, an eccentric fascist leader who married an American heiress, failed to bolster the cause.

10. *NCH*, Aug. 31, 1938.

11. *NCH*, Aug. 24, 1938.

12. General I. E. Tsumanenko taught at the Russian Commercial School and the Pushkin Memorial School. *NCH*, Nov. 30, 1938.

13. In a police report dated Dec. 2, 1938 (SMPD 8902), Deputy Sub-Inspector A. Prokofiev noted that the Chusan Road Russian Club had been founded in June 1932 as a professional military organization and reorganized into a club in 1936; when the Sino-Japanese conflict broke out in 1937, the

club was suspended, but it reopened in December 1938. Prokofiev produced numerous reports for the Shanghai Municipal Police on the Russian refugee community in the 1930s.

14. *Shankhaiskaia Zaria*, Dec.12, 1938.

15. Purin was allegedly an informer for the Japanese consular police. See SMPD 7784.

16. *NCDN*, Nov. 7, 1938, p. 6.

17. Stephan, *Russian Fascists*, pp. 173–74.

18. *NCDN*, Nov. 11, 1938.

19. *NCDN*, Nov. 14, 1938, p. 3.

20. *China Press*, June 15, 1939. Police report SMPD 5002A provides a listing of the bodies, dates of formation, leaders, and membership of sixty Russian public organizations. For discussion of Japanese manipulation and control of the Korean and Taiwanese diasporas in China, see Barbara J. Brooks, "Japanese Colonial Citizenship in Treaty Port China."

21. *China Press*, June 15, 1939.

22. Police report, June 6, 1939, in SMPD 5002A.

23. *NCH*, Nov. 6, 1940.

24. Ibid. Other sources citing the figure 25,000 are: *Shanghai Times*, June 4, 1939; *China Press*, June 21 and July 3, 1940; and *Shanghai Evening Post and Mercury*, Oct. 28, 1940.

25. "In the Russian Colony," *NCDN*, Oct. 3 and Oct. 31, 1939.

26. *China Press*, June 21, 1940; *Shanghai Evening Post and Mercury*, July 3, 1940.

27. Police report, Aug. 4, 1940, in SMPD 801C. See also *Novosti Dnia*, June 2, 1940.

28. Another recent arrival from the north was N. L. Karganov, who became head of the Shanghai branch of the Russian Fascist Union. See "In the Russian Colony," *NCDN*, Feb. 1, 1940.

29. *Rus*, June 6, 1940. *CWR*, June 8, 1940, reported on the organizational changes. See also *NCDN*, June 4, 1940, p. 9.

30. My emphasis added. See police report, Aug. 1, 1940, in SMPD 80C.

31. *China Press*, June 4, 1940; *Novosti Dnia*, June 2, 1940.

32. An article about the assassination noted that Metzler was currently manager of the motor car and casualty insurance department of the American Asiatic Underwriters Company. See *NCH*, Aug. 7, 1940, and *NCDN*, Aug. 3, 1940. The popular column "In the Russian Colony" never appeared again after Metzler's death, suggesting that Metzler wrote it.

33. Nikolai Alekseevich Ivanov was educated at the Viatsk gymnasium and in 1908 graduated from St. Petersburg University with a diploma of the highest rank. He began a diplomatic career in 1910 with appointments to the Russian consulates in Beijing, Harbin, Kul'dzhu, and Shanghai. When the Russian

consulate in Shanghai was closed, Ivanov became senior general executive secretary of the Bureau of Russian Affairs and, at the same time, assessor of the consular corps for trials of Russian cases in foreign courts in Shanghai. See Zhiganov, *Russkie v Shangkhaie*, p. 35.

34. "Interview with Mr. N. A. Ivanoff," police report, Aug. 5, 1940, in SMPD 5002A.

35. U.S. Office of Strategic Services reports from Shanghai claim that Karpov was suspected of complicity in the murder of Metzler. Karpov had worked for Japanese intelligence in both Shanghai and Tianjin. U.S. National Archives and Records Administration, OSS China/Shanghai, RG-182A, box 2, folder 13.

36. "Interview with Mr. N. A. Ivanoff," p. 3.

37. Ibid., p. 4.

38. Ibid., p. 5.

39. Ibid., p. 6.

40. Ibid., p. 7.

41. *Far Eastern Times* (*Dal'nevostochnoe vremia*), Jan. 21, 1941.

42. The Reformed Government of the Republic of China was formed on March 28, 1938; its officials resided in Shanghai until November, when its offices moved to Nanjing. See Shanghai Municipal Council, *Report, 1938*, p. 17. Wang Jingwei's inauguration took place on March 30, 1940.

43. Police notes, May 1942 in SMP-MIS-17, p. 1. After Mayor Fu Xiaoan was slashed to death by a house servant in October 11, 1940 (see *NCDN*, Oct. 12, 1940), he was succeeded by Acting Mayor Su Xiwen, until the appointment of Chen Gongbo as mayor on November 5, 1940.

44. *NCDN*, Sept. 16, 1941.

45. *NCDN*, Sept. 29, 1941.

46. *NCH*, Feb. 23, 1938.

47. Russian Emigrants Committee, SMP-MIS-17, p. 4.

48. English translation of *Shankhaiskaia Zaria* article, Nov. 25, 1941.

49. *CWR*, Mar. 1, 1941. In a category of the Shanghai Municipal Police Files called "Other Records," there are microform copies of Registration Cards for Russian Emigrants, 1940–45, and microform copies of Registration Certificates for the Russian Emigrants Committee, 1944–45.

50. *Shanghai Times*, Mar. 10, 1942.

51. Russian Emigrants Committee, May 1942, in Shanghai Municipal Police File designated SMP-MIS-17, p. 8.

52. The figure 6,000 appears in the *Shanghai Evening Post and Mercury*, Oct. 28, 1940. *China Press*, June 21, 1940, speaks of from 6,000 to 8,000 Russian Jews in Shanghai.

53. *Shanghai Evening Post*, Oct. 28, 1940; *China Press*, June 21 and July 3, 1940; *NCDN*, Oct. 29, 1940.

54. Police report, Mar. 31, 1942, in SMPD 5471.

55. *NCDN*, Oct. 30, 1941.

56. *NCDN*, July 26, 1941.

57. *NCDN*, Oct. 27, 1941. An article in the *CWR* reported that the leaflets came from the German Nazi Propaganda Bureau located in the Park Hotel across from the Race Course. It charged that the material was dropped from a Bureau window on the sixteenth floor and blew across the street onto a football game being played at the Race Course. *CWR*, Nov. 1, 1941.

58. The All-Russian Fascist Union had branches in Tianjin, Beiping, Qingdao, and Chefoo. See *NCH*, Apr. 24, 1940.

59. *Nash Put*, May 10, 1942.

60. *Nash Put*, Aug. 16, 1942.

61. *Novoe Vremia*, Aug. 19, 1942.

62. Police report, Sept. 12, 1942, in SMPD 7478.

63. "North China Nazi Party," *NCH*, May 7, 1941.

64. *CWR*, Sept. 6, 1941.

65. Kirby, *Germany and Republican China*, p. 175. Chinese fascism found its clearest expression in the Blue Shirts, a brief but virulent GMD political movement. See Eastman, "Fascism in Kuomintang China."

66. See Kreissler, *L'action culturelle allemande in Chine.*

67. A barter trade developed in which loans to the Chinese paid for German industrial products and were repaid by shipments of raw materials such as tungsten, antimony, hog casings, bristles, feathers, and wool. Presseisen, *Germany and Japan*, pp. 148–49.

68. U.S. National Archives and Records Administration, "History of the Nazi Party in China," n.d., declassified secret, RG-226, box 10, folder 86, p. 2. This 18-page report, containing a personal name index and Nazi Party organizational chart, was based on postwar interviews with leading German officials, Germans residing in Shanghai, and captured Japanese documents.

69. Kreissler, "In Search of Identity," pp. 16, 18, 22.

70. U.S. National Archives and Records Administration, "List of Germans in Shanghai," RG-226, box 8.

71. Dirksen, *Moscow, Tokyo, London*, pp. 177–79. Germany recognized Manchukuo on May 12, 1938, ending the arms shipment and supply of military advisors to Chiang's regime.

72. *Landesgruppenleiter* Siegfried Lahrmann also held the title of director of German State Railways, China Branch.

73. U.S. National Archives and Records Administration, "History of the Nazi Party in China," pp. 2–3.

74. Carey, *War Years at Shanghai*, pp. 108–9.

75. Analysis provided by Dr. Ernest Halpern, attached to the Special Tax Department of the Shanghai Special Municipal Government, in U.S. National

Archives and Records Administration, "History of the Nazi Party in China," p. 4.

76. Written deposition by Puttkammer quoted in U.S. National Archives and Records Administration, "History of the Nazi Party in China," p. 3.

77. U.S. National Archives and Records Administration, RG-319, report on Josef Meisinger by the 81st Counter Intelligence Office, dated Sept. 30, 1945. Meisinger left Berlin on March 16, 1941, crossed the Soviet Union by rail, and arrived in Tokyo on April 2, 1941.

78. U.S. National Archives and Records Administration, RG-226, box 7, folder 12, tab 45, report on the interrogation of Captain Ernest Dello, German Luftwaffe, captured by the U.S. military in the Atlantic on the blockade runner *Rio Grande.*

79. See U.S. National Archives and Records Administration, Josef A. Meisinger, IRR Files XA51-42-60 and XE-003304 in RG-319, box 362. Meisinger was taken into custody by U.S. forces on September 6, 1945. After a brief stay at the Interrogation Center in Alexandria, Virginia, he was flown to the Oberursel Interrogation Center near Frankfurt, Germany, on November 20, 1945. The Polish authorities won extradition of Meisinger to Poland, where he stood trial for war crimes and was hanged in March 1947.

80. U.S. National Archives and Records Administration, Josef A. Meisinger, IRR case file XA51-42-60, RG-319, folder 1.

81. Ibid.

82. In 1954, former Shanghai refugees made notarized statements about their experiences in Shanghai. Two of them reported doing so in order to claim restitution from the German government. These two statements, notarized by Helmut Erlanger in San Francisco on June 26, 1954, and July 2, 1954, were given by Gertrud Johanna Schnellenberg and Julius Wolff. Other statements were by Margaret Wolff, July 2, 1954; Erich Faerber, June 12, 1954; Fritz Wiedemann, Jan. 22, 1951; and Robert Peritz, Jan. 11, 1952. These affidavits were provided to the author by Paul Rosdy, Vienna, Austria. See also Wasserstein, *Secret War*, p. 144.

83. Inuzuka, *Yudaya mondai to Nihon no kōsaku*, p. 397. A check of the Japanese foreign consular posts did not include a listing for M. Shibata in Shanghai. One of the key missions of the more than 300 consultants in Shanghai was to find ways to access the Sassoon wealth remaining in Shanghai after his departure.

84. Fritz Kauffmann, "Die Juden in Shanghai im 2. Weltkrieg," pp. 13–23, based on a presentation given to the Tiffin Club of New York, Feb. 12, 1963, and revised by the author for publication.

85. Robert Peritz, signed statement, Sydney, Australia, Jan. 11, 1952. Peritz went on to claim that many in the Shanghai ghetto were starving because they could not earn money.

86. Kauffmann, "Juden in Shanghai im 2. Weltkrieg," p. 21.

87. Telephone interview with Genia Topas Bloch, daughter of Boris Topas, Feb. 11, 1996. Ms. Bloch identified the committee secretary as a Russian Jew named Podolsky and not Peritz. Podolsky reportedly died in the Bridge House.

88. Telephone interview with Laura Topas Popper, daughter of Boris Topas, Nov. 14, 1994.

89. Scattered volumes of *Yudaya kenkyū* are available at the Library of Congress.

90. The Greater East Asia Co-Prosperity Sphere, announced in August 1940, covered Japan, China, Manchukuo, and the former Dutch, French, and British colonies in South East Asia. It was later extended to the Philippines. The slogan was "Asia for Asiatics."

91. Wasserstein, *Secret War*, p. 108.

92. The formal military agreement setting out separate spheres of German-Japanese operations, in which Japan was assigned a broad area, including China, is found in Meskill, *Hitler and Japan*, pp. 59–60, 199–202.

93. U.S. National Archives and Records Administration, Japanese prisoner of war account marked secret, Japanese Special Services in China, OSS SSU, Detachment 202, RG-226, box 10, folder 78, p. 10.

94. U.S. National Archives and Records Administration, Dello interrogation, RG-226, box 7, folder 12 (cited n. 78 above).

95. For discussion of these points, see Chalmers Johnson, *Instance of Treason*, pp. 154–62.

96. Presseisen, *Germany and Japan*, pp. 318–20; Meskill, *Hitler and Japan*, pp. 182–89.

97. U.S. National Archives and Records Administration, U.S. Army, Records of the Office of the Judge Advocate General, War Crimes Branch, RG153, entry 143, file 100–146.

98. Chalmers Johnson, *Instance of Treason*, pp. 74, 184–85.

99. U.S. National Archives and Records Administration, Joseph A. Meisinger, RG-319, folder 1, p. 4, and folder 2.

100. Carey, *War Years at Shanghai*, p. 64.

101. Wiedemann's testimony as to the Nazi influence is found in Kranzler, *Japanese, Nazis and Jews*, p. 488 and n. 18c, p. 509.

Chapter 7

1. Shanghai Municipal Archives, Conseil d'Administration municipale de la Concession française, *Compte rendu 1941/Budget 1942*, p. 208.

2. Shanghai Municipal Archives, Shanghai Municipal Council, *Annual Report 1941 and Budget 1942*, p. 5.

3. Shanghai Municipal Archives, Shanghai Municipal Council, *Municipal Gazette, 1942*, Jan. 30, 1942, p. 9.

4. Shanghai Municipal Archives, Shanghai Municipal Council, minute book, 1942, minutes of a meeting of the council on Jan. 7, 1942, attended by Theodore Chang, A. Glathe, Y. Hanawa, Jabin Hsu, K. Okazaki, R. von der Crone, Y. Yazima, and L. T. Yuan. Resigning members were Chairman J. H. Liddell, Dr. R. J. McMullen, F. A. Pollock, and C. J. Schaap.

5. Shanghai Municipal Archives, Conseil d'Administration municipale de la Concession française, *Bulletin Municipal, 1942*, Feb. 5, 1942, proclamation no. 1071.

6. Lu, *Beyond the Neon Lights*, pp. 219–20. Wakeman notes that in Taiwan the Japanese in applying the system punished entire neighborhoods for acts of resistance. Wakeman, *Badlands*, p. 135. For a historical account of the system and evidence of its earlier ineffectiveness, see Hsiao, *Rural China*, pp. 72–83. For documentary information on the *baojia* system in the French Concession and International Settlements, see Shanghai Municipal Archives, Conseil d'Administration municipale de la Concession française, *Bulletin Municipal, 1942*, May 30, 1942, Ordinance no. 163, and Shanghai Municipal Council, *Municipal Gazette, 1942*, May 29, 1942, p. 61, and "*Pao-chia* Regulations," Notification 6112, Oct. 2, 1942, p. 149.

7. Shanghai Municipal Archives, Shanghai Municipal Council, *Annual Report 1942 and Budget 1943*, p. 158.

8. Shanghai Municipal Archives, Shanghai Municipal Council, minute book, 1940, minutes of a meeting of the Council on July 24, 1940, p. 344.

9. Shanghai Municipal Archives, Shanghai Municipal Council, *Annual Report 1941 and Budget 1942*, p. 94. The move to new quarters at the Race Club took place on Nov. 9. Members of the Russian Detachment supported the police on street patrols, in search posts on Bund pontoons, and as drivers, guards, and in other duties. Reportedly, the SMP had to compete for recruits with the French Municipal Police, who paid their Russian staff more.

10. Shanghai Municipal Archives, Shanghai Municipal Council, minute book, 1942, minutes of meeting on Sept. 2, 1942.

11. Shanghai Municipal Archives, Shanghai Municipal Council, *Municipal Gazette, 1942*, Sept. 25, 1942.

12. Carey, *War Years at Shanghai*, pp. 35–36.

13. Proclamation by Japanese Army Headquarters, Shanghai, Sept. 28, 1942, p. 68; Finnane, *Far From Where?* p. 103; Lee, *Letter to My Aunt*, letters dated Sept. 22 and Oct. 1, 1942, pp. 66, 68–69.

14. Lee, *Letter to My Aunt*, letter dated Sept. 30, 1943, p. 191. This source, written as a diary by a Canadian married to a Chinese professor, contains a series of letters prepared by the author between October 1941 and March 1946 and includes copied and translated current documents, proclamations, and newspaper articles, etc. Reportedly, the Japanese placed Italian officials under house arrest, seized properties and froze Italian assets, and initiated surveillance measures.

15. Horowitz, *Rose Jacob Horowitz: An Oral History*, p. 30. For discussion of the camps, see Carey, *War Years at Shanghai*, pp. 89–101.

16. The U.S. Treasury closed donor accounts of both Japanese citizens and aliens who had been dealing with Japan before the war, releasing only small monthly payments to account holders. See *Personal Justice Denied*, p. 31. This source was called to my attention by Warren Tsuneishi, a resident of the Heart Mountain (Wyoming) Relocation Center.

17. For reports from internees at the Zhabei camp, see Mark Williamson, "Internment in Shanghai," *China Connection*, Spring 1999, the first of a three-part series. The Pudong camp also included British and Dutch internees. See Grover and Grover, *Captives of Shanghai*, p. 108.

18. Laura Margolis, press release, Dec. 31, 1952, Independent Jewish Press Service, Inc., p. 1D.

19. Longhua Camp became a major focus of J. G. Ballard's autobiographical novel *Empire of the Sun*.

20. Interview with Gertrude Bryan, wife of Shanghai Municipal Advocate Robert Bryan, Jan. 21, 1989; J. B. Powell, *My Twenty-Five Years in China*, p. 327.

21. Carey, *War Years at Shanghai*, p. 98. January 1943 also saw the end of extraterritoriality in China.

22. Police report, Nov. 20, 1942, in SMPD 5422A. Others in attendance included L. M. Rogovin, chairman of CENTREJEWCOM, and Dr. Berglas, chairman of the Kitchen Fund *Kuratorium*.

23. Japan, Ministry of Foreign Affairs, "Jikyoku ni tomonau Yudaya-jin taisaku," a highly restricted draft for the decision of the 1942 ministerial liaison conference. For its appearance as a formal decision, see Japan, Ministry of the Army, Military Affairs Section, "Jikyoku ni tomonau Yudaya-jin no toriatsukai" (Mar. 11, 1942). The formal decision reads as follows:

> 1. Prohibit all Jews from coming to Japan, Manchukuo, and China, and other occupied areas, except those with special reasons.
> 2. Jews residing in Japan, Manchukuo, China, and other occupied areas will be treated in the same manner as citizens of those countries except that, in light of the special ethnic/racial characteristics [*minzoku teki tokusei*], strict surveillance of their residences and places of business will be carried out, and any enemy-like actions/maneuvers [*tekisei sakudō*] will be rejected and suppressed.
> 3. Those Jews who can be used by Japan will be strictly selected and provided appropriate treatment, but they must not provide any support to the Jewish racial/ethnic movement [*minzoku undō*].
>
> NOTE: The outline of the Jewish policy decided at the five ministers' conference on December 6, 1938 is hereby abolished.

24. Japan, Ministry of the Army, Military Affairs Section, "Jikyoku ni tomonau Yudaya-jin no toriatsukai," File T1111 R118-F31254.

320 Notes to Pages 191–94

25. Japan, Ministry of Foreign Affairs, "Jikyoku ni tomonau Yudaya-jin taisaku," File S-9460-3-2559.

26. "Shanhai ni okeru Yoroppa hinan Yudaya-jin no sankanen" [Three Years of the European Refugee Jews in Shanghai], a Japanese translation of an article written in German by Heitsu Genteron (romanized name) in December 1942, reports a total of 19,451 Jews. See Library of Congress Japanese Ministry of Foreign Affairs microfilm collection, File S-9460-3-2785.

27. This plan, which had been discussed with the Japanese embassy in Nanking, was forwarded from the Japanese consulate general in Shanghai to the Ministry of Greater East Asian Affairs. See Japan, Ministry of Foreign Affairs, "Yudaya-jin taisaku ni kansuru ken," in File S-9460-3-2556.

28. Reportedly, after the situation of the Jews in Shanghai had been studied, a top secret report by the Japanese consulate general in Shanghai was forwarded to Tokyo. It contained most of the contents of the Feb. 18 proclamation, although instead of using the term Jew, the proclamation refers only to "stateless refugees." See Japan, Ministry of Foreign Affairs, "Yudaya-jin ijū ni kansuru ken," sections 4–8 in S-9460-3-2563. *Shanghai Times*, Feb. 18, 1943, p. 1. The *Shanghai Times* account includes a map of the designated area with the proclamation. Follow-up reporting, much of it repeating its own earlier account of Feb. 18, appeared in the *Shanghai Times* on Feb. 19 and 20. The *Shanghai Times* was British-owned but, owing to financial difficulties, had accepted loans from the Yokohama Specie Bank. During the war, it became the official Japanese mouthpiece in English for Shanghai.

29. Japan, Ministry of Foreign Affairs, "Jikyoku ni tomonau Yudaya-jin taisaku," File S-9460-3-2559. In May 1942, the Japanese ambassador to Germany, Oshima Hiroshi, met in Berlin with the Third Reich's minister of Eastern Occupied Territories, Alfred Rosenberg, who told him that Japan should segregate the Jews in Shanghai before they dispersed to various regions of East Asia and created problems for Japan. See File S-9460-3-2880.

30. Japan, Ministry of Foreign Affairs, "Jikyoku ni tomonau Yudaya-jin taisaku." File S-9460-3-2559.

31. Interview with Henry Compart, July 10, 1994; Zeitin, "Shanghai Jewish Community," pp. 54–68.

32. National Socialism had a variety of meanings to different Chinese political factions, but most examined its features for their possible relevance to China's strengthening and national recovery. See Kirby, *Germany and Republican China*, pp. 152–75.

33. "Shanghai, Hunting Ground of Thriving Jewish Racketeer," *Shanghai Times*, Mar. 16, 1943, p. 4. Another version of the Wang speech, carried in the *Xinwan Bao*, is noted in Kranzler, *Japanese, Nazis and Jews*, p. 487.

34. Japan, Ministry of Foreign Affairs, "Yudaya-jin taisaku ni kansuru ken." File S-94604-3-2556. See also Lee, *Letter to My Aunt*, letter dated Feb. 26,

1943, pp. 103–4. And see the Japanese document "Measures Pertaining to Jewish People" cited in Kranzler, *Japanese, Nazis and Jews*, pp. 482–83.

35. "Summary Report as per February 28, 1943," in SMPD 5422A.

36. Japan, Ministry of Foreign Affairs, Japanese consular police report to the Japanese consulate general, July 9, 1943. File S-9460-3-2652.

37. Japan, Ministry of Foreign Affairs, Japanese consular report. File S-9460-3-2653.

38. Lee, *Letter to My Aunt*, letter dated Apr. 3, 1943, pp. 117–19.

39. This description is reported by Sh. Mendelsohn, "The Battle of the Warsaw Ghetto," *Unser Leben* (Our Life), Apr. 19, 1943, English Supplement, pp. 38–41.

40. Examples of reports of Hongkou German refugees taking their lives appear in the *Shanghai Times*, Mar. 2 and 3, 1943.

41. By October 1937, 371,270 persons had been repatriated to their native places since hostilities began. Shanghai Municipal Archives, Shanghai Municipal Council, *Municipal Gazette* 30 (Dec. 3, 1937): 341–60; Yeh, *Wartime Shanghai*, pp. 4, 10.

42. The Polish government in exile was originally established in Paris on September 20, 1939, and reported to a national council and parliament in exile. In its reconstituted form, it was located first in Angers, France, and subsequently in London.

43. Kranzler, *Japanese, Nazis and Jews*, pp. 354–55.

44. Information provided by Ewa Barteczko, Polish National Library, 1994.

45. Fiszman, "Quest for Status," pp. 10–11.

46. The Polish Record Book shows that of the 206 Polish refugees who entered Shanghai between 1934 and 1936, 76 (37 percent) were Jews.

47. Zeitin, "Shanghai Jewish Community," p. 64.

48. Police report, May 28, 1943, in SMPD 5422A.

49. Dr. J. A. J. Cohn's birth name was Jan Weinberg. His parents came from Romania. After they died in Nagasaki, Japan, a German physician, Dr. Cohn, adopted Weinberg, who then took the name Cohn. Letter dated Dec. 31, 1984, from Rudolf Loewenthal. Another report mentions that Dr. Cohn helped local Zionists in Nagasaki "with the disposal of the Nagasaki Synagogue to the Japanese Government." See *IM*, May 9, 1924, p. 21.

50. "Jüdische Gemeinde, 1934–1944," *SJC*, Jan. 16, 1944, p. 5. Other articles dealing with this key organization, its functions and budget, appear in this same journal on July 18, 1943, Aug. 8, 1943, and Aug. 29, 1943.

51. Police report, May 4, 1943, in SMPD 5422. Besides L. M. Rogovin, the new leadership included R. R. Glaser, Fr. J. Wolff, E. Starer, E. Mendschein, and G. G. Abraham.

52. Speech by T. Kubota, *SJC*, May 9, 1943.

53. Kranzler, *Japanese, Nazis and Jews*, pp. 523–25.

54. *SJC*, May 9, 1943.

55. A Japanese Ministry of Foreign Affairs list of people exempted, dated March 1944, with the category of exemption and their English names and addresses, is in the Library of Congress microfilm collection, File S-9460-3-2873.

56. *SJC*, May 9, 1943.

57. *SJC*, Aug. 29, 1943; statistics show that about 30,000 pass renewals were handled during the ghetto period. See *CWR*, Nov. 17, 1945, p. 67.

58. Wartenberger, "Memoirs," p. 47, says Ghoya called himself "King of the Stateless Refugees."

59. *SJC*, Aug. 29, 1943, p. 1.

60. Rubin, *Ghetto Shanghai*, p. 123.

61. A typical daily list included 30–40 special passes. See, e.g., *SJC*, Nov. 14, 1943.

62. *SJC*, Sept. 29, 1943, p. 5.

63. *SJC*, Oct. 25, 1943, p. 3.

64. Wartenberger, "Memoirs," pp. 55–56.

65. *SJC*, Sept. 21, 1943, p. 3.

66. Budget records of the AJJDC for the years 1943–44 show no expenditures for Shanghai relief. See American Jewish Archives, AJJDC, 1940–49, Nearprint Special Topics, "30 Years: The Story of the JDC" (1945) and "Report of the Secretary — Moses A. Leavitt" in "The JDC in 1944." In the latter report, Shanghai is not mentioned at all.

67. Chou, *Chinese Inflation, 1937–1949*, p. 23.

68. Lee, *Letter to My Aunt*, letters written between August 1943 and August 1945, pp. 174, 190, 319, 392, 439.

69. Ibid., p. 46.

70. *SJC*, Nov. 23, 1943.

71. Telephone interview with W. Michael Blumenthal, Feb. 12, 1996.

72. Telephone interview with Genia Bloch, Tel Aviv, Feb. 11, 1996.

73. Interview with Joseph Ganger and Benjamin Fishoff, Shanghai, Apr. 1994.

74. Interview with W. Michael Blumenthal, June 10, 1993.

75. Japan, Ministry of Foreign Affairs, Japanese consular police report. File S-9460-3-2655.

76. "Kitchen Fund report on Bread Tickets for Inmates of the Camps as per February 28, 1943," in SMPD 5422A. Of the 2,764 camp residents, 2,243 received tickets; 521 did not. A breakdown of figures for each of the five camps is included.

77. Leo Baeck Institute, Jerome Agel Collection, box 1, folder 4. This source reports that 20 percent of the Hongkou refugees were on public assistance by the end of 1944.

78. Tickets were issued in values of 5, 10, 20, 25, 30, and 50 cents and $1 and could be obtained at the Jüdische Gemeinde office or at the Doumer Cinema in the French Concession. See police report, Apr. 2, 1943, in SMPD 5422A; Kranzler, *Japanese, Nazis and Jews*, p. 544.

79. Wang, *Shanghai E qiaoshi*, p. 340; Kranzler, *Japanese, Nazis and Jews*, p. 545.

80. Leo Baeck Institute, Jerome Agel Collection, box 1, folder 2.

81. Interview with W. Michael Blumenthal, June 10, 1993.

82. Interview with Henry Compart, July 10, 1994.

83. Wartenberger, "Memoirs," pp. 70, 78–79.

84. Coble, "Chinese Capitalists and the Japanese," in *Wartime Shanghai*, pp. 66–67; Iriye, *Power and Culture*, pp. 98–99.

85. *SJC*, Sept. 29, 1943, p. 5.

86. Police report, Sept. 9, 1943, in SMPD 5422A, vol. 2.

87. T. Kubota in *SJC*, Aug. 29, 1943.

88. *SJC*, Aug. 29, 1943, p. 5.

89. Ibid.

90. *SJC*, Jan. 9, 1944, p. 3. It is very likely that a long period of time elapsed before HICEM in Shanghai received the letters, especially from camps like Westerborg. Jews from this camp had been shipped to the East by early 1944. Publishing the name of the sender and addressee of letters in this newspaper was one important service of the *Shanghai Jewish Chronicle*.

91. Interview with W. Michael Blumenthal, June 10, 1993. The acronym ORT derives from the Russian Obschestvo Remeslenovo i. zemledelcheskovo Trouda (Society for Trades and Agricultural Labor), created in 1880 to assist Jewish trade schools and establish new colonies, agricultural schools, and model farms.

92. Louis Kemp, a civil engineer, was head instructor. He began his teaching in August 1939 when he set up a similar school at the Pingliang Road Camp. See police report, June 23, 1942, in SMPD 5422.

93. Police report, June 16, 1942, in SMPD 5422. Students at the Gregg School paid monthly tuition of $30 each.

94. Interview with Henry Compart, July 10, 1994.

95. Wartenberger, "Memoirs," pp. 48–49.

96. Institute of Jewish Affairs, WJC, Information Series, no. 9, Feb. 18, 1949, p. 6.

97. Pan Guang, "Shanghai's Case in the Annals of Jewish Diaspora," p. 7.

98. *IM*, Jan. 13, 1922, p. 10.

99. For discussion of the Shanghai Sephardim's involvement in the World Zionist Movement and the weakening of its initial enthusiasm, see Meyer, "Sephardi Jewish Community of Shanghai," pp. 246–75. The Theodor Herzl Zionist Organization, named after its founder, the journalist son of a Hungar-

ian merchant who spent his life trying to solve the Jewish question through the establishment of a Jewish homeland in Palestine, was the most conservative Zionist body. His organizational skills produced a worldwide Zionist movement. A different approach came from the New Zionist Organization founded by Vladimir Jabotinsky. Frustrated by the slow progress made by the Herzl Zionists, this movement supported militant political action aimed at realizing a Jewish state. Along with the conservative revisionist youth group Brit Trumpeldor, popularly named Betar, the New Zionists became known as the "revisionists" and enjoyed support especially from Russian Jews. A membership list for the Shanghai Theodor Herzl Zionist Organization appears in SMPD 5422, vol. 2.

100. Police report, June 7, 1943, in SMPD 5422, vol. 2.

101. Police report, Aug. 5, 1943, in SMPD 5422A, vol. 2.

102. For details on Shanghai Zionism, see Pan Guang, "Zionism and Zionist Revisionism in Shanghai," pp. 267–76.

103. U.S. National Archives and Records Administration, "History of the Nazi Party in China," pp. 8–9. H. Essen headed the KDF in Shanghai; Carl Puttfarcken was the overall head in China.

104. Ibid., p. 11. The formal name of the Hitler Youth overseas organization was Reichsdeutsche Jugend im Ausland. Kreissler, "In Search of Identity," p. 12, notes that more than 85 percent of the Kaiser Wilhelm School's German students were enrolled in it in 1939–40. Its leader in Shanghai was Helmut Wiedemann; Gretel Pflug led the Girl Guides.

105. Wartenberger, "Memoirs," p. 100.

106. Ibid., pp. 105–15. Wartenberger was an active participant in tending to the dead and wounded during this disaster.

107. Ibid.

108. Ibid., p. 111–12.

Chapter 8

1. Wang Zhicheng, *Shanghai E qiaoshi*, p. 221. Money sent to the Soviet embassy in London was returned, but the names of donors were recorded.

2. "Exiled Russians in Shanghai Rally to Aid Fatherland," *NCDN*, Oct. 12, 1941.

3. Interview with Nikita Moravsky, June 16, 1995.

4. Interview with Mouza Zumwalt, Mar. 8, 1996.

5. According to the July 1942 *baojia* census, there were 1,666 registered Soviet citizens in the three areas of Shanghai. Russian Emigrants Committee, SMP-MIS-17, p. 9. Key Soviet organizations in Shanghai in 1943 were the "Circle of Soviet Citizens," with 355 members (N. S. Zephyrov, president); the Soviet Red Cross; the Association of Young Friends of the Soviet Red

Cross; the Association of Soviet Women; the Commercial Association of Soviet Citizens; and the Mutual Assistance Society of Soviet Citizens. See French police report, Feb. 27, 1943, in SMPD 13, "List of Soviet Organizations in Shanghai."

6. Interview with Joseph Froomkin, Sept. 1995.

7. *NCDN*, Dec. 3, 1941, p. 4.

8. *Shen bao*, Oct. 26, 1941.

9. Interview with Nikita Moravsky, June 16, 1995.

10. Balakshin, *Final v. Kitae*, 1: 32.

11. *NCDN*, Oct. 22, 1942, p. 4.

12. *Russian Orthodox Church*, p. 123.

13. Interview with Amir Khasimutdinov, Apr. 9, 1996.

14. Wang Zhicheng, *Shanghai E qiaoshi*, p. 222.

15. Police report, Jan. 30, 1942, and *NCDN*, Oct. 22, 1941, p. 2. See *CWR*, Mar. 1, 1944, pp. 439–41, for discussion of the *Vozvrashchenchestvo*, or "returning" movement, which sought and found an ideological home in Soviet communism.

16. *NCDN*, Oct. 22, 1941.

17. "Letter from L. V. Grosse," *NCDN*, Oct. 22, 1941, p. 4

18. "Letter in Reply to Grosse," *NCDN*, Oct. 24, 1941, p. 5.

19. "Letter in Reply to Basil," *NCDN*, Oct. 26, 1941, p. 6.

20. "Letter from Grosse," *NCDN*, Nov. 27, 1941, p. 4.

21. "Letter in Reply by Grosse," in *NCDN*, Oct. 25, 1941, p. 4.

22. Ibid. Managers of *Slovo* were identified as M. V. Val', Altadukov, and General Sychev; the editor was a Dr. Zaitsev. Olga Lembitch owned *Shankhaiskaia Zaria*. Other occasional publications were the *Russian Scout* (Russkii Rasvedchik), an organ of monarchist Russian youth; and the *Standard*, a religious monarchist organ. Both of the latter two publications supported Japanese aims, which they saw as benefiting their own. *CWR*, Mar. 1, 1941, p. 440.

23. "Letter" in *NCDN*, Nov. 5, 1941, p. 4. This probably was the "Circle of Soviet Citizens" organization referred to in n. 5 above.

24. *NCDN*, Oct. 17, 1941.

25. Wang Zhicheng, *Shanghai E qiaoshi*, pp. 308–9.

26. *Shanghai Times*, Jan. 1, 1943.

27. *Shankhaiskaia Zaria* and *Novoe Vremia* (English translation), Dec. 8, 1942, in SMPD 7478.

28. *Shanghai Times*, Jan. 5, 1943.

29. Russian Emigrants Committee, SMP-MIS-17, p. 2.

30. Ibid., p. 3.

31. *Shanghai Times*, Feb. 14 and 15 and Mar. 31, 1943.

32. "Russians Told Not to Carry Dual Papers," *Shanghai Times*, Mar. 17, 1943.

33. A list of voters who participated in the general election of December 24, 1944, is reportedly found in bundle 33 of the Russian Emigrants Committee files, according to the SMP files index, but not included in the SMP files collection.

34. Russian Emigrants Committee, SMP-MIS-17, p. 4.

35. Police report, Apr. 2, 1944, in SMPD 5002A; Russian Emigrants Committee, SMP-MIS-17, p. 4.

36. Police report, Apr. 3, 1944, in SMPD 5002A.

37. Interview with Nikita Moravsky, June 16, 1995.

38. Fomin received 235 votes; Bologov, 433; and Sereinikov, 360. See Russian Emigrants Committee, SMP-MIS-17, pp. 5–6.

39. Police report, July 14, 1942, in SMPD 5471, p. 5.

40. Other leaders included A. N. Vonsovich and S. I. Vasiliev, vice-chairmen; Y. A. Mariash, secretary; A. A. Avdienko, treasurer; and P. A. Boiko-Sokolsky and G. F. Totsky, members at large. The Board of Auditors included N. M. Krivenko, chairman; G. Melnichenko, member; and E. Ilchook, secretary. See police report, July 15, 1942, in SMPD 5471, p. 5.

41. Ibid., p. 6.

42. Erich Koch, as quoted in Dallin, *German Rule in Russia*, p. 167.

43. Police report, June 24, 1942, in SMPD 5471. Daily broadcasting, which began in May 1942, changed to a one-hour program, from 2:00–3:00 on Sunday afternoons, in September. Police report, Oct. 9, 1942.

44. English translations of *Nash Put*, June 21, 1942, in SMPD 7478.

45. Police report, June 24, 1942, in SMPD 5471, pp. 3–4.

46. The new Ukrainian National Committee in East Asia had its headquarters at 261 Gordon Road, in the western part of the International Settlement. Its chairman, J. V. Sweet, had been a journalist and editor in Vladivostok until 1922, when he went to Harbin, where he continued his journalist career until 1941. In Shanghai, he worked as a journalist and stamp dealer. A. I. Drobiazko, the committee's vice-chairman, had escaped in 1918 to Harbin, where he worked as a horticulturalist. In 1939, he was appointed by the Tianjin Anti-Comintern Committee to the Economic Section of the Beiping branch. After coming to Shanghai in August 1940, he worked for the *Ukrainian Voice of the Far East*. M. I. Pirogov, the committee's secretary, an alumnus of the Kiev Military Academy, had been recruited by Admiral Kolchak's government in 1918 and had fled to Manchuria in 1924. He had arrived in Shanghai in 1933 and was involved in various business enterprises there. At this time, he worked for the German Machine Company on Canton Road. Other members of the committee included Sweet's wife, M. Milko and wife, and K. Opadchy. See police report, June 24, 1942, in SMPD 5471, p. 2.

47. English translation of *Novoe Vremia* article, Aug. 6, 1942, in SMPD 5471.

48. Deputy Sub-Inspector A. Prokofiev made two lengthy reports on the Ukrainian organizations and their aspirations within the space of just two days. Reports dated June 22 and 24, 1942, in SMPD 5471.

49. Police report, June 22, 1942, in SMPD 5471, pp. 7–8. A list of 164 names of members of the Ukrainian Representatives Committee exists as an attachment to this document.

50. In SMPD 5471.

51. Letter dated Sept. 18, 1943 (?), in SMPD 5471.

52. Ibid.

53. Letter in police report, Sept. 30, 1944, SMPD 5471, p. 2.

54. Ibid., p. 4.

55. Ibid., p. 5.

56. Police report, Aug. 8, 1942, in SMPD 5471, noting this observation by Commissioner of Police M. Watari concerning Ukrainian registrations.

57. Other members of the All-Russian Fascist Union included G. A. Hofen, "Head of the Shanghai group"; V. V. Ivanchenko, secretary; and E. N. Chetverikov, head of the Women's Section. Police report, Apr. 30, 1942, in SMPD 7478, p. 7.

58. Steklov edited the *Russian Vanguard*, which ceased publication owing to his illness on November 9, 1941. Police report, Jan. 26, 1942, in SMPD 5835.

59. Translation of 1941 *Novoe Vremia* article in SMPD 5835.

60. "The All-Russian Fascist Union," police report, Apr. 30, 1942, in SMPD 7478, p. 7. The report is signed by Deputy Inspector A. Prokofiev.

61. English translation of article "Regarding Karganov-Spasovsky's Letter," in *Novoe Vremia*, Aug. 19, 1942.

62. English translation of this article in *Nash Put*, Oct. 26, 1942, in SMPD 7478.

63. English translation of an article entitled "Explanation Regarding the Incident Involving M. M. Spasovsky" in *Novoe Vremia*, Aug. 26, 1942.

64. Police report, Sept. 12, 1942, in SMPD 7478.

65. Police report, Oct. 27, 1942, in SMPD 7478.

66. A meeting for renaming the organization the Union of National Workers of Russia drew 110 followers. Police report, Oct. 14, 1943, in SMPD 7478.

67. Police reports for 1943 in SMPD 7478.

68. E. M. Kojevnikov is referred to throughout the documentation as "Hovans," but "Khovans" is a more accurate rendering of the name. "Eugene Pick," "Eugene Kruger," "Eugene Pavlov," and "Dr. Karl Luge" were among his other aliases. U.S. National Archives and Records Administration, China Theater X-2 Branch Report, Oct. 12, 1945, p. 2. See also Wasserstein, *Secret War*, pp. 44–47, 113–14.

69. Hovans reportedly purloined a diary and report on foreign warships at

Hankou from Borodin, which he was able to sell to the French consul. SMPD 2911/8. Hovans's role as a G.P.U. agent is also noted in police report, July 31, 1941, in SMPD IO-7926. See also *CWR*, Sept. 20, 1941, p. 98.

70. U.S. National Archives and Records Administration, RG-226, China Theater X-2 Branch Report, Sept. 7, 1945, p. 2.

71. Wang Zhicheng, *Shanghai E qiaoshi*, p. 365.

72. U.S. National Archives and Records Administration, RG-226, OSS report, Oct. 12, 1945, p. 3

73. U.S. National Archives and Records Administration, RG-226, China Theater X-2 Branch Report, Sept. 7, 1945, p. 3.

74. Ibid., p. 3.

75. *NCDN*, June 18, 1931, in SMPD 2523.

76. U.S. National Archives and Records Administration, RG-226, China Theater X-2 Branch Report, Sept. 7, 1945, p. 4.

77. U.S. National Archives and Records Administration, RG-226, 182A, folder 70.

78. On Mamontov's murder, see Wasserstein, *Secret War*, pp. 93–94, 113.

79. Hovans also was suspected of being involved in the murder of Ch. Metzler, chairman of the Russian Emigrants Committee, through his agent "Karpoff," probably V. I. Karpov, who claimed to be an advisor to the Japanese Military Headquarters. U.S. National Archives and Records Administration, RG-226, OSS China/Shanghai, folder 13, and China Theater Branch Report, Sept. 7, 1945, p. 2. For his appearance before the Second District Court, where testimony was given by three White Russians regarding S. Marmontov's murder, see *NCDN*, Oct. 30, 1941; *Shanghai Times*, Oct. 30, 1941. Another report claimed that Hovans instigated Marmontov's murder because he had refused to participate in the murder of Metzler's successor, Ivanov. See *CWR*, Sept. 27, 1941; Oct. 11, 1941.

80 Wang Zhicheng, *Shanghai E qiaoshi*, pp. 365–66.

81. U.S. National Archives and Records Administration, RG-226, OSS/Shanghai, folder 122. Hovans admitted in court that he had worked for the German consul general in Shanghai. See *NCDN*, Nov. 18, 1941, p. 7.

82. U.S. National Archives and Records Administration, OSS report, Oct. 12, 1945.

83. U.S. National Archives and Records Administration, RG-226, China Theater Branch Report, Oct. 12, 1945, p. 2; War Department, Office of the Assistant Secretary of War, Headquarters, Strategic Services Unit, China Theater Report, Dec. 28, 1945, p. 5.

84. U.S. National Archives and Records Administration, RG-226, 182A, folder 49.

85. Ibid., date of information March 1943.

86. U.S. National Archives and Records Administration, RG-226, 182A, folder 8; folder 19.

87. U.S. National Archives and Records Administration, RG-226, "Miscellaneous German Activities in China," folder 62, pt. 2.

88. For discussion of Miorini's activities, see Wasserstein, *Secret War*, pp. 153–54.

89. U.S. National Archives and Records Administration, RG-226, "Germans in China," folder 55.

90. Ibid.

91. Fonteyn, *Autobiography*, pp. 24, 29.

92. Rena Krasno, *Strangers Always*, p. 165.

93. Interview with Nikita Moravsky, Mar. 22, 1996. Alexander Vertinsky's song "Those Were the Days," popularized by Gene Raskin of the Limelighters, was chosen by Paul McCartney for the Welsh singer Mary Hopkin's debut in the late 1960s.

94. *NCDN*, July 27, 1941. On one occasion, V. A. Chilikin, publisher of the *Russian Daily News*, celebrated with the White Russians. See ibid., Aug. 28, 1941, p. 2.

95. Reported to the author at the Shanghai reunion of former Jewish refugees, September 1994.

96. Interview with Mouza Zumwalt, Mar. 8, 1996.

97. Interview with Joseph Froomkin, June 16, 1993, whose father headed the coordinating committee responsible for allocating the funds.

98. Rena Krasno, "Russian Jews in Shanghai," p. 6.

99. Interview with Mouza Zumwalt, Mar. 8, 1996.

100. Japan, Ministry of Foreign Affairs, Japanese consular police report, July 9, 1943. File S-9460-3-2658.

101. Telephone interview with Laura Topas Popper, who expressed the view that the Sephardi Jews who had enormous wealth could have done more to aid the ghetto, but were inhibited by their superior attitude.

102. Joseph Froomkin, unpublished MS, p. 79.

103. Ibid., p. 83.

104. Russian Emigrants Committee, SMP-MIS-17, p. 6.

105. Ibid., p. 6.

Chapter 9

1. Wartenberger, "Memoirs," p. 116.

2. Ibid., pp. 116–17.

3. Ibid., p. 118.

4. For an account of the experiences of the advance U.S. naval forces upon reaching Shanghai, see Elmo R. Zumwalt, *On Watch*, pp. 3–22.

5. Wartenberger, "Memoirs," pp. 121–22.
6. Interview with Nikita Moravsky, June 16, 1995.
7. Joseph Froomkin, unpublished MS, p. 118.
8. Ibid.
9. Grebenschikoff, *Once My Name Was Sara*, p. 103.
10. Interview with Stanley Bergman, Apr. 23, 1995.
11. Wang, *Shanghai E qiaoshi*, p. 332; Hershatter, p. 62; SMPD 7042.
12. U.S. National Archives and Records Administration, U.S. Marine Corps Records, RG-313, box 6129, cable from commander, U.S. Navy Port Facilities, Shanghai, to commander, Naval Forces, Western Pacific, May 19, 1948. I am grateful to Yang Zhiguo for making these records known to me.
13. Vorda Hounold, "Memories of Shanghai," p. 16.
14. Wartenberger, "Memoirs," p. 132.
15. Ibid., p. 119.
16. Rubin, *Ghetto Shanghai*, p. 153.
17. Wartenberger, "Memoirs," p. 131.
18. "UNRRA in China," by Harry B. Price, assistant director and historian, China Office, UNRRA, in *Almanac Shanghai 1946/47*, ed. Lewin, p. 27.
19. Dai, *Summary Report on UNRRA*, p. 4; *Fifty Facts about UNRRA*, p. 24.
20. *Almanac Shanghai 1946/47*, ed. Lewin, p. 29.
21. Chou, *Chinese Inflation, 1937–1949*, pp. 24–26, 138.
22. Hounold, "Memories of Shanghai," p. 20.
23. Joseph Froomkin, unpublished MS, p. 5; Ben-Eliezer, *Shanghai Lost*, p. 223.
24. Joseph Froomkin, unpublished MS, pp. 5–6.
25. Ibid., p. 49.
26. Ibid., p. 50.
27. In 1967, the AJJDC reassigned Charles Jordan to Czechoslovakia, where he traveled extensively organizing relief for Jewish refugees behind the Iron Curtain. A reliable refugee source reports that he left his home to buy a newspaper one morning but never returned. His body was found in Prague's Vltava River. The doctor who examined his body reported that Jordan had been murdered by injection of a drug. The doctor "committed suicide" shortly afterward. The Prague government claimed Jordan died during interrogation at the Egyptian embassy in Prague, where he was believed to be an Israeli spy. See also *New York Times*, Feb. 4, 1974.
28. Estimates were that 10,191 persons each received 12 oz. of bread daily; 9,000 bags of flour and 35,000 cases of foodstuffs were transported monthly; from January to November 1946, 26,690 pieces of men's clothing, 25,927 pieces of women's clothing, and 12,711 blankets were distributed by the Joint Clothing Department. "The American Jewish Joint Distribution Committee in Shanghai," *Almanac Shanghai 1946/47*, ed. Lewin, p. 37. The World Jewish

Congress China Section reported the distribution of clothing and shoes as follows: the Jüdische Gemeinde received 65 percent of the goods; Polish refugees, 15 percent; Russian Jews, 8 percent; Sephardi Jews, 7 percent; Czech Jews, 5 percent. Letter dated May 7, 1946, WJC MS collection, 361, box H87.

29. "Abstract of a Statistical Survey of 13,475 Refugees in Shanghai, China, as of March 31, 1946," AJJDC Research Department, Nov. 25, 1946. Countries are broken down as follows: Germany 7,498; Austria 4,337; Poland 654; Czechoslovakia 181; other 805.

30. *Almanac Shanghai 1946/47*, ed. Lewin, p. 38. For a detailed discussion, including layout of the Chinese lane or alleyway housing, see Lu Haochu, *Beyond the Neon Lights*.

31. *Almanac Shanghai 1946/47*, ed. Lewin, p. 39.

32. Rubin, *Ghetto Shanghai*, p. 153.

33. *Almanac Shanghai 1946/47*, ed. Lewin, p. 13.

34. HIAS established contact with relatives abroad for 7,094 refugees. *Almanac Shanghai 1946/47*, ed. Lewin, p. 43.

35. Ibid., p. 43.

36. Ibid., p. 46.

37. Memorandum from the AJJDC to Dr. Tartakower, World Jewish Congress, Oct. 1, 1946, WJC MS collection, 361, box H87.

38. *CWR*, Feb. 2, 1946; *Shanghai Herald*, Mar. 12, 1946.

39. Letter dated Sept. 17, 1945, from the American Jewish Conference and World Jewish Congress to Tsui Tsuen-ling, first secretary, Embassy of the Chinese Republic, in WJC MS collection, box H87. Quoting newspaper reports, the letter noted that these Chinese actions would be canceled if the refugees could acquire "valuable guarantees, either Chinese or foreign."

40. Ray, *UNRRA in China*, p. 48.

41. *Almanac Shanghai 1946/47*, ed. Lewin, p. 40.

42. Description contained in letter from Bertold Glanz, Dec. 15, 1945.

43. "Constitution of the International Refugee Organization," pp. 13–14.

44. Interview with Nikita Moravsky, Aug. 21, 1996.

45. Ibid.

46. Joseph Froomkin, unpublished MS, p. 80.

47. Ibid., p. 7; interview with Nikita Moravsky, June 16, 1995.

48. Interview with Nikita Moravsky, June 16, 1995.

49. Wang, *Shanghai E qiaoshi*, pp. 117–21. Another estimate puts the figure at "about 5,000." See Fedoulenko interview, p. 127.

50. Interview with Nikita Moravsky, June 16, 1995.

51. Truman in *Public Papers of the Presidents of the United States, April 12 to December 31, 1945*, pp. 572–78.

52. Ibid., pp. 572–73.

53. Ibid., p. 577.

54. Letter from Kurt Grossman to Dr. Tartakower, Feb. 15, 1949, WJC MS collection, box H88.

55. Memorandum, July 5, 1945 from Dr. Arieh Tartakower, WJC MS collection, ser. A, Central Files, box A75.

56. "Statement of Refugees who left Shanghai since the End of the War 'Til Dec. 31st 1947," WJC MS collection, box H88.

57. Memorandum, Oct. 11, 1948, from the Political Department, WJC, to Members of the Executive Committee (American Branch), p. 3.

58. Memorandum, Aug. 4, 1946, from Dr. I. Schwarzbart, Organization Department, WJC.

59. Letter from Walter Sternberg, Migration Committee of the Council of European Refugee Organizations, Feb. 8, 1949, to Kurt R. Grossman.

60. *Almanac Shanghai 1946/47*, ed. Lewin, p. 37.

61. "Statement . . . Summary of Refugees Remaining in Shanghai," World Jewish Congress, Dec. 31, 1947.

62. Letter from Charles Jordan, Apr. 24, 1946.

63. I. Jacob and J. Dobekirer, "Report of Activities of China Section of Jewish World Congress Covering Two Years: From End of 1945 to 1947," WJC, 1948, p. 2.

64. Memorandum from Dr. A. Tartakower, Sept. 1945, WJC MS collection, box A75.

65. Letter from William Deman to Kurt Grossman, WJC MS collection, Jan. 25, 1948.

66. U.S. Public Law 774, in *U.S. Statutes at Large: Displaced Persons Act of 1948*, pp. 1009–14.

67. Truman, "Statement by the President upon Signing the Displaced Persons Act," in *Public Papers of the Presidents of the United States, January 1 to December 31, 1948*, pp. 382–84.

68. "Appeal to Truman," *Aufbau: Reconstruction* (New York), Nov. 19, 1948.

69. Letter from Walter Sternberg to Kurt Grossman, Feb. 8, 1949, WJC MS collection, box H88.

70. Memorandum from Kurt R. Grossman, WJC, to Dr. Robert Marcus, Mar. 18, 1949, WJC MS collection, box H88,

71. Report, Nov. 16, 1949, WJC MS collection, box H88.

72. Memorandum from Kurt Grossman, Jan. 24, 1949, in WJC MS collection, box H88.

73. AJJDC records reported 1,500, a figure that may have overlooked those Jews arriving under private sponsorship. The Jewish Welfare Society reported the 2,500 figure, which seemed to consider the initial 700 refugees plus the annual quota increases of 300 immigrants. See Rutland, *Edge of the Diaspora*, pp.

236–38. For firsthand reports from refugees attempting to settle in Australia, see Finnane, *Far From Where?* pp. 182–92.

74. William Deman letter to Kurt R. Grossman, Dec. 27, 1948.

75. Truman in *Public Papers of the Presidents of the United States, April 12 to December 31, 1945*, pp. 575, 578.

76. Letter from Walter Sternberg to Kurt Grossman, Aug. 10, 1949, WJC MS collection, box H88.

77. Letter to Walter Sternberg of the Council of European Refugee Organizations, Feb. 14, 1949, from Kurt R. Grossman, WJC MS collection, box H88.

78. Letter from William Deman to Kurt R. Grossman, Jan. 16, 1949.

79. An AJJDC document, "Shanghai: Departures since the Beginning of Evacuation" (Feb. 1949), notes that of the 3,408 passengers (2,562 DPs and 846 residents), 145 had the United States as their destination; 29, Canada; 53, Latin America; 109, Australia and New Zealand; and 11, Europe; 327 chose repatriation; and 58 remain unknown.

80. WJC MS collection, "Argentine Measures Hit DPs," memorandum, Dec. 25, 1948.

81. Memorandum from Phil Baum to Dr. Robert Marcus, June 29, 1950.

82. Memorandum from Phil Baum, American Jewish Congress, to Dr. Marcus dated June 20, 1950.

83. U.S. Public Law 555, *Displaced Persons Act of 1948 — Amendment* (June 16, 1950), p. 224.

84. The figure 5,500 appears in the Fedoulenko interview, pp. 131–32. The *New York Herald Tribune*, Apr. 20, 1949, speaks of 4,000 refugees.

85. Interview with Nikita Moravsky, including newspaper clippings provided during the interview, Aug. 21, 1996.

86. Letter from Walter Sternberg, Feb. 8, 1949, to Kurt R. Grossman.

87. This censorship inspired a heated exchange of letters to the editor from family members of Samar refugees in the *NCDN*, Feb. 10, 19, 14, 17, 1949.

88. Interview with Nikita Moravsky, June 16, 1995.

89. Ibid.

90. *Our Herald*, souvenir issue, Jan. 1951, prepared aboard the USS *General W. G. Haan*, which carried 1,117 refugees from Samar to the United States. On board were 989 Russians, 52 Poles, 26 Ukrainians, and 17 Latvians. The remaining nationalities numbered fewer than 10 each.

91. Ibid. Within this group, 852 were Eastern Orthodox; 129 were Protestant; 81 Roman Catholic; 18 identified as Baptists, and 13 Lutherans. The remainder numbered fewer than 10.

92. Memorandum from Kurt R. Grossman to Dr. Robert Marcus, May 6, 1949.

93. Fedoulenko interview, p. 150. Fedoulenko served as vice-chairman of the Russian Emigrants Committee in the camp community.

94. During Archbishop Ioann's visit to the United States, he initiated work on the establishment of the Russian Orthodox Cathedral of St. John the Baptist, now located on 17th Street in Washington, D.C., where a mural depicts him. Mention is also made in the WJC MS collection, series H, of negotiations undertaken by George Hoague, Jr., "personal representative of the IRO Director General to General MacArthur," who traveled to Washington on behalf of the Samar community.

95. *Manila Times*, Nov. 15, 1949.

96. U.S. Public Law 203, *Refugee Relief Act of 1953*, Chapter 336, p. 444.

97. *Our Herald*, Jan. 1951.

98. "A Delayed Haven: 1,131 Russians End a Flight from Communism," *San Francisco Chronicle*, Jan. 26, 1951, p. 25; "Years of Wandering End for Russian DPs Here," *San Francisco Examiner*, Jan. 26, 1951, p. 9.

99. "To Our Future," by "A.N.K." [Aleksei Nikolaevich Kniazev], in *Our Herald*, 1951.

100. Schwarzbart, "400 Jews Left," p. 1.

101. Abraham, *Council of the Jewish Community of Shanghai*.

102. Ibid., p. 8. In 1954, the Sephardi Communal Association numbered 46 members; the Ashkenazi, 120 members. Including family members, the total number of Jewish residents in Shanghai was 310.

103. Schwarzbart, "Dwindling Jewish Community in China," p. 2.

104. Schwarzbart, "Last Jews," p. 1.

105. Schwarzbart, "Dwindling Jewish Community," p. 2.

106. Schwarzbart, "400 Jews Left," p. 2.

107. Ibid., p. 13.

108. Schwarzbart, "400 Jews Left."

109. Letter from F. R. Bienenfeld to Dr. Nehemiah Robinson of the European Division, WJC, Oct. 29, 1952, WJC MS collection, box 88.

110. Paul Rosdy made copies of affidavits available to this author. They include one by Robert Peritz, a leader of the International Committee; one by his assistant, Dr. Erich Faerber; and one by Fritz Wiedemann, former German consul general in Tianjin. They all support the story related to them by Japanese Vice-Consul Shibata that the Japanese were planning to act against the Jews at the bidding of the Germans. The Wiedemann testimony also appears in Kranzler, *Japanese, Nazis and Jews*, p. 488; Kranzler mentions the Faerber and Peritz affidavits on p. 473.

111. Letter from Dr. Nehemiah Robinson to Dr. F. R. Bienenfeld, WJC, Nov. 6, 1952, in WJC MS collection, box H88. The research also found that refugees of Austrian nationality could not benefit under the terms of the Allied-Japanese Peace Treaty.

112. U.S. National Archives and Records Administration, United States of America vs. Lothar Eisentraeger (Ludwig Ehrhardt), RG-153, vol. 22, box 560. This case took place in the courtroom of the Ward Road Jail in Hongkou.

113. Letter from N. Wylie to Office of the U.S. General Counsel, Frankfurt, Sept. 19, 1950, in RG-153.

114. Letter from Damon M. Gunn, judge advocate, to N. Wylie, Office of the Legal Adviser, Sept. 29, 1950, RG-153.

115. See the legislation enacted on June 29, 1956, to compensate victims of National Socialist persecution (*Bundesentschädigungsgesetz*, or *BEG*). The Final Federal Compensation Law enacted in September 1965 increased the number of persons eligible for compensation as well as the assistance offered.

116. "Current eligibility criteria of the Article 2 Fund," attachment to a letter to the author from Joseph M. Spraragen, Conference on Jewish Material Claims Against Germany, Inc., dated Oct. 23, 1996. For a description of this fund, see Article 2 of the "Agreement on the Enactment and Interpretation of the Unification Treaty" (in German), ratified on Sept. 18, 1990, in *Bundesgesetzblatt* 2, no. 35, beginning at p. 885.

117. Telephone interview with Ingrid Richardson, Austrian Embassy, Washington, D.C., Sept. 25, 1996. The one-time payment is administered in Austria by the National Fund of the Republic of Austria for the Victims of Persecution.

118. Schwarzbart, "Last Jews," p. 1; id., "Dwindling Jewish Community," p. 1.

119. Ibid., p. 2.

120. Peter Humphrey, "Death Leaves Just One Jew in China," *South China Morning Post*, Feb. 24, 1982; Christopher Wren, "A Jewish Legacy Draws to a Close in North China," *New York Times*, Feb. 27, 1983.

BIBLIOGRAPHY

Archives and Papers

AMERICAN JEWISH ARCHIVES, CINCINNATI, OHIO

American Jewish Joint Distribution Committee Collection
David Brown Papers
M. S. Bloch (The Morris Company)
Rabbi Betram W. Korn papers
Rabbi Joseph Zeitin Collection
World Jewish Congress Collection

WILLIAM DEMAN. LETTERS AND CORRESPONDENCE PROVIDED BY
JOAN R. DEMAN, 1995.

DEPOSITIONS PROVIDED BY PAUL ROSDY, VIENNA, AUSTRIA

Erich Faeber, June 12, 1954
Robert Peritz, Jan. 11, 1952
Gertrud Johanna Schnellenberg, June 26, 1954
Fritz Wiedemann, Jan. 22, 1951
Julius Wolff, July 2, 1954
Margaret Wolff

LEAGUE OF NATIONS ARCHIVES, GENEVA

"Commission of Inquiry into the Traffic of Women and Children in
the Far East," COL 155-128, 1928–32, itinerary, interviews, and
selected documents

File R 4691-92, cotes des séries 13457, listes 22, reports, letters, and clippings, 1933–37

"Position of Women of Russian Origin in the Far East," August 15, 1935, A.12, 1935, in file R4692

"Situation des femmes d'origine Russe en Extrême-Orient," Aug. 14, 1935, A.12 in file R4692

"Traffic in Women and Children: Conference of Central Authorities in Eastern Countries, Bandung, Indonesia," C.228.M.164, [February] 1937 IV

"Traffic in Women and Children," C.476.M.318, [December] 1937 IV

LEO BAECK INSTITUTE, NEW YORK, SHANGHAI ARCHIVES, JEROME AGEL RESEARCH COLLECTION YEARBOOKS

POLISH RECORD BOOK, 1934–41 (CONSULATE GENERAL OF POLAND, SHANGHAI)

SHANGHAI MUNICIPAL ARCHIVES

Conseil d'Administration municipale de la Concession française à Changhaï

Comptes Rendus/Budgets, 1922–43

Bulletin Municipal, 1922–43

Shanghai Municipal Council

V. F. Grosse. Reports to the Commissioner General, Shanghai Municipal Council, 1925–31, File U-1-3-3002

Ch. A. Metzler, Memorandum to Secretary, Shanghai Municipal Council, Oct. 1932, file U-1-3-3001

Municipal Gazette of the Council for the Foreign Settlement of Shanghai, 1933–43

Minute Books, 1933–43

Annual Reports and Budgets, 1933–43

U.S. NATIONAL ARCHIVES AND RECORDS ADMINISTRATION

Central Intelligence Agency Files, RG 263, Shanghai Municipal Police Files

General Records of the Department of State, RG 59, decimal files 893.55 and

893.48. Records of the Foreign Service Posts of the Department of State, RG84, Shanghai Consulate Files

Office of Strategic Services Archives, RG 226, series 182A

"Hebrew Society for the Study of Nipponese Culture"

"History of the Nazi Party in China," folder 134

"Interrogations of Captain Ernest Dello," folder 12

"List of Germans in Shanghai"

"OSS China/Shanghai"

Records of the Army Staff, RG 319: Investigative Records Repository, Josef A. Meisinger, case files XA51-42-60 and XE003304

Records of the Naval Operating Forces, RG 313: U. S. Marine Corps

Records of the Office of the Judge Advocate General, U.S. Army, War Crimes Branch, RG 153: "United States of America vs. Lothar Eisentraeger (Ludwig Ehrhardt)," proceedings before a Military Commission by Command, Shanghai, China

Interviews

NOTE: Interviews were conducted by the author unless otherwise indicated.

Ballerand, Hélène (Loula). Apr. 3, 1998. Oakton, Va.

Bergman, Stanley. Telephone interview, Apr. 23, 1995

Bloch, Genia Topas. Telephone interview, Feb. 11, 1996.

Blumenthal, W. Michael. June 10, 1993 (taped); telephone interview, February 12, 1996.

Boguslavsky, Boris W. May 15, 1996 (taped). Washington, D.C.

Bryan, Gertrude. Feb. 11, 1989. Arlington, Va.

Compart, Henry. June 12 and July 10, 1994 (taped). Silver Spring, Md.

Fedoulenko, Valentine Vassilievich. Interview by Boris Raymond, 1966: "Russian Émigré Life in Shanghai." University of California Berkeley Oral History Project. Glen Rock, N.J.: Microfilming Corp. of America, 1978.

Fielden, Grant A. Telephone interview, May 6, 1992.

Fishoff, Benjamin. May 1994. Shanghai.

Froomkin, Joseph. June 16, 1993. Washington, D.C.

Ganger, Joseph. May 1994 (taped). Shanghai.

Glass, Werner B. 1996 (tapes provided).

Hamburg, Eva. Telephone interview, Feb. 21, 1996.

Hounold, Vorda. Jan. 24, 1993. Washington, D.C.

Hu, Wen-an and Peggy Hu. Feb. 26, 1995. Bethesda, Md.

Ishiguro, Kenji. Sept. 11, 1996. Washington, D.C.

Jordan, Colonel Jim. Feb. 21, 1989. Alexandria, Va.

Jarblum, Laura Margolis. Interview by Menahem Kaufman, Apr. 26, 1976, pp. 1–44. Tel Aviv. Interview provided by Kurt Maier.

Kahn, Margot. 1992. Interview provided by Pan Guang. Shanghai.

Kamkin, Elena. Telephone interview, Feb. 3, 1993.

Khasimutdinov, Amir. Apr. 9, 1996. Honolulu.

Moravsky, Nikita. Mar. 22, May 17, June 16, and Aug. 21, 1996 (taped). Washington, D.C.

Penners, Sheila. Telephone interview, June 20, 1996.

Petrov, Viktor. Feb. 15, 1993. Silver Spring, Md.

Popper, Laura Topas. Telephone interview, Nov. 14, 1994.

Richardson, Ingrid. Telephone interview, Sept. 25, 1996.

Schriner, Herta. Oral presentation, Leo Baeck Institute, May 1995.

de Stackelberg, Baroness Garnett. Telephone interview, Mar. 23, 1989.

Tokmakova, Irena A. July 15, 1994. Washington, D.C.

Tsuneishi, Warren. Telephone interview, February 17, 2001.

Wang, Zhicheng. May 1992. Shanghai.

Willens, Liliane. Aug. 5, 1996. Washington, D.C.

Zumwalt, Mouza. Mar. 8, 1996 (taped). Arlington, Va.

Newspapers and Other Periodicals

Bulletin/Igud Yotsei Sin (Association of Former Residents of China), English Section, Tel Aviv

The China Connection (a quarterly newsletter edited by Oscar Armstrong, published in Bethesda, Md.)

China Press

China Weekly Review

Israel's Messenger

Kokusai Himitsu-ryoku no kenkyū (Research on the International Secret Power)

North China Daily News

North China Herald

Novoe Vremia (New Times)

Oriental Affairs

Our Life (English supplement to *Unser Leben*)

Points East (Sino-Judaic Institute, Menlo Park, Calif.)

Shanghai Evening Post and Mercury

Shanghai Jewish Chronicle

Shanghai Pictorial

Shanghai Times
Shankhaiskaia Zaria
Yudaya Kenkyū (Jewish Research)

Other Sources

Abend, Hallet. *My Life in China, 1926–41.* New York: Harcourt, Brace, 1943.
———. *Treaty Ports.* Garden City, N.Y.: Doubleday, 1944.
Abraham, R. D. *Council of the Jewish Community of Shanghai: Report for July 1953–June 1954 and Statement of Account for January–December 31, 1953.* Shanghai: N.p., 1954.
Agel, Jerome, and Eugene Boe. *Deliverance in Shanghai.* New York: Dembner Books, 1983.
Ahlers, John. "Proposal to Send 100 Thousand German Jewish Refugees to Yunnan Province." *China Weekly Review,* July 22, 1939, pp. 226–27.
All about Shanghai: A Standard Guidebook. Hong Kong: Oxford University Press, 1983.
Almanac Shanghai 1946/47. Edited by Ossie Lewin. Shanghai: Shanghai Echo, 1947.
Amano, Keitarō. *Dai tōa shiryō sōran* [Directory of Materials on Greater East Asia]. Tokyo: Daigadō, 1994.
American National Red Cross. *Annual Report of the American Red Cross for 1923.* Washington, D.C.: American National Red Cross, 1924.
Anderson, Benedict. *Imagined Communities: Reflections on the Origins and Spread of Nationalism.* London: Verso, 1991.
Bakich, Olga, ed. *Rossiiane v Azii* [Russians in Asia]. Annual. Toronto: University of Toronto, 1994.
Balakshin, Petr P. *Final v Kitae: Vozniknovenie, Razvitie, i Ischeznovenie Beloi Emigratsii na Dal'nem Vostoke* [Finale in China: Formation, Development, and Disintegration of the White Russian Emigration in the Far East]. 2 vols. San Francisco: Kn-vo Sirius, 1958–59.
Ballard, J. G. *Empire of the Sun: A Novel.* New York: Simon & Schuster, 1984.
Barber, Noel. *The Fall of Shanghai.* New York: Coward, McCann, & Geoghegan, 1979.
Bauer, Yehuda. *A History of the Holocaust.* New York: Franklin Watts, 1982.
Baum, Vicki. *Shanghai '37.* 1939. Reprint. New York: Oxford University Press, 1986.
Ben-Eliezer, Judith. *Shanghai Lost, Jerusalem Regained.* [Israel]: Steimatzky, 1985.
Bergère, Marie-Claire. *The Golden Age of the Chinese Bourgeoisie, 1911–1937.* New York: Cambridge University Press, 1989.
———. "'The Other China': Shanghai from 1919–1949." In *Shanghai: Revolu-

tion and Development in an Asian Metropolis, ed. Christopher Howe, pp. 1–34. Cambridge: Cambridge University Press, 1981.

——. *Sun Yat-sen*. Stanford: Stanford University Press, 1999.

Best, Gary Dean. "Financing a Foreign War: Jacob H. Schiff and Japan, 1904–05." *American Jewish Historical Quarterly*, no. 4 (June 1972): 313–24.

Betta, Chiara. "The Rise of Silas Aaron Hardoon (1851–1931) as Shanghai's Major Individual Landowner." *Sino-Judaica: Occasional Papers of the Sino-Judaic Institute* 2 (1995): 1–40.

——. "S. A. Hardoon (1851–1931): Marginality and Adaptation in Shanghai." Ph.D. diss., London School of Economics and Political Science, University of London, 1997.

Bi Chunfu and Ma Zhendu. "A Plan to Settle Jewish Refugees in China." *Sino-Judaica: Occasional Papers of the Sino-Judaic Institute* 2 (1995): 66–84.

Bickers, Robert A. *Britain in China: Community, Culture and Colonialism, 1900–1949*. Manchester: University of Manchester Press, 1999.

——. "Shanghailanders: The Formation and Identity of the British Settler Community in Shanghai, 1843–1937." *Past & Present*, no. 159 (May 1998): 161–211.

Bickers, Robert A., and Christian Henriot, eds. *New Frontiers: Imperialism's New Communities in East Asia, 1842–1952*. Manchester: Manchester University Press, 2000.

Bickers, Robert A., and Jeffrey N. Wasserstrom. "Shanghai's 'Dogs and Chinese Not Admitted' Sign: Legend, History and Contemporary Symbol." *China Quarterly*, no. 142 (June 1995): 265–87.

Boyle, John Hunter. *China and Japan at War, 1937–1945: The Politics of Collaboration*. Stanford: Stanford University Press, 1972.

Bresler, Boris. "Harbin's Jewish Community, 1898–1958: Politics, Prosperity, Adversity." In *The Jews of China: Historical and Comparative Perspectives*, ed. Jonathan Goldstein, 1: 200–215. Armonk, N.Y.: M. E. Sharpe, 1999.

Brooks, Barbara J. "Japanese Colonial Citizenship in Treaty Port China: The Location of Koreans and Taiwanese in the Imperial Order." In *New Frontiers: Imperialism's New Communities in East Asia, 1842–1952*, ed. Robert A. Bickers and Christian Henriot, pp. 109–45. Manchester: Manchester University Press, 2000.

Brown, Mendel. "The Jews of Modern China." *Jewish Monthly* 3, no. 3 (June 1949): 158–63.

Cabanowski, Marek. *Tajemnice Mandzurii: Polacy w Harbinie* [Mysterious Manchurians: The Poles in Harbin]. Warsaw: Muzeum Niepodleglo'sci, 1993.

Cambon, Marie. "The Dream Palaces of Shanghai: American Films in China's Largest Metropolis." M.A. thesis, Simon Fraser University, 1993.

Candlin, Enid Saunders. *The Breach in the Wall: A Memoir of the Old China.* New York: Macmillan, 1973.

Carey, Arch. *The War Years at Shanghai, 1941–45–48.* New York: Vantage Press, 1967.

Chang, Kia-Ngau. *The Inflationary Spiral: The Experience in China, 1939–1950.* Cambridge, Mass: MIT Press, 1958.

Chen, Joseph T. *The May Fourth Movement in Shanghai: The Making of a Social Movement in Modern China.* Leiden: E. J. Brill, 1971.

The Chinese Yearbook, 1940–1941. Shanghai: N.p.

Chou, Shun-hsin. *The Chinese Inflation, 1937–1949.* New York: Columbia University Press, 1963.

Clausen, Søren, and Stig Thøgersen. *The Making of a Chinese City: History and Historiography in Harbin.* Armonk, N.Y.: M. E. Sharpe, 1995.

Clifford, Nicholas R. *Spoilt Children of Empire: Westerners in Shanghai and the Chinese Revolution of the 1920s.* Middlebury, Vt.: Middlebury College Press, 1991.

Coble, Parks M. *Facing Japan: Chinese Politics and Japanese Imperialism, 1931–1937.* Cambridge, Mass.: Council on East Asian Studies, Harvard University, 1991.

———. *Shanghai Capitalists and the Nationalist Government, 1927–1937.* Cambridge, Mass.: Council on East Asian Studies, Harvard University, 1986.

Cohen, Paul A. *History in Three Keys: The Boxers as Event, Experience, and Myth.* New York: Columbia University Press, 1997.

Cohen, Robin. *Global Diasporas: An Introduction.* Seattle: University of Washington Press, 1997.

Cohn, Norman Rufus Colin. *Warrant for Genocide: The Myth of the Jewish World Conspiracy and the Protocols of the Elders of Zion.* Chico, Calif.: Scholars Press, 1981.

"Constitution of the International Refugee Organization." *Treaty Series*, no. 25. London: His Majesty's Stationery Office, 1950.

Cosman, Tania Manooiloff. *My Heritage with Morning Glories: A White Russian Growing up in China.* Washington, D.C.: Creative Communication Services, 1995.

Dai, Poeliu. *Summary Report on UNRRA Activities in China.* New York: International Secretariat, Institute of Pacific Relations, 1947.

Dallin, Alexander. *German Rule in Russia, 1941–1945: A Study in Occupation Policies.* New York: St. Martin's Press, 1957.

Darwent, E. C. *Shanghai: A Handbook for Travellers and Residents.* Shanghai: Kelly & Walsh, 1920.

Davidson-Houston, J. V. *Yellow Creek: The Story of Shanghai.* London: Putnam, 1962.

Davies, Norman, and Antony Polonsky. *Jews in Eastern Poland and the USSR, 1939–1946.* New York: St. Martin's Press, 1991.

Deacon, Richard. *Kempei Tai: The Japanese Secret Service Then and Now.* New York: Beaufort Books, 1983.

Deng, Ming, ed. *Survey of Shanghai, 1840s–1940s: Shanghai bainian lueying.* Shanghai: Shanghai People's Fine Arts Publishing House, 1993.

Dicker, Herman. *Wanderers and Settlers in the Far East: A Century of Jewish Life in China and Japan.* New York: Twayne, 1962.

Dirksen, Herbert von. *Moscow, Tokyo, London: Twenty Years of German Foreign Policy.* Norman: University of Oklahoma Press, 1952.

Disaster and Salvation: The History of "Vaad Hatzala" in America. Introduction by Rabbi Eliezer Silver. New York: Vaad Hatzala Book Committee, 1957.

Dorfman, Ben. "White Russians in the Far East." *Asia,* Mar. 1935, pp. 166–72.

Drucker, Olga Levy. *Kindertransport.* New York: Holt, 1992.

Duara, Prasenjit. "Why Is History Antitheoretical?" *Modern China* 24, no. 2 (Apr. 1998): 105–20.

Duus, Peter, Ramon H. Myers, and Mark R. Peattie, eds. *The Japanese Informal Empire in China, 1895–1937.* Princeton: Princeton University Press, 1989.

Eastman, Lloyd. "Fascism in Kuomintang China: The Blue Shirts." *China Quarterly,* no. 49 (Jan.–Mar. 1972): 1–31.

Elvin, Mark. "The Administration of Shanghai." In *The Chinese City Between Two Worlds,* ed. Mark Elvin and G. William Skinner, pp. 239–62. Stanford: Stanford University Press, 1974.

Emigranten Adressbuch. Facsimile edition. Hong Kong: Old China Hand Press, 1995.

Encyclopaedia Judaica. 16 vols. New York: Macmillan, 1972.

Fairbank, John King. "The Creation of the Treaty System." In *The Cambridge History of China,* vol. 10, ed. Denis Twitchett and John K. Fairbank, pp. 213–63. New York: Cambridge University Press, 1978.

———. *Trade and Diplomacy on the China Coast: The Opening of the Treaty Ports, 1842–1854.* Stanford: Stanford University Press, 1969.

Fedorova, Nina. *The Family.* Boston: Atlantic Monthly Press, 1940.

Feetham, Richard. *Report of the Honorable Richard Feetham, C.M.G., Judge of the Supreme Court of the Union of South Africa to the Shanghai Municipal Council.* 3 vols. Shanghai: North China Daily News and Herald, 1931.

Fifty Facts about UNRRA. New York: United Nations Information Office, 1946.

Finch, Percy. *Shanghai and Beyond.* New York: Scribners, 1953.

Finnane, Antonia. *Far From Where? Jewish Journeys from Shanghai to Australia.* Melbourne: Melbourne University Press, 1999.

Fiszman, Joseph R. "The Quest for Status: Polish-Jewish Refugees in Shanghai, 1941–1949." Paper presented at the symposium, "Jewish Diasporas in China: Comparative and Historical Perspectives," Harvard University, Aug. 1992.

Fletcher, Joseph. "The Heyday of the Ch'ing Order in Mongolia, Sinkiang and Tibet." In *The Cambridge History of China*, vol. 10, ed. Denis Twitchett and John K. Fairbank, pp. 351–408. New York: Cambridge University Press, 1978.

Fogel, Joshua A. "Integrating into Chinese Society: A Comparison of the Japanese Communities of Shanghai and Harbin." In *Japan's Competing Modernities: Issues in Culture and Democracy, 1900–1930*, ed. Sharon A. Minichiello, pp. 45–69. Honolulu: University of Hawaii Press, 1998.

Fonteyn, Margot [Margaret Hookham]. *Margot Fonteyn: Autobiography*. New York: Knopf, 1976.

Frank, Benis M. "The Jewish Company of the Shanghai Volunteer Corps Compared with Other Jewish Diaspora Fighting Units." Paper prepared for presentation at the conference "Jewish Diasporas in China: Comparative and Historical Perspectives," Harvard University, Aug. 1992.

———. "The Shanghai Volunteer Corps: A Socio-Military History." Unpublished manuscript.

Fu, Poshek. *Passivity, Resistance, and Collaboration: Intellectual Choices in Occupied Shanghai, 1937–1945*. Stanford: Stanford University Press, 1993.

Fulcher, Helen McCracken. "The McCrackens of Shanghai: A Family Portrait." Unpublished manuscript, May 1974.

———. *Mission to Shanghai: The Life and Medical Service of Dr. Josiah C. McCracken*. New London, N.H.: Tiffin Press, 1995.

Gao Wangzhi. "The Contributions of Jewish Communities in Shanghai Viewed in Their Sino-Jewish Perspective." *Points East* 2, no. 1 (Feb. 1987): 1, 4–8.

Ginsbourg, Anna. *Jewish Refugees in Shanghai*. Shanghai: China Weekly Review, 1940.

Glenny, Michael, and Norman Stone. *The Other Russia*. New York: Viking Penguin, 1991.

Glines, Carroll V. *The Doolittle Raid: America's Daring First Strike Against Japan*. New York: Orion Books, 1988.

Goldstein, Jonathan, ed. *The Jews of China: Historical and Comparative Perspectives*. 2 vols. Armonk, N.Y.: M. E. Sharpe, 1999–2000.

Goodman, Bryna. *Native Place, City, and Nation: Regional Networks and Identities in Shanghai, 1853–1937*. Berkeley and Los Angeles: University of California Press, 1995.

Goodman, David, and Masanori Miyazawa. *Jews in the Japanese Mind: The History and Uses of a Cultural Stereotype*. New York: Free Press, 1995.

Goto-Shibata, Harumi. *Japan and Britain in Shanghai, 1925–31*. New York: St. Martin's Press, 1995.

Graves, William S. *America's Siberian Adventure, 1918–1920.* New York: P. Smith, 1941.

Grebenschikoff, Betty. *Once My Name Was Sara.* Cape May, N.J.: Original Seven Publishing Co., 1992.

Grover, David H., and Gretchen G. Grover. *Captives of Shanghai: The Story of the President Harrison.* Napa, Calif.: Western Maritime Press, 1989.

Hauser, Ernst O. *Shanghai: City for Sale.* New York: Harcourt, Brace, 1940.

Henriot, Christian. *Belles de Shanghai: Prostitution et sexualité en Chine aux XIXe–XXe siècles.* Paris: CNRS Éditions, 1997.

———. *Shanghai, 1927–1937: Municipal Power, Locality, and Modernization.* Translated by Noël Castelino. Berkeley and Los Angeles: University of California Press, 1993. Originally published as *Shanghai, 1927–1937: Élites locales et modernisation dans la Chine nationaliste* (Paris: Éditions de l'École des hautes études en sciences sociales, 1991).

Heppner, Ernest G. *Shanghai Refuge: A Memoir of the World War II Jewish Ghetto.* Lincoln: University of Nebraska Press, 1993.

Hershatter, Gail. *Dangerous Pleasures: Prostitution and Modernity in Twentieth-Century Shanghai.* Berkeley and Los Angeles: University of California Press, 1997.

———. "The Hierarchy of Shanghai Prostitution, 1870–1949." *Modern China* 15, no. 4 (October 1989): 463–98.

Ho, Allan, and Dmitry Feofanov, eds. *Biographical Dictionary of Russian/Soviet Composers.* New York: Greenwood Press, 1989.

Hōkōshi [pseudonym of Colonel Yasue Norihiro], trans. *Sekai kakumei no rimen* [What is Behind the World Revolution?]. N.p.: N.p., 1936.

Honig, Emily. *Creating Chinese Ethnicity: Subei People in Shanghai, 1850–1980.* New Haven: Yale University Press, 1992.

———. *Sisters and Strangers: Women in the Shanghai Cotton Mills, 1919–1949.* Stanford: Stanford University Press, 1986.

Horowitz, Rose Jacob. *Rose Jacob Horowitz: An Oral History, Shanghai, 1927–1949.* Michael Paul Onorato, interviewer and editor. Fullerton, Calif.: Old China Hand Project, California State University, 1991.

Hounold, Vorda. "Memories of Shanghai." Unpublished manuscript, Mar. 1989.

Hsia, Ching-lin. *The Status of Shanghai: A Historical Review of the International Settlement.* Shanghai: Kelly & Walsh, 1929.

Hsiao Kung-chuan. *Rural China: Imperial Control in the Nineteenth Century.* Seattle: University of Washington Press, 1960.

Huebner, Jon W. "Old Shanghai Revisited." *American Asian Review* 5, no. 3 (Fall 1987): 84–104.

Hunter, Janet E., comp. *Concise Dictionary of Modern Japanese History.* Berkeley and Los Angeles: University of California Press, 1984.

Il'ina, Natalia Iosifovna. *Dorogi*. Moscow: Sovetskii pisatel', 1983.

Inuzuka, Kiyoko. *Yudaya mondai to Nihon no kōsaku* [Japanese Activities and the Jewish Question]. Tokyo: Nihon Kōgyō Shinbunsha, 1982.

Inuzuka, Koreshige [see also Utsunomiya, Marehiro, below]. *Shina ni okeru Eikoku no dōkō to Yudaya no seiryoku* [British Trends and the Influence of Jews]. Tokyo: Kokusai Seikei Gakkai, 1938.

Iriye, Akira. *Power and Culture: The Japanese-American War, 1941–1945*. Cambridge, Mass.: Harvard University Press, 1981.

"The Ivanoff Murder and Japanese Intrigue in the Local Russian Community." *China Weekly Review*, Sept. 27, 1941, pp. 97–99.

Jackson, Stanley. *The Sassoons*. New York: Dutton, 1968. Reprinted as *The Sassoons: Portrait of a Dynasty* (London: Heinemann, 1989).

Japan. Ministry of the Army. Military Affairs Section. "Jikyoku ni tomonau Yudaya-jin no toriatsukai" [Treatment of Jews in View of the Current Situation].1942. Washington, D.C.: Library of Congress, microfilm collection, File T1111 R118-F31243-45, 31254-56.

Japan. Ministry of Foreign Affairs. Archives. Japanese consular report to the Japanese consulate general, July 9, 1943. Washington, D.C.: Library of Congress, microfilm collection, File S-9460-3-2652.

———. "Jikyoku ni tomonau Yudaya-jin no taisaku: Renraku Kaigi kettei-an" [Measures to Be Taken Vis-à-vis Jews in Relation to the Present Situation: Draft Decision of the Liaison Conference]. 1942. Washington, D.C.: Library of Congress, microfilm collection, File S-9460-3-2557-60.

———. "Shanhai ni okeru Yoroppa hinan Yudaya-jin no sankanen" [Three Years of the European Refugee Jews in Shanghai]. Written in German by Heitsu Genteron (romanized name) in December 1942 and translated into Japanese (no German version included) and transmitted as "confidential." Library of Congress microfilm collection, File S-9460-3-2776-2857.

———. "Yudaya hinanmin shūyō chiku" [The Area for Assembling the Jewish Refugees]. May 1940. Library of Congress microfilm collection, File S-9460-3-2146-51.

———. "Yudaya-jin ijū ni kansuru ken" [Report on the Transfer of Jews]. Declassified top secret memo, Feb. 9, 1943. Library of Congress microfilm collection, File S-9460-3-2563.

———. "Yudaya-jin taisaku ni kansuru ken" [Concerning Measures vis-à-vis Jews]. Declassified top secret memo no. 69, Nov. 18, 1942. Library of Congress microfilm collection, File S-9460-3-2556.

"Jewish Refugees in Shanghai: A Heartbreaking Problem." *Oriental Affairs*, June 1940, pp. 290–94.

Johnson, Chalmers. *An Instance of Treason: Ozaki Hotsumi and the Sorge Spy Ring*. Stanford: Stanford University Press, 1990.

Johnson, Linda Cooke. "Shanghai: Emerging Jiangnan Port, 1683–1840." In *Cities of Jiangnan in Late Imperial China*, ed. Linda Cooke Johnson, pp. 151–81. Albany: State University of New York, 1993.

———. *Shanghai: From Market Town to Treaty Port, 1074–1858.* Stanford: Stanford University Press, 1995.

Johnston, Tess, and Deke Erh. *Frenchtown, Shanghai: Western Architecture in Shanghai's Old French Concession.* Hong Kong: Old China Hand Press, 2000.

———. *A Last Look: Western Architecture in Old Shanghai.* Hong Kong: Old China Hand Press, 1993.

Johnstone, William C., Jr. *The Shanghai Problem.* Stanford: Stanford University Press, 1937.

Jones, Francis Clifford. *Shanghai and Tientsin, with Special Reference to Foreign Interests.* New York: American Council, Institute of Pacific Relations, 1940.

Karns, Maurine, and Pat Patterson. *Shanghai: High Lights, Low Lights, Tael Lights.* Shanghai: Tridon Press, 1936.

Kauffmann, Fritz. "Die Juden in Shanghai im 2. Weltkrieg: Erinnerungen eines Vorstandsmitglieds der Jüdischen Gemeinde" [The Jews in China in the Second World War: Memoirs of a Member of the Executive Committee of the Jewish Community]. *Bulletin des Leo Baeck Instituts* 73 (1986): 13–23.

Kirby, William C. *Germany and Republican China.* Stanford: Stanford University Press, 1984.

———. "The Internationalization of China: Foreign Relations at Home and Abroad in the Republican Era." *China Quarterly*, no. 150 (June 1997): 433–58.

Koffsky, Peter. *The Consul General's Shanghai Postal Agency.* Washington, D.C.: Smithsonian Institution Press, 1972.

Kokusai Seikei Gakkai [Society of International Politics and Economics]. *Kokusai himitsu-ryoku no kenkyū* [Research on the International Secret Power]. 1936–41.

———. *Shina o meguru seiji keizai narabini senden ni katsuyaku-suru Shanhai Yudaya meikan* [Directory of Shanghai Jews Involved in Politics, Economics, and Propaganda Involving China]. 1937.

———. *Yudaya Kenkyū* [Jewish Research]. 1941–43.

Komor, Paul. "European Refugees." In *Proceedings of the Joint Committee of Shanghai Women's Organizations* (Eleventh Annual Conference of Women's Clubs in Shanghai, May 7 and 18, 1939), 42–48.

Kotenev, A. M. *Shanghai: Its Mixed Court and Council.* Shanghai: North China Daily News & Herald, 1925.

———. *Shanghai: Its Municipality and the Chinese.* Shanghai: North China Daily News & Herald, 1927.

Kotkin, Stephen, and David Wolff, eds. *Rediscovering Russia in Asia: Siberia and the Russian Far East*. Armonk, N.Y.: M. E. Sharpe, 1995.

Kounin, I. I. *Eighty-Five Years of the Shanghai Volunteer Corps*. Shanghai: Cosmopolitan Press, 1938.

Kranzler, David. *Japanese, Nazis and Jews: The Jewish Refugee Community of Shanghai, 1938–1945*. Hoboken, N.J.: KTAV, 1988.

Krasno, Rena. *Strangers Always: A Jewish Family in Wartime Shanghai*. Berkeley, Calif.: Pacific View Press, 1992.

———. "Russian Jews in Shanghai: Historic Perspective of an Eyewitness." *Points East* 9, no. 2 (Aug. 1994).

Kreissler, Françoise. *L'action culturelle allemande in Chine, de la fin du XIXe siècle à la Seconde Guerre Mondiale*. Paris: Éditions de la Maison des sciences de l'homme, 1989.

———. "In Search of Identity: The German Community in Shanghai, 1933–1945." Paper prepared for the Conference on Foreign Communities in East Asia, Lyon, France, 1997.

Kremer, Roberta, ed. *Diplomat Rescuers and the Story of Feng Shan Ho*. Vancouver: Vancouver Holocaust Education Centre, 1999.

Lee, Elizabeth. *A Letter to My Aunt*. New York: Carlton Press, 1981.

Lee, Leo Ou-fan. *Shanghai Modern: The Flowering of a New Urban Culture in China, 1930-1945*. Cambridge, Mass: Harvard University Press, 1999.

Leitner, Yecheskel. *Operation — Torah Rescue: The Escape of the Mirrer Yeshiva from War-Torn Poland to Shanghai, China*. New York: Feldheim Publishers, 1987.

Leventhal, Denis A. "From Your Historical Society: A Jewish Tour Guide to Shanghai." N.p., n.d.

Levin, Nora. *The Holocaust: The Destruction of European Jewry, 1933–1945*. New York: Crowell, 1968.

Levine, Hillel. *In Search of Sugihara: The Elusive Japanese Diplomat Who Risked His Life to Rescue 10,000 Jews from the Holocaust*. New York: Free Press, 1996.

Lidin, N. "Russkaya emigratsiya v Shankhaie" [The Russian Émigré Group in Shanghai]. *Russkiye Zapiski* [Russian Annals (Paris)] 2 (1937): 308–19.

Lincoln, Anna. *Escape to China*. Woodhaven, N.Y.: Maryland Books, 1982.

Lipschitz, Chaim U. *The Shanghai Connection*. New York: Maznaim Publishing, 1988.

Löwenthal, Rudolf. "The Jewish Press in China." *Nankai Social and Economic Quarterly* (Tianjin) 10, no. 1 (Apr. 1937): 104-13.

Lu, Hanchao. *Beyond the Neon Lights: Everyday Shanghai in the Early Twentieth Century*. Berkeley and Los Angeles: University of California Press, 1999.

Lukas, Richard C. *The Forgotten Holocaust: The Poles under German Occupation, 1939–1944*. Lexington: University of Kentucky Press, 1986.

Luke, Iguman. "The Glorification of Saint John of Shanghai and San Francisco." *Orthodox Life Magazine*, July–Aug. 1994.

McGee, Barbara B., and Ruth Dorval Jones. *Barney: Journals of Harry Virden Bernard*. N.p.: B. B. McGee, 1982.

Maier, Kurt-Salomon. *Shanghai Sabbath: An Historical Tragicomedy in Four Acts*. Arlington, Va.: Russo Publishing, 1988.

Mancall, Mark. *China at the Center: 300 Years of Foreign Policy*. New York: Free Press, 1984.

Marrus, Michael R. *The Unwanted: European Refugees in the Twentieth Century*. New York: Oxford University Press, 1985.

Martin, Brian G. *The Shanghai Green Gang: Politics and Organized Crime, 1919–1937*. Berkeley and Los Angeles: University of California Press, 1996.

Maynard, Isabelle. *China Dreams: Growing Up Jewish in Tientsin*. Iowa City: University of Iowa Press, 1996.

Maruyama, Naoki. "The Shanghai Zionist Association and the International Politics of East Asia until 1936." In *The Jews of China: Historical and Comparative Perspectives*, ed. Jonathan Goldstein, 1: 251–66. Armonk, N.Y.: M. E. Sharpe, 1999.

Meskill, Johanna Menzel. *Hitler and Japan: The Hollow Alliance*. New York: Atherton Press, 1966.

Meyer, Maisie. "The Sephardi Jewish Community of Shanghai, 1845–1939, and the Question of Identity." Ph.D. diss., London School of Economics and Political Science, University of London, 1994.

———. "Three Prominent Sephardi Jews." *Sino-Judaica: Occasional Papers of the Sino-Judaic Institute* 1 (1995): 85–110.

Millard, Thomas. *China: Where It Is Today and Why*. Shanghai: Kelly & Walsh, 1928.

Miller, G. E. *Shanghai: Paradise of Adventures*. New York: Orsay Publishing, 1937.

Murphy, Rhoads. *Shanghai: Key to Modern China*. Cambridge, Mass: Harvard University Press, 1953.

Nakashige Kiichi. *Yudaya-jin mondai ni kansuru chōsa hōkokusho* [Report Concerning the Jewish Question]. Tokyo: Kōa-in Kachū Renraku-bu, June 1941.

New, Christopher. *Shanghai: A Novel*. New York: Summit Books, 1985.

Nish, Ian Hill. *The Origins of the Russo-Japanese War*. London: Longman, 1985.

———. "An Overview of Relations Between China and Japan, 1895–1945." *China Quarterly*, no. 124 (Dec. 1990): 601–23.

"Origins and Future of the Local Russian Community." *Shanghai Sunday Times*, five-part ser., 1936.

Pan Guang. *Youtairen zai Shanghai: The Jews in Shanghai*. Shanghai: Shanghai Pictorial Publishing, 1995.

——. "Qianjin di'er shijia dazhen qijian Shanghai de Youtai nanmin" [Survey of Shanghai Jewish Refugees During World War II]. *Shanghai Shekeyuan xueshu jikan*, no. 2 (1991): 112–20.

——. "Zionism and Zionist-Revisionism in Shanghai, 1937–1949." In *The Jews of China: Historical and Comparative Perspectives*, ed. Jonathan Goldstein, 1: 267–76. Armonk, N.Y.: M. E. Sharpe, 1999.

——. "Shanghai's Case in the Annals of Jewish Diaspora: An Appreciation." *Points East* 9, no. 2 (Aug. 1994): 7.

Pan Ling. *In Search of Old Shanghai*. Hong Kong: Joint Publishing Company, 1982.

——. *Old Shanghai: Gangsters in Paradise*. Hong Kong: Heinemann Asia, 1984.

Pan, Lynn. *Shanghai: A Century of Change in Photographs, 1843–1949: The End of an Era*. New York: New Amsterdam Books, 1990.

Patent, Gregory. *Shanghai Passage*. New York: Clarion Books, 1990.

Peattie, Mark R. "Japanese Treaty Port Settlements in China, 1895–1937." In *The Japanese Informal Empire in China*, ed. Peter Duus, Ramon H. Myers, and Mark R. Peattie, pp. 166–209. Princeton: Princeton University Press, 1989.

Perry, Elizabeth J. *Shanghai on Strike: The Politics of Chinese Labor*. Stanford: Stanford University Press, 1993.

Perekrestov, Peter, trans. and comp. *Man of God: Saint John of Shanghai and San Francisco*. Redding, Calif.: Nikodemos Orthodox Publication Society, 1994.

Personal Justice Denied: Report of the Commission on Wartime Relocation and Internment of Civilians. Washington, D.C.: Commission on Wartime Relocation and Internment of Civilians, 1982.

Petrov, Viktor P. *Shankhai na Vampu: Ocherki i rasskazy* [Shanghai on the Whangpoo]. Washington, D.C.: Izd. Russko-amerikanskyogo istoricheskogo ob-va, 1985.

——. "The Town on the Sungari." In *The Other Russia*, ed. Michael Glenny and Norman Stones, pp. 206–21. New York: Viking, 1991.

Polansky, Patricia. "Russkaia Pechat' v Kitae: City of Shanghai." Paper presented at the Fourth World Congress on Soviet and East European Studies, Harrogate, England, July 1990.

Pott, F. L. Hawks. *A Short History of Shanghai, Being an Account of the Growth and Development of the International Settlement*. Shanghai: Kelly & Walsh, 1928. Reprint. New York, AMS Press, 1973.

Powell, John B. *My Twenty-Five Years in China*. New York: Macmillan, 1945.

Presseisen, Ernst L. *Germany and Japan: A Study in Totalitarian Diplomacy, 1933–1941*. The Hague: Martinus Nijhoff, 1958.

Raeff, Marc. *Russia Abroad: A Cultural History of the Russian Emigration, 1919–1939*. New York: Oxford University Press, 1990.

Ray, J. Franklin, Jr. *UNRRA in China*. Secretariat Paper No. 6. New York: Institute of Pacific Relations, 1947.

Rigby, Richard W. *The May 30 Movement: Events and Themes*. Canberra: Australian National University Press, 1980.

Ristaino, Marcia R. *China's Art of Revolution: The Mobilization of Discontent, 1927 and 1928*. Durham, N.C.: Duke University Press, 1987.

———. "New Information on Shanghai Jewish Refugees: The Evidence of the Shanghai Municipal Police Files in the National Archives, Washington, D.C." In *The Jews in China: Historical and Comparative Perspectives*, ed. Jonathan Goldstein, 2: 135–51. Armonk, N.Y.: M. E. Sharpe, 2000.

———. "The Russian Diaspora Community in Shanghai." In *New Frontiers: Imperialism's New Communities in East Asia, 1842–1952*, ed. Robert Bickers and Christian Henriot, pp. 192–210. Manchester: Manchester University Press, 2000.

———. "Russian Women as Icons in Republican Era Shanghai." Paper delivered at the East Asia–Saint Petersburg–Europe Conference: Inter-civilization Contact and Perspectives on Economic Cooperation, Saint Petersburg State University, Russia, October 2–8, 2000.

———. "Russische Flüchtlinge im 'gelben Babylon.'" In *Der grosse Exodus: Die russische Emigration und ihre Zentren, 1917 bis 1941*, ed. Karl Schlögel, 329–45. Munich: C. H. Beck, 1994.

———. "White Russian and Jewish Refugees in Shanghai, 1920–1944, as Recorded in the Shanghai Municipal Police Archives, National Archives, Washington, D.C." *Republican China* 16, no. 1 (1990): 51–72.

Ross, James R. *Escapte to Shanghai: A Jewish Community in China*. New York: Free Press, 1994.

Roth, Cecil. *A History of the Jews*. New York: Schocken Books, 1961.

Robinson, Nehemiah. *Convention Relating to the Status of Refugees: Its History, Contents, and Interpretation*. New York: Institute of Jewish Affairs, 1952.

Roland, Joan G. "Baghdadi Jews in India and China in the Nineteenth Century: A Comparison of Economic Roles." In *The Jews of China: Historical and Comparative Perspectives*, ed. Jonathan Goldstein, 1: 141–56. Armonk, N.Y.: M. E. Sharpe, 1999.

Rose, Father Seraphim, and Abbot Herman. *Saint John the Wonderworker: A Preliminary Account of the Life and Miracles of Archbishop John Maximovich*. Platina, Calif.: St. Herman of Alaska Brotherhood, n.d.

Rowe, William T. *Hankow: Conflict and Community in a Chinese City, 1796–1895*. Stanford: Stanford University Press, 1989.

Rubin, Evelyn Pike. *Ghetto Shanghai*. New York: Shengold Publishers, 1993.

The Russian Orthodox Church. Moscow: Progress Publishers, 1982.

Rutland, Suzanne D. *Edge of the Diaspora: Two Centuries of Jewish Settlement in Australia*. Sydney: William Collins, 1988.

Sakamoto, Pamela Rotner. "The Policy of the Japanese Ministry of Foreign Affairs Towards Jewish Refugees." Ph.D. diss., Fletcher School of Law and Diplomacy, Tufts University, 1997.

Samoylov, Nikolay. "Role of the Russian Ecclesiastical Mission in Beijing in Sino-Russian Ecclesiastical and Cultural Contacts." Paper delivered at the East Asia–Saint Petersburg–Europe Conference: Intercivilization Contact and Perspectives on Economic Cooperation, Saint Petersburg State University, Russia, October 2–8, 2000.

Schickman-Bowman, Zvia. "The Contruction of the Chinese Eastern Railway and the Origins of the Harbin Jewish Community, 1898–1931." In *The Jews of China: Historical and Comparative Perspectives*, ed. Jonathan Goldstein, 1: 198–199. Armonk, N.Y.: M. E. Sharpe, 1999.

Schrecker, John E. *Imperialism and Chinese Nationalism: Germany in Shantung*. Cambridge, Mass.: Harvard University Press, 1971.

Schurtman, William, "Report on the Jewish Refugee Community of Shanghai." Jan. 1954. Typescript provided to the author by Pan Guang, Shanghai, 1992.

Schwarzbart, Dr. Isaac I. "The Dwindling Jewish Community in China: A Comparative Report on the Last Chapter of the Life of the Jewish Community in China (1954/55–1955/56)." WJC, Oct. 30, 1956.

——. "The Last Jews in China Prepare for Emigration." WJC report, Oct. 19, 1955.

——. "400 Jews Left Among 600,000,000 Chinese: How They Struggle to Keep Jewishness Alive." WJC Organization Department Report No. 4, Sept. 25, 1957.

Seagrave, Sterling. *The Soong Dynasty*. New York: Harper & Row, 1985.

Sergeant, Harriet. *Shanghai: Collision Point of Cultures, 1918–1939*. New York: Crown Publishers, 1990.

Shatzkes, Pamela. "Kobe: A Japanese Haven for Jewish Refugees, 1940–1941." *Points East* 3, no. 1 (Feb. 1993): 10–16.

Shillony, Ben-Ami. *The Jew and the Japanese: The Successful Outsiders*. Rutland, Vt.: Charles E. Tuttle, 1991.

——. *Politics and Culture in Wartime Japan*. Oxford: Clarendon Press, 1981.

Shirer, William L. *The Rise and Fall of the Third Reich: A History of Nazi Germany*. New York: Simon & Schuster, 1960.

Simpson, John Hope. *Refugees: Preliminary Report of a Problem*. London: Royal Institute of International Affairs, 1938.

——. *The Refugee Problem: Report of a Survey*. London: Oxford University Press, 1939.

Smith, Canfield. *Vladivostok under Red and White Rule: Revolution and Counter-revolution in the Russian Far East.* Seattle: University of Washington Press, 1975.

Snyder, Louis L. *Encyclopedia of the Third Reich.* New York: McGraw-Hill, 1976.

Sopher, Arthur, and Theodore Sopher. "China and Japan's Need: A Role for the Jew." *Israel's Messenger,* Nov. 1, 1935, pp. 7, 14.

Steele, A. T. *Shanghai and Manchuria, 1932: Recollections of a War Correspondent.* Tempe: Center for Asian Studies, Arizona State University, 1977.

Stephan, John J. *The Russian Far East: A History.* Stanford: Stanford University Press, 1994.

——. *The Russian Fascists: Tragedy and Farce in Exile, 1925–1945.* New York: Harper & Row, 1978.

The Story of the "Jacquinot Zone" Shanghai, China. Shanghai: Nantao Supervisory Committee, 1938.

Stranahan, Patricia. *Underground: The Shanghai Communist Party and the Politics of Survival, 1927–1937.* Lanham, Md.: Rowman & Littlefield, 1998.

Strand, David G. *Rickshaw Beijing: City People and Politics in the 1920s.* Berkeley and Los Angeles: University of California Press, 1989.

Sugihara, Yukiko. *Visas for Life.* Translated by Hiroki Sugihara with Anne Hoshiko Akabori. Edited by Lani Silver and Eric Saul. Introduction by Sir Edmund L. de Rothschild. San Francisco: Edu-Comm. Plus, 1995. Published in Japanese as *Rokusennin no inochi no biza* (Tokyo: Taisho Shuppan, 1993).

Sugiyama, Gen. *Sugiyama memo.* 1967. 2 vols. Tokyo: Hara Shobo, 1989.

Tata, Sam, photographer. *Shanghai 1949: The End of an Era.* Introduction by Ian McLachlan. New York: New Amsterdam Books, 1990.

Tobias, Sigmund. *Strange Haven: A Jewish Childhood in Wartime Shanghai.* Urbana: University of Illinois Press, 1999.

Tokayer, Marvin. *The Fugu Plan: The Untold Story of the Japanese and the Jews During World War II.* New York: Paddington Press, 1979.

Truman, Harry S. "Harry S. Truman: Containing the Public Messages, Speeches, and Statements of the President." In *Public Papers of the Presidents of the United States, April 12 to December 31, 1945.* Washington, D.C.: GPO, 1961.

——. "Statement and Directive by the President on Immigration to the United States of Certain Displaced Persons and Refugees in Europe." December 22, 1945, pp. 572–76.

——. "Directive by the President on Immigration to the United States of Certain Displaced Persons and Refugees in Europe." December 22, 1945, pp. 576–78.

——. "Statement by the President upon Signing the Displaced Persons Act,

June 11, 1948." In *Public Papers of the Presidents of the United States, January 1 to December 31, 1948*, pp. 382–84. Washington, D.C.: GPO, 1964.

U.S. Department of State. *Foreign Relations of the United States: Diplomatic Papers, 1940*, vol. 4: *The Far East*. Washington, D.C.: GPO, 1955.

U.S. Public Law 774. June 25, 1948. 80th Cong., 2d sess., June 25, 1948. In *U.S. Statutes at Large*, vol. 62, pt. 1: *Public Laws. Displaced Persons Act of 1948*. Washington, D.C.: GPO, 1949.

U.S. Public Law 555. 81st Cong., 2d sess., June 16, 1950. *Displaced Persons Act of 1948 — Amendment.*

U.S. Public Law 203. 83d Cong., 1st sess., Aug. 7, 1953. *Refugee Relief Act of 1953.*

Utsunomiya Marehiro, or Kiyō [pseudonym of Inuzuka Koreshige]. "Kokusai Yudaya zaibatsu no Shina keizai seiha masani kansei sentosu" [Total Control of the Chinese Economy Is About to Be Completed by the International Jewish Zaibatsu]. *Kokusai Himitsu-ryoku no kenkyū* 3 (1937): 103–29.

Uyehara, Cecil H. *Checklist of Archives in the Japanese Ministry of Foreign Affairs, Tokyo, Japan, 1868–1945*. Washington, D.C.: Library of Congress, 1954.

Wakeman, Frederic, Jr. *Policing Shanghai, 1927–1937*. Berkeley and Los Angeles: University of California Press, 1995.

———. *The Shanghai Badlands: Wartime Terrorism and Urban Crime, 1937–41*. Cambridge: Cambridge University Press, 1996.

Wakeman, Frederic, Jr., and Wen-hsin Yeh, eds., *Shanghai Sojourners*. Berkeley, Calif.: Institute of East Asian Studies, 1992.

Wang, Zhicheng. *Shanghai E qiaoshi* [A History of the Russian Emigré Community in Shanghai]. Shanghai: Sanlian shudian, 1993.

Wartenberger, Horst. "My Shanghai Memoirs." Unpublished manuscript, 1952.

Wasserstein, Bernard. *The Secret Lives of Trebitsch Lincoln*. New Haven: Yale University Press, 1988.

———. *Secret War in Shanghai: Treachery, Subversion and Collaboration in the Second World War*. London: Profile Books, 1998

———. *Vanishing Diaspora: The Jews in Europe since 1945*. Cambridge, Mass.: Harvard University Press, 1996.

Wasserstrom, Jeffrey. *Student Protests in Twentieth-Century China: The View from Shanghai*. Stanford: Stanford University Press, 1991.

Wei, Betty Peh-t'i. *Shanghai: Crucible of Modern China*. Hong Kong: Oxford University Press, 1987.

Who's Who in China. 5th ed. Shanghai: China Weekly Review, 1936.

Who's Who in China. Supplement to the 5th ed. Shanghai: China Weekly Review, 1940.

Whyte, William Foote. *Street Corner Society: The Social Structure of an Italian Slum*. Chicago: University of Chicago Press, 1943.

Willoughby, Charles A. *Shanghai Conspiracy: The Sorge Spy Ring, Moscow, Shanghai, Tokyo, San Francisco, New York*. New York: Dutton, 1952.

Wischnitzer, Mark. *Visas to Freedom: The History of HIAS*. New York: World Publishing Company, 1956.

Wolff, David. *To the Harbin Station: The Liberal Alternative in Russian Manchuria, 1898–1914*. Stanford: Stanford University Press, 1999.

Woźniakowski, Krzysztof. "Polonia Chińska w latach 1897–1949 i jej życie kulturalno-literackie" [The Polish Community in China in the Years 1897–1949 and Its Cultural And Literary Life], pt. 1. *Przeglad Polonijńy* 1 (Jan. 1976): 97–109.

Yang Haijun. "Zhongguo Youtairen yanjiu 80 nian" [Eighty Years of Research on the Jews of China]. *Zhongguo shehui kexue* 3 (1994): 146–56.

Xu, Buzeng. "Jews and the Musical Life of Shanghai." In *The Jews of China: Historical and Comparative Perspectives*, ed. Jonathan Goldstein, 1: 230–38. Armonk, N.Y.: M. E. Sharpe, 1999.

———. "Youtai yinyuejia zai Shanghai" [Jewish Musicians in Shanghai]. *Yinyue yishu* [Art of Music], nos. 3–4 (1991).

Xu, Xin. "Chinese Research on Jewish Diasporas in China." Paper presented at the symposium "Jewish Diasporas in China," Harvard University, Aug. 1992.

Xu, Xin, and Ling Yiyan, eds. *Youtai baike quanshu* [Encyclopedia Judaica]. Shanghai: Shanghai renmin chubanshe, 1993.

Yamashita Hajime. "Shanhai no bōmei Yudaya-jin to Nihon" [Jewish Exiles in Shanghai and Japan]. *Asahi Shimbun*, Feb. 23, 1989.

———. "Shanhai no Doitsu Yudaya-jin" [The German Jews of Shanghai]. *Doitsu bungaku* [German Literature], nos. 31–33 (1987).

Yasue, Hiroo. *Dairen tokumu kikan to maboroshi no Yudaya kokka* [The Dairen Intelligence Post and the Phantom Jewish State]. Tokyo: Yahata Shoten, 1989.

Ye, Xiaoqing. "Shanghai Before Nationalism." *East Asian History*, no. 3 (June 1991): 33–52.

Yeh, Wen-Hsin. "Shanghai Modernity: Commerce and Culture in a Republican City." *China Quarterly*, no. 150 (June 1997): 375–94.

———, ed. *Becoming Chinese: Passages to Modernity and Beyond*. Berkeley: University of California Press, 2000.

———, ed. *Wartime Shanghai*. New York: Routledge, 1998.

Zeitin, Joseph. "The Shanghai Jewish Community: An Historical Sketch." *Jewish Life* 12, no. 4 (Oct. 1973): 54–68.

Zhiganov, Vladimir Danilovich. *Russkie v Shankhaie* [Russians in Shanghai]. Shanghai: N.p., 1936.

Zimmels, H. J. *Ashkenazim and Sephardim: Their Relations, Differences, and Problems as Reflected in the Rabbinical Responsa*. London: Oxford University Press, 1958.

Zumwalt, Elmo R., Jr. *On Watch: A Memoir*. New York: Quadrangle/New York Times, 1976.

Zuroff, Efraim. "Rescue via the Far East: The Attempt to Save Polish Rabbis and Yeshivah Students, 1939–41." *Simon Wiesenthal Center Annual* 1 (1984): 153–81.

Zweig, Ronald W. *German Reparations and the Jewish World: A History of the Claims Conference*. Boulder, Colo.: Westview Press, 1987.

Abraham, D. E. J., 145
Abraham, R. D., 134, 154
Air raids on Shanghai, 158–59, 202, 212–13
AJJDC. *See* American Jewish Joint Distribution Committee
All-Russian Emigrants Committee, 218–19, 221, 224, 227. *See also* Russian Emigrants Committee
All-Russian Fascist Union, 173–74, 229–32
American Community Church, 35
American Jewish Congress, 149
American Jewish Joint Distribution Committee (AJJDC), 104, 120, 124, 129, 119–22 *passim*, 134, 141–46 *passim*, 156, 157, 202, 252, 257–59, 272
Americans, 4–10 *passim*, 16, 27, 41, 55–56; anti-Semitism, 112; attitudes toward refugees, 3, 4–5, 6, 99; business, 31–32, 86; internment of, 185–86, 188–90, 214; Japanese and, 150, 152, 154, 156–57; Japanese internees in U.S., 189; European refugees and, 99, 117–18, 133, 142–4, 150, 154; Nazis and, 176; in post–World War II era, 243–46, 254–55, 259–65, 268–69; radio station XHMA, 133, 210; refugee legislation and policy (post-war), 254–57, 259–65; Russians and, 35–36, 41;

treaties, 7; in World War II, 185–91 *passim*, 213, 214, 220, 222, 233–34, 280
Anti-Semitism, 4–5, 95, 112, 194, 230, 278; of Japanese, 5, 48–49, 96–97, 150–52, 173–75; among Jews, 144; Nazi-based, 96–97, 180–81, 194; origins, 30–33; of White Russians, 5, 49, 96, 148, 231, 265, 280
Arbitration Courts, 134–37. *See also* Jewish Arbitration Court of CFA; International Committee Arbitration Court; Jüdische Gemeinde, Arbitration Court
Ashkenazi, Meir (Rabbi of Shanghai), 25, 96, 105, 134, 142, 210, 211
Ashkenazi Communal Society of Shanghai, 116
Ashkenazi Jewish Communal Association, 147, 152, 270
Ashkenazi Jews, 21, 23–24, 32, 33, 67, 97, 155, 275, 277, 279; Russians and, 27–28, 95–97 *passim*; Sephardim and, 23–26, 270. *See also* Shanghai Ashkenazi Collaborating Relief Communal Association (SACRA); Shanghai Ashkenazi Jewish Communal Association (SAJCA)
Ashkenazi Philanthropic Society of Shanghai, 32
Assassination of political leaders, 159, 166–70 *passim*, 187, 215, 279